City of a Million Dreams

Set in Miller and Desire Pro by Tseng Information
Systems, Inc.

Manufactured in the United States of America

The University of North Carolina Press has been a
member of the Green Press Initiative since 2003.

Cover illustrations: Front, "Creole Dancer" (NOL04),
© Herman Leonard Photography, LLC; back, Louis
Armstrong and Leon René, author's collection, gift of
the late Leon René.

Library of Congress Cataloging-in-Publication Data
Names: Berry, Jason, author.
Title: City of a million dreams : a history of
New Orleans at year 300 / Jason Berry.
Description: Chapel Hill : The University of North
Carolina Press, [2018] | Includes bibliographical
references and index.
Identifiers: LCCN 2018020837 | ISBN 9781469647142
(cloth : alk. paper) | ISBN 9781469664026 (pbk. : alk.
paper) | ISBN 9781469647159 (ebook)
Subjects: LCSH: New Orleans (La.)—History.
Classification: LCC F379.N557 B47 2018 |
DDC 976.3/35—dc23 LC record available at
https://lccn.loc.gov/2018020837

For Melanie McKay, my wife and soul mate,

with love and gratitude.

. . .

And in memory of

Kenny M. Charbonnet: paterfamilias, attorney,

godfather of my youngest.

Jeff Gillenkirk, "Lefty": author, social critic.

Hoya Saxa.

The past is not decent

or orderly, it is made up

and devious.

The man was correct

when he said it's not

even past.

—ROBERT PINSKY, "GULF MUSIC"

CONTENTS

Galleries of illustrations begin on pages 127 and 219.

City of a Million Dreams

Prologue

Funerals are an art form in New Orleans. One follows them with a careful eye on beauty and decay.

The November 20, 2015, send-off for Allen Toussaint resembled an affair of state. Internationally renowned and effervescent at seventy-seven, Toussaint had been in Madrid, felled by a heart attack at the hotel after a final bow at the piano. The body came home amid a furor over Mayor Mitch Landrieu's decision to dismantle four Confederate monuments in the wake of the Charleston shooting massacre of nine African American churchgoers by a white nationalist. In that aftermath, South Carolina governor Nikki Haley had ordered the removal of the Confederate flag from the statehouse. Mayor Landrieu called for a landmarks commission to find another place for the memorials. "Symbols should reflect who we really are as a people," he said.

The funeral of a beloved black musician promised respite from a roiling debate over myth, memory, and politics. Events surrounding the Toussaint burial pageant magnified a theme of this book: how the beguiling image of New Orleans grew from a culture of spectacle in tension with a city of laws, an official city the popular culture challenged.

Sixteen hundred people filled the downtown Orpheum Theater, finally restored a decade after Hurricane Katrina. Rock, jazz, and rhythm-and-blues artists joined politicians, cultural leaders, media folk, and music aficionados center-aisle to greet the family beneath the stage. White blossoms, shaped like a treble clef, adorned the casket. Elton John sent carnations.

"The tunes you gave us are the soundtrack of our lives," said Landrieu in the first eulogy. The musicians kept on script: give a personal tribute, sing a song, surrender the

1

podium. They included Elvis Costello, Jimmy Buffett, Boz Scaggs, John Boutté, Irma Thomas, Dr. John, Cyril Neville, Davell Crawford with Trombone Shorty, and the Preservation Hall Jazz Band. Toussaint had many hits in his 800-title catalog: "Mother-in-Law," "Optimism Blues," "What Do You Want the Girl to Do," "Make A Better World," and "Southern Nights," among others. Most of the mourners had grown up dancing to his hip-romantic lyrics as sung by a range of vocalists. Imagine the honeyed baritone of Benny Spellman:

> Lipstick traces
>   On a cigarette
> Every memory of you
>   Lingers yet
>   I've got it bad
> Like I told you before
>   I'm so in love
>   with you
> Don't leave me
>   no more!

Toussaint produced songs for vocalists as varied as Paul Simon, Aaron Neville, and Patti LaBelle. When Katrina smashed the city in 2005, the flood swallowed his workspace, the piano, his wardrobe, the works. Toussaint escaped to New York. In the new world, he shed his reluctance to perform and cut an elegant figure on stage. Out of that rebirth came *Bright Mississippi*, a gem of jazz standards, and *Songbook*, recorded live at Joe's Pub, featuring Toussaint on solo piano singing his favorites. Eventually, he moved back home, the cool man of music coasting in a Rolls Royce, lending his time and celebrity to good causes.

After the funeral tributes, Preservation Hall drummers began a solemn tolling of the dirges. People stood. The bass drum pounded through the theater—*boom ... boom ... boom ... boom*—hard, deep thuds of grief calling mourners to follow the band and pallbearers as they pushed the coffin up the aisle, through the lobby, into the sunlight. The percussive thunder shifted to staccato flutters of the snare drum, building tension as the grand marshal in tuxedo and top hat emerged in slow, stately steps, leading the procession into the street opposite the Roosevelt Hotel. Several thousand people, cordoned off by police, hovered in a semicircle around the white hearse, a forest of cameras and iPhones held high, the limousine door open, awaiting the casket for what Jelly Roll Morton had once called "the end of a perfect death."

Landrieu hugged a distraught John Boutté, the vocalist whose career had soared in *Tremé*, the HBO series. As pallbearers, singer Cyril Neville and pianist A. J. Loria, a charming lounge lizard and easy rider with the private Toussaint, lodged the coffin into the vehicle. Then the band broke into the up-tempo anthem for a soul cut loose from earthly ties, "Didn't He Ramble," and those surrounding the hearse went sashaying in the street, pumping umbrellas and waving handkerchiefs.

Toussaint was driving another Rolls Royce, in 1996, when I called him for an interview. "Your place does fine," had come the silken voice. A few days later he sat on my couch, eyeing the bookshelf. I asked if he had a set time for composing. After dinner, he said. "Because it's so quiet. The night air ... even if you're inside, the hum of the city is down to a minimum, whereas in daytime you hear that between B-and-B-Flat hum." He paused. "The electrical hum of the cities in England is different—the power source, the amount of voltage is different."

"New Orleans has a B-flat hum," I said, coveting the phrase.

"Oh, absolutely. The city is B-flat all the way."

The city's B-flat humming had shifted to a weird cacophony over the months before he died. In an irony that Toussaint, who lived on Robert E. Lee Boulevard in Lakeview, would have savored, he became a posthumous player in the tinderbox dispute over Robert E. Lee, arms folded, standing sixty feet above the St. Charles Avenue streetcar tracks atop a pale Doric column. The Lee Circle statue was a flash point for preservationists and conservatives who filed a court challenge to halt Landrieu's plan to take down the Lee and three other Confederate monuments. In response, Glen David Andrews, a swaggering trombonist and high-octane singer, made his stand. One of fifteen children raised in a citybed of poverty, his kin lines suggest a dynastic saga out of a Gabriel García Márquez novel. Glen David Andrews had eight cousins named Glen Andrews; three Glens played in the same band. Surveying the jagged divide, Glen David Andrews tweeted, "Rename Lee Circle after Allen Toussaint. Perfect place to honor our hero."

As Black Lives Matter galvanized protestors nationwide over police shootings, a New Orleans drive supporting Andrews's call for a renamed Toussaint Circle rallied 8,000 signatures. A Facebook group, Save Our Circle, claiming 27,000 signatures, accused Landrieu of "an attempt to 'hide' history." The group's founder, Tim Shea Carroll, told me, "The statue never bothered anybody for the forty-eight years I've been in New Orleans, until this tragic event in South Carolina, and anything related to it became a pariah. Let's not tear down for political correctness."

How did Robert E. Lee become an icon on St. Charles Avenue?

"Lee had the least connection to New Orleans, having passed through when he was a United States Army officer," reported Campbell Robertson of the *New York Times*, in coverage of the controversy.

The Lee statue was erected in 1884 amid a movement for Southern redemption that mythologized the Confederacy's defeat as the Lost Cause. As Confederate statues went up across the South, the cultural narrative (later popularized by *Gone with the Wind*) softened the grisly post-Reconstruction politics that regained power in a reign of lynching and other violence targeting African Americans. In the Lost Cause story line, the Civil War had never been about slavery but rather was about an agrarian society, steeped in chivalry and kind to its slaves, that fought in resistance to an industrializing Northern economy. The Lost Cause was a force in molding how history was taught to generations of Southerners, me among them.

As Mardi Gras became a late nineteenth-century floor show for the aristocracy, black men costumed as Indians paraded out of a roots culture that began with massive ring dances of enslaved Africans before the Civil War. The "Masking Indians" charged into the twentieth century, singing coded lyrics of resistance and often clashing with cops during their Mardi Gras marches. The Zulu parading club emerged in 1909, dripping satire. The king in his lard can and banana stalk scepter was a vaudevillian swipe at Rex the king of Carnival. "Zulu caricatured Rex; a black Lord of misrule upsetting the reign of the white lord, a mocker of a mocker ... a black Carnival parade that commented on white Carnival parades," writes the historian Reid Mitchell.

The black culture of spectacle melded with Carnival season as a stage for identity pageants in a city polarized by the politics of race. The narrative that shadowed the Lost Cause took decades for city leaders to absorb—the flowering of jazz, a new art form, an African American epic, in song lines and musical dynamics, risen from deep memory, gaining authority over time. The parading culture had its own evolution. Louis Armstrong rode as King of Zulu in 1949, a triumphant joy-maker transcending satire. As the Zulu Social Aid and Pleasure Club, with its elaborately decorated floats, grew in membership, it became a political powerhouse.

Moon Landrieu (Mitch's father) became mayor in 1970 as segregation was eroding; he hired African Americans in City Hall and for public projects, pushing the idea of the city on a new path. Landrieu was long out of office when a majority-black city council, in 1993, declared the "Liberty

Place" monument—which commemorated an 1874 white revolt against the Reconstruction governor—to be a public nuisance and, after a legal battle with the monument's die-hard supporters, had the obelisk removed from Canal Street and wedged behind the Aquarium of the Americas, next to an up-ramp for the parking lot of an elevated mall. That White League obelisk, the Lee icon, and two other statues were on Mayor Mitch Landrieu's hit list as the city prepared for its 2018 Tricentennial.

The clash of icons, Lee versus Toussaint, animated a town fabled for its music, parties, and bars that rock till dawn. Here was the city of laws—the official city, *the government*—changing sides under a mayor whose plan appalled a fair number of New Orleanians. As a native son, I know lots of them in both camps. Walker Percy once wrote that people in New Orleans are happiest when making money, caring for the dead, or "putting on masks at Mardi Gras so nobody knows who they are." Now the masks were coming down, and people accustomed to the charming Southern way of complimenting the roses while ignoring the cadaver at the garden party were peering at each, asking, "What is our history?"

I began work on this book well before that bombastic urban drama of the monuments began, but as it played out, my thoughts turned to the founder of New Orleans, Bienville, a tattooed warrior who guided the survival of the port town in a raw, hostile world, and how the city opened into a series of adventures in which its identity kept shifting, like a great diva changing costumes in a succession of operatic roles. Resurrection dramas rose from the floods, fires, slave revolts, epidemics, wars, corruption, riots, and crime. Through all of that an African American culture grew into a life force of dancing, parading, and music to resist a city of laws, anchored in white supremacy for much of our history.

Allen Toussaint's funeral was doubly poignant for extending a lineage of burial marches begun as early as 1789 with the lavish memorial for Carlos III, when the city was a Spanish property. Funerals in New Orleans are caravans of memory; they hold a mirror to the society at given points in time. In following a leitmotif of how funerals influenced the culture of parading, I cast this narrative as a character-driven history, training a viewfinder on selected people whose lives held a mirror to the changes in daily life. As the city became a crossroads of humanity, migrants filled out map-of-the-world neighborhoods; they forged a Creole culture, rich in foodways, music, and a good deal more—tradition-bearers in the story of a grand American city.

. . . .

Bienville

JOURNEY INTO THE INTERIOR

Snakes crawled across his body, coils tattooed on flesh: signs to the Choctaw and other tribes that the founder of New Orleans fought as fiercely as anyone. "They are all nude and wear only a belt around their bodies [with] a piece of cloth," a French admiral noted of the Indians in a 1720 diary. "They have their skins covered with figures of snakes which they make with the point of a needle. Mr. de Bienville who is the general of the country has all of his body covered in this way and when he is obliged to march to war with them he makes himself nude like them. They like him very much but also fear him." He wanted their fear for what he had to do.

The tension between spectacle and law that would shape the city was written on the body of its founder. Sent by the Crown to tame a wilderness and impose order, Bienville's skin illustrated his power in the clash between French interests and those of Native Americans.

Indigenous people from Canada down to deep Louisiana used the living body to convey visual memory, "acts of bravery performed by the tattooed man," writes Arnaud Balvay. Their body art also displayed weapons, lizards, skulls, flowers, the moon and stars, even Jesus's words learned from missionaries. European trappers and colonizing soldiers had their bodies inked to showcase their achievement and courage, suggesting a shared terrain for natives to trust. Sometimes it worked.

In March 1718, the commandant general Jean-Baptiste Le Moyne, Sieur de Bienville, guided barges to an elevated bank of the Mississippi and led his team of thirty French convicts, six carpenters, and four Canadian *voyageurs*, hacking through canebrakes and trees, clearing the area to build where silt layers had settled in the shape of a crescent.

On that oxbow where Indians hunted, Bienville chose France's strategic port. Ninety miles north of the Gulf of Mexico, *La Nouvelle Orléans* would link the vast colony to the Atlantic world, Mexico and Peru. Here would rise a fort to blunt Spanish forays out of Florida, or British forces ranging down from the Carolinas with Chickasaw mercenaries seeking Indian slaves.

Bienville was thirty-eight and knew the region well. His crew included salt smugglers, petty criminals deported from France for evading Louis XIV's taxes, now hoisting planks for the carpenters. For several years, French soldiers and Canadian trappers good with the gun had clawed out an existence at Bienville's military base, far east on Mobile Bay, as around them people died of famine or malaria, the men finding beds with Indian women. During that grim ordeal, Bienville had sent letters to the palace in Versailles, seeking greater assets from Count Pontchartrain, who had never set foot in Louisiana. Nor had Louis XIV, the Sun King for whom the vast Louisiana colony was named.

In August 1715, the king lay dying in Versailles, a leg enflamed by gangrene. After seventy-two years on the throne, Louis XIV had buried three sons and a grandson; he was leaving a far-flung empire, a bloated war debt, and a demoralized populace. Count Pontchartrain had orders to have the king's heart surgically removed after death, a gift to the Jesuits of Paris. The king appointed his nephew, Philippe II, duc d'Orléans, to rule as regent until his five-year-old great-grandson, Louis XV, reached maturity. This boy had been the dauphin, for whom a Gulf island off the Alabama coast was named.

Philippe d'Orléans went through women as some men sample wine; but ruling as regent for the boy king, Orléans tackled France's economic crisis with a bold plan by John Law, a Scottish financial wizard. Law created a French national bank, folding the royal debt into a massive stock sale to develop Louisiana. A Crown partnership with Law's company sent ships with women, money, wine, and supplies to the plantation economy, promoted grandiosely in the French press as a land of horses and buffalo, primed for silver mine profits.

The plan to move France's garrison at Mobile Bay, north of the Gulf of Mexico coast, to a site named for d'Orléans, upriver on the Mississippi, provoked debate among officials. Where to situate the port? Bienville, eager to solidify his authority, preempted them by breaking ground at the site he chose. With a new Cross of Saint Louis, a pay raise and land concession at Horn Island in the Gulf, he had two corporate officials *above him*! He, who had done more than any human being to turn this outback into a speck of French civilization, *was not governor*. He wanted that; he wanted more.

The city began as a cluster of palmetto-thatched huts and cypress sheds on a riverfront clearance somewhere in today's French Quarter. "We are working on New Orleans with such diligence as the dearth of workmen will allow," Bienville reported to French officials that summer of 1718. "Everything will grow there." A company agent stewed in disagreement: "Crayfish abound, so that tobacco and vegetables are hard to raise.... The air is fever-ridden [with] an infinity of mosquitoes."

Bienville wanted the new town to feed commerce with *concessionaires'* plantations grouped along the river. The challenge for everyone was to stay alive. Smallpox, other epidemics, and tribal wars had cut through Gulf South peoples like a scythe. "Of the seven thousand whites who entered the Lower Mississippi Valley from 1717 to 1721, at least half of them perished or abandoned the colony before 1726," writes Daniel H. Usner. Of Africans, in nearly equal number between 1718 and 1731, about half died at sea or soon after arrival.

Bienville needed stable Indian ties to anchor the food supply. New Orleans was a village clearing when he sent André Pénicaut, a carpenter adept at Indian dialects, sixty miles upriver to the grand chief of the Chitimacha. Bienville's punitive expedition of 1706 had killed fifteen Chitimacha warriors and executed a headman for the murder of a missionary priest and three *voyageurs* at a river camp. Count Pontchartrain supported eye-for-an-eye retribution. To the Chitimacha, reduced by disease deaths and tribal slave raids, Pénicaut proposed peace. First, the chief must free their few French prisoners and accept the loss of Chitimacha captives already sold as slaves. There was more: Bienville wanted the chief to uproot and resettle his people downriver, twenty-five miles south of the port. Bienville envisioned the crops, meat, and hides of Indians meshing with a plantation economy. "I told them," wrote Pénicaut, "they would have to come to New Orleans to sing their calumet of peace to M. de Bienville." The calumet was a smoking pipe.

The Chitimacha stepped out of their pirogues, moving in rhythm with pebble-filled gourds, the men in bright colors jostling along, chanting and swaying in a sinuous dance of tribute. The interpreter was a remarkable Chitimacha woman owned by Antoine-Simone Le Page Du Pratz, later the author of the colony's first history. A Dutchman with expertise as both a soldier and an architect, Le Page had a cabin on Bayou St. John (which Bienville had named for the precursor of Christ, and incidentally himself, Jean-Baptiste). "I purchased from a neighbor a native female slave to have someone to cook for us," wrote Le Page. "My slave and I did not speak each other's language: but I made myself understood by means of other signs."

One night, as she made a fire, Le Page was startled by "a young alligator, five feet long." Fetching his musket, he was more startled at "the girl with a great stick in her hand attacking the monster!" As the battered reptile slithered off, "she began to smile and said many things which I did not comprehend."

Le Page's enslaved woman translated for the Chitimacha headman. From his account, we learn a new detail: Bienville demanded the head of another Chitimacha responsible for the 1706 killing of the priest, based on the intelligence that he had gathered in the intervening years. Draped in a beaver-skinned robe, the Chitimacha's "word-bearer" smoked the calumet of peace and handed the pipe to Bienville with presents of deer skin and hides. This negotiator told Bienville that they had delivered the head of "the bad man, in order to make peace." Justice had been rendered by the hatchet of "a true warrior" who had lost his wife and child in previous years of war. Through the Chitimacha woman's translation, the word-bearer's speech then soars: "Formerly the sun was red, the roads filled with brambles and thorns, the clouds were black, the water was troubled and stained with blood, our women wept unceasingly, our children cried with fright, the game fled far from us, our houses were abandoned, and our fields uncultivated . . . our bones are visible."

From the ravages of war he pivots to a verbal painting of paradise. "The water is so clear that we can see ourselves within it . . . our women dance until they forget to eat, our children leap like young fawns."

Seasoned in the diplomacy that involved Indians' costumed parades, Bienville filled his role in a culture that negotiated power through ritual dancing. The commandant general accepted the pipe, inhaled, and offered food, cementing terms of peace. He reported to France of his good ties with the Acolopissa across the lake for "fresh meat that is consumed at New Orleans."

He spent much of 1718 shuttling between New Orleans and Gulf Coast outposts, dealing with Company bureaucrats and painted Indians.

"Chance and Bienville's cunning are what determined that New Orleans would have a future," writes Lawrence N. Powell in *The Accidental City*. Company officials variously wanted the d'Orléans site at Mobile Bay, or Biloxi, or 120 miles upriver at Natchez. Ignoring them, Bienville kept on building. French ships were anchoring at Dauphin Island, a three days' haul to the mouth of the Mississippi and upriver against hard currents to the embryonic port. The colony had so few medium-sized vessels that 600 people got stranded on Dauphin Island for three miserable months. Facing a shortage of carpenters and nails, Bienville complained to the Navy Council of his "infinite embarrassment" over substandard craftsmen.

Meanwhile, John Law peddled land grants to 119 *concessionaires* as feudal lords with indentured servants and slaves shipped from West Africa. Law coaxed the duc d'Orléans to move denizens in French public hospitals to ships with beggars and inmates doing time for "murders, debauchery, and drunkenness," writes Gwendolyn Midlo Hall. To provide wives, Law herded prostitutes, and women from dungeons onto ships, one "accused of fifteen murders," others charged with "blasphemy . . . and assassination"— not the matrimonial candidates Bienville envisioned. In September 1719, as the abductions became known, 150 women at La Rochelle "threw themselves like furies on their guards, ripping out their hair, biting and pummeling them, which forced the guards to shoot at these poor creatures, killing six and wounding a dozen more." Law recruited prostitutes from Paris's Salpêtrière hospital, promising dowries to those who would marry. On September 18, 1720, after a group wedding of eighty pardoned criminals and as many women, the newlyweds had their shackles removed as the voyage set sail. After riots at two prisons, the Crown halted the forced emigration.

In 1719, titanic rains drove the Mississippi over the embankment, leaving a matchstick village in water for weeks. Law's company ordered a work halt and building of the capitol at Biloxi. Facing the crisis, Bienville stalled. He had a residence for himself built at Biloxi; meanwhile, at *La Nouvelle Orléans*, his men built new sheds and cabins and dug canals to channel water to the back swamp. As Bienville's cat-and-mouse game continued with Company of the Indies officials, Law's "Mississippi Bubble," arranged like a Ponzi scheme on revolving debt, crashed in 1720. The new bank heaved from losses. Law fled to Venice.

With so much at stake in Louisiana, Company men hunkered down. Bienville drew heightened scrutiny for failure to deliver speedy profits. In Paris, poverty and crime spread. A plague struck France in 1720, with 100,000 deaths. Shipping halted at key ports.

Bienville held a card: *La Nouvelle Orléans*, though prone to floods and illness, numbered 519 people by 1721. He awarded himself twenty-seven acres near the king's plantation across the river, and cultivated an ally in Adrien de Pauger, a French engineer. Pauger had been bickering with his boss, chief royal engineer Louis-Pierre Le Blond de La Tour, down in Biloxi, where a faction wanted the d'Orléans port to be built. Pauger was sent up the Mississippi to see if they might do better north of Lake Pontchartrain at Bayou Manchac. At Bienville's site, gazing at the few riverfront cabins and clumps of trees, Pauger envisioned a city. He designed a grid of sixty-six squares, eleven parallel to the river, six on perpendicular lines. A roof and a garden were "necessities of urban life," Pauger wrote La Tour. Bienville, who built a large house below the riverfront clearance, provided Pauger with land and slaves.

A copy of Pauger's map anonymously reached Paris, "the last thing that the Biloxi faction wanted to see," writes Powell. Bienville, obviously, sent it. La Tour joined Pauger at New Orleans, helping to execute the urban parallelogram with a riverfront parade grounds, the Place d'Armes (today's Jackson Square). The French engineers emulated the Spanish plaza as a garden-like space with shrubs and floral beauty, framed by a church and garrison, with Place des Vosges in Paris as added inspiration. They named key thoroughfares for royalty—Bourbon, Royal, Orléans, Burgundy; cross streets for royal cousins, Conti and Chartres, plus Toulouse and Dumaine for Louis XIV's out-of-wedlock sons. Both engineers, La Tour and Pauger, would die soon of diseases. Their design endured as the city grew.

Bienville planted orange trees. He had struggled more than two decades in this region, seeking some promise in the existence he had forged a world away from his early life of privilege. His one documented romance ended badly. Perhaps that failure was unrelated to his appearance, bare-chested with glistening skin. Those tattooed snakes formed a striking mosaic on the body of a nobleman, as if *le sieur* had been in the tropics too long.

· · · · · · · · · ·

ROOTS OF THE FOUNDER

Charles Le Moyne was one of New France's richest men when Jean-Baptiste, the twelfth child, was born in Montreal about February 23, 1680. His birth furnished his father a yearly bonus of 400 livres (roughly $4,000 today) from Louis XIV's policy for rewarding prolific families of suitable pedigree. Shipping out from Normandy at fifteen, Charles Le Moyne, under the guidance of Jesuits in Quebec, went to live with Hurons, in keeping with the religious order's immersion strategy, learning a language and customs. When they baptized Indians, the priests pronounced them Christians and subjects of Louis XIV, an idea glorious and vague in equal measure. Rising from trapper to a merchant of deer hide and mink, Le Moyne married Catherine Thierry. Buying up land, he paid the Crown to secure his barony at Montreal. He gave his sons titled names for localities of his French youth; they had no land value, but a title opened doors to career advancement with approval of the king.

Jean-Baptiste's father died when he was five; his mother when he was ten. Taken in by his eldest brother's family, he became a French naval cadet at twelve. At sixteen he joined the crew of his thirty-four-year-old sibling,

Pierre, Sieur d'Iberville (the third eldest brother). Iberville had routed British forces at Port Nelson in 1695 and sailed to France with 51,997 pounds of deerskin booty from which he garnered wealth. In 1697, at Hudson Bay, an outnumbered Iberville sank a British man-o'-war. Bienville, seventeen, was wounded but returned a victor to France.

Iberville, the war hero with a wife and estate in France, was Bienville's role model and a commanding presence to Count Pontchartrain, Jérôme Phélypeaux, whose father had bequeathed him the title and office. Limping, his face scarred from childhood smallpox, Pontchartrain was Iberville's superior at Versailles as he prepared for Louisiana.

In 1682, on mudflats where the mouth of the river met the Gulf of Mexico, Robert Cavalier, Sieur de La Salle, had planted a cross and named the huge Mississippi Valley *La Louisiane* for Louis XIV. Pitching the Mississippi's huge potential as a shipping lane from New France to the West Indies, La Salle gained Crown support to found a colony; but in 1685 his ship got lost. On a maddening overland trek to rediscover the Mississippi, La Salle's men murdered him with a shot to the head. In 1699, Iberville set sail to complete La Salle's dream with Bienville aboard.

"We looked with admiration at the beauty of this river," wrote Pénicaut, the carpenter. Over time, the river would prove a godlike force capable of great destruction. Turkey, geese, and teal fluttered over a lush world as fifty men on longboats, pushing away from three ships anchored in the Gulf of Mexico, passed riverbanks with savannas of billowing saw grass, bamboo clusters, and moss-bearded oak.

"It is almost certain that Iberville first viewed the future site of downtown New Orleans on the calm Saturday of March 7, 1699," writes Richard Campanella. Bison grazed on levees formed by sediment. Annocchy Indians came forward, rubbing their faces and bellies in a sign of welcome. Iberville gave them axes, knives, and glass beads; the Indians shared buffalo meat and provided a guide to help him track clues from a missionary's journal that Iberville carried from La Salle's first trip as they moved upriver, eyeing potential sites for settlement.

On March 14 they met a canoe with four Mougoulacha Indians, a Choctaw branch, and pulled ashore. A chieftain robed in bearskin extended a calumet. Iberville traded knives and axes for corn and meat. They followed the natives into a village shared with the Bayogoula, warmly greeted by their chief. Iberville counted 107 windowless huts with beds but scant furniture; two temples made of timber with a conical roof had tables stacked with skins and beef. The 250 men went naked. Iberville saw few children; women wore girdles of tree bark; the younger ones had tattooed faces and breasts and blackened their teeth. One-fourth of the village had died of smallpox. Bodies lay on platforms covered by cane mats; the stench "attracts many buzzards," noted Iberville.

The scene clashed with the explorers' memories of candlelit solemnities at church funerals, a view of death as doorway to salvation. Mourners processed to tingling chimes. In France, wills prescribed fees for robed monks as sacred escorts, with torch carriers and children from orphanages to enhance the delegation. Funerals in Canada were less grand. Explorers feared dying alone, mindful of the adage, "He who goes unburied shall not rise from the dead." Iberville's journal records sharp contrast with the burial rites of "beggarly" Indians, naming those of his men who died, with no account of prayers over an earthen grave.

Bienville, nineteen, proved adept at Indian languages, ferreting out information in stops as they rowed past palmetto rooftops posting bear and fish heads, offerings to the gods. Iberville and his men planted a cross, a French flag, and went searching for the Houmas tribe mentioned in accounts of La Salle's trip. When a bear lunged out, Bienville shot the beast and supplied the men with supper meat.

The party found a landing near present-day Baton Rouge. Iberville and a small group set out for the Houmas compound. Tribal lieutenants met them and after smoking the calumet led them singing to the village. The chief, stout and dignified, hosted a reception in a wooden temple with an exchange of gifts, the Houmas yelling, "Hou! Hou! Hou!" About 350 people gathered in a plaza, rattling drums and gourds, lacing rhythms as twenty young men paraded past, then "fifteen of the prettiest young women," marveled Iberville, "all of them naked," save for feathered fur sashes "painted red, yellow and white, their faces and bodies tattooed or painted," swishing fans to mark time.

The chief hosted a supper with a bonfire; young men carrying bows and arrows sang war dances with the feathered women until midnight. The Houmas leader knew of no fork in the river, contradicting the missionary's journal. He led 150 people following Iberville's team back to the river and another night of torch-lit dances. "They offered the women to our officers, who politely thanked them," wrote the second-in-command, Ensign Sauvolle, then lapsing into silence.

The French team faced a long return to their ships in the Gulf. Sending Sauvolle and Bienville down the Mississippi, Iberville took a southeastern route in pirogues led by an Indian guide across an arterial bayou he named Manchac. The waterway sloped into interlocked lakes. Iberville named the more distant one Maurepas, for the peerage in France that the elder Count Pontchartrain had given his son. The larger, lower-lying body of water shouldered a cypress swamp on its southern shore that would one day become the city's Lakeview neighborhood. Iberville named the big lake Pontchartrain, after the father and son.

Meanwhile, the river pulled Bienville's retinue to a Bayogoula village where he learned of a letter that the explorer Henri de Tonti had left for La Salle after they failed to meet on that doomed final trip. Tonti was a legendary explorer who had lost his right hand in a war with the Spanish and was thereafter outfitted with prosthetic hook. Indians called him the "Iron Hand." Bienville traded a hatchet for the Iron Hand's letter.

At the Bayogoula camp, the priest in Bienville's party, unable to find his breviary and journal, threw a fit. The chief was offended, refusing to provide them with a guide. Bienville bargained, swapping a gun and bullets for a twelve-year-old captive Indian; the boy wailed on being sent off with strangers. Enslaved to Bienville, the sobbing boy sinks into historical oblivion. Colonial documents reference Bienville's fluency in Indian languages; the boy may have been a way to sharpen those skills.

Some 3,500 Indians from six nations lived within a few days' travel of the Gulf Coast, facing deadly epidemics and slave raids from the Atlantic coast. Iberville fostered ties with natives in building a settlement at present-day Ocean Springs on the Gulf Coast. He sailed to France, but Pontchartrain, his finances strained by war, sent him back without enough to seed a colony. Iberville asked the Crown for a county near Mobile, lead mine concessions, a license to import African slaves, a beaver fur monopoly, and a warehouse at the mouth of the Mississippi. Instead, Pontchartrain sent him to fight the British in the West Indies.

Invading the island of Nevis, Iberville took a load of milled sugar and 1,309 Africans, whom he sold for personal profit at Saint-Domingue, the engine of Caribbean sugar production. A web of people around Iberville—several brothers, cousins, kinfolk by marriage, and bottom-feeders—had profiteered while Louis XIV was melting palace silverware to help fund his war with Spain. Pontchartrain ordered an investigation of Iberville's assets that spanned two decades, forcing restitution from his remarried widow.

Pontchartrain's view of Bienville darkened, but he needed continuity in Louisiana. Bienville, twenty-four, with scant memory of his father, looked to older men in proving himself. The garrison moved to Mobile Bay. Henri de Tonti, three decades his senior, moved down from Arkansas and, though Bienville's subordinate, became a mentor, riding with him into Indian areas, trying to keep a fragile peace. In 1704, the Iron Hand's home at Mobile took up residence in Bienville's two-story townhome with a mansard roof, "the most beautiful house in the city," the young postulant Marie Madeleine Hachard wrote to her father on April 24, 1728. "We have a courtyard and a garden, which adjoin each other on one side, and at the end are all wild trees of prodigious height and girth." Beaubois was their confessor.

Ignoring hospital work as they had no cloister, the nuns set up a girls' school that soon had twenty Europeans boarding, and seven enslaved Africans, Indians, and "Negresses" as day students, furthering the Ursuline vision of forming a Christian society. Company officials, facing budget issues, stalled at building the cloister. But the school flourished.

In 1728 the King's Council annulled land grants on the lower Mississippi, usurping most of Bienville's property. In New Orleans, his ideal of an orderly French society advanced with the arrival of *filles à la cassette*, "the casket girls" from good middle-class families, each with a small chest given by the Company with dresses and clothing.

The new governor, Étienne Boucher de Périer, was a former naval officer employed by the Company; Périer sent the hard-drinking Étienne de Chépart to Fort Rosalie as commandant. The Superior Council convicted the short-tempered Chépart of "acts of injustice" for jailing an officer, but Périer pardoned him. At Natchez plantation 30 soldiers provided security for 200 Frenchmen, 82 Frenchwomen, 150 children, and 280 Africans. With plans for a land partnership with Périer, Chépart threatened to send an Indian in manacles to New Orleans if he failed to pay a harvest debt, a bad signal. Great Sun and Tattooed Serpent had died; Sun rulers, allied with village leaders, saw a bedraggled graveyard dishonoring French ancestors. The French let their animals gobble vegetables from Indian gardens, while showing exquisite concern for their Africans' grounds. Natchez headmen saw a portent in Chépart's threats: they, too, might end up French slaves one day. The Natchez forged ties with the majority of the African slaves. Indian hunting parties borrowed French weapons for a hunt, promising deer meat and corn in return.

Alerted by seven of his men to Indian tensions, Chépart put them in leg irons. After a long night drinking and enjoying women provided by the new Great Sun, Chépart arose on November 28, 1729, to Indians parading into his compound. He was killed early in the massacre of 145 men, 36 women, and 56 children. Marauding warriors pillaged homes, burned farms, the fort, boat launch, and acres of tobacco. The Natchez gained control over most of the Africans, and captured 50 white women and children. When a clutch of survivors reached New Orleans, "some of these people completely naked, others in their drawers, maimed," noted a company clerk, "we heard these people speak ... everything was on fire and covered in blood in Natchez." The Ursulines took in 30 dazed orphan girls.

New Orleans resembled a French village, with weddings, house parties, young men paying visits to girls who boarded at the Ursulines' convent— a small society pitched into terror as reports from Natchez detailed atrocities committed against prisoners and the silence of African slaves, who had been alerted to the pending assault. French fears of Indian attacks fed new paranoia of a revolt by Africans and Indians. New Orleans had a sixty-soldier garrison vulnerable to a large army. Sending for French forces, Périer cast lines to Bienville's Choctaw allies. He drafted Africans into a company that invaded a village of Chaouachas *south* of town, capturing women and children, slaughtering men in a foolhardy, genocidal retaliation unrelated to the Natchez far upriver.

In early 1730 Périer sent out two punitive forces, leading the second with 200 French and 500 Choctaw warriors. Fifteen blacks were among the troops sent against the Natchez. After long pursuit into central Louisiana, Périer returned with the ragged Sun hierarchs among his prisoners. Shipped to Saint-Domingue, they were sold as slaves.

Fear of Indians marked New Orleans in the summer of 1730, when an Illinois delegation arrived with Chief Chicagou, who had gone hunting with Louis XV five years earlier. Leaders of the Michigamea and Kaskaski had come downriver with him to express solidarity with *La Nouvelle Orléans*. Townsfolk packed St. Louis Church to see Indians in colorful dress sing Gregorian chant. Ursuline nuns sent up intonations of the first Latin couplet; "the Illinois continued the other couplets in their language in the same tone." The Indians took "more delight and pleasure in chanting these holy Canticles," a Jesuit noted, "than the French receive from chanting their frivolous and often dissolute songs."

Company of the Indies officials responded to its catastrophic losses at Natchez by washing their hands of Louisiana, returning control to Louis XV. In 1732, the king sent Bienville, fifty-two, back as governor.

. . . .

THE BIG MAN AT TWILIGHT

Bienville was livid at Périer for sending a drunken idiot to Natchez, wrecking Bienville's truce. He saw Périer as a weak Company man and paltry general. Finding the garrison run down and troops demoralized, he ordered Périer to vacate his residence immediately or see his clothes out on the road.

Bienville reported to Count Maurepas, minister of colonies at Versailles,

In "The Head of Luís Congo Speaks," the poet Brenda Marie Osbey performs a judgment of history via the psyche of the executioner, whom she imagines decapitated by Africans for being a traitor to them, his "head rotting in some farmer's field."

> i am the severed head of luís congo
> i speak for him—
> in the name of the fear and hatred you once knew of me
> give me please
> i beg of you
> a bit of your cool
> > fair
> > water

. . . .

PRELUDE TO ST. MALÓ

Behind the facade of a mannered French plantation elite lay the sexual hodge-podge of a society that defied *Code Noir* strictures; the urges for intimacy hatched a multicolored map of humanity whose lines of culture and habit often relied on legal loopholes. As the Canadian yeoman had found sexual sustenance with Indian women, enslaved Africans of both sexes found beds with area Indians; the black-Indian progeny would find a legal designation, *griff.* Though the *Code Noir* barred interracial marriage, Frenchmen who had children by African women sidestepped the prohibition and freed their illicit offspring by petitioning the Superior Council for manumission of negresses and dark children, typically for loyal service. "When very young slaves were manumitted, they were clearly being rewarded for something other than their years of good service to their masters," writes Jennifer M. Spear.

The landed class tolerated errant Frenchmen who paired off with dark women because the colony had too few Frenchwomen, or Creole daughters of the earliest *concessionaires*. The overarching fear of the slaveholders was slave rebellion. The maroons, or runaways (from *marronage*) raised those fears among the slaveholders. Africans fled to secluded areas below town, a sprawling marshland forest with inlets and hamlets stretching down to the Gulf. The maroons subsisted by stealing crops and livestock from the estates where they had toiled.

Marronage was a shadow of the slave dances, a bold freedom quest beyond resistance language in the dance. Tolerating the ring dances as a means to defuse emotions of slave labor, the planters feared that the maroons would destabilize their world—a fear that persisted for several decades before the city of laws confronted a revolutionary leader called St. Maló. The lives of Luís Congo and St. Maló did not overlap, but the maroon rebel was the Africans' response to people like Luís Congo, who gained freedom as soldiers, strong arms for officialdom, or spies who helped pacify the enslaved Africans. St. Maló emerged from a succession of events as the colonists absorbed a major identity change.

Twenty years after the founding, many French couples sent unwillingly to Louisiana had divorced. In this group, "senior delinquents ran fencing operations outside of town that traded with slaves for stolen goods, making burglary a problem in New Orleans, not for the last time," writes Ned Sublette. "They bartered with the Indians to sell them liquor and ran the prostitution business with an experienced eye. A hospital for venereal disease was in operation by the end of the decade."

In 1743, when Bienville departed, the town had survived financial convulsions, floods, hurricanes, food shortages, a slave revolt, Indian tensions, maroons, and smugglers in a black market. Police criticized slave owners for allowing blacks to gather and drink at weddings and dances. *Code Noir* enforcement was slippery. For the gentry importing wine and chocolate, it was vital to maintain the élan, or at least the patina, of French town life. Their bottom line for slaves was productivity.

The generation of Creoles inheriting power looked to Paris as their lodestar and as dutiful French subjects welcomed the new governor, Pierre de Rigaud, the marquis de Vaudreuil. Like Bienville, Vaudreuil was a military officer of Canadian nobility, but he was no rugged Indian fighter. A man of cultivated tastes, Vaudreuil enjoyed life. As soldiers skimmed funds from the trading posts, the governor yawned, too, at his wife selling under-the-table apothecary items from their "little Versailles" of a home. The new Creole generation delighted in Vaudreuil's "grandeur and elegance," as Grace King wrote, "his gracious presence, refined manners, polite speech, beautiful balls, with court dress *de rigueur*." The festive aristocracy did little to give *La Nouvelle Orléans* better standing in Paris, however. The port town of 6,000 was still a losing proposition for the Crown. Plantations on Saint-Domingue had booming profits from exporting tons of sugar with 100,000 slaves, who vastly outnumbered the ruling class.

THE CHURCH, SLAVERY, AND THE SHIFT TO SPAIN

In 1760, Montreal fell to the British, leaving France without control of Canada. Meanwhile, Britain captured much of the French Caribbean and most of America east of the Mississippi. In 1762, Louis XV offered New Orleans to Carlos III of Spain, his cousin in the Bourbon dynasty, as compensation for losing Florida. Louis XV washed his hands of the port with its profits sapped by a smugglers' black market. For Carlos III in Madrid, New Orleans was attractive as a riverine bulwark against British sights on Mexican silver. Under the Treaty of Paris, the royal cousins agreed to keep the transfer secret until 1764.

In 1763, the Jesuits became the targets of a French reactionary movement: the Jansenists derided them as morally flexible, overtolerant of human sin in a fallen world. With more than 22,000 priests and 700 schools and colleges in Europe, the Society of Jesus had a web of missionaries in far-flung cultures and had become a force in colonial economics. The New Orleans community had a thriving indigo plantation with slaves. In contrast, the Jesuits had thirty missions in Paraguay among the Guarani people, herders who farmed yerba and cotton, furnishing textiles for trade with Spanish towns. In 1750, Spain gave Portugal the right to 400,000 square kilometers in that region, which included seven Jesuit missions. In 1754 the Guarani revolted against a forced migration and great cost in lost lives, land, and a way of life. The Jesuits tried to keep communities intact.

The Portuguese prime minister accused the Jesuits of abetting Guarani warfare and pressured Pope Benedict XIV to investigate the order for bloodthirsty vices. In 1761, an incensed Carlos III responded by abrogating the treaty over Portugal's refusal to deliver certain lands. The king of Portugal then confiscated Jesuit properties in his country, deported 1,100 Jesuits to Italy, recalled their missionaries, and "stuffed [them] into underground dungeons where they were left to rot away," writes John O'Malley, S.J.

The crackdown was fueled by the Jesuits' role in Martinique. As in New Orleans, the Society of Jesus priests were important actors in that island's economy. They established Martinique's first sugar plantation in 1640, becoming the island's second-largest slave owners. In 1756, the Jesuit operation had overextended debts. British ships captured thirteen vessels with export crops for Europe. Creditors sued the Society in France. The Jesuits lost. In August 1762, after Louis XV's failed efforts at intervention, the Paris Parlement barred the Jesuits from France and confiscated their buildings.

In 1763, people in New Orleans were unaware that their city was a Spanish property. The Jesuit plantation made the priests among Louisiana's largest slaveholders. Religious orders owned slaves in a moral myopia tied to the Crown, though they sometimes treated the enslaved better than other owners did. In Haiti, the Jesuits educated 25,000 slaves. The papacy was conflicted over slavery, believing that Indians who populated the vast Spanish empire were capable of belief in Jesus; but the structural church adhered to a Western economy, whose monarchies relied on enslaved labor. Missionary practices varied widely. In Paraguay, Jesuits sided with Indians. The Ursulines in New Orleans promoted family groupings among enslaved families in their community, relying on slave labor for their plantation. Creole planters saw the Jesuits, who paid no taxes, as unfairly advantaged. With the news from Paris, the Superior Council accused the Jesuits of ignoring missionary duties "to increase the value of their buildings and land" and ordered the seizure of the acreage, 10 buildings in the compound, 140 slaves, 280 books and sundry items. The auction ran eight days. "The church ornaments, sacred vessels and vestments were turned over to the Capuchins," wrote a historian. "The chapel of the Jesuits was razed and the graves on the plantation desecrated."

Had the Spanish taken power in New Orleans earlier, Carlos III would probably have spared the Jesuits, given his title of Royal Catholic Majesty. In 1773, Pope Clement XIV, pressured by other monarchs, suppressed the Jesuits. Thanks to sympathetic royals in Russia and Poland, the order survived, waiting to rebuild under a future pope.

In 1765, Spain assumed control of *Nueva Orleans*. Several Creole leaders, a Bienville nephew among them, sailed to France, hoping to persuade the king to change his mind. In Paris they tracked down the founder, seeking gravitas for their case; Bienville, white-haired at eighty-four, living alone on a pension, served instead as an ironic symbol of their plight. The king refused to see them.

Spain sent a governor, Don Antonio de Ulloa, a fifty-year-old distinguished scientist and diplomat. He had recently married a young Peruvian aristocrat, and her dowry gave him financial stability. Avoiding the Creoles' social swirl, the Ulloas made few friends. When a 1768 colonial decree ordered the port to trade within Spain's empire, a clutch of Creole planters and merchants, furious at losing French markets that allowed a free hand to smuggle, fomented a rebellion. Ulloa and his wife fled before a shot was fired. The city drifted in political limbo until August 1769, when Alejandro O'Reilly, a Dublin-born inspector general of the Spanish military, arrived with twelve ships and 2,056 soldiers.

O'Reilly had the rebel leaders arrested and tried, six of them shot by firing squad and six others shipped off to prison in Havana. Paying off government debts, O'Reilly replaced the Superior Council with the Cabildo, a town council. He oversaw the transfer from the *Code Noir* to Spanish slave law, which was more flexible in giving slaves the right to own property and for *coartación*, to petition for their own freedom by an adjudicated amount which an owner could not refuse. By 1791, 1,330 blacks had gained their freedom out of a population of 4,897. "The effect this had on slave morale can be imagined," writes Ned Sublette.

As the new administration shifted exports to Havana and Madrid, the city's economy improved. More than a generation had passed since the last ship from Africa had anchored in New Orleans. Spain opened the port to vessels laden with a range of enslaved Africans, particularly from Kongo. To maintain control, Spanish authorities offered selected slaves a chance for freedom by tracking down runaways. As Spanish jurists gave slaves some leeway to buy their freedom, more blacks owned weapons—a double-edged sword for the system of control. In September 1779, 80 free colored men joined a force of 670 in defeating the British in Florida. In the early winter of 1781, a rowdy river of free blacks and slaves rolled through streets in search of Carnival dances, a boisterous rebuke of laws to punish slaves circulating without a master's permit. The attorney general asked the Cabildo to restrict blacks from wearing masks that mimicked whites. "With so many strangers in the city, officials found it difficult to identify the race of masked revelers," writes Kimberly S. Hanger.

· · · · · · · · · ·

ST. MALÓ'S CHALLENGE

The French frontier town of New Orleans turned into a small Spanish city where most people spoke French. The Cabildo levied a planters' tax to compensate any owner whose slave died while leased out for work or on military patrol. By 1781, several maroon groups had compounds in the wilderness southeast of the city near Lake Borgne. The maroons called their village Ville Gaillarde, meaning a community for those who were strong, healthy, free, and clever. Governor Esteban Miró, a Spaniard who had married into a prominent local family, worried that in Ville Gaillarde maroons could live on yams, "fish and shell fish, and abundant wild life." He calculated that 500 *maroons* could defend their camp indefinitely. The local bayous were too thin for military ships to ramrod an overpowering assault.

The maroon leader, Juan Maló, had fled an upriver plantation in an area called the German Coast, after German colonists of the 1720s. Biographical details for Maló are sketchy; but he was a Creole, born a generation after the first Africans. For French speakers of French origin, the first association would be with Saint-Malo, the port city in Brittany. People called him San Maló—spelled St. Maló. *Malo* means "bad" in Spanish; to Bamana-speakers, it meant "shame." Calling him "San" may have been a coded articulation of *sans* (French for "without"). To the Bamana, a shameless man threw off conventions, a rebel from the social order.

As African people peeled off to join St. Maló's village, planters were staring at losses in fields without enough labor. "The runaways left in families," writes historian Gwendolyn Midlo Hall, "a substantial number of women and children among them." Captured maroons testified that they had fled with extended families because of the owners' cruelty.

Sunday dances in the field behind the town pulsed with a yearning for freedom. Africans knew that to join St. Maló brought the risk of being caught, tortured, and executed. St. Maló, in stealing supplies from plantations (tools, meat, and food through allies in slave quarters), was a rising threat to the system. In 1782, a Spanish commander set out with a battalion of colored troops, guided by four maroons-turned-spies. St. Maló's troops ambushed them, killing one man and wounding several others by gunfire. A second expedition went out, but St. Maló's maroons beat them back.

A captured maroon testified that St. Maló claimed to have killed four Englishmen in a boat en route to Mobile and had taken their weapons. In March 1783, a third battalion left the city for the maroon village guided by a slave who had negotiated his freedom, plus 200 pesos, to get them there. Seven pirogues crossed Lake Borgne, carrying armed slaves and free blacks in a force led by French and Spanish Creoles. Landing on firm ground, they saw Africans scatter into the woods and fired, killing one man and capturing twelve. Ten others fled into the marsh. In St. Maló's village, the troops seized eight more men, tied them up, and marched them back to the pirogues. As the flotilla paddled across the lake, a pirogue with four maroons drew close to the helm of Macnamara, a slave owner. The advancing rebels began shooting, killed one of their own captured men and wounded another *captif.* Macnamara fired back, hitting a maroon who keeled over, causing the canoe to capsize, guns sinking in the water. The marshland rebels swam toward his boat: Macnamara readied his men for their surrender. A voice roared out of the water: *"Use force!"* The maroons gripped the pirogue, pushing and shaking, trying to capsize it. Macnamara and his men hammered them with gun butts. One maroon sank dead in the water; Macnamara's men pulled a wounded man and two others into the pirogue as prisoners. St. Maló swam away, escaping to shore.

St. Maló

The prisoners revealed that outside Ville Gaillarde lay another compound and more homes. Maroons continued raiding plantations, leaving dead cattle in the fields. Governor Miró calculated that to capture St. Maló he needed an expedition with provisions for two weeks. A year passed with an unusually long winter. St. Maló was moving among several settlements as more maroons fled. With a price of 200 pesos on his head, St. Maló was a target for slaves willing to spy.

Governor Miró traveled to Florida in May to negotiate a treaty with Indians; he entrusted an aide, Francisco Bouligny, to attack St. Maló's band. A slave revealed that St. Maló had thirty-three men roaming the region, aided by networks on plantations with another maroon village south of the city at Barataria.

Prodded by wealthy planters, the Cabildo issued warnings of a potential economic collapse and launched a fourth expedition. The troops spent three days scouring Ville Gaillarde and the surrounding area, which was empty. A secondary force of five armed pirogues moved through arterial bayous off Lake Bourne, surprising a clutch of maroons along a bank who bolted into the marsh, trailed by gun blasts. The maroons sank into soggy muck, the soldiers kept shooting, and as smoke cleared they surrounded seventeen men; several of the outliers were wounded. A soldier discovered St. Maló among them. With a bullet wound in the arm, the maroon leader begged to be finished off. The troops knew immediately that St. Maló was much more valuable alive.

As the pirogues pushed upriver toward the Plaza de Armas, white people came to the levee to cheer the flotilla and the state's military superiority over an infinity of Sunday dances by African-blooded people.

The government hauled in forty men and twenty women among St. Maló's followers; a dozen were slaves complicit in aiding the maroons. Four collaborators were branded on the cheek with an *M*, for maroon, and released to their owners. Three men were given 300 whip lashes each and banished from Louisiana; it is hard to imagine them surviving the loss of blood.

In prison, St. Maló's wound turned to gangrene. In a book on the Cabildo, Gilbert C. Din and John E. Harkins write that the maroon leader complied with authorities, "confessed his crimes, and implicated others (Bouligny described him as acting as a fierce *fiscal* or prosecutor), even coaxing his lieutenants to admit their knowledge." Gwendolyn Hall doubts the validity of St. Maló's confession. Governor Miró expected to oversee the trial on his return. Bouligny ordered the prosecutor, Don de Reggio, to take depositions. Reggio did so and, without a trial, pronounced the prisoners guilty. A man in agony from a rotting wound can say anything. St. Maló knew that his execution was coming; what he "confessed" was also a way of *getting his story out*. The man who had yelled, *"Use force!,"* as the maroons shook the enemy boat, causing two of his captured followers to be shot, was an all-or-nothing warrior. Dying, reeling in pain, knowing his men were doomed, he may have wanted to spare them from torture while getting some final truth encoded. St. Maló had another concern: his wife, Cecilia Canuet (considered his ally in crime by officials), was sentenced to the gallows. Cecilia claimed she was pregnant. Did the confessions St. Maló induced help gain a suspension of her execution?

St. Maló faced the noose on the Plaza de Armas on June 12, 1784. Planters, free folk, slaves, Indians, *petit bourgeois*, German, Spanish, and French Creole planters massed under hot skies to watch the floggings and shrieks of minor figures before the execution of the ringleaders outside the church. A grotesque religious scandal erupted.

The Capuchin priests owned a man named Baptiste who, according to an official, had been identified by St. Maló as a member of his group when it had ambushed the Englishmen on a boat in Bay St. Louis. Baptiste had been working on his day off when arrested; he denied the accusation. Bishop Cirilo Sieni de Barcelona had stood approvingly with officials as the condemned men filed into the Plaza de Armas; but on seeing the priests' slave brought up for the whip, Bishop Cirilo and his clerics were outraged: Reggio had convicted Baptiste on a rush to judgment. Sentenced to 200 lashes, he was tied beneath the gallows. St. Maló, awaiting his noose, shouted that Baptiste and another slave laid bare for whipping were innocent. Shock hit the crowd as the clerics, on a balcony above the plaza, refused their customary role of hearing confessions of the condemned and walking with them to the gallows and whipping post. Cirilo shouted his protest of injustice to the slave Baptiste, tied up, no cleric at his side—an odd display of social conscience.

After that gory afternoon, when St. Maló was hanged and Baptiste shredded, Bishop Cirilo sent a letter of protest to Carlos III in Spain and a copy to the Cabildo. Bouligny's report to the Cabildo stated that citizens were relieved now to sleep in peace with maroons no longer roaming—justifying his judicial tactics. The slaves were "happy with the imprisonment and punishment of St. Maló and his companions … as just and indispensable." Over the next few months forty more prisoners were tied up for public lashings and several executed by hanging.

Slaves left no written accounts of their thoughts on St. Maló. Even those few who were literate would not dare to, given the state's overpowering rituals of death. Instead a symbolic language was growing at the Sunday marketplace behind the rampart, dancing by people from a larger map of African regions, before larger crowds than anyone had seen there. The spectacle upset Bishop Cirilo. In a 1786 pastoral letter he lamented, "Negroes who at the vespers hour, assembled in a green expanse called 'Place Congo' to dance the bamboula and perform the rites imported from Africa by the Yolofs, Foulahs, Bambarras, Mandigoes and other races." In identifying Africans by regional group, calling the commons the "Place Congo," *and* by singling out a dance, *bamboula*, the bishop sent us a flare on how the ritual psyche of danced memory had grown since the embryonic 1740s.

Slave ships under the Spanish had brought new African peoples to New Orleans, notably from Kongo. The name of the *bamboula* dance stems from the smaller of two cyndrical drums, *babula*, each held by a percussionist between the legs, the man astride the smaller-skinned surface hitting a swifter undercurrent of lines to the pounding rhythm of the larger drum. *Bambula* in the Kikunga language of Kongo means "to remember" or "to remind." What were the Place Congo dancers remembering? The upsurge of African peoples diversified a vocabulary of rhythm, movement, and chant lines of call-and-response. In northern Kongo, the spirits of those who die by violence can induce a writhing state of possession in devotees. We have no evidence of whether that happened at the Place Congo; but the trauma of St. Maló's death two years earlier surely was burned into the minds of dancers in their performances of memory.

Africans of different nationalities rejuvenated the Place Congo as twilight fell on the eighteenth century. By one inventory in the 1790s, 160 Africans of 584 shipped to New Orleans were from Kongo, the largest single group. In New Orleans, after some seventy years—more than two generations—in which the seminal Senegambians had grown old, or died, and their children became adults with families, the community absorbed people from Kongo and other regions in a Creole culture of adaptability, forging something new in an art of reassembling. *Bamboula* and other dances spread through islands of the Caribbean and Gulf of Mexico, north to New Orleans with variations on male dancers, inside the ring, prancing erotically around women who shimmied to undulating polyrhythms.

The erotic intensity of the dancing and power of the drums, coupled with Bishop Cirilo's letter, drove Governor Miró's stern order of 1786. Certain specifics show how the loopholes in the black code had been exploited. Though he did not outlaw Sunday slave dances, Miró restricted Africans from dancing in public squares during evening Mass—an indication of how widely spread they were. The order provides a freeze frame on that porous society: slaves could no longer rent apartments, and slaves and Indians could not buy liquor. As one can imagine, "enforcement" of these laws was a legal satire. Miró also heeded the sexual insecurity of white females by denouncing free colored women as "lascivious" for the feathers worn in their curls. Ordered to forego plumes and cover their hair, women of color responded with colorful, improvisational tunics called *tignons* that inspired portrait artists in years to come.

A deeper change began at this time in the emergence of voodoo, a West African belief system transplanted to New Orleans from Saint-Domingue as more ships carried enslaved people from the island.

For Fon people from Dahomey, *vodun* meant "genius" or "protective" spirit. Believers kept ancestral memory alive in a pantheon of once-living people, gods, and goddesses under a Creator. The *loa* (or *lwa* as spelled today in Haiti) were spirits of great energy who possessed the bodies of worshippers in ceremonies. In the swell of *captifs* from different West African nationalities sent to Caribbean islands—along with Brazil, Venezuela, and other New World outposts—a fusion of beliefs surged from spiritual need.

"Actually, *vodun* was Africa *reblended*," writes Robert Farris Thompson. "The encounter of the classical religions of Kongo, Dahomey, and Yorubaland gave rise to a creole religion." The altar of ancestral spirits found a welcoming belief in Roman Catholic liturgies and "saints who were said to work miracles."

Dancers in the *vodun* huts of Saint-Domingue found thrones of the once-living, altars where ancestral shades melded with visages of Catholic saints and umbrellas fringed with small flags representing ancestors for use in burial processions. The umbrella was an icon of African royalty. The ecstasy in trancelike possessions of death-in-life spirits radiated through slave villages, firing the passion for freedom in Saint-Domingue. When the 1789 revolution in Paris began spreading across France, the impact reached the island, where white planters felt superior to mulatto slave owners. In 1791, a plantation headman and high priest named Boukman launched a revolt in Le Cap Français. "Voodoo was the medium of conspiracy," C. L. R. James has written. The uprising failed, with Boukman decapitated and others brutally executed; but the spark was lit, the fires of revolution raged off and on through twelve years of butchery and massacres on all sides, culminating in a black victory and in 1804 the declaration of the Republic of Haiti. News of the rolling battles seared the white Southern mind. In 1792, New Orleans banned slave ships from the West Indies, fearing the worst.

In 1883, a brilliant, eccentric, and nomadic journalist named Lafcadio Hearn, working in New Orleans, took a boat south of the city for a piece in *Harper's Weekly* on Saint-Maló, a remote village in St. Bernard Parish. He found a lighthouse and cottages on stilts in an enclave of Filipino migrants. "The steel blue of the western horizon heated into furnace yellow, then cooled off into red splendors of astounding warmth," wrote Hearn in one of several evocative descriptions. The story-behind-the story eluded him. "It is said that the colony was founded by deserters—perhaps also by desperate refugees from Spanish justice."

St. Maló's resistance burrowed into the memory of African Americans, like a force made from the powder of crushed bones.

Shortly after the Civil War, an elderly African American woman in St. Bernard Parish sang "Dirge of St. Maló," in old Creole, for a scholar who later shared it with the writer George Washington Cable. Cable's translation appeared in a *Century Magazine* piece in 1888.

Alas, men, come make lament

For poor St. Maló in distress
They chased, they hunted him with dogs,
   They fired a rifle at him.
   They dragged him back from the cypress swamp
His arms they tied behind his back,
   They tied his hands in front of him;
   They tied him to a horse's tail,
   They dragged him up into the town.
   Before those grand Cabildo men
   They charged that he had made a plot
   To cut the throats of all the whites.
   They asked him who his comrades were.
Poor St. Maló said not a word!
The judge his sentence read to him,
   And then they raised the gallows tree.
   They drew the horse—the cart moved off
   And left St. Maló hanging there!
   The sun was up an hour high.
   They left his body swinging there
   For carrion crows to feed upon.

Oral traditions distill an essence, a story in the mind of a people, using or discarding certain facts. A dirge is a song of lamentation. A century after his death, this one became a praise song to St. Maló, absolving him of betrayal, with a telling silence on whether he planned to kill the whites. The *vodun* and *vodou* of Saint-Domingue, the island that cast off its name in becoming Haiti, reached New Orleans with the late eighteenth-century slave ships. The transplanted rituals ripened in the city's culture of spectacle. As African gods melded with images of Catholic saints, a new figure appeared in the pantheon. "St. Marron, a folk saint unique to New Orleans, was the patron of runaway slaves," writes Carolyn Morrow Long in a biography of the *vodou* priestess Marie Laveau.

Marronage spread in Saint-Domingue as runaways fled the cruelties of a regime, just as St. Maló's followers did in the marshes south of New Orleans. St. Marron reached New Orleans as a resurrected memory of Haiti, if not as a spiritual descendant of St. Maló; the figure assumes an image similar to St. Anthony in the city's voodoo pantheon. Anthony is the saint to whom Catholics pray for finding things they have lost. St. Maló survived, too, in oral traditions of Mardi Gras Indians, blacks who celebrate Native Americans for having harbored fugitive slaves; the tradition is rooted in Congo Square dance.

In the early 1990s, Bruce "Sunpie" Barnes, a rocking zydeco bluesman and leader of the Louisiana Sunspots band, began hearing shards of the St. Maló story from older black Indian chiefs. Raised in the Arkansas delta, Barnes is a brawny former football player who moved to New Orleans in 1987 as a researcher with the National Park Service; he pursued a music career while lecturing at the National Jazz Historic Park. In meeting Creole folk in bayou parishes south of the city, he found "stories about St. Maló well known among people who have household altars and remember him. In the plantation country around Vacherie"—in the vicinity of the estate that St. Maló fled—"the older people talk about him. I know people down around Bayou St. Maló who remember him. The village is underwater now from coastal erosion." In 2017, Sunpie and the Louisiana Sunspots released a song, "San Malo," with Barnes's booming voice and throbbing accordion rhythm:

> Saint Malo, you are hiding in the woods.
>   Soldiers are looking for you.
> Saint Malo you are very bad,
>   But you are also tough.
> *Oh Saint Malo, wiri wawawiri-oh!*
> *Oh Saint Malo, wiri wawiwir-oh!*
>
> Saint Malo, you are a real scoundrel,
>   but you make good magic.

The others who are amazed, and for the whites,
   you are a very high price.

Oh Saint Malo, wiri wawawiri-oh!
Oh Saint Malo, wiri wawiwir-oh!

Saint Malo made a big maroon village
   to free all of the slaves over there,
A lot of people came
   To save their lives.

Oh Saint Malo, wiri wawawiri-oh!
Oh Saint Malo, wiri wawiwir-oh!
   Saint Malo, you hid over there.
      Soldiers are searching for you.
   Saint Malo, you are bad,
      You are the most powerful spirit.

Oh Saint Malo, wiri wawiwir-oh!

3

*The Great Fire and Procession
for Carlos III*

In 1788, four years after the execution of St. Maló, *Nueva Orleans* had 5,388 people living in about a thousand houses among the nineteen streets laid out by the early French engineers. Most buildings faced the Mississippi for access to river breezes. Land near the levee ran higher than the rampart, a log-in-mud wall between the city and outback—the Congo field, a brickyard, military fort, and the great cypress swamp.

A network of ditches ran along the wood-plank sidewalks, called *banquettes*. In heavy rain the ditches spilled muck into streets where pigs wallowed and errant cows got stuck. Just inside the rampart, St. Peter Street cemetery lodged the dead of all colors, as an archaeological excavation discovered in the 1980s. Roads by the rampart, sparsely populated, sprouted thickets of weeds and shrubs. The near-river streets that led toward the Plaza de Armas, like Bourbon, Royal, and Chartres, had cottages and townhouses interspersed with two-story homes, shops for meat, wine, and dry goods close to the Cabildo, church, and stockade at the square. The city as yet had no newspaper or public library; eight private schools, teaching in French, had 400 pupils, in addition to the Ursuline school for girls.

Shingled cottages of brick and mortar typically had small yards. The two-story cypress homes with steep Norman roofs and wraparound balconies, called galleries, had room for gardens of ornamental beauty, a lasting influence of French aesthetics. People crossed footbridges over the *banquettes* to reach residences. The small city at times had a glow from radiant wildflowers and pink azaleas, a French transplant. The finer homes harmonized with an elegant vision of Pauger's 1721 street grid. People tended orange and lemon trees, the seedlings originally from Saint-Domingue. The Plaza de Armas, the soldiers' parade ground, functioned as a park when not used for military band concerts or executions.

Louis XV had transferred to Carlos III a city with serious deferred maintenance. Workers fortified the levees, but water seepage left damp streets, adding mud to the mounds of rubbish. Poor folk occupied hovels that put out odors from chicken coops, goat dung, and rabbit cages. The night sky emboldened rats, snakes, bull roaches, even alligators slithering over the *banquettes*, streets, and yards. "The puddles, hoofs, feet, wheels, and wind eroded Calle Borbon unevenly," writes Richard Campanella in *Bourbon Street: A History*. "Horses and carriages, pedestrians, frolicking children, stray dogs, occasional livestock, the Cabildo-paid town crier, and peddlers" singing French-Creole sales of pork, beef, fowl, and fish animated street life. Mule-drawn carts toted off human waste from home privies in a sanitation policy myopic to the mule plop that rainwater washed into ditches; poor drainage drew virus-laden flies. People with means slept behind netting to avoid insect bites.

The city had worn-down military defenses, too. In fealty to a distant ruler, His Royal Catholic Majesty, Carlos III, in Madrid, the French Creoles began welcoming Spanish soldiers and administrators, many of them bachelors. Unlike his French royal cousins, who supported mistresses and confessed to trusted clerics, Carlos III, known for probity, sired thirteen children with Queen María Amelia; five died young. "Carlos III hunted nearly every afternoon from one o'clock till dusk, roaming the countryside in pursuit of wolves and foxes that preyed on his subjects' farms and livestock," writes Jon Kukla. He kept a three-decade kill tally: 5,323 foxes, 539 wolves. A benevolent despot, he created "hospitals, free schools, savings banks ... asylums and poor houses."

After the suppression of the Jesuits, bishops in Spain's far-flung colonies sent their priests to Jesuit Indian missions that hung portraits of the king and queen. A catechism for Indians in Bolivia reads as follows:

Question: Who are you?
Answer: I am a loyal vassal of the King of Spain.
Q: Who is the King of Spain?
A: He is a Lord so absolute that he recognizes no greater temporal authority.
Q: And where does this King derive his royal power?
A: From God himself.

Crown and Church saw Indians as capable of rational thought, given correct spiritual training, a view that encouraged the intermarriage of natives and Spaniards in parts of the Latin American empire.

Like Louisiana's French kings, Carlos III never saw New Orleans; yet he was more deeply involved in its issues and left lasting marks. The elegant thoroughfare begun in 1835, St. Charles Avenue, honored Carlos III with the name of his patron saint, Charles Borromeo.

The Spanish king needed a well-armed port to block British vessels' access to the Gulf. Half of Spain's export trade came from the silver mines of Mexico, one-fifth of which went straight to the Crown. The superintendent of the king's mint in Mexico sent silver pesos to New Orleans, via Havana, to float the local economy. As the American Revolution began, British forces drove the Spanish out of Florida and moved into Louisiana, taking Baton Rouge. General O'Reilly, on capturing New Orleans, had expelled English merchants and traders. A bevy of exiles regrouped west of Lake Pontchartrain at Manchac, a way station for bayou commerce with Baton Rouge. The Crown prohibited trade with Britain; Spanish officials in the city tolerated a black market of smugglers selling corn, flour, and necessities in the New Orleans area. Anglo-Americans had overtaken Indians as suppliers in the food chain.

After decades as a French outback, New Orleans was reborn in the 1770s as a transshipment point for Spanish support of the American Revolution. Oliver Pollack, an Irish-born merchant, worked with Governor Luís de Unzaga y Amézaga to smuggle gunpowder from the king's warehouse to American rebels in Virginia. On January 1, 1777, Lt. Gen. Bernardo de Gálvez, the nephew of Spain's minister for the Indies, succeeded Unzaga as acting governor. A seasoned soldier, the thirty-year-old Gálvez worked with Pollack in channeling medical supplies, weapons, and gunpowder from Cuba up the Mississippi, using the Spanish flag for diplomatic passage, avoiding inspections at British-held ports. The charismatic Gálvez, meanwhile, charmed a young widow, Félicie de St. Maxent d'Estréhan, a daughter of one of the wealthiest Creole planters. Ten months later, despite a prohibition barring top Spanish officials from marrying into local families, Bernardo and Félicie exchanged vows before Cirilo de Barcelona, the vicar general and future bishop of Louisiana. Her father included slaves in the dowry.

For a general to raise an army in New Orleans turned on stark concessions to racial reality: a black majority blanketed the city and suburban plantations (about 8,000 people total) with a limited pool of white males. French governors followed Bienville's strategy of recruiting Africans to earn their freedom by fighting against Indians. When General O'Reilly stepped off his warship at the plaza to bugles and booming cannons in 1769, he had eighty black soldiers among 2,062 troops. O'Reilly secured an oath of allegiance to Carlos III from prominent citizens and groups, including thirty-four soldiers from "La Compagnie des Mulâtres et Nègres Libres de cette colonie de la Louisiane." Some signed their names "X." Gálvez continued recruiting the black militia as he gathered troops in the summer of 1779.

To boost Louisiana's population, Spain provided ships for 2,000 "Isleños" from the Canary Islands, soldiers and their families who arrived in New Orleans from late 1778 through the summer of 1779. Many of them settled in marshlands south of the city, near the area where St. Maló and the maroons had retreated in today's St. Bernard Parish (so named for Bernardo de Gálvez, as was Galveston, Texas). In August 1779, Gálvez learned from an intercepted letter that the British had moved 400 troops to Manchac as a wing before sending 1,500 soldiers from Pensacola to invade New Orleans. Planning his defense, Gálvez sent Lt. Col. Esteban Miró with 260 troops, 100 of them black, to positions below Manchac.

On August 18, days before Gálvez's launch, a hurricane smashed the city, destroying dozens of buildings, killing farm livestock, and sinking most of his gunboats. Gálvez called a mass meeting at the Plaza de Armas. After receiving official notice that elevated him from "acting" to "Governor," he waited for a prime moment to reveal the news. Now he had it. Gálvez told the crowd of his sympathy and support for the battered city. "Although I am disposed to shed my last drop of blood for Louisiana and for my king, I cannot take an oath which I may be exposed to violate, because I do not know whether you will help in resisting the ambitious designs of the English. What do you say? Shall I take the oath of governor? Shall I swear to defend Louisiana?"

The crash of applause raced his blood; volunteers came forth.

On August 27, Gálvez led the troops west on the road along the Mississippi, marching upriver past the German Coast, a force of 667 men, the majority Spaniards, 89 of African descent, 60 white Creoles, 9 American volunteers. They covered 115 miles over eleven days in heat so brutal that men were falling out like flies; the army was also a moving magnet, pulling in armed Indians and white militiamen, pushing the numbers to 1,427 when Gálvez camped on September 6, a mile outside of Manchac. The next morning in thick fog he ordered the attack; they encountered only two dozen troops. Manchac surrendered quickly; a handful of men ran away.

Gálvez had several gunboats trail the army along the Mississippi. After Manchac, he rested his troops several days, off-loaded cannons and pushed ahead to within firing distance of Baton Rouge. As troops dug placements to embed the artillery, Gálvez sent soldiers out to cut firewood, a distraction to draw enemy fire. The cannons blasted the Baton Rouge defensive wall, forcing a surrender that included all British forts on the Mississippi. Gálvez's return to New Orleans elated citizens trailed by memories of Bienville's failed campaigns against the Chickasaw: a *victory*! Gálvez honored ten black militia leaders with silver medals for service to King Carlos; several black officers were promoted. Amassing a larger army, Gálvez captured Mobile, and later Pensacola.

"The grand tradition began of New Orleanians of color playing in a military band," writes Ned Sublette. Mulatto soldiers, called *pardos*, wore the round hat with crimson cockade, white jacket, and a collar of inlaid gold buttons, marching in trousers and knee boots, advancing to cadences of the drummers and fifers. Spanish policy gave dark-skinned blacks, called *morenos*, a green jacket with white buttons and lapels. Musicians played the rousing Spanish and French melodies, extending a European tradition of marching with troops bound for battle to trumpets and kettledrums. For whites, the appetite for parades mingled pride and a sense of security in marching soldiers as a guardian force, a symbol of protection. Authorities required colored officers of both groups to be proficient "in reading and writing, ability to command, and a proper lifestyle reflective of the officer's social position," writes Kimberly S. Hanger. Nevertheless, Cabildo authorities worried that maroon outliers had blood ties to black soldiers or free colored families. *Gens de couleur libres* constituted 9.8 percent of the population in 1778. And yet nearly two-thirds of them owned at least one slave. Family ties among black people made the porous society more unpredictable to those at the top.

Despite the anxiety of its ruling class, had New Orleans been a democracy, Gálvez would have been unbeatable. His victories over the British won the admiration of George Washington, strengthening Spanish ties with the emergent United States. In the winter of 1781, as Gálvez prepared to attack Pensacola, the season of balls that began after the November harvest, when the planters and their families moved to their homes in town, rolled on with music and dancing into the spring. Later that year, after Galvez's victory in Florida, Carlos III sent him to Havana as captain general. Gálvez's second-in-command, Esteban Rodriguez Miró, took his place. In 1784, Carlos elevated Gálvez to a new pinnacle, as viceroy to Mexico.

The Great Fire and Procession

The Cabildo, which met in a building on the Plaza de Armas, functioned as both town council and judiciary. The governor presided over eight men with an *escribano*, the royally appointed scribe, a notary public fluent in Spanish and French who earned handsome fees for sideline work. Six councilmen, major owners of property and slaves, were called *regidores perpetuos*—they purchased seats-for-life, which could be sold at auction or passed on to heirs should the *regidor* die. Two *alcaldes ordinarios*, or civil judges, competed in annual elections. The eight officials formed the council's voting body. The *regidores* held collateral offices overseeing city governance, with lesser scribes producing official documents in ornate prose. The *alcaldes ordinarios* ruled in civil disputes but held no authority over the military or the Church.

People in the Spanish city had an ample food chain. The Indian trade begun by Bienville meant a supply of ducklings, geese, water hens, venison, turkey, and rabbit, among the fowl and game that Africans hunted, too. The Gulf, the bayous, and the saltwater Lake Pontchartrain yielded oysters, bass, catfish, redfish, speckled trout, croaker, and flounder. In 1779, the Cabildo opened a public market for beef and mutton at the levee, just above the plaza, with inspectors to insure cleanliness and fair scales. Fish vendors had designated spots at the area that would become the French Market, selling to taverns, cabarets, eateries, and cooks for private kitchens. Private gardens provided some seasoning apart from the traffic in filé powder, bay leaves, garlic, and peppers. The era of grand restaurants was yet to come, but people ate well.

Governor Miró was a battle-tested soldier who, like Gálvez, had married a daughter of the landed class. Miró and the *regidores* "were the disciples of rival ministries and court cliques in Spain," writes Christina Vella in *Intimate Enemies*. She likens the Cabildo to an aquarium where "the biggest fish randomly and continually nipped at each other and the governor, so as to control as much of the fishbowl as possible."

Andrés Almonaster y Roxas was the biggest local fish. Born in 1728 in a village near Seville, Almonaster as a young man moved to Madrid and became a royal notary, sealing transactions as an official witness. Madrid was a congested city of 150,000 people whose roaming pigs on slop-ridden lanes led Carlos III to raze slums, erect public gas lights, and pave and clean the streets. Almonaster's wife had died when he sailed to New Orleans with General O'Reilly in 1769. The city's mucky side probably struck him as a miniature Madrid. On March 16, 1770, the arriviste Spaniard stood before "The Illustrious Cabildo," the term of the recording secretary who read the royal edict: "His Majesty honors Don Andrés Almonaster y Roxas with the position of Secretary for all his Kingdom ... [and] as Public Secretary for War in charge of the Royal Treasury" in Louisiana. Following the declaration, the Cabildo *regidores*, each in turn, placed the royal edict on top of their heads, in a ritual of submission to the king.

Almonaster earned a tidal flow of money; the notary's job was to authenticate all evidence submitted to a court. He was the paid public witness for countless transactions and acts, such as certifying that horrible punishments of convicted slaves were carried out. "Hundreds of documents sent to the captain general in Cuba every few months had to be inspected and signed by a notary," writes Vella.

Upon his arrival and purchase of land and slaves, Almonaster became a builder, buying and selling real estate. With a modest home in town and a brickyard and plantation on Bayou Road, he bought lots bordering the Plaza de Armas from *regidores* and built additional dwellings. With a fortune and no family, Almonaster in his fifties became a philanthropist. Funding worthy projects was fulfilling and enhanced his image with the king.

In 1782, his offer to rebuild Charity Hospital unloosed jealousies among members of the Cabildo. Endowed in 1735 by the will of a sailor, Jean Louis, for "the founding of a free hospital for the poor and needy sick," the longest-operating Charity Hospital in the United States (until 2005) was first housed in a former residence at Chartres and Bienville Streets: the Hospital of St. John, as originally named, was unrelated to the Royal Hospital staffed by Ursuline nuns. The indigents' hospital moved into a new building in the 1740s on a large lot near the rampart by the St. Peter Street cemetery. Supported by donations, under the auspices of the Superior Council, the hospital was in disrepair as the French era ended. Under Spanish law, control fell to the governor and His Catholic Majesty's religious representative, Cirilo Sieni de Barcelona, the provincial vicar. The hurricane of 1779 demolished the building, leaving a kitchen and storehouse as a makeshift hospital with six beds.

Almonaster's 1782 offer to fund the rebuilding sparked a power struggle. The Cabildo *regidores* announced that they would appoint a hospital superintendent and treasurer. Incensed at the challenge to his authority, Cirilo protested to Gálvez (still the titular governor) in Havana: "It is clear from the Spanish laws that they have no right." Cirilo had traveled as military chaplain with Gálvez's troops and officiated at the governor's wedding. Gálvez blocked the *regidores*' move.

But for acting governor Esteban Miró, letting Almonaster build the hospital was an easy call. They were friends, fellow Spaniards, and the Cabildo men hadn't lifted a finger for the barely functional hospital in three years since the brutal storm. Almonaster's generosity reflected well on Governor Miró, whose baby girl Cirilo had baptized. To be doubly safe, Almonaster wrote King Carlos, seeking the permission he naturally received. The *regidores* protested that a new hospital would complicate street expansion in the underpopulated area—and Almonaster planned to use recycled bricks! Miró stymied them. Almonaster established two large stores and three smaller ones close by, producing rental income for operating funds at the Charity Hospital of San Carlos, named for the king. Almonaster chose the superintendent, specifying details on food, sanitation of utensils, and a private bed for each patient. In 1785 when the hospital opened, he also built a smaller facility for lepers, a safe distance behind his Bayou Road plantation.

Standing above the fray of the hectoring Cabildo men, Almonaster had the confidence of wealth, Miró's solidarity, and the friendship of a Spanish missionary priest who arrived in 1781. Antonio de Sedella, thirty-one, was two decades younger than Almonaster. The Grenada-born Capuchin's personality was so mesmerizing that Creoles called him "Père Antoine," as if he were French, instead of "Padre Antonio." Cirilo made him director of Charity Hospital, providing an alliance with Almonaster, whose patience was stretched by the Cabildo *regidores* scheming to control his largesse. The aging bachelor and the dynamic young priest became fast friends. When Cirilo traveled to Cuba in 1784 to be elevated as a bishop, Sedella was auxiliary vicar, governing church operations. Wearing sandals and the brown robe of his Capuchin order (a division of the Franciscans, vowed to poverty and work with the poor), Antonio de Sedella was pastor of the church at the Plaza de Armas.

In a city where black people, enslaved and free, brought infants for baptism and worshipped at St. Louis Church, the popular Père Antoine in 1786 achieved a secret status known to few people beyond Miró: the ecclesiastical court in Cartagena, Colombia, named Sedella a commissary, or secret agent, of the Holy Office of the Inquisition. The Inquisition's dark history of persecuting European heretics, burning some at the stake, fed on paranoia over power. Church officials of the Spanish empire, fearful of the French Enlightenment's free-thinking poisons, created Inquisition tribunals in Mexico and Colombia, among other colonies. Miró, though Catholic, was a pragmatist. Despite routine communications with Sedella over church administration, he was uneasy with the idea of a cleric spying on people to advance prosecutions for blasphemy in a church tribunal, or forcing unwanted cases on the Cabildo. Sedella routinely closed his letters to Miró, "I kiss the hand of Your Lordship."

At Sedella's suggestion, Almonaster built a brick chapel for the Ursulines. On March 20, 1787, Almonaster, then fifty-nine, married a twenty-nine-year-old Creole, Louise de La Ronde. Their house on a corner of the Plaza de Armas was staffed by forty-four slaves, with "a constant and more or less furtive traffic of black men coming to visit the women servants."

Meanwhile, Père Antoine was gaining popularity at St. Louis Church, while the commerce that encouraged Miró brought sailors and merchants from upriver American states or territories, which were grounded in the separation of church and state. In His Catholic Majesty's colony, the last thing Miró needed was some zealot targeting apostate braggarts in any of the city's seventy-five taverns that produced $1.85 million in revenue (and prostitution profits untold) or trying to root out sinful literature in private French libraries. Miró had begun a family in this exotic city, so different from his native Catalonia. He did not want Sedella gumming things up.

King Carlos had authorized benefits to Acadian exiles fleeing Nova Scotia after the British invasions between 1755 and 1764. Spain helped French-speaking farmers and ranchers in the diaspora of *le grand dérangement* (the great expulsion) find land in Louisiana's southern prairie and bayou country. The policy of gifts to Indian leaders was paying off, too. In 1787, the once-menacing Chickasaw sent a peace delegation with the Choctaw, thirty-six chiefs in all, as city folk watched the parade of feathers, chanting, dancing, and shaking gourds. Miró gave a welcoming speech, smoked the calumet, bestowed medals, and hosted them at a ball where the Creole ladies in fine dresses dazzled the chiefs.

The sheer size of the country expanding to the north, from the Carolinas over to Tennessee, down into Mississippi and Alabama as whites pushed deeper, rendered New Orleans vulnerable to ships carrying troops larger than his army, Miró realized. Determined to keep the city safe, he recognized the complexities of a fluid society.

But he could not protect the city from its fate on Good Friday, March 21, 1788.

After morning liturgy at St. Louis Church, Vicente José Núñez, a twenty-seven-year-old army paymaster, walked home to 619 Chartres Street, a block upriver from the Plaza de Armas. A Spaniard who kept a devotional altar at home, Núñez lit upward of fifty votive candles and after prayers retreated for the afternoon meal. Possibly he took a nap. The candle heat swelled like a furnace and at about three that day the ceiling burst into flames and spread to adjacent buildings. A terrific wind swept in from the river, stoking the flames into a fireball whose tentacles stretched from roof-top to rooftop, igniting shingles of chip wood, ranging down the dry walls of stucco or cypress that crackled like kindling—the flames gorged on rugs, chairs, tables, toys, curtains, and beds, people bolted out of doors, crowds retreating along the levee or upriver toward plantations. The blaze raged across the Plaza de Armas into St. Louis Church, flames eating the empty pews and icons of saints.

Sedella reported to a Cuban bishop that he ordered men to sprinkle the rooftops with water, thus reducing the spread of the fire—a claim contrary to other eyewitness accounts, which said the town had few buckets or emergency water. St. Louis Church burned to rubble; so did the priests' lodging, the Cabildo hall, the military barracks at the plaza, and the stockade where guards released prisoners to save their lives. The billowing trail of fire left scorched lots where houses had stood at noon; the flames raged along St. Peter Street to cross-streets below the Plaza de Armas amid a boom of explosions from loaded weapons people had illegally stored in their homes. The holocaust burned with a ferocity no one there had ever seen. In less than five hours, 856 buildings were destroyed, eight-tenths of the homes, the core of the business district, and most of the mansions of French design, a smoking semicarcass of the city as flames sputtered out toward eight that night.

"With dawn the scene appeared more horrible and pitiful," a numbed Miró wrote in his report to Havana, "seeing along the road in the most abject misery so many families who, a few hours before, enjoyed large fortunes and more than average comforts of life." Only one person died. Miró had seen soldiers die in battle, yet he was unnerved by the sobbing and "ghastliness" of faces in the ruins of "a city that was the product of seventy years of labor."

From government offices upwind of the fire, Miró and Martín Navarro, the Crown tax collector, secured the colonial archives and King Carlos's funds. They threw themselves into emergency relief, giving out military tents to house the hundreds of homeless, with rice, biscuits, and petty cash for basic needs. At Miró's behest, outlying plantation owners sent corn and peas; he sent ships with money to Philadelphia and other ports for medicine, nails, food, and supplies. "Soon Madrid was pouring silver into the rebuilding of New Orleans," writes Lawrence N. Powell.

The Good Friday fire of 1788 destroyed most of the French colonial city; the Spanish rebuilding efforts maintained the tradition. As homeowners, slaves, colored artisans, and soldiers, black and white, cleared away charred beams and burned remains of houses, Bertrand Gravier and his wife, who owned a large plantation on the near-upriver side of the city, decided to sell off tracts to facilitate a new suburb, Faubourg Sainte-Marie. On April 1, the royal surveyor drew out squares with three cross-streets, four roads running perpendicular to the river, and an angular street named Gravier (in today's central business district). Another street, San Carlos, was named for the king.

Miró insisted on stronger timber and materials for reconstruction, while preserving the French grid, yards, and spacing of lots. The Plaza de Armas eventually gained a breezeway supported by thick round pillars of Spanish colonial style for the spacious Cabildo—completed in 1799, a classic structure today—lodged between the church and the Presbytère, all funded by Almonaster. Slave labor was pivotal to the reconstruction that followed the 1788 fire. So, too, was a well-trained corps of blacksmiths, enslaved and free, who forged a rich, wrought-iron balcony style in years to come, reflecting Havana's influence. Several months after the event, a *London Chronicle* dispatch called New Orleans the "most regular, well-governed, small city in the western world."

And yet the scope of suffering grew in the months after the Great Fire. Tons of charred rubble and soot shoveled out of burned buildings sent up a filthy haze, full of toxins. Illnesses spread; a fever contagion struck in the fall. People were dying so fast that the cemetery could no longer accommodate the bodies. Miró wrote Sedella on October 25, citing the "epidemic which has raged" as a result of the fire, the river flooding, and "the evil odor coming from the cemetery." In a swipe at the Cabildo, Miró added that "public opinion not being influenced this time by the prejudices usual in a matter of this kind, agrees that the cemetery will be removed"—meaning, they had to bury the dead across the rampart, against royal policy, which mandated burials in the church or St. Peter Street graveyard. Miró wanted a new "provisional cemetery" behind Charity Hospital. "The old," he continued, "is not to be destroyed till the reception of the royal approval." In securing the auxiliary vicar's consent, Miró signaled that Sedella was a player in the ring of power. Digging began on the new St. Louis Cemetery, 90,000 square feet between the Congo field and the garden behind Charity Hospital.

On Christmas Eve 1788, Carlos III died in Madrid, surrounded by his family. It took four months for the news to reach *Nueva Orleans* by ship. Miró and the Cabildo members immediately planned a state funeral. Almonaster now sat on the Cabildo, having outmaneuvered the *regidores* who had schemed against him.

"Because of isolation and ignorance, colonial New Orleanians suffered from boredom," report Cabildo historians Gilbert C. Din and John E.

Harkins. "No ceremonial event in New Orleans in the Spanish period compared to those held in 1789 to commemorate the death of King Carlos III and the accession to the throne of his son, Carlos IV."

The record of the "Illustrious Body," as the Cabildo scribe, Pedro Pedesclaux, calls the *regidores*, opens a window on a traumatized people seeking hope.

For the funeral procession on April 22, 1789, Governor Miró dispatched two commissioners, draped in black mourning colors, behind "the two mace-bearers of the city,... also in mourning, to accompany the publishing of the ceremony," noted the scribe, "with all the pomp and splendor which the limited funds of the City Treasury will permit." Financially battered by the fire, the town would spare no expense for the memory of the king. Following the mace-bearers, two infantry battalions in full finery paraded forth; the record does not say if black troops marched in a unit, but it is impossible to imagine the *pardo* and *moreno* soldiers, honored with medals by King Carlos, holding back or being barred from the procession of "distinguished persons of this Capitol" to the chapel at Charity Hospital, the available sacred space since the fire. Almonaster must have taken some solace in that.

The altar was transformed into a "majestic sepulchral bier." The canopy that nearly touched the ceiling must have taken several days' work to complete, with insignias of the king and medals of royalty sewn into the four arched festoons that "covered in mourning the main chapel, the contour of the altar, its furnishings and pulpit adorned with sixty Royal Coat of Arms placed in symmetrical harmony." Inside the canopy on the majestic bier rested an urn draped in a mantle of blazing red violet, on top of which rested a pillow with golden tassels and braid. Across the pillow lay a "scepter and gilt crown with bright beautiful enamel, which resembled precious stones."

And then, in one of those choice scenes that rise from the words of a distant past like the clarion call of a culture, the Cabildo scribe marvels at how the flames in "large torch holders and candlesticks, the large number of lights giving splendor to the mournful display, presented a strange spectacle equally respectful and demonstrative as was the high object to whom it was dedicated as the veneration and tender love of those offering the same."

Strange splendor, indeed: notables of a city that had lost 80 percent of its building stock in a fire thirteen months earlier, people who had sobbed and buried kith and kin in the train of death over recent months from the fever plague, members of the "Illustrious Body," survivors all, sat in pews lit up by gigantic candles to mourn a king they had never seen. The late April heat from that torch-and-candle power was thick enough to spring ringlets of sweat about the necks of the women and men, perspiring to darken garments and underarms even with fluttering hand fans. The French and Spanish Creoles clung to a belief in royalty and their places in a hierarchy transplanted from the Old World. In a very real sense they were celebrating themselves and their endurance. Welcoming them at the altar, notes the scribe, stood "the Reverend Father Friar Antonio de Sedella, Religious Capuchin Priest, Ex-Lecturer of Sacred Theology, Commissary of the Church, Parish Priest, Parson, Ecclesiastical Judge of this said City who with his distinguished eloquence and Christian fervor eulogized the well-known exalted virtues of the August deceased King, vivifying them with energetic descriptions of the paternal love with which he always held the good will of his subjects, the real sorrow and tears of the audience in such a grievous loss concluded the ceremony," followed by artillery bursts from the infantry, "discharging volleys as ordered at Royal funerals, and about midday this Illustrious Body returned in the same order and with the original accompaniment to the Government Building where courteous leave taking took place."

Members of the Illustrious Body then went home for siesta.

At four in the afternoon they reassembled, Governor Miró, the Cabildo *regidores*, the military officers, the mace-bearers, the infantry troops in full dress, and the society notables moving to "the sound of their drums and music, and completing this retinue, the Picket of Mounted Guards of Dragoons," marching to the home of the perpetual commissioner and royal ensign of the city who had charge of the royal banner under Spanish code. The royal ensign was Don Carlos de Reggio, who had prosecuted St. Maló and the maroons five years earlier. At his home another ceremony ensued, followed by "delicious refreshments ... served to a large number of persons," with a spillover crowd served beneath awnings erected in the yard for the occasion. Then Reggio, flanked by the military entourage and trailed by the Illustrious Body, escorted the royal banner back to the Cabildo and then to the hospital chapel, where Friar Sedella, several priests, and a deacon received it from the hands of the royal ensign and placed it before the altar for the blessing. Everyone then sang the "Te Deum," the Latin song of praise to the Lord that La Salle and his men had intoned 107 years earlier on discovering the mouth of the Mississippi River.

The Illustrious Body marched back "in the same formation, escort and retinue, increased by the clergy" to the recently constructed council chambers. The ensign stood on the balcony facing the Plaza de Armas, waving the royal banner to the cheering crowds. With the formal announcement of the new king, Carlos IV, came three artillery salvos and more cheers. The celebration ran three nights, with "sweet music from a large orchestra," the staging of two comedies, and dances attended "by all the prominent people of both sexes who were served with abundant and delicious refreshments in the Saloon." The festivities were courtesy of the governor and city funds in "the amount of 201 pesos and 7 reales, which [Cabildo members] found very reasonable, in comparison to the high prices of everything, at the present time."

The lavish prose omits what music the military band played in the procession or the orchestra for dancing by the Illustrious Body. Nevertheless, the picture of a marching military band and prominent citizens processing extends the line of European funereal custom, wrapped in power and privilege. The Cabildo report of Carlos III's funeral is our first account of musicians parading to honor the dead in New Orleans, a tradition that would magnify as parades became a winding mirror on the evolution of society in generations to come.

The Cabildo's glowing account of Antonio de Sedella's sermon masks the trouble he faced. As the historian Richard E. Greenleaf observed, "What is clear from diocesan records is that long before his clashes with Governor Esteban Miró, Père Antoine was acting as judge in cases normally handled by the Inquisition in New Spain."

Bishop Cirilo de Barcelona, still in Cuba, was vexed on learning that the young cleric he had entrusted as vicar, or chief administrator of the Louisiana church, was an agent of the Inquisition. Cirilo lobbied Havana bishop Santiago José de Echevarría y Eleguezúa to intervene with higher church authorities and revoke Sedella's judicial post. Echevarría and Cuba's captain general Las Casas agreed with Cirilo, fearing "grave disturbances" from a campaign against heretics in heavily French Louisiana, a sponge for foreign merchants, sailors, and flatboatmen of whatever faith or none. Echevarría of Havana ordered the suspension of Sedella as an Inquisition official; Bishop Cirilo wrote King Carlos IV on July 13, 1787, seeking his support. On January 9, 1788, Carlos upheld the suspension. Sedella remained the vicar of Louisiana in Bishop Cirilo's absence.

In the chaos, suffering, and agonizing losses between the Great Fire and funeral for the king, Père Antoine gained popularity with the people, while polarizing the local clergy into Spanish and Cuban camps. When Bishop Cirilo returned to New Orleans on August 30, 1789, to inspect the state of the Church, peasants were rioting in France, and a radicalized National Assembly in Paris had abolished the feudal rights of the clergy and aristocracy. Far from the early explosions of the French Revolution, Cirilo, a legal purist, viewed Sedella as a troublemaker who mocked the virtue inherent in obedience. After an investigation, Cirilo reported to Havana's new bishop, José de Trespalacios, that Sedella had hidden accounts on the Church books; moreover, he had improperly performed weddings. On November 20, 1789, he wrote Trespalacios asking for Sedella's removal. The Cuban bishop gave Cirilo the approval for a canon law process to remove Sedella.

Sedella in turn wrote Trespalacios, portraying himself as victim of a hostile bishop; he rallied the support of Almonaster, Ursuline nuns, military officers, judges, and shopkeepers in 250 pages of testimonials. Cirilo offered to drop the punitive proceeding if Sedella would return to Spain voluntarily; the bishop asked him to go to Pensacola, but Sedella balked, further angering Cirilo. The bishop turned to Miró for help. In consulting his advisors, the governor realized that Père Antoine had allies in his own inner circle. The clerics' feud put Miró between a rock and a hard place.

At nine o'clock on the night of April 28, 1790, Sedella showed up at Miró's residence brandishing a trump card: an order from the Spanish Inquisition, dated December 5, 1789, empowering him to confiscate seditious literature. Miró could imagine what might lurk in the libraries of Creole grandees and their fury at such zealotry. He did not need that. Sedella gave Miró a letter of his own, requesting that the military "furnish me immediately the soldiers whom I may request to carry out my duties." "Your Lordship will please advise me of the place, to which you will communicate your orders for my guidance."

Miró was gravely noncommittal.

The next day, an emboldened Sedella sent a letter to Miró, asking that "Your Lordship will please communicate to me, without delay, the secret orders I requested yesterday." He warned that "the success of my mission is imperiled by such tardy measures"—he needed those soldiers. That night, to his delight, a group of soldiers knocked on Père Antoine's door after the dinner hour, only to shock him by placing him under arrest, making him leave without time to pack. They took Sedella to the river dock, where Bishop Cirilo put him on a barge, guarded by soldiers. Soon Père Antoine was on a ship bound for Cadiz, back to Spain, a nuisance no more.

4

City of Migrants

On the morning of January 21, 1793, Louis XVI knelt before the guillotine in a public square of Paris. A hushed crowd watched the blade drop, and when the executioner held up the king's severed head, "blood flowed and cries of joy from eighty thousand armed men struck my ears," wrote a revolutionary polemicist, a tad dazed. "I saw people pass by, arm in arm, laughing, chatting familiarly as if they were at a fête." The Revolution sent France into war with Spain and Britain.

The Reign of Terror in Paris put Creole descendants of the Bienville era on a psychological tightrope between their French identity and their status as subjects of the king of Spain. Spanish coffers paid for the city's defense and rebuilding after the 1788 fire. By 1792, Jacobin partisans of the French Revolution had become brash figures on Calle Borbón and old streets named for a tottering monarchy. People fleeing the French island of Saint-Domingue—planters, white and colored, as well as physicians, artisans, teachers, and the enslaved—told traumatic tales of killings and lives disrupted by the slave revolt.

In 1788, Saint-Domingue's estimated 452,000 slaves, 40,000 whites, and 28,000 free blacks fueled France's most profitable colony, exporting $130 million worth of sugar, coffee, and other crops. Slaves' life expectancy was so low from overwork and sadistic punishment that French ships brought 220,000 Africans to replenish the dead between 1784 and 1790. Two-thirds of them had been free a decade earlier.

The world changed in 1789 when the French National Assembly broke the grip of Church and Crown. The Declaration of the Rights of Man, championing *liberté, égalité,* and *fraternité*, sent depth charges to Saint-Domingue. Free black men seeking equal status with the white elite led an uprising; the leaders, soon captured, were publicly tortured and executed. The 27,548 free blacks did not initially advocate ending slavery. "The quarrel between whites and Mulattoes," wrote C. L. R. James, "woke the sleeping slaves."

The 1791 slave insurrection at the port of Le Cap Français, "Pearl of the Antilles," had a searing impact far beyond the island. As the revolt spread, a leader emerged in Toussaint Louverture, a forty-eight-year-old planter's coachman with a superb mind who would guide an army that gradually consolidated power over much of Saint-Domingue. The larger island, Hispaniola, included a Spanish side, Santo Domingo.

"Louisiana was the most desirable region in North America for the Creole refugees to reconstruct their shattered lives," writes Alfred N. Hunt. The 1791 New Orleans census of 4,446 inhabitants, down by about 900 from three years earlier, reflected the death toll from the fever epidemic after the Great Fire. By 1797, the population had nearly doubled, to 8,056: 3,948 whites, 1,335 free blacks, 2,773 enslaved. A conservative estimate of 1,000 people from Saint-Domingue reflects the city's new role as a sanctuary for refugees from the Caribbean island war.

On December 30, 1791, François Louis Hector, baron de Carondelet, succeeded Esteban Miró as governor of Louisiana and Spanish Florida. Carondelet was greeted at the outskirts by his official escort into town, Don Andrés Almonaster, the royal ensign for Carlos IV and representative of the Cabildo. "The public Buildings are capacious and elegant," noted a Virginia gentleman who had recently passed through. "The private Houses generally neat and commodious."

Born in 1747 in Cambrai, France, Carondelet at age fifteen entered the Spanish military and served in the Caribbean during the American Revolution. In 1777, Carondelet married María de la Concepción Castaños y Aragorria, a baroness from a family close to the king. In 1781, he won distinction fighting at the Battle of Pensacola. With a brother in the priesthood, Carondelet equated law and virtue with royal paternalism. As a governor in Guatemala, he expanded the army's presence with little regard for budget and founded sixty towns for Indians displaced by Spanish colonizing. In New Orleans, as Jacobins raised bloodthirsty songs, Carondelet sent his wife and children to Havana for safekeeping.

New Orleans now had a theater on St. Peter Street. Imagine the flare of Carondelet's jowls on seeing Frenchmen in the seats singing "Ça ira," with its refrain, "Les aristocrates à la lanterne" (Hang the aristocrats from the lamppost). The governor's noble title was mocked and twisted into "cochon de lait" (sucking pig) in a ditty sung in taverns and cafés:

When we will be republicans,
we will hang all the rascals,
Quachodelait will be the first ... to be guillotined.

New Orleans riveted the motherland that had abandoned it a generation earlier. France's new minister to America, Edmond-Charles Genêt, a
son of privilege who spoke five languages and played the harpsichord, had
been expelled from his diplomatic post in Russia by Empress Catherine II
for championing the French Revolution. Genêt arrived in America, charged
with seeking debt repayment or credit for the French economy. George
Washington's administration kept neutral toward France in its wars with
Britain and Spain. "Hot headed, all imagination, no judgment," simmered
Secretary of State Thomas Jefferson in a letter about Citizen Genêt. Jefferson saw Spanish Louisiana's major port as a place of value when Genêt
issued a pamphlet, *The Freemen of France to Their Brothers in Louisiana.*
It reached the desk of Governor Carondelet in October 1793. "The French
nation, knowing your sentiments, and indignant at seeing you the victims of
the tyrants by whom you have been so long oppressed, can and will avenge
your wrongs," wrote Genêt. The six-page call-to-arms was an ironic pitch to
Creoles invested in slave labor.

> Now is the time to cease being the slaves of a government to which you
> were shamefully sold; and no longer to be led on like a herd of cattle,
> by men who with one word can strip you of what you hold most dear—
> liberty and property.... know ye, that your brethren the French, who
> have attacked with success the Spanish Government in Europe, will in
> a short time present themselves on your coasts with naval forces; that
> the republicans of the western portion of the United States are ready to
> come down the Ohio and the Mississippi in company with a considerable
> number of French republicans and to rush to your assistance under the
> banners of France and liberty; and that you have every assurance of suc-
> cess. Therefore, inhabitants of Louisiana, show who you are; prove that
> you have not been stupefied by despotism and that you have retained in
> your breasts French valor and intrepidity ... to seek your own freedom.

To Creole descendants of the early *concessionaires* steeped in French
civilization, what was France, after chopping off the king's head? American colonists had broken the yoke of Britain's monarchy, while maintaining slavery. That equation of freedom and ownership of human property
tempted Creole gentry who might resent the *idea* of Spanish overlords, if

not Carondelet personally. Blacksmiths, tailors, wheelwrights, and mid-ranking workers, without slaves, saw the brawny American republic sending ships and flatboats with flour, supplies, and cargo to a port governed by Spanish regulations. Each piece of news on Toussaint Louverture's forces beating back British and Spanish troops angling for the French island economy stoked fear in the Southern big house of slave rebellions. On June 23, 1793, the African army again attacked Le Cap Français, driving 10,000 people into the harbor, rescued by ships and carried off to Cuban and Atlantic ports.

Short, stout, and fastidious, the baron de Carondelet had seen the blood-spattering of warfare. He petitioned Havana for more troops and ordered new fortifications behind the rampart and at outposts up and down the Mississippi. He demanded an oath of loyalty to Spain from all people who had arrived since 1790; he deported a French trader, a free black tailor from Saint-Domingue, and sixty-eight assorted men he deemed a threat to public order. Carondelet's fear of a revolutionary French invasion matched his concern for public safety in unruly New Orleans. "Taverns, gambling-dens and bawdy-houses ignored the laws by which they were supposed to be regulated," noted Hebert Asbury, "and kept open at all hours to accommodate drunken, brawling crowds."

When Genêt failed to raise funds to send Kentucky troops to Louisiana, in a scheme to establish an independent state, the Jefferson administration protested to Paris that Genêt's machinations violated French neutrality. Genêt's recall notice left him fearing the guillotine; he received permission to stay, married well, and settled quietly in New York.

To Carondelet, the raffish city of many-colored peoples speaking different tongues begged for discipline. People of New Orleans dumped garbage in gutters that the Cabildo paid workmen to scoop out; the streets reeked after bad rain. Carondelet created four wards, each with a police house. To reduce crime, he erected sixty-eight street lamps lit by oil, paid for by a tax on bread and butchered meat.

Almonaster wrote Crown officials opposing Carondelet's appeal for funds to support more military salaries and weapons. Carondelet bristled. Almonaster's honors included the title of "colonel and adjutant major of the Battalion of New Orleans Militia [which caused] a large exodus of members so that drills and parades had to be cancelled," writes Jack D. L. Holmes. Almonaster's artillery company could not muster enough men for target practice. "Generally, historians have seen fit to praise Almonaster for his wonderful charitable spirit, but few of his contemporaries regarded him with anything but contempt and loathing."

Holmes's critique of the philanthropist-builder may be overly harsh; but Almonaster's attempt to thwart Carondelet's military authority was an overreach of inflated pride. Carondelet had a personality, easy to offend, and his sense of honor, burnished by his military background, took umbrage at a military halo bestowed by the Crown for courage unproven. Build a hospital, sure; a church, great; but what did you do in the war, Andrés?

Carondelet maneuvered around him to rebuild esprit de corps, beef up troops, and staff the outposts, keeping diplomacy with the Choctaw, Chickasaw, and other tribes, reminding the chiefs that the Spanish, unlike the French and British, did not traffic in Indian slaves. Indian troops were a key strand in his military strategy.

In 1794 he ordered the digging of a canal just beyond St. Louis Cemetery and linked it to a turning basin on Bayou St. John. Patrician women took swims there. The waterway led to Lake Pontchartrain and was an easterly route to Lake Borgne and beyond to the Gulf. Carondelet Canal failed to expand seafaring traffic, however; it later closed.

On December 8, 1794, boys playing with matches caused a fire that ravaged through Royal and other streets in the area near the Plaza de Armas, destroying 212 buildings in barely three hours. As Carondelet and the *regidores* threw themselves into emergency response, Almonaster was relieved that the flames had spared his nearly completed cathedral on the plaza where St. Louis Church had burned in 1788. He had work yet to complete on the Cabildo and Casa Curial (today's Presbytère), the residence for the Capuchin monks beside the church, facing the riverfront plaza.

Carondelet arranged rebuilding loans for people who lost their homes, specifying use of brick and plaster to reduce the threat of future fire. Cypress was too flammable. Spanish building codes and design show today in the plane of housing exteriors near the sidewalk's edge, a firewall of sorts in the masonry of brick and stucco. The facades of pastel hues and iron-lace balconies, curled into arabesques, are elegant specimens of Spanish architecture. So are the cool courtyards with flowerbeds out back, reached by the *loggia*, the area at the end of the carriageway, beneath Moorish arches, with access to the stairwells. Creole townhouses featured low-pitched Spanish tiled roofs (some were flat, furnishing rooftop terraces), dormers, and gables.

··········

MIRRORS OF CHURCH AND STATE

For Carondelet, Almonaster, the Cabildo *regidores*, military officers, colonial officials, and prominent citizens of the Illustrious Body, the ceremonial processions in St. Louis Cathedral (so designated by the Crown) melded respect for high ritual with a blooming culture of human display. The march of military bands, the parades of Indian delegations, masked balls at Carnival, and the stately processions of ecclesiastical figures on holy days of the Catholic calendar gave the French orphan city and Spanish foster child a ripening public square. As the Illustrious Body enjoyed the city for its celebration of life, the powerful rhythms of spiritual memory in the African dances across town on the Congo field nurtured an identity of resistance in the musical hothouse.

"The *French* and *Spanish* Subjects of Louisiana are strict *Romanists*, and therefore, enthusiastically fond of Pageantry and their religious Festivals," wrote a Virginia traveler, Col. John Pope, of the 1791 Good Friday procession. "Traitor Judas, for political reasons, appeared in the Regimental Uniform of a *Spanish* Soldier, under Sentence of Death, for having divulged the Countersign to the Enemy in Consideration of a *Bribe*." Costuming Judas as a Spanish traitor reminded spectators on the streets that in a fallen world His Catholic Majesty's governor and troops personified security. As the American Revolutionary War ended in 1782, Spanish soldiers passed through New Orleans en route to Havana. Miró groused to a captain general that he needed clarinetists, trombonists, and a music director for his regimental orchestra.

The Roman Catholic Church in which Almonaster was so invested was the city's ceremonial heart, with choirs, musicians, and trains of priests and acolytes in stately movement to the altar, bathed in candle glow, as well as open-air processions for funerals and feast days. According to one study, at least half of the 214 Catholic burials between 1796 and 1798 featured four or more singers, averaging two funerals per week in those two years alone. However jaded or detached certain planters and rich merchants felt about the faith, given the Church's paradoxical role as a slaveholder and yet protector of slaves, supporting their self-purchase, Creole society gave allegiance to the king, who appointed the priests in consultation with bishops. Rituals of the Church calendar, like affairs of state, drew the Illustrious Body, cloaked in finery, into the pews, to see and be seen, as free blacks and the enslaved watched with imaginations whirring.

In that fishbowl society, with military parades and religious processions as high moments, the Church had its own upheavals. Upon his arrival in 1772, Cirilo of Barcelona was appalled to find Spanish Capuchins with eighteen slaves in the friary of their French brethren, including ten women and four children who lived among the priests, serving their meals on china.

Cirilo was aghast on seeing the friars, vowed to poverty and service to the poor, snorting snuff like rich planters. One woman, he wrote, was "the concubine of the friars, for such is the reputation she bears." The woman's sister, unmarried and pregnant, lived in the religious house where other negresses snuck out at night to meet their lovers—a sign of decadence to Cirilo. When he sought to confront these matters, he met resistance from then-governor Luís Unzaga. New Orleans had many white men who, laws notwithstanding, sired children with dark women; the governor wanted no Pandora's box of a clergy scandal. Besides, the French Capuchins were transitioning out of *Nueva Orleans*. Cirilo and his monks soon settled in, embracing the Crown's standard of protecting slaves from extreme cruelty, however difficult to enforce. Seeing the Capuchins' own Baptiste whipped in the Plaza de Armas before St. Maló's hanging fanned Cirilo's frustration about the limits of religious authority.

Bishop Cirilo evinced a monastic strain of humility as he went house to house, begging for alms, showing people that away from sacred mysteries of the altar he was not a man robed in pride. In 1795, he suffered a stunning setback. Church documents from Havana disclosed that Antonio de Sedella, the lionized "Père Antoine" he'd shipped to Spain five years earlier, had appealed to Carlos IV and won a reversal.

Sedella in his Spanish exile sent to Madrid a fat file of testimonials from New Orleanians with a lawyer's brief arguing that he was wrongly displaced and deserved the right of return. As the months rolled into years, Père Antoine's supporters had written Bishop Trespalacios in Havana, objecting to his abrupt deportation. Cirilo complained of Sedella's poor record keeping, how he spent money, and his practice of letting people sign as wedding witnesses who weren't present. These were serious lapses under Church law, but were they enough to expel a priest from a country?

Fray Antonio de Sedella coveted popularity and flouted rules. His charisma mingled with Cirilo's rule-bound personality like acid on silk. When Sedella had confronted Miró, the governor saw a power-addled monk poised to invade people's homes, seize bad books, and dump a witch hunt on the Cabildo. The bishop wanted him gone. Miró washed his hands and sent the menace off. But why did Sedella force Miró's hand, daring him *not* to provide guards for his heresy probe? The priest had a Machiavellian turn of mind. As Père Antoine, the populist pastor knew that Cirilo wanted him evicted. Bishops hold the upper hand. In provoking Miró, Sedella got booted by the bishop pulling rank. The unruly cleric did not imagine that his appeal would take five years; but he prevailed, securing his station in New

Orleans with its porous laws, a place that suited him like a hand in glove. The Church historian Roger Baudier called his career "probably the stormiest of any priest who served in Louisiana."

Reviewing files in Havana, Bishop Trespalacios fumed that his authority had been usurped by Cirilo, an auxiliary bishop. "You have exceeded your powers; you have acted contrary to law," Trespalacios wrote him, "and you have done wrong by sending off Father Sedella." Reading the accounts of other priests whom Cirilo had removed, Trespalacios wanted him out. Cirilo sent a letter of twenty-two self-justifying pages to the Crown with documents to buttress his case; after a mission to Pensacola, Cirilo returned to Havana. Trespalacios sent him back to Spain, a bishop in title only, his career in tatters.

In July 1795, Sedella sailed back to his city in the sun. When the new bishop, Luís Peñalver y Cárdenas, arrived and reviewed the files, he decided that the more serious charges lacked proof. Victorious, Père Antoine returned to St. Louis Cathedral as a pastor. Carondelet had no fear of an investigative zealot. But Sedella's zealotry would swing from harsh enforcement of laws to a cult of personality, the likes of which the city had never seen.

Spanish rule molded a three-tier society, unique in the South, of whites, slaves and *gens de couleur libres*. Saint-Domingue émigrés strengthened the society's French roots and increased the ranks of free colored people who hoped for equality with whites—an aspiration that intensified the 1790s island revolt. Carondelet walked a thin line, relying on the free black militia to man outposts and maintain order in the city. As his worries rose that Jacobin *provocateurs* would gain a foothold, he ordered a two-year prison sentence in Havana for a black militiaman who had espoused "universal equality among men."

On February 4, 1794, the French National Assembly abolished slavery in the colonies. In Saint-Domingue, some planters welcomed British warships seeking to capture French territory and remake the slave economy. Toussaint Louverture, however, negotiated a military alliance with France.

"To preserve emancipation, Louverture decided that he must preserve the plantation economy and encourage the return of white planters who had fled," writes Laurent Dubois. "Locked in conflict with ex-slaves who had a very different vision of what freedom should mean, he maintained and perfected a coercive system that sought to keep them working on plantations." Fighting with the French, Toussaint prevailed in the next phase of war, defeating the British.

France, however, was soon experiencing new convulsions that would change its politics of empire. In Paris, during October 1796, the five-man Directory, having wrested control from the Jacobins, turned to Napoléon Bonaparte, a Corsican general in the army, to defeat a mob threatening the new government. Bonaparte's troops and artillery left 1,400 dead, securing the Directory's control. Promoted to major general, Bonaparte saw France's destiny as his own, leading troops against Austria and Italy (taking the pope as prisoner) and into a triumphant invasion of Egypt.

Half a world away, Carondelet's warning to the Cabildo of "undercover plots" was borne out in April 1795 with the foiling of a slave rebellion, upstream from Baton Rouge at the Pointe Coupée estate of Julien Poydras, a French native and one of Louisiana's wealthiest planters. The plan was to set fire to a Poydras building; when nearby planters arrived to quench the flames, the rebels would kill them with weapons from Poydras's arsenal and shoot slaves disloyal to the revolt. But a plotters' conversation, overheard and reported to overseers and planters, ignited the crackdown before a match was lit. Carondelet sent reenforcement troops and ordered a tribunal. Testimony revealed that the conspirators "were well informed about the war between France and Spain [and] the French Convention's abolition of slavery in all French colonies," writes Gwendolyn Midlo Hall. The ringleaders had rallied followers with hopes pinned on a French invasion of Louisiana. Fifty-seven slaves and three white collaborators were convicted; twenty-three slaves were hung, their heads cut off and nailed to posts along the river road from Pointe Coupée to New Orleans.

In those human faces shorn of bodies lay an evil taunting of the spiritual beliefs invested in the carved masks worn in memory dances to West African ancestors. The dancing rings on the Congo field, without masks, now forbidden, charged survival as a quest for freedom.

As Carondelet scrambled to stave off French-inspired rebellion and maintain slavery, Toussaint Louverture gained power in Saint-Domingue by providing certain planters with freed slaves he pressed back into servitude while trying to foster a profit-sharing scheme for restored plantations; whipping and savage punishment were outlawed. A Catholic and now a landowner, the "black Spartacus" wanted reconciliation, hoping the Africans would gain skills from the educated mulattoes and returning French. Saint-Domingue was still a powder keg with regions under control of rival leaders; France wanted to regain control of the sputtering economy. Santo Domingo, the Spanish side of the island, was still a slave state.

In banning slave ships from Saint-Domingue in 1792, Carondelet wanted to block Africans fired by revolutionary dreams; but Spanish ships had already brought an influx of people from Kongo, in west-central Africa (today part of Angola), where the Catholic Church had deep roots. Portuguese missionaries converted a fifteenth-century king, who took the baptismal name João I. Eighteen years later, in 1509, his successor, Alfonso I, from the capital Mbanza Kongo, guided the building of churches and the spread of Catholic teaching. Kongo royalty adopted coats-of-arms like European kings, with swords that symbolized a historic link between ironwork and African monarchy.

"Beyond heraldry, swords appeared in the Christian Kongo during coronations, elite burials, and ceremonial displays of allegiance," writes Cécile Fromont. "They shone in particular in *sangamento* dances, where they swayed in the hands of elite men whose acrobatic leaps and bounds made awe-inspiring showcases of strength and agility." An account of the 1622 funeral procession of King Alvaro III of Kongo—led by the governor, trumpeters and drummers, "the crosses of the brotherhoods, the clergy and dignitaries, and six nobles who carried a litter with the king's weaponry and his corpse covered with a pall of the Order of Christ"—foreshadow the Illustrious Body's procession for Carlos III in 1789. On a stage of public theater, mock warriors of *sangamento* fused Kongo and Catholic rituals in a line of danced memory that superseded burial choreographies of the earliest Africans in New Orleans. With real swords off limits, enslaved dancers improvised a body language of ritual feints, attacks, and gyrating rings of exaltation.

When European empires seized on slave labor to milk the resources of colonial lands, the Portuguese trade in human property began to erode the Kongo kingdom. About 40 percent of African slaves shipped across the Atlantic came from Kongo. *Sangamento* spread a tradition in which "the election ritual of a Kongo king in the diaspora involved a mock war performance," writes Jeroen Dewulf in *From the Kingdom of Kongo to Congo Square*.

A traveler in 1819 marveled at how New Orleans slaves "meet on the green, by the swamp, and rock the city with their Congo dances." By that time, a second generation of Kongo people had emerged—Afro-Creoles, absorbing the larger folkways of the town. Ritual dancing to simulate violence, one strand in the web of Place Congo performance, would infuse the street theater of Carnival season. The Mardi Gras Indians, parading as mock warriors in the late nineteenth century, carried the cultural memory of Congo Square and paid homage to a lineage of Big Chief leaders, suggesting *sangamento* as a mythic root. "The Kongo dance, in fact, should be understood as part of a ritual to invest royal authority in a tale narrating the military achievements of the illustrious kings," writes Dewulf. Africans torn away from tribal monarchies with communal dancing transplanted roots of myth in the Congo field, memories of ancestry and kingship in the rhythms and lines and rings radiating into forbidden parts of town. Black obsessions with royalty had an ironic mirror in the Creole balls of lords and ladies in Carnival season.

Music and dancing coursed across the racial divide like a current of electricity charging both cultures. In 1800, free black militia members secured permission from the Cabildo to attend Saturday dances at the popular hall of one Bernardo Coquet, whose Sunday dances were for white customers, from November until Carnival season ended at Ash Wednesday. Slaves attended the balls illegally. "They dance in the country, they dance in the city, they dance everywhere," a French refugee from Saint-Domingue observed in 1802.

People of color in the emergent social mosaic had layers as complex as the whites of different ethnic roots. The city's first known burial society was the Persévérance Benevolent and Mutual Aid Association, founded by blacks in 1783 to provide dignified burials. Saint-Domingue exiles fostered Masonic lodges for fraternal solidarity.

When the traveler Francis Baily passed through in 1797, he walked the riverfront "between the levée and the front row of houses"—the butchers' arcade established several years earlier—and saw "a kind of market by that miserable class of men who swarm here in great numbers—I mean, the unfortunate blacks ... to fix their little stalls, and retail the several articles they had to vend, whereby to raise a scanty pittance." Two years after the Pointe Coupée slave revolt, African-blooded vendors had moved from the Congo field, behind the rampart, into the stalls off the Plaza de Armas, a venue for greater commerce, the future French Market.

Baily is a precursor of the traveling memoirists in the nineteenth century whose words enlarge our view of the changing city. "The inhabitants of this place are a mixture of English, Irish, Scotch, American, French and Spanish," he wrote, "somewhat altered by the natural progress of assimilation, owing to such a promiscuous combination of different characters." Scornful of a laziness and "love of ease" that relied on slavery, he took note of the popularity of pool tables and the French theater, a small playhouse with an amphitheater overlooking the pit, a row of boxes and a gallery. "The plays are performed in French and they have a tolerable set of actors."

On Sunday, Baily observed, "the fore part of the day was kept in a religious performance of a few forms and ceremonies ... under the roof of the church." One performance gave way to another:

Scarcely had the priest pronounced his benediction, ere the violin and fife struck up at the [cathedral] door, and the lower classes of the people indulged themselves in all the gaiety and mirth of juvenile diversions. Singing, dancing and all kinds of sport were seen in every street ... particularly amongst the negroes who in *this* country are suffered to refrain from work on that day. Here, arrayed in their best apparel, forgetful of the toils they had endured the preceding part of the week, and let loose from the hand of the master, they would meet together on the green and spend all day in mirth and festivity ... as if they were enjoying themselves in the midst of their friends and relatives, and had never been snatched from their own country by the cruel hand of the Christians.

Baily doesn't say whether "the green" was behind the rampart. Another writer, two years later, found "vast numbers of negro slaves, men, women, and children, assembled together on the levee, drumming, fifing, and dancing in large rings"—across the legal line of the rampart. Eleven years after Bishop Cirilo's 1786 pastoral letter complained of dancing on the Congo field at evening prayer, African dancers had flowed out to a stretch of the levee in town, violating the restriction of Sundays on Place Congo, a law loosely enforced as the century ebbed.

Two-thirds of the baptisms at St. Louis Cathedral in the late 1790s were for infants of African ancestry, enslaved and free, with colored militia members frequently standing as godfathers. Visions of salvation preached in the pulpit held promise in the life force of danced memory. Under Père Antoine, the cathedral tolerated dancers coursing on streets behind a bishop's procession.

At the Plaza de Armas on the feast of Corpus Christi, June 15, 1797, the visiting Baily marveled at streets leading from the Cathedral "planted with green boughs and bushes on both sides, and strewed with a kind of gravel. A mixed multitude of men, women and children surrounded the church, waiting for the coming out of the sacred treasure"—the communion chalice. With so many black Catholics, the mixed multitude surely included Kongo people. Soldiers preceded priests "in different habits, carrying tapers, crosses ... [and] the host on a bier dressed round with flowers." The bishop walked solemnly "underneath a canopy supported by half a dozen priests." Carondelet and his attendants came next, with mounted soldiers "to keep off the rabble which followed behind." Cavorting behind musicians in the march, held back by troops on horseback, "the rabble" must have included Africans, jostling to the processional tempo, a forerunner of today's "second-line" dancing behind funeral marches or parading clubs. "The houses on each side were lined with visitors, who strewed flowers upon the head of the venerable bishop as he went by, and kneeled to the host as it passed along."

Almonaster, who died in 1798, was buried inside the Cathedral with liturgical honors. Three weeks later, his widow, Louise de La Ronde Almonaster, cited the agreement by which the *regidores* would reimburse Almonaster for the construction of the Cabildo; she requested an installment from the treasury surplus, which they paid. The Cabildo was completed the following year, a majestic specimen of Spanish colonial architecture. The fortune that Almonaster bequeathed to his three-year-old daughter, Micaela Leonarda, included the buildings and lots on opposite sides of the Plaza de Armas, framing her father's legacy: the Cabildo, St. Louis Cathedral, and the Presbytère.

Almonaster's wealthy widow had no intention of giving away money. The third jewel in the Almonaster crown, the Presbytère, is a two-story brick structure with urns along the balustrade and a ground floor arcade of elliptical arches. It was originally called the Casa Curial, or ecclesiastical house, built for the Capuchin community of Almonaster's friend Père Antoine. Almonaster was overseeing the construction when he died. His widow halted payments. Bishop Luís Peñalver y Cárdenas sued her to finish the job; she petitioned the court that to do so would impose on her two young daughters a reduction in their standard of living. The judge ruled for the bishop. The widow appealed to Carlos IV in Madrid, who in consideration of the substantial donations by Don Andrés Almonaster y Roxas, relieved her of further cost. "The Presbytère was not completed until 1813," writes Christina Vella. As construction lumbered along, the church rented out rooms for stores. "It was never used as a rectory."

· · · · · · · · · ·

NAPOLEONIC HUBRIS PRODUCES THE PURCHASE

The revolutionary changes churning between Paris and Saint-Domingue made New Orleans attractive to France a generation after it had given the city to Spain. A power shift in 1799 hoisted Napoléon Bonaparte to the rank of first consul. Talleyrand, the foreign minister, shared Bonaparte's desire to rebuild France's massive sugar industry, which had struggled during Saint-Domingue's long revolution. Bonaparte saw New Orleans as a fort to undercut U.S. smugglers selling goods to Saint-Domingue, and he wanted a wedge between the United States and Britain in its quest for empire.

As Carondelet finished his term and left New Orleans, Napoléon bargained with Carlos IV for the return of Louisiana; he offered a kingdom in northern Italy for the king's brother-in-law, the duke of Parma. In a secret treaty signed March 21, 1801, the duke's son received the throne of Florence and a swath of Tuscany. France got six Spanish warships and Louisiana; Napoléon waited, however, before taking control. Louisiana, he assured Carlos, would be French.

President Thomas Jefferson had his own view of the port on the lower Mississippi. "There is on the globe one single spot, the possessor of which is our natural and habitual enemy," he famously noted in a letter to America's ambassador to France, Robert Livingston. "It is New Orleans, through which the produce of three-eighths of our territory must pass to market." In 1802, as Livingston and delegate James Monroe began talks in Paris to purchase "the Isle of Orleans," Bonaparte sent 30,000 troops by ship, planning to defeat Toussaint Louverture's forces, secure a peonage economy, and restore slavery on the island. Jefferson feared that if Saint-Domingue fell, France would invade New Orleans. Toussaint Louverture controlled most of the slave-free island.

Bonaparte's brother-in-law, Gen. Charles Victoire Emmanuel Leclerc, led the invasion. "Rid us of these gilded negroes," Napoléon wrote Leclerc, in reference to the black generals. As French forces gained ground, Louverture sent word that he would negotiate. At a meeting with other black leaders and Leclerc, Louverture negotiated his French military rank, pay, and retirement to his plantation. Leclerc's forces soon began losing battles, for which he blamed Louverture's behind-the-scenes influence. Invited to another lunch in June 1802, Louverture arrived with a light force of guards who were quickly overwhelmed. Stunned by the grenadiers surrounding him with bayonets, Louverture braced at the words of Leclerc's aide-de-camp: "General, we have not come here to do you any harm. We merely have orders to secure your person." He was bound and taken to a ship, his wife, two sons, and a niece arrested, too. His house plundered, his plantation destroyed, he was shipped to France and put in prison.

Bonaparte's deceit took out the one leader with a mass following and the skills to negotiate peace. Other black commanders doubled down to fight.

Leclerc's momentum sank in a yellow fever epidemic; French troops buried their dead at night in a vain effort to hide the impact of a military tide turning against them.

Jefferson authorized Livingston and Monroe to offer France as much as $10 million for New Orleans. As prospects dimmed for his slave empire, Bonaparte added bait. "It is not only New Orleans that I will cede, it is the whole colony," he said. "I renounce it with the greatest regret. . . . I require money." Like Louis XV, who sold Louisiana in 1763 over military debt, Napoléon needed funds for his war with Britain. The French counter of $15 million was steep, but startled the Americans by including the entire Mississippi Valley, a land mass of 909,130 square miles reaching west to the Rocky Mountains, and upriver to Canada, doubling the size of the United States overnight.

In March 1803, France dispatched Pierre-Clément de Laussat to New Orleans to oversee the transfer from Spain. Bonaparte concealed from him information on the sale. A seasoned diplomat who had kept his head, literally, through the Terror, Laussat anticipated a long tour of duty, guiding the restoration of *La Nouvelle Orléans*, a society he found suitably elegant with dancing and the arts.

On April 7, 1803, Toussaint died of pneumonia in prison.

On April 30, Livingston and Monroe signed the Louisiana Purchase Treaty with their counterpart, François Barbé-Marbois. The treaty was kept secret, allowing for the weeks to send word across the Atlantic and give Jefferson time to announce and execute the transfer.

Laussat had dismissed speculations of a New Orleans deal. Jefferson's July 4 announcement of the treaty, sending it to Congress for ratification, put Laussat in a scramble for credibility. He had to persuade Creoles that the second coming of *La Nouvelle Orléans* would prosper as an emancipated French city in America. Carlos IV, faced with Napoléon's broken pledge for a French city, lacked the military power or financial motivation to renege on their deal. On November 2, 1803, as Laussat was making his preparations, General Leclerc died in Le Cap Français of yellow fever. By then, 24,000 of the 34,000 troops sent by Napoléon had died in battle or from illness, with another 8,000 in hospitals, writhing in chills and vomiting black bile from yellow fever. Bonaparte sent another 10,000 troops; French forces were losing ground to Jean-Jacques Dessalines's army. As the French retreated, Dessalines's warriors massacred the remaining whites, a fate that Toussaint Louverture had wanted to prevent. On New Year's Day 1804, Dessalines proclaimed the Republic of Haiti.

"More than 50,000 European soldiers, plus an estimated eighteen generals," writes Lawrence N. Powell, "had perished because of Napoléon's racist fantasy that the island's black majority could be returned to slavery."

Fears and animosities surged before Spain's transfer of New Orleans to the French. Barely a decade had passed since the Jacobins decapitated Louis XVI, a Bourbon cousin of Carlos IV. Shock gripped the Ursuline convent. The Revolution had shuttered religious houses in France; the mother superior and fifteen sisters, in a community of twenty-five, decided to leave for Havana. The prefect Laussat appealed to them for trust. "One of the elder women, breaking through conventual restraint and habitual timidity, poured forth upon him a fierce denunciation of the power he represented," Grace King writes. The mayor, "upon his knees to the mother superior," pleaded that they not abandon their mission. Amid heavy sobbing, nine remaining sisters stood in the convent garden, filled with women who had studied there as the sixteen nuns departed. "Slaves bearing lanterns walked before them. The vicar-general, Governor Salcedo, the Marquis de Casa-Calvo, and a long cortege of citizens followed them to their vessels and saw them embark."

Laussat did his best to bring off a smooth transfer; but when a dozen Spanish officers invited to a fête at his home failed to show (an absence for which he blamed his rival envoy, the former governor Casa-Calvo), Madame Laussat denounced the Spaniards as "souls of filth" to a roomful of stunned guests. An American present so noted in a letter alerting William C. C. Claiborne, soon to arrive as Jefferson's designated governor of the Orleans Territory.

In the late morning of November 30, 1803, Pierre-Clément de Laussat, escorted by sixty French Creoles, walked across a Plaza de Armas bulging with people. A brig on the river fired a salute. Spanish soldiers stood straight. A drumroll announced Laussat's arrival in the Sala Capitular, the Cabildo's ceremonial room. He greeted Spain's last governor, Juan Manuel de La Salcedo, who walked with difficulty, and the Marqués de Casa-Calvo (Sebastián Calvo de La Puerta y O'Farrill), a Cuban soldier-diplomat and sugar baron with a cordial front to shroud his cynical thoughts.

Salcedo gave Laussat silver keys to outlying forts; they signed papers. The Spanish flag came down; that of France went up. Laussat made the rounds of receptions, dinners, toasts, and dancing that continued till dawn. In his three weeks as French prefect, Laussat restored the *Code Noir*, scaling back the slaves' right to self-purchase; terminated the municipal council called the Cabildo and established the grand colonial building with the same name as the seat of government to come. To a society becoming more French, with

Saint-Domingue migrants a vibrant presence at the Café de Réfugiés on St. Philip Street, and the riverfront square returned to its original name, the Place d'Armes, Laussat had to soften the fears of an epic change. "France has ceded Louisiana to the United States of America," he declared. "You, Louisianians, will thus become a living monument to that friendship between the two Republics, which cannot but increase from day to day and which must strengthen so powerfully their common peace.... Louisianians, you are raised at once from the status of colonials to that of metropolitan citizens with a constitution and a free government.

"May Louisianians and Frenchmen always call one another by the sweet name of 'Brother' no matter where on earth they may meet and may this title alone from now on describe the relationship between them in their eternal attachment and free dependency."

In early December, Governor Claiborne and Brig. Gen. James Wilkinson, with 350 troops, marched south from Natchez, the soldiers making camp on the outskirts of New Orleans. "Claiborne and Wilkinson knew that their actions were being watched closely in Louisiana and throughout the country," writes Jon Kukla in his notable history of the Louisiana Purchase, *A Wilderness So Immense.*

> Genteel toleration of cultural and ethnic difference was one thing— New Orleans cuisine was delicious, its music agreeable, its people handsome—but *armed* free people of color were dangerously reminiscent of St. Domingue. Militia companies of free men of color represented a frightening assertion of political demands and social aspirations.... Claiborne accurately characterized his confrontation with diversity as the "principal difficulty" he faced as governor of the new territory.

The end of the European city brought no euphoric hopes of its rebirth. At the Cabildo on December 20, 1803, Laussat signed papers of transfer to Claiborne, who stood high in Jefferson's confidence. As the twenty-nine-year-old American and fifty-three-year-old Frenchman witnessed the rise of the third flag of nationality in three weeks over the Place d'Armes, scattered shouts and a flurry of tossed hats sank into a larger "lugubriousness of silence and immobility of the rest of the crowd," a French traveler wrote.

The city steamed with hopes, schemes, and plots to challenge any politician, even one as shrewd as Claiborne. Within a year, his wife and young daughter would die on the same day.

5

···

Claiborne

A CITY EMBATTLED

In the 1790s, as planters sold off land for *faubourgs*, or neighborhoods, New Orleans branched out like the slow unfolding of a lady's fan.

A major subdivision lay behind the rampart, between, to the west, the Congo field, Carondelet Canal, and a military fort, and, to the east, brickyards and farms on Bayou Road. Claude Tremé carved out tracts of this expanse for early nineteenth-century roads and dwellings that included shotgun houses, an import from Haiti: the doorway and front window, close like the barrels of a gun, providing an airway through rooms to the back. The urban village featured brick cottages of inlaid posts, stucco facades in tones of earth and sky, and raised manor houses with wraparound galleries.

Certain porches were close enough to hear the percussion and cross-rhythms at Place Congo on Sunday. A short walk enabled residents to gaze at the swirling human rings. A visitor in 1808 observed

> twenty different dancing groups of the wretched Africans, collected together to perform their *worship* after the manner of their country. They have their own national music, consisting for the most part of a long kind of narrow drum of various sizes, from two to eight feet in length, three or four of which make a band. The principal dancers or leaders are dressed in a variety of wild and savage fashions, always ornamented with a number of tails of the smaller wild beasts. . . . These amusements continue until sunset, when one or two of the city patrole [*sic*] show themselves with their cutlasses, and the crowds immediately disperse.

Today, the neighborhood that filled out the area is famous for parade clubs, brass bands, and the HBO series *Tremé*, which dramatized the post–Hurricane Katrina struggle through the music culture. The imagery of John Boutté's title song captures life far removed from the roots.

Hangin' in the Tremé
    Watchin' people sashay
Past my steps
    By my porch
In front of my door

Church bells are ringin'
    Choirs are singing
While the preachers groan
    And the sisters moan
In a blessed tone

Claude Tremé was an unlikely namesake for today's enclave of soul-rocking resilience to the NOPD sirens and young gunshot victims.

· · · · · · · · · ·

A PLACE NAME OF BLEEDING IRONY

The twenty-eight-year-old native of Sauvigny reached New Orleans in 1783. Established as a hatmaker, Tremé bought and sold at least one slave and went before the Cabildo in minor civil disputes in his early thirties. Tremé was living in a rented room on Dauphine Street near the rampart on October 20, 1787, when he woke up to barking dogs at 4 A.M. He grabbed a gun, went out, saw a man carrying a sack, yelled "stop thief," and fired. Alejo, a thirty-year-old slave, went down. A crowd gathered, a surgeon came; authorities took statements. Alejo, a sawmill worker who lived across the river, had been visiting the woman he planned to marry at her mother's house. He was returning "to his habitation," a report to the Cabildo stated, when

> some dogs barked and at this instant a man whom he did not know opened the door asking Alejo to declare himself and to stop, but Alejo said that he continued on his route without wanting to stop. Alejo went a short distance and the man shot him and commenced to shout "thief" six times, then he quit. The slave, knowing himself to be gravely ill, dragged himself as well as he could to the lodging of his mother which is one

block distant from the site of the shooting, where he entered and they put him to bed in the *sala principal,* or main room.

Père Antoine presided at his funeral.

The Cabildo filed charges against Tremé for the killing. His housekeeper, a free woman of color, testified that two Negro robbers had been menacing the neighborhood. Colleagues and friends vouched for Tremé. Governor Miró sentenced him "to five years imprisonment in the garrison of this plaza ... [and] he must pay the cost of the trial by the seizure of all his goods." An inventory of his possessions included a showcase of seventy-six hats, a walnut writing desk, a bed with mosquito netting, assorted buttons of gold and silver, and twelve pieces of gold braid.

Tremé had his charm. With jail time done, his petition to marry Julie Moreau, "a pure white person by birth, respectable and of distinguished qualities," came five days after Carondelet approved him to reopen the hat business. And so they wed. A year later, Julie inherited her grandfather's plantation off Bayou Road, perpendicular to which her husband sketched a line for rue Saint-Claude, stamping his saint's name (and thus his own) on the embryonic grid. The developer who had killed a black man was color-blind when it came to sales. "Enumeration of thirty-seven persons who bought lots in the Faubourg Tremé between 1798 and 1810 reveals a pattern of purchases by free persons of color, French and Spanish colonial settlers, and recent immigrants," note the architectural historians Roulhac Toledano and Mary Louise Christovich. The Tremés used sale profits to purchase a plantation two miles below town; they raised seven children and had thirty-four slaves when Claude died in 1828.

Life in an emergent *faubourg* presented challenges, as the prefect Laussat recalled of the summer of 1803. "Our lodgings at the gates of this city, some thirty paces from the ramparts, were still regarded as being beyond the city limits"—walking distance from the Tremé lots. "The country is so infested with snakes that one day, in my poultry yard, my cook, having picked up a setting turkey, found his bare arm immediately entwined by a large puff adder that was eating the eggs. The poor man got off with a good scare." On the porch, as after-dinner conversations ebbed, "We cursed hundreds of times the swarms of gnats and mosquitoes which devoured us." Yet to Governor William C. C. Claiborne, the bustle of workers carving roads, laying the wooden planks for *banquettes,* building houses, and people planting gardens (and killing snakes) made Faubourg Tremé a bright spot in his high-pressure toil.

Writing on December 23, 1803, to Secretary of State James Madison, Claiborne conceded "much anxiety" about how to handle the "large corps of people of color ... highly esteemed as soldiers" by the Spanish. The sight of black soldiers, celebrating the new U.S. city, unnerved the governor and Brig. Gen. James Wilkinson; they sent a request for more troops to President Jefferson and the secretary of war. Wilkinson feared "Horrible Scenes of Bloodshed & rapine ... [as] in St. Domingo."

Jefferson cynically told his cabinet, "The militia of colour shall be confirmed in their posts, and treated favorably, till a better settled state of things shall permit us to let them neglect themselves"—scant help to Claiborne, down in the moment, as the black soldiers asked to meet.

Playing for time, Claiborne began organizing a white militia. Haiti's revolution haunted Louisiana planters; but many colored soldiers had blood ties and complicated relationships with whites. Governor Casa-Calvo in 1802 had put the black militia under the authority of the Cuban military, exempting them from taxes; as the city became American, he was unable to pull their loyalties to Spain. Now, as Spain's special envoy, Casa-Calvo was in no hurry to leave New Orleans. Spain controlled parts of Florida, Alabama, and a western area of present-day Louisiana, stretching into Texas, where he was scouting boundaries, allowing fugitive slaves to defect in support of Spain. French loyalists yearned for Napoléon, now emperor, to send ships and reclaim the city for France.

Claiborne arrived with 350 soldiers and General Wilkinson, an older man, "heavy, squat [and] good natured" who had secretly renounced his citizenship in the 1780s, pledging loyalty to Spain, wangling money from Governor Miró for organizing Kentuckians to rally behind Carlos III. The plan failed; Miró kept Wilkinson on a $2,000 annual retainer as a spy. Wilkinson was lobbying for a pension with Casa-Calvo, who settled with him for $12,000. Casa-Calvo also had tentacles of intelligence from Père Antoine, a Spaniard with a pension. As Claiborne monitored the inflow of roustabouts, peddlers, and deal-makers seeking a stake in New Orleans, a nest of French pirates, by way of Haiti, had taken root in marshlands south of town. Wilkinson was scheming with the disgraced Aaron Burr, who had killed Alexander Hamilton in a duel, to invade Mexico, cement ties with Spain, and blunt U.S. expansion into Ohio. In a portrait of the time, Claiborne, in a dark waistcoat with gold trim and matching epaulets, white collar, brown curls, and a polished face, shows resolve. He needed a lot to manage the politics of a snake pit.

CLAIBORNE AND JACKSON

Born in 1775 to William and Mary Leigh Claiborne in Sussex County, Virginia, William Charles Cole Claiborne was one of five children in an ancestral line from Westmoreland County, England. In 1621, an ancestor, William Clayborne, moved to Jamestown as a plantation supervisor for a London firm. Six generations later, the father of the future governor, Col. William Claiborne, fought against the British in the Revolution. The boy grew up in the heady expectations of a new republic. Connections helped. At fifteen, William got a job in the clerk's office of Congress, then in New York, and followed its move to Philadelphia, watching laws get made. Jefferson gave him access to his personal library. He found a mentor in Tennessee representative John Sevier. Back in Virginia, after studies at William and Mary College, Claiborne read law in an attorney's office, passed the bar, and moved to Tennessee to get his start.

Claiborne rose with speed, saving money as he made it. In 1796, at twenty-one, he took part in the convention at Knoxville to draft a state constitution and met Andrew Jackson, a state solicitor of twenty-nine whose life would color Claiborne's with cosmic force.

A descendant of Scotch-Irish immigrants, Jackson grew up in the Waxhaws region on the border of North and South Carolina, his quicksilver personality forged from a survival quest like nothing the patrician Claiborne had known. Andrew was named for the father who died before Elizabeth Jackson gave birth to him in 1767, the youngest of three sons. With the provider dead, they moved in with the family of Elizabeth's invalid sister. "The Jacksons needed a home, the Crawfords needed help, and a bargain was struck," writes Jon Meacham in his biography of Jackson. "Even in his mother's lifetime, Jackson felt a certain inferiority to and distance from others."

He was thirteen when British troops captured Charleston. His oldest brother, Hugh, died in battle for the rebels. The Tories invaded Waxhaw, "systematically destroying the household belongings of Mrs. Crawford, before her eyes and those of her children. . . . the modest accumulation of a family's lifetime was ruined in minutes," writes H. W. Brands in *Andrew Jackson: His Life and Times*. Sliced in the hand and gashed in the head by a sword-wielding Tory, the boy was taken forty miles with his brother Robert to a prison rife with smallpox. Elizabeth Jackson made it there and persuaded British officials to exchange her sons for British prisoners "their American captors couldn't afford to keep." Andrew walked barefoot alongside his determined mother and ill brother, who rode horseback on the cold wet return. Robert died the second day home. Smallpox ravaged Andrew, shivering under blankets, nursed by his mother. As he improved, the dutiful Elizabeth went back to rescue her nephews; she died along the way. A bag with her clothes arrived for the fourteen-year-old boy, now an orphan. Rage at the British fused with a fierce will to live. He worked, read, scraped, and studied law in North Carolina. A woman who knew the young lawyer recalled, "His face was long and narrow, his features sharp and angular and his complexion yellow and freckled. But his eyes *were* handsome. They were very large and a kind of steel-blue, and when he talked to you he always looked straight into your own eyes ... as much as to say, 'I have nothing to be ashamed of and I hope you haven't.'"

After the Tennessee convention, John Sevier, now governor, appointed Claiborne, twenty-one, to the state supreme court. Jackson won a U.S. House race, and several months later vaulted to the Senate as a seat became vacant. Claiborne resigned from the court and, with Sevier's support, successfully ran for Jackson's previous seat. In November 1797 the congressman went to Philadelphia, three years below the mandated age of twenty-five. Seasoned at cultivating older men, Claiborne kept his seat. Congress moved to Washington, D.C., in 1800. A year later, Claiborne cast a crucial vote for Thomas Jefferson as president over Aaron Burr in the runoff decided by the House. President Jefferson rewarded the loyalist, appointing him territorial governor of Mississippi as it prepared for statehood. In 1801 Claiborne married seventeen-year-old Elizabeth Lewis of Nashville, with whom he moved to Natchez. In 1803, Jefferson gave Claiborne a more pivotal job in the emerging geography, governor of Orleans Territory.

· · · · · · · · · ·

"A MERE STRANGER HERE"

Speaking no French, he got off to a rocky start. On January 2, 1804, Claiborne wrote Secretary of State James Madison, confiding that in Louisiana, the capacity for elective governance was "an enigma that at present bewilders them." He faced outrage when the letter leaked to a Federalist paper; a Creole grandee called him "a mere stranger here." Eliza stayed in Nashville at her parents' home with their infant daughter while Claiborne got situated in New Orleans. Social gatherings were more lavish than in Washington. Three weeks before the U.S. flag rose at the Place d'Armes, Laussat hosted a party for "as many Spaniards as Americans and Frenchmen." Men began gambling at tables, breaking for food and dance: "Two sumptuous servings were interrupted by three toasts—the first was made with a white champagne, to the French Republic and Bonaparte; the second, with a pink champagne, to Charles IV and Spain; the third with a white champagne, to the United States and Jefferson. Each of these toasts was accompanied by three salvos of twenty-one guns fired from the batteries."

The Illustrious Body in full dress, bidding adieu to monarchy, partied hard till the sunrise of an odd new world, democracy.

"Coffee was served when crowds of people began to come inside," continues Laussat, uncertain how many were returning from a break or were late arrivals for a bash heating up. The Frenchman widens his lens:

A hundred women attended, most of them beautiful or pretty and all of them well built, elegant and gorgeously dressed. One hundred fifty to two hundred men moved in and out in three lively quadrilles, while card tables were set up everywhere. They danced in a flood of lights within the various rooms, whose doors I had ordered taken down. English quadrilles interrupted every third French one. To open the ball, the Marquis de Casa-Calvo danced a minuet with Madame [Louise de La Ronde] Almonaster....

We had supper at three in the morning. Here were two tables; the large seated fifty persons and the small one, twenty. Little by little, the gentlemen and ladies took their leave. At five o'clock, however, two quadrilles were in full swing. At seven o'clock, the *danse des bateaux* and *galopade* were still holding forth, and eight persons were still dancing when the last gamblers broke up.

Claiborne had to oversee the formation of state laws aligned with the U.S. Constitution, fortify a slave economy, build up the militia, and foster unity in a city of about 8,000 people, less than half of whom were white. Despite fears of a black majority, an immediate hostility churned against Anglo-Americans. On January 8, 1804, a public ball nearly erupted in violence when the orchestra struck up a French quadrille, and an American threatened to club a fiddler with his walking stick. Claiborne was present and negotiated for the musicians to play alternate songs in French and English. The quadrille resumed, an American yelled for a song in English. Someone shouted, "If the women have a drop of French blood, they will not dance!" Women fled the hall. A young lady stood on a bench, pleading in French, "We have been Spanish for thirty years and the Spanish never forced us to dance the fandango; neither do we want to dance the reel or jig!" General Wilkinson ordered a waltz and escorted her to the dance floor. Three ladies sought sanctuary at the table where Casa-Calvo, playing cards, ordered gumbo.

"There you have a picture of the feelings that stir up people," Claiborne fumed to Laussat, who had watched it all.

"See to it that they do not clash over things more serious and more important," the Frenchman replied.

But the clashes over identity at public balls *were* important, as Claiborne learned. January began Carnival season, several weeks with balls and revelry down the social ladder. "Insofar as slaveholding planters regarded themselves as aristocracy," writes Samuel Kinser, "they had an obligation to continue the masking and dancing which since the sixteenth century were standard parts of royal and aristocratic behavior. The court-as-spectacle was an integral part of policy."

As public balls attracted people of new nationalities, some dancehalls became a social tinderbox. City authorities ordered the balls to program two French quadrilles, one in English, then a waltz. Tempers exploded at a dance on January 22, 1804, with an officer and fifteen soldiers stationed on Claiborne's order. Thirty men broke into a brawl, troops pulled them apart. At Wilkinson's order the band raised "Hail, Columbia" and French voices rose, "Vive la République!" A letter to the *Gazette* railed that "the blame of these misfortunes are imputable solely to the Governor"—he was guilty of thinking people ignorant of "the blessings of a free government," and indifferent to "rights annihilated, their laws, languages, manners and custom trampled on."

In high relief from that volatility came the French-speaking black soldiers, whose esprit de corps impressed Claiborne. The uniforms—black boots, white breeches, white vests, white waistcoats topped by a crimson cockade—were a Casa-Calvo legacy. The small delegation had come to pledge the loyalty of 300 comrades: many had fought with Gálvez against the British, others joined under Miró and Carondelet, manning patrols to track maroons and guard outlying forts. Noël Carrière, fifty-eight, was influential, his story a snapshot of *gens de couleur* society.

Born in 1746 to an African father with a wife in the Ursuline slave community, Carrière carried the surname of his mother, who raised him in a different part of town. "Noel Carriere, a skilled tanner and cooper, apparently continued to live in the household of his owner, Marguerite Trepagnier Carriere, and was inventoried as part of her estate in 1769," writes the historian Emily Clark. On purchasing his freedom at twenty-five, Carrière had "somehow managed to acquire two servants widely recognized to be *his* slaves while still in his teens. This improbable feat was an indication of the energetic personality that would preside over the remaking of a large swath of free black society in late colonial New Orleans." Carrière was thirty-two when he exchanged vows at St. Louis Church with Mariana Thomas, a freewoman; her father, Pierre Thomas, a black soldier, became his role model. In 1780, Second Lieutenant Carrière earned a medal for fighting the British at Baton Rouge. Black military men embraced a Spanish ideal of honor, protecting women in marriage. During the 1790s, Carrière served as a witness at eighteen weddings, notes Clark. Père Antoine was the pastor during half that time: "Carriere officially witnessed roughly half of the weddings of free people of color during this period [1790–1804], including the marriages of nearly half of the militia members who wed. . . . Half of all weddings of free people of color in the 1790s involved militia members as grooms, witnesses, or both, and many different militiamen participated in this way, though no witness approached Carriere's virtuosity."

The Carrières had ten children; the eldest son, Noël II (born in 1780), joined the battalion before his father's death in late 1804. If Carrière *père* personified a colored Catholic establishment, Pierre Bailly, whose son also joined the militia, was "the period's foremost black agitator," writes Kimberly S. Hanger. Born a slave in 1750, freed in 1776 by Josef Bailly, Pierre became Pedro in Spanish documents. At twenty-eight he married a recently freed woman and in 1781 purchased his mother's freedom. The blacksmith acquired property, rented out storage space, bought and sold slaves. Promoted to second lieutenant for service at Baton Rouge, Mobile, and Pensacola, he "almost single-handedly tried to incite revolt among *pardos* [mulattoes] and improve their status." Bailly went on expeditions to capture maroons; in the peacetime militia he stanched levee breaks and made night patrols.

Absorbing the revolutionary news from Paris and Le Cap Français, Bailly bristled over white officers not eating at the same table with *pardo* soldiers; he resented orders for manual labor. Despite the beheading of Louis XVI, he liked the French, saying, "They have conceded men their rights." Accused of feigning illness to avoid manual labor, his image stained by avoiding the Corpus Christi procession, Bailly's real crime was free speech. In 1794 Carondelet convicted him of "tirades against the Spanish government . . . a manifest follower of the maxims of the French rebels." He spent two years in a Cuban prison. On return, his militia standing a memory, Bailly rebuilt his finances. Listed as head of household with thirteen people, including eight slaves, in a 1798 census, he had a notary certify his second lieutenant rank of 1792. Thus, he signed the 1804 document given to Claiborne with fifty-four other signatures of militia members, his son Pierre's among them, pledging "fidelity and zeal ... to the Government as a corps of volunteers agreeable to any arrangement which may be thought expedient."

As he awaited instructions from Washington on military organization, Claiborne told the militia members to maintain their established positions. On the advice of Secretary of War Henry Dearborn, he soon presented the leaders with a silk brigade flag. A sullen white crowd gathered at the Place d'Armes for the presentation ceremony, with guards stationed to prevent violence. The black company were not pleased at having white officers, but in a power-shifting city, they kept a cool front.

Slavery cut an ideological chasm in the early republic; Vermont abolished enslavement in its constitution of 1777. As other Northern states followed, mandating gradual steps for emancipation, Congress passed an 1804 law "to prevent the emergence of an internal slave trade while allowing slave owners to migrate to Louisiana with their human property," writes Adam Rothman. In a city where smuggling had long fed a black market economy, illegal traffic in slaves provided planters a pool of coerced labor, notwithstanding national law.

Claiborne's spirits lifted in June 1804 when Eliza and three-year-old Cornelia Tennessee arrived from Nashville. The United States had purchased a city block on Levee Street (today Decatur) on the riverfront near the Place d'Armes. The governor's residence occupied a corner at Toulouse Street with a garden so large it gave the Spanish family across the street an easy view. Tropical heat and drenching rains brought sickness; by August all three Claibornes were down on sopping sheets. The 1804 yellow fever epidemic followed by eight years the first record of the disease in New Orleans and foreshadowed lethal tides of epidemics that would roll across the city in the nineteenth century.

Yellow fever is an arbovirus spread by a mosquito, the *Aëdes (Stegomyia) aegypti*. Historically, the insect thrived in cities, particularly warm weather ports. "The female of the species needs the protein found in human blood to ovulate," writes Benjamin H. Trask. "After the virus has spread and incubated in the mosquito for a couple of days to a few weeks, the mosquito can infect other humans for the rest of [its] short life." Scientists did not pinpoint the source of the epidemics until the early twentieth century. Trask cites a prevailing scientific view that "slave traders imported the disease to the Americas from West Africa." The mosquito drew blood from primates and carried the pathogen on ships. "With the importation of millions of African slaves," writes Trask, "the virus became endemic in South America and the larger islands of the Caribbean Sea. In the 1800s commercial traffic criss-crossed the Gulf of Mexico [and western Atlantic Ocean].... Infectious mosquitoes, ill crew members, and passengers carried the disease to the United States."

Yellow fever brought piercing chills, headaches, retching of dark bile, back and kidney pains, jaundice, aching muscles, and inflammation of the eyes, face, and tongue. "The climate and spells of excessive heat retarded my convalescence," Laussat wrote of his July 1803 illness, presumably caught from mosquitoes on his porch. "I was laid up for twenty-five days and did not feel my natural self until after four months." On September 16, 1804, Claiborne wrote Jefferson that his secretary, Joseph Briggs, had died of the virus. Claiborne was physically robust enough to survive yellow fever. He tended his wife and child, "sponged their burning faces and mopped away their black vomit." Eliza and Cornelia died within hours of each other on September 26, 1804.

Bottling his grief in an environment of political enemies ever lurking, Claiborne drew consolation from his secretary (and late wife's brother), Micajah G. Lewis. Claiborne's fuming about the inadequacy of his $5,000 salary became gossip fodder he didn't need. An anonymous 1805 *Louisiana Gazette* piece scoffed at rumors of Claiborne's courting wealthy women (thus putting the rumors into print); a second piece had a lady in rustling silk (the late Eliza) outside a mansion with music and her husband inside, as if seeking a new wife while she "bent her willing steps toward the graves of Louisiana." Micajah Lewis learned the writer's identity, challenged him to a duel over his late sister's honor, and died of the gunshot wound. In fourteen months, Claiborne had survived yellow fever but lost his wife, child, and a secretary to the disease and his brother-in-law to gunshot.

· · · · · · · · · ·

BATTLE OF THE PEWS

As Claiborne defused the "war of the quadrilles," a surreal battle erupted in the city's ceremonial heart. Père Antoine, the Spanish monk in sandals and robe, had a charisma and popular following to make politicians wince in envy. Carlos IV's control of the New Orleans church was done. Beyond the Hispanic world, the Vatican appointed bishops. Bishop Peñalver left in 1801 for Guatemala, appointing two Irish priests as vicar-generals, or seconds-in-command. One soon died. Many Spanish-speaking clerics left. Not Antonio de Sedella: he clashed with the vicar, Rev. Patrick Walsh, over the control of St. Louis Cathedral. Casa-Calvo, who arranged funds to ease the transition for the faithful to cover the costs for clergy, nuns, and churches, backed Père Antoine in a letter to Walsh. The Irish vicar retorted that the king of Spain had no standing.

The Vatican had given authority of the Orleans Territory to Bishop John Carroll of Baltimore, a Jesuit helping his order survive, a confidante of Benjamin Franklin, and a founder of Georgetown College. Walsh advised the Vatican office, Propaganda Fide (Propagation of the Faith), that he had revoked Sedella's faculties—the right to say Mass; officiate at baptisms, funerals, and weddings; or take confessions. Disobedience to church authority was the issue. On March 14, 1805, the *Moniteur de la Louisiane* announced a meeting to elect a pastor and parish board. Walsh wrote to the mayor and aldermen: church law forbade electing a pastor. Hostility to federal control channeled into the pews; people roared, "We want Père Antoine as pastor!" The monk rose, thanking his flock, affecting humility—alas, he was under Walsh's order.

Mayor James Pitot asked Sedella if he believed in his suspension, or could he be the pastor people wanted? The priest said that since His Catholic Majesty had appointed him, he should ask conditional consent of the king's envoy, Casa-Calvo, and seek a canon law opinion. Casa-Calvo's support was assured. A former lieutenant governor of West Florida, degreed in civil and canon law, provided an opinion that supported Sedella. Backed by a canon lawyer and Casa-Calvo, Père Antoine became the pastor, subject to a board of wardens, called *marguilliers*. The arrangement undercut the Roman Catholic Church's monarchical structure in which the pope, relying on a hierarchy's recommendations, appointed a bishop. The bishop assigned or removed priests. Sedella was out of bounds. Walsh announced that rituals at the cathedral were invalid, telling people to attend the Ursuline chapel. He petitioned the territorial high court to subject Sedella to his authority. Louisiana was melding its Franco-Spanish code into laws aligned with the U.S. Constitution, which barred any state role in affairs of faith. Casa-Calvo, in transferring authority for church property to the *marguilliers*, gave the court a precedent in ruling that the *marguilliers*, as owners of the church, could choose their pastor, which His Royal Catholic Majesty never permitted. This put the cathedral, which Almonaster had built for a global church, in an opaque legal limbo.

From Rome, a Propaganda Fide cardinal wrote Bishop Carroll, asking if the New Orleans government could help enforce Church law (and oust Sedella). Carroll wrote Secretary of State Madison, accusing the "artful Spanish friar" of a plot by which a supporter had gone to Paris with $4,000 to offer Napoléon if he would recommend Sedella as bishop. "The attempt has completely miscarried," Carroll advised Madison. The bishop asked if the administration would support a French bishop for New Orleans. "The case is entirely ecclesiastical," Madison replied: the Church could appoint any bishop. "The accounts here agree with the character you have formed of [Sedella]," he added in a private coda.

Walsh asked Claiborne to intercede, calling Sedella "as dangerous to politics as religion." Constitutionally restricted, the governor was suspicious of Sedella's ties to Casa-Calvo, who was still in Louisiana, inspecting Spanish borders in an area near Baton Rouge, uncovered by the Louisiana Purchase, amid reports that he was encouraging slaves to defect for freedom with Spain. Claiborne summoned the rebel priest and made him swear allegiance to the United States. Bruised in the press, Claiborne must have felt a tinge of jealousy for a man so popular among the new Americans and haughty in his sinecure from the king of Spain.

Walsh died of yellow fever on August 22, 1806. Bishop Carroll dispatched his Baltimore vicar-general, Rev. John Olivier, to take over the New Orleans church. In enemy territory, Father Olivier hired a notary to document his June 15 appearance at the cathedral where he asked "for the keys to the said church, to which demand the woman answered, 'He [Père Antoine] was gone out.' . . . The vicar general next presented himself at the house of the Reverend Father Antonio Sedella, Capuchin friar, who keeps the said church, where the said crowd, being then considerably increased and riotous opposed themselves to the said vicar general ... [and] became more riotous and disturbed the peace of the territory by uttering cries and threats."

Claiborne wrote Jefferson that a "mob" of "low Spaniards, free Mullatos, and negroes" blocked Father Olivier, a move that cut across lines of race and class while pleasing planters who despised the Church. Feeling threatened, the vicar left town. Père Antoine now led the one institution where people voluntarily gathered across the color line; he had also carved a schism that the Vatican and Carroll wanted to mend.

· · · · · · · · · ·

WILKINSON ASCENDANT

Even with his $12,000 payoff from Casa-Calvo, who returned to Cuba in mid-1806, Brig. Gen. James Wilkinson had trouble holding onto money. That problem, coupled with his cynical patriotism, made him a natural ally for Aaron Burr, the disgraced former vice president. In the fall of 1806, Wilkinson sensed that Burr's scheme to pull Western states into an invasion of Mexico was doomed. Burr had visited New Orleans the year before, trolling for support. To curry favor with President Jefferson, Wilkinson double-crossed Burr by securing a border zone in east Texas; he thundered into New Orleans, arresting a clutch of Burr supporters. Claiborne worried after a foreboding letter from Andrew Jackson, who had left the Senate to build farmland wealth and commanded the Tennessee militia. "Keep a watchful eye on our General," he wrote. "I fear there something rotten in the State of Denmark." Wilkinson had several alleged Burr conspirators shipped out of state; he arrested but then released the *Orleans Gazette* editor and, after more unconstitutional maneuvers, called off his dogs in mid-January 1807. Burr was captured, arrested for treason, and taken to Richmond; he was tried that summer, acquitted, and moved to Europe.

Claiborne's life took a sweeter turn in 1806; he married Clarisse Duralde, twenty-seven, who came from a wealthy family in the prairie town of Opelousas. Her charms failed to tame his rage when Daniel Clark, an Irish-born wheeler dealer and the delegate to Congress, baited him in public for favoring a Negro militia over whites. Claiborne, who signed 1806 legislation that meted out harsher treatment of slaves, challenged Clark to a duel. On June 8, 1807, they rode separately into Spanish territory at Manchac, walked ten paces, turned, and fired. Claiborne fell with a bullet to the thigh. Clark won the *affaire d'honneur* but lost his next congressional race to Claiborne ally Julien Poydras.

In all of this machismo and violence, Clarisse's words elude us. Did she try to talk him out of the duel? In his wounded weeks in bed (during which he wrote Jefferson to "apologize for my imprudence"), did she brood on the hubris of men? He recovered. In 1808, she gave birth to William C. C. Claiborne II. Later that year, on November 29, Clarisse Duralde Claiborne died of yellow fever. Twice a widower, the governor had a baby boy.

· · · · · · · · · ·

HAITI'S LONG REACH

In 1809, after an empire-hungry Napoléon invaded Spain, Cuba deported Haitian refugees who had settled there: 9,059 of them poured into New Orleans—2,731 whites, 3,102 free persons of color, and 3,226 slaves. More came in 1810, doubling the overall population to 17,242 in barely six months, making the city at once blacker and more French. Relief committees formed to help the émigrés, who had exerted a profound imprint on New Orleans before 1809. A former Saint-Domingue jurist, Louis Moreau Lislet, drafted the digest of Louisiana civil law. Schooled in varied professions, including music, theater, and opera, the island French and *gens de couleur libres* settled in Tremé or Marigny, a new *faubourg* that a plantation owner developed downriver from the plaza. Newspapers offered the exiles free listings. A music teacher living above a Bourbon Street ballroom advertised in 1809: "He repairs instruments and makes guitars on a handsome Paris model and composes a varnish for the instruments."

As benevolent societies and other groups cushioned the once-propertied refugees, port authorities assumed that those listed on ship manifests as *criados* (servants) were slaves. France had abolished colonial slavery in 1794. "In what sense and by what right, were thousands of men, women, and children once again to be held as 'slaves'?" asks the legal scholar Rebecca Scott. Cuban ships plowing up the Mississippi defied an 1807 congressional ban on importing foreign slaves. "Governor Claiborne was caught between a recently enacted federal law," continues Scott, "and the practical problem of what to do with inadmissible refugees. . . . Among the thousands of arriving migrants whom Claiborne counted as free were many men and women who insisted that their only source of support was the labor of persons who accompanied them, whom they designated slaves. Therefore the challenge of providing for the refugees deemed free was entangled with the question of the status of persons whom the refugees wished to have recognized as slaves."

Claiborne and area planters pressed Congress to forego fines of Cuban ship captains for importing slaves. Under an act of March 16, 1810, by the governor and legislative council, owners could "possess, sell and dispose" of their human property, regardless of freedom conferred by French law. "The free status of any refugee of discernable African descent [was] at risk, unless he or she could quickly produce credible proof of individual freedom," writes Scott. The historian Edward E. Baptist notes that of "the 3,000 people sold as slaves in New Orleans between 1809 and 1811," 16 percent belonged to the Haitian refugee community. How many of those people sold were, in fact, legally free?

In a city that so readily bent its laws, the Congo dances pulsed with freedom, body rhythms laced out in rings among folk in costumes, celebrating to percussions and strings, nurturing a tradition within the larger culture of feast-day processions of priests and musicians, military parades, public balls, and music in theaters. New Orleans in the early 1800s had three opera companies before New York had one. For a city of nearly 20,000 souls in 1810, the society teemed with diversity. As Congo dances riveted visiting ministers and writers, a cunning mentality circulated among certain onlookers. An 1810 newspaper ad suggests the man who placed it directed a sharp gaze at dancing folk, enslaved and not.

50 Dollars Reward

Will be given to any person for apprehending a mulatto fellow PIERRE, (tho' he may have changed his name) Creole of the Cape; about 5 feet one inch high ... between 28 and 30 years of age; much pitted with the small pox, in consequence of which his beard is in spots: his face is thin and the nose a little turned up. *He was last seen last Sunday with a Tambourine unstrung in his hand,* and a pair of razors from which it is presumed he plays on, and also may have been a barber, having been, as a boy, at a barbers shop in Charleston, where I purchased him. I understand he was a drummer at the Cape after he ran away from me. When he was seen last Sunday, he wore a large white tapped hat, a whitish coat with blue stripes of the stuff the French call *candelit*, a pair of Nankeen pantaloons and boots. He has been a runaway for 16 years. Speaks good English and lately kept a barbers shop in Boston, where he has lived 8 months and has recently come to this country. He will no doubt endeavor to pass for a free man. He is extremely cunning and artful.... Claud Guillaud. July 20.

"The Cape" means Le Cap Français, where Pierre was born about 1781 in then-Saint-Domingue; at some point, he was shipped to Charleston and re-sold. Guillaud on buying the boy branded his initials, C. G., on Pierre's chest, another ad reveals. Pierre, about fifteen, fled back to Le Cap. On reaching Boston, he had been legally free half his life. Did Pierre know the risk of returning to New Orleans? Wearing pantaloons, a hat, and a white coat with blue French stripes, he must have thrummed his tambourine at Congo Square or levee gatherings. Pierre La Puce, as he called himself at his barber shop in Faubourg Marigny, was recaptured.

Most accounts of Congo Square were by whites from farther north or foreign countries—fresh eyes on the memory tides that washed past locals as so much ephemera. Cultural impact registered in subtler ways. The police force, founded in 1805 to bolster slave control, issued an 1809 ordinance on funerals, revealing evidence of things unseen in the press:

Art. 9—As to the custom observed by several Africans and people of colour of assembling during the night, on occasion of the death of some of their acquaintance, these meetings shall be tolerated *only when confined to the relations of the deceased,* and when everything is conducted at them with decency. But if the tranquility of the neighborhood be interrupted with cries, singing or dancing &c. on such occasions, the Commissary of Police and the patrols, are required to take up all persons found at such meetings after the hour of retreat [italics added].

An assemblage at night by "Africans and people of colour" (no mention of slaves) was now "a custom." Tolerating the songs and dancing of kinfolk at funerals erected a pseudo-legal standard. How did the police know who was related to whom without breaking up the dance?

Newspaper ads offering rewards for fugitive slaves speak volumes about the owners' emotions and the staggering psychological distance of the enslaved.

A Negro WENCH, Named Therese, 22 ... of the *Congo nation*, she had on when she went away, a green flannel petticoat, with a wrapper of brown cloth, and a cloak. She absconded on the 7th last. She is of an ordinary stature and has a middling handsome countenance, and appears to be pregnant.

A generous reward will be given to any person will bring said wench to Berthe Grima, No. 9, on the square.

"Wench" meant a working-class woman or a prostitute, and in this context raises inevitable questions about whether Mr. Grima, a wealthy merchant, had more than descriptive interest in her "middling handsome countenance." If indeed pregnant, Therese may have fled to keep her future child from becoming his property, too. Enslaved women who were pregnant or with young children not infrequently ran off. The language of the notices for runaway slaves is often accompanied by generic drawings, like gentle cartoons of a woman with a bag or a man with a satchel, suggesting affection or emotional closeness to soften the message of human beings fleeing from lives of fear and subjugation. A "negro boy named CIPIO, well known in town as a bread seller," fled with "an iron collar fastened with a French padlock, though probably he may have got it off." When he came back with the proceeds of selling bread, the owner locked his neck as in some dungeon nightmare. The understatement of such cruelty is breathtaking, yet Southern society accepted barbaric punishments as the price of upholding a way of life.

An 1808 reward posted for "my maroon Mulatress, named CITE, creole from the French port of St. Domingue, age of 24," by a widow signals that if Cite lived on the island after age twelve she should have been free.

Pierre La Puce escaped again, according to a *Courier* ad in the late summer of 1811. His new owner, C. Gallate, references the initials branded on his chest by the previous owner, describing him as "a barber, plays the drums and tambourine . . . and has some marks of the cowskins on his hips"—meaning scars from where he had been whipped. "The said mulatto took with him a great quantity of clothes and his tambourine."

The tambourine players at Congo Square were a world away from sugar plantations forty miles upriver on the German Coast, so-named after early settlers, where many wealthy families now had French names. America's largest slave revolt erupted there in early 1811, just after the sugarcane harvest, with the gentry preparing for Carnival season and parties in town. The attack was well planned by plantation slaves with an "extensive network of maroon colonies running up and down the river on both sides . . . [and] in the rear of the city of New Orleans," writes Albert Thrasher. "On foot or by boat, maroons moved regularly and quickly . . . to another carrying information." The scholar Edward E. Baptist cautions, "We only know what we know from confessions made by some of the captured rebels. Perhaps 'knew' is not the right verb to use when the information comes from tortured people desperate to save their own skins."

On the chilly midnight of January 8, 1811, a *commandeur*, or overseer, called Charles Deslondes broke into Col. Manuel Andry's big house with about twenty-five rebels from several plantations, hacking to death the grown son, Gilbert Andry, and wounding the father. Manuel Andry managed to run to the river and escaped in a pirogue. Deslondes and several lieutenants discarded their cheap work clothes, slipped on Andry's military uniforms, and set out on horseback. By midmorning on January 9, a growing force, estimated by some as 500 rebels, was moving along the levee toward the city, thirty-six miles south, hitting plantations, gathering horses, guns, swords, cane knives, hatchets, and farm tools, drawing slaves and maroons from fugitive enclaves into "parade formation, marching to military drums, singing and chanting, 'On to New Orleans!'" Slaves loyal to owners hid white family members in cane fields and helped them flee to the city. Planter Jean-François Trepagnier stayed in defiance; a house slave chopped off his head. Deslondes's forces burned three plantation houses on the march.

Claiborne had previously sent troops after "brigands" who had waylaid a mail carrier on horseback. When news of the revolt reached the Cabildo midmorning on January 9, Claiborne canceled a military excursion to Spanish Florida and sent the local militia, including a battalion of blacks, to River Road. At four that afternoon, after two days' march, the insurgents were camped twenty miles out from the city at a plantation near Lake Pontchartrain, which they raided for food and drink. Gen. Wade Hampton's troops, including a militia led by Colonel Andry, attacked Deslondes's camp before dawn on January 10 and sent the rebels scrambling. After an aching fifteen-mile retreat, the slaves regrouped at a plantation, low on bullets; meanwhile, a force of armed planters led by Manuel Andry attacked from the rear. The slave army faced a fusillade that killed sixty-six rebels, some executed at close range, with twenty-two captured and twenty-seven missing if not dead in the woods. Deslondes was taken back to the plantation where it began. Andry chopped off his forearms, shot him, and threw him into a fire.

"Local authorities orchestrated the rebels' executions to magnify the degrading and terrorizing effects of their punishments," writes Adam Rothman. An outlying court sent captives back to their owners for execution and decapitation in front of the slave communities and posted the heads on stakes posted along river road to seed fears. "Others were tried in New Orleans before a jury composed of leading planters." The Place d'Armes again became an execution site, as did Fort Ferdinand, abutting Congo Square, where one of the rebels was executed. Baptist estimates that "close to one hundred" of the rebel slaves were killed.

As newspapers domestic and foreign ran articles on the insurrection, the territorial legislature awarded planters $300 for each slave killed or executed, and up to a third of the appraised cost of houses burned. Advocates for statehood argued that Louisiana, with its agricultural wealth and anchoring port, should join the United States. By admitting Louisiana in April 1812, the United States cemented itself to a slave economy, the debate over which would burn hot in decades to come.

After eight years as appointed governor, Claiborne won election to the office in the spring of 1812. That fall, he married Cayetana Bosque, sixteen, alternately called Suzette and Susanna, a Spanish Creole who eight years earlier at her parents' home opposite the governor's mansion had seen the big yard where Claiborne's late young daughter played. He was thirty-seven; with a four-year-old son, he needed domestic stability. "Claiborne's third marriage was a rushed affair," writes Peter J. Kastor. "Susanna was apparently pregnant at the time, for references to a daughter, Sophronia, appeared only a few months after the November 1812 wedding."

Père Antoine presided at the ceremony.

···

Pirates, Black Soldiers, and the
War under Jackson

Napoléon's defeat in Haiti opened the Mississippi Valley for a vast expansion of slavery. The Non-Importation Act of 1806 banned certain goods from Britain in an effort to force British ships to respect American sovereignty at sea and halt the abduction of commercial sailors. The subsequent embargo choked the port economy of New Orleans, while smugglers moved goods along the bayous. In 1807, Congress banned international slave trading to protect the status of coerced black labor as a U.S. enterprise. Governor Claiborne considered slavery a natural law of the economy. He also needed African American troops to strengthen the militia. Louisiana legislators opposed a free colored militia as a threat to the social order, fearing that free blacks would conspire with slaves.

In 1813, as Claiborne struggled to build a militia, he was incensed at the defiance of slave-smuggling French pirates in a renegade colony thirty-nine miles south of the city at Barataria Bay, an inlet off the Gulf of Mexico. Evading revenue laws, the brothers Pierre and Jean Laffite used privateer ships flying the flag of Cartagena, the Caribbean port that had broken with Spain. Spanish vessels were a main target for maritime mercenaries like the Laffites, living among sailors and servants on the barrier island of Grand Isle, raiding vessels like bandits on a highway, bringing back goods and slaves to sell in Louisiana.

William C. Davis's *The Pirates Laffite* pinpoints their origins in the village of Paulliac, in the Médoc region of France. Pierre Laffite was born about 1770. His mother soon died, his father remarried, and in or about 1782, Jean Laffite was born. Pierre shipped out for Louisiana in May 1802, by way of Saint-Domingue. "He stopped at Cap Français on the way and narrowly escaped the street fighting as French troops battled black revolutionaries," writes Davis. "By March 1803, Pierre had reached New Orleans, bringing with him a mulatto mistress and a son." Pierre moved on to Pensacola, and by 1805 was involved with another mulatto woman who gave birth to more children.

Pierre's move to Louisiana suggests a symbiotic tie with his half-brother, younger by a dozen years. Jean Laffite's back pages are blank before his 1809 arrival in the New Orleans. Pierre's brief period in Saint-Domingue may have meant a reunion with Jean, as a sailor or mercenary honing the piratical skills that would later secure the Barataria base south of New Orleans, where maroons once roamed. New Orleans was a cocoon of Saint-Domingue émigrés, with taverns catering to all comers. Pierre, who established a residence and office in the city, was a "robust, powerfully built man of above middle height," writes Davis. He had "a light complexion and light brown hair ... piercing dark eyes" and teeth "brilliantly white." Jean Laffite, a sturdy inch or two above six feet, had "side whiskers down his chin, and the pale cast of his skin despite his time at sea created an arresting contrast with his large dark hazel eyes and dark hair." Pierre's house was on Royal Street, where Jean sometimes stayed, or at a boardinghouse whose guests appreciated him as a convivial presence at dinner. Tough and gregarious, the Laffites wanted both worlds: acceptance in the city and the financial feast from trafficking in goods plundered at sea by their men or other buccaneers, who unloaded their catch in the slips at Grand Isle.

Claiborne, the former Tennessee high court justice, frowned at the Creole society's permissive take on the law; when the governor denounced slave-smuggling as criminal behavior in social settings, certain ladies airily replied that men of their families, who had trafficked slaves under the Spanish, were never suspected of dishonesty. Pleasure-loving Creoles who yawned at probity were a thick pill for Claiborne to swallow in social rituals that can try the patience of governors. The Barataria pirates had shot and wounded two customs agents seeking to halt their activities on a bayou, and a revenue agent hit by a bullet had fallen into the water and drowned. That mattered to Claiborne.

For Claiborne, the Laffites' stronghold heightened the urgency of mustering a strong militia. British generals in 1812 were sending troops by sea and overland in the northeast, determined to recapture America thirty-eight years after the Declaration of Independence. If Claiborne couldn't smash a nest of pirates, how could he defend the city from a British invasion moving up from the Gulf?

Britain's advances outraged Claiborne's fellow Tennessean, Andrew Jackson. In 1812, Jackson was forty-five; he had left the U.S. Senate in 1797 and returned to his home state, serving six years as a judge. In 1802, he defeated Governor John Sevier in the election for major general of the Tennessee militia. Settled in a happy marriage, Jackson had a cotton plantation outside Nashville and business dealings to keep a normal man at peace. But whether because of losing two brothers and his mother in South Carolina during the Revolution, or his own boyhood scar at the hands of the British, Jackson maintained a "hot temper, prickly sense of honor, and sensitivity to insult that embroiled him in a series of fights and brawls," notes Daniel Feller. In 1806 he got into an argument over a horse race. A duel resulted; Jackson was hit in the chest but shot the other man dead. He carried on with the piece of lead embedded in his body.

By Jackson's lights, Jefferson and Madison as presidents had failed to take aggressive moves needed to blunt Britain's continuing military harassment. Jackson believed that westward-moving white yeomen were strengthening the country. He had no qualms about using slaves on his plantation, Hermitage, or selling them—slavery was in the Old Testament, and he read the Bible daily. In Andrew Jackson's clear-cut view, you fought to survive and to prevail.

When the United States declared war on Britain in June 1812, Jackson received orders from the Madison administration to go to New Orleans; he headed south with 2,071 volunteers, reaching Natchez in March 1813.

Claiborne lacked Jackson's commanding personality; more than a decade had passed since their political interactions in Tennessee. Trying to raise a sufficient base of troops, Claiborne met resistance from a planter-dominated legislature and a Creole ambivalence about the United States. A Louisiana infantry division had been summoned north to fight the British. It must have been difficult for Claiborne to write Jackson, saying that he was prepared for a defensive war yet needed reinforcements. Both men were surprised by a shift in Federal strategy; at Natchez, Jackson received an order to return to Tennessee—New Orleans was no longer an immediate line of defense. Jackson was irate. He wrote Governor Willie Blount that he would "make every sacrifice," leading his troops 500 miles back through a chilly late winter.

Claiborne wrote Louisiana's congressional delegation, seeking greater support. In a letter dated July 9, 1813, the governor painfully admitted to President Madison that the "heterogeneous mass" of people had not produced enough men to defend the city. A decade after the Louisiana Purchase, New Orleans lacked a coherent American identity and allegiance for which to fight. The secretary of war sent 2,000 muskets, giving Claiborne some comfort. He had a city, and laws, to defend.

His first order of business involved the brothers Laffite. On November 24, 1813, Claiborne issued a proclamation detailing the smugglers' crimes, offering a $500 reward to "any person delivering the said John Lafitte to the Sheriff of the Parish of Orleans." Like a cock-of-the-walk, Jean Laffite himself had a circular posted in the city offering $5,000 "to any person delivering Governor Claiborne to me at Isle au Chat"—Cat Island, in the Gulf off Bayou Lafourche. Meanwhile, authorities arrested Pierre Laffite, who was living openly in New Orleans.

The Laffites ran a black market economy that allowed them to live well and mingle in plantation society. At Barataria, Grand Isle, and Cat Island they sold slaves taken from ships at sea to planters, particularly French Creoles. A leading New Orleans merchant complained to Claiborne that people were paying $150 to $200 a head in Barataria for slaves who would cost $700 each in the city. As pirates gamed the laws, Claiborne struggled to raise an army to protect people against the British.

· · · · · · · · · ·

JACKSON ON THE WARPATH

On Jackson's return trek to Tennessee, 150 men got sick, a third of them too ill to sit up. With only eleven wagons, he ordered officers to surrender their horses for ailing men. As he had done as a boy for his brother sick with smallpox on the road back to their home in South Carolina, he gave up his own horse, winning the affection of men who nicknamed him Old Hickory, tough as wood, on that hard trip home.

Back in Nashville that fall, Jackson got into another fight after serving as second to a brigadier general in a duel with one Jesse Benton. Jesse was the brother of Thomas Hart Benton, a Jackson aide-de-camp (later a U.S. senator from Missouri and great-uncle and namesake of the twentieth-century artist). In the raw frontier culture of the time, bullish men often fought duels over insults and trivial issues. Tom Benton, who was away at the time, blamed Jackson for the bullets that peppered his brother's posterior. "You conducted it in a savage, unequal, unfair and base manner," Tom Benton railed in a letter to Jackson after the duel. In early September, after learning that the Bentons were staying at City Hotel in Nashville, Jackson rode into town, dismounted with a horse whip and pistol and approached Tom Benton at the hotel.

Benton and Jackson both fired.

Benton's first bullet blew into Jackson's left shoulder, piercing an artery and splintering bone. The second hit his left arm; the third shot missed.

A brawl erupted. Jackson's allies carried the wounded general to another hotel, where he lay on a bed swooning in pain as the blood drenched two mattresses; the physicians recommended amputating his arm. Jackson refused. Finally, they bound him up and sent him home, with bolts of pain that stayed with him for years.

As Rachel Jackson tended to her suffering husband, a civil war was building in the Creek nation across the northeastern area of present-day Alabama. As whites encroached on lands, some Creeks were inclined to assimilate; others, called Red Sticks (after their painted war clubs), rose to the war-for-survival speeches by the roaming chief Tecumseh. White settlers began seeking safe areas like Fort Mims, a ramshackle trading post well north of Mobile. The catalytic event came August 30, 1813, when 726 Red Sticks launched a lightning attack on the fort, slaughtering upward of 250 people, mostly white, but with Indians and blacks among the victims, and horrific atrocities committed against women and children. "Half of the 100-man garrison of Mississippi Territorial Volunteers died with their commander," writes Gregory A. Waselkov.

Terror engulfed the region. From President Madison down to the governors of Georgia, Mississippi, and Tennessee (Alabama was neither a state nor a territory), the fear of further massacres and a southeastern Indian front that was forging ties with the British ignited a military response. Cherokee and Choctaw warriors joined U.S. troops against the Creek rebels.

With his bullet-blasted shoulder and weak arm, General Jackson took Governor Willie Blount's news of the call for troops with righteousness. Animated by the thought of Indians marching to scalp and pillage, he issued a call to "Brave Tennesseans!" The avenger got on his horse and led his troops into Alabama, speeding along under warm fall skies.

Leading about 2,500 Tennessee volunteer infantrymen, Jackson reached Huntsville, meeting up with Brig. Gen. John Coffee and 1,300 cavalry men. On November 3, they reached the outskirts of a Red Stick camp at Tallushatchee; Jackson sent the cavalry ahead. Coffee's forces annihilated the Creeks, taking 186 lives, including women and children. Coffee blamed warriors taking refuge in houses with families for the accidental death of innocents. "We now shot them like dogs; and then set the house on fire, and burned it up with the forty-six warriors inside it," the volunteer David Crockett boasted. The Tallushatchee massacre sent convulsions through the Creeks not aligned with the Red Sticks.

Jackson's letter at this juncture to his beloved Rachel reflects a biting paradox in his personality. The war tactician praises General Coffee's "elegant style" in executing orders; he also tells his wife, "I send on a little Indian boy for Andrew," their adopted son, as a playmate and family member. The Creek infant was ten months, his family lost in the blood tide. Indian chiefs whose forces wiped out white settlements occasionally took surviving infants. Jackson seems to have pitied the Creek baby, named Lyncoya. "Jackson and the baby were both members of the same brotherhood of orphans," writes Steve Inskeep in *Jacksonland*. "Jackson had never met his own father and lost his mother to disease when he was a boy during the Revolution."

Jackson's forces kept moving. At Talladega they killed 300 more Red Stick Creeks. In March 1814, Jackson received 3,300 reinforcements, which included U.S. Infantry members, Tennesseans with 700 cavalry, as well as 500 Cherokee and 100 Creek warriors. They marched toward Horseshoe Bend, a forested peninsula on the Tallapoosa River. A thousand Red Sticks who huddled with 350 women and children "were nearly a spent force, desperate members of a society near collapse," writes Inskeep, describing "a shelter from marauding horsemen ... less a citadel than a refugee camp."

Jackson ordered the attack at 10:30 A.M. on March 27. The cannons under Coffee's command pounded the wall to war drums and Red Stick warriors screaming their defiance. Meanwhile, Cherokee and Creek fighters in Jackson's army crossed the river from the far side, setting fires and battling toward the fort. At the sight of rising smoke, Jackson ordered his attack; fighting raged throughout the day, with 557 Red Stick warriors killed on the ground and an estimated 300 in the river. Jackson lost 49 men, with 154 wounded. Jackson the conqueror pressured the defeated Creeks into a treaty that surrendered 23 million acres in tribal homelands to the United States, constituting most of present-day southwest Georgia and central Alabama. "Thirty-four of the thirty-five Creek leaders who signed the treaty of surrender had supported the United States during the war," writes Adam Rothman, "and they were understandably astonished and embittered to find themselves stripped of much of their land."

While Jackson's forces were fighting at Horseshoe Bend, the British army defeated the French at Toulouse and Bonaparte abdicated. Britain was the commanding European power. After a bout of dysentery, Jackson in late summer headed toward Mobile. Buoyed by victories abroad, British troops set their sights on America, once again, heading south from Canada, taking towns through the Chesapeake, freeing slaves to pull in as combatants. Then the unthinkable happened: on August 24, 1814, the British broke through the ill-prepared troops guarding Washington, D.C. As Madison, his family, staff, and other officials fled, the redcoats set fire to the Capitol, the Supreme Court, the Library of Congress, and the White House; the flames, soot, and smoke wrecked furniture, paintings, and books but left the presidential mansion built by slaves charred and standing. The glow from the burning of Washington was visible fifty miles away.

Clerks at the Department of State packed certain archives of the country into linen sacks and loaded them onto wagons—the Declaration of Independence, the Constitution, international treaties, and the correspondence of George Washington. They toted the material by horseback thirty-five miles to Leesburg, Virginia, where they hid the early archives of American history in the cellar vault of an empty house and gave the keys to the sheriff.

. . . .

LAFFITE'S GAMBIT

As Washington burned, Pierre Laffite sat in a stockade behind the Cabildo, his bail set at $12,514.52 because of a legal judgment he had ignored. The federal grand jury laid on new charges for having "commanded, counseled, & advised ... acts of piracy & robbery upon the high seas ... & repeatedly introduced goods, wares & merchandising arising from such piratical captures into this District." Down at Grand Isle, Jean Laffite engaged a lawyer who arranged for the publication of a letter, a strange appeal to public opinion intended to benefit Pierre, stressing the need "to prevent *monopoly*.... the public ought to generally share the profits of this advantageous trade." Laffite impishly signed his letter "Napoleon Jr.," appealing to the city's French core against Anglo-American legal standards.

Laffite's fluency in English, if slightly flawed, suggests a keen mind, a criminal with wit and a grasp of market dynamics. He abided by a certain code in robbing ships; he did not steal the personal belongings of passengers nor allow his men to rape or gratuitously beat their victims; piracy was business—steal the slaves, dry goods, seasoning, wine, and sundry other commercial items to resell in lower Louisiana. Laffite was eyeing a shift of operations to the coast of Mexico as the Mexican independence war from Spain intensified when the British handed him a plum.

On September 3, 1814, Capt. Nicholas Lockyer of the warship *Sophie* arrived at Grand Isle. Laffite subdued his angered French outlaws, who loathed the British. Escorted into his house, Lockyer gave Laffite material: a proclamation from British lieutenant colonel Edward Nicolls urging Louisiana citizens to revolt. Nicolls's personal letter to Laffite included a carrot: "You may be a useful assistant to me." Lockyer also held out a stick: the choice for Laffite of collaborating with the British or seeing his ships and buildings destroyed. Laffite detained Lockyer overnight as a sop to his infuriated men and sent him back the next day promising to think it over.

He immediately sent the documents to a Saint-Domingue émigré in New Orleans, asking him to give them to authorities. With this signal of national loyalty, he hoped to gain leverage with Claiborne; he also asked for the release of Pierre, who was ill.

Just then, however, Pierre escaped the Cabildo jail. Claiborne, meanwhile, was frustrated by Louisiana legislators resisting black military troops in the wake of Washington's destruction and British ships roaming the Gulf. "With a population differing in language, customs, manners and *sentiments*," he wrote Jackson, surely embarrassed, "I should not with entire certainty calculate on the support of the people."

"They must be for us or against us," replied Jackson, now given command by the president for all military operations in Tennessee, Louisiana, and the Mississippi territory. His remark about free colored troops sent a flared message to all people. "No objections can be raised by the citizens of Norleans [*sic*] on account of their engagement."

Claiborne did not have enough men answering the call to military duty, a "perfectly sincere insubordination of the individual's liberty and opinion to the common welfare," George Washington Cable wrote with telling hindsight. Claiborne stressed to Jackson that Laffite and his men might be useful. From his field camp, Jackson hurled a thunderbolt at the legislature, calling black soldiers "sons of freedom" in a proclamation Claiborne posted. "Your intelligent minds are not to be led away by false representations. Your love of honor would cause you to despise the Man who should attempt to deceive you." He offered black volunteers the same $124 and 160 acres of land that white soldiers would get.

One can almost hear Jackson spitting out the words "wretches" and "hellish banditti" in responding to Claiborne about the Baratarians. He wanted Lafitte and his men in jail. Claiborne was also dealing with Master Commandant Daniel T. Patterson of the federal navy station at New Orleans. Patterson, twenty-seven, was a New Yorker by birth and hostile to amnesty for robbers at sea; he had orders from Washington to attack them. Claiborne, shifting to a morally flexible view of the Laffites (the enemy of my enemy is my friend), would not feud with Washington over Patterson's order. While the British waited for Laffite's reply and the pirate waited on Claiborne's, Patterson's flotilla went down to the coast.

On September 15, Jackson's guns at Mobile Point beat back British forces. The next morning, at Grand Isle, Jean Laffite was hosting a buyers' breakfast with stocked warehouses when the federal ships came in view. The New Orleans clients jumped in their boats and fled. Unwilling to fight Americans or risk having Pierre recaptured, Jean Laffite ordered his dozens of men to flee and did so himself by pirogue, threading up the bayous toward German Coast plantations where he had friendly clients. Commandant Patterson nevertheless took eighty pirates prisoner and a bigger prize, eight ships of various tonnages, burning several more among the nineteen vessels deemed not seaworthy. His men also torched forty wood-and-palmetto roof cabins and hauled a load from the aborted warehouse sale, as chronicled by Davis in *The Pirates Laffite*. The list of confiscated goods included

> medicinal herbs and flowers, bags of anise seed, boxes and barrels of glassware, more than ten thousand gallons of wine, seventy-five demi-johns of spirits, ships' sails, a ship's cable, boxes of soap, glass tumblers, a lot of German linen, hundreds of silk stockings, poplin sheeting, sewing thread, coffee, bales of paper, cocoa, rope grass bales, window glass, duck canvas, and more—all the real plunder of pirates rather than the doubloons and jewels of fiction. The flower ran to 163 barrels, and that had been Jean Laffite's own goods. The *Santa Rita* had aboard her cloves, coffee, cinnamon, 17,200 cigars, sherry, Málaga wine, 769 gallons of brandy, raisins, candles, 483 pounds of chocolate, cocoa and more. Just the duty being evaded on the cargo amounted to $10,766.39.

Patterson bagged good money, too, some $3,327 in several currencies or specie, and "letters of several New Orleans merchants of good standing, documentation of their businesses with the Laffites that the court could use to institute prosecutions," writes Davis, calculating that the full value of assets "may have run to $200,000."

Hiding at a plantation twenty miles above town, Jean Laffite cast a line to a prominent attorney immersed in the city's preparations for war, hoping that he might gain leverage with the help of Edward Livingston.

. . . .

FOR CLIENT AND COUNTRY

If Edward Livingston and the Laffites had one thing in common it was a personal investment in the river port city crowded with people seeking to remake their lives. As British ships from Jamaica moved toward Louisiana, the pirates found a brilliant legal advocate.

Born in 1764, schooled as a boy by tutors in Albany, Livingston graduated from College of New Jersey (later, Princeton); he studied law with Alexander Hamilton and Aaron Burr, won a New York congressional seat and delivered the state delegation's vote to Thomas Jefferson for president in the

1800 election decided in the House of Representatives. Livingston's wife died after Jefferson appointed him federal attorney in New York, a post in which he served while also being mayor, as some politicians did at the time. Livingston crashed in 1803. On recovering from yellow fever he learned that $100,000 in his offices had disappeared with a clerk. Livingston resigned both his positions, sold property toward repayment of the debt, and in 1804 moved to New Orleans, seeking a clean break.

His brother, Robert Livingston, had helped draft the Declaration of Independence and in Paris helped negotiate terms of the Louisiana Purchase. Fluent in French, Edward Livingston rejuvenated his legal career in the city of many colors and customs. The people of New Orleans, he wrote to his sister up in New York, were "hospitable, honest, and polite, without much education, but with excellent natural abilities ... people with whom a man who had nothing to regret, might pass his life as happily as can be expected in any part of this uncertain world." In 1805, Livingston married Marie Louise Magdaleine Valentine d'Avezac de Castera Moreau de Lassy, a widow from Haiti. She was nineteen; he was forty-two.

As newspapers covered Jackson's victory at Mobile, Livingston in October launched the Committee for Public Safety, pressing officials for a swifter, stronger build-up. Frustrated by lawmakers, Claiborne resented Livingston's reach into his area of authority; but the lawyer saw the need for serious forces to secure New Orleans and the life he had made. He also wanted access to Jackson; they had served in Congress together years before.

As eighty pirates sat behind bars, the federal grand jury issued eleven indictments based on the Grand Isle documents, including one for a purchasing client of the Laffites. As merchants contacted Livingston for legal defense, he wrote President Madison seeking a general amnesty to halt prosecutions of the Laffites, their imprisoned gang members, and clientele. Livingston echoed his request in a letter to Jackson.

Jackson was then marching to Pensacola in pursuit of Red Stick Creeks and to seize the Spanish fort overtaken by Lt. Col. Edward Nicolls, who had tried to lure Jean Laffite. The British were forcibly pulling in recruits from blacks and Indians and laying plans to invade New Orleans. As Jackson's army came barreling down, British frigates in retreat destroyed two nearby forts with powerful shelling. Once Pensacola was secured, Jackson took his soldiers to Mobile to regroup. After a bad bout of dysentery, he began his march to New Orleans in late November.

Jackson reached New Orleans on December 1 with three military aides, trailed by 1,500 volunteers from Tennessee and Kentucky, men looking less like a spit-shine army than backcountry hunters. Greeted by Governor Claiborne and Mayor Nicholas Girod, Jackson was given a Royal Street headquarters—three stories and a balcony. His reunion after many years with Edward Livingston was mutually beneficial. Jackson needed a trusted guide to the strange city. The French-speaking Livingston became his translator and confidential secretary. When Jackson stepped onto the balcony to greet the public, he was forty-seven, tall and gaunt at 145 pounds from his stomach illness, his hair like iron bristles. Alert to human divisions in the century-old cobblestone streets beneath him, the general promised, leaving pauses filled by Livingston's French, to "drive enemies into the sea, or perish in the effort."

"Good citizens," he intoned, "You must rally around me in this emergency, cease all differences and divisions, and unite with me in patriotic resolve to save this city from dishonor and disaster which a presumptuous enemy threatens to inflict upon it."

Planters agreed to let slaves be used to build up fortifications, dig trenches and thicken earthen mounds at command posts surrounding the city. Jackson immediately called out the 350 free colored soldiers under Col. Joseph Savary, a Haitian mulatto, military veteran, and soldier of fortune with ties to the Laffites. Savary raised a second battalion, many of whose members had fought as French loyalists against Toussaint Louverture. Several men, like Noël Carrière and Pierre Bailly, were namesake sons of African Creoles who had fought in New Orleans for the Spanish. Others, from Haiti, made new lives in the Creole city.

Lieutenant Colonel Nicolls, meanwhile, was moving through parts of Florida, southwest Louisiana and Texas, luring slaves to fight for Britain, with offers of uniforms, guns, and provisional freedom.

New Orleans had never been invaded; but with reality bearing down, people were on edge. General Jackson's arrival in New Orleans forced the society into an identity shift; however French the city was at its core, however Latin in its tolerance and committed to a belief in life lived well, its people saw their survival in embrace of the American identity, the agenda of a long-frustrated Governor Claiborne.

Appeals to Jackson that he grant amnesty to the Laffites and their men met an icy wall: the former judge would not breach the legal process. Bernard de Marigny de Mandeville, a Creole potentate, neighborhood developer, and gambler, had joined Livingston's safety committee; Marigny and another member met with Dominic Hall, the federal judge overseeing the Barataria case, and stressed the need for every available man to fight. Hall advised Marigny to secure a resolution in the legislature, seeking a suspension of procedure in his own court. For lawmakers who had supporters who were clients of the Laffites, the vote for amnesty was an easy call and included a suspension of bankruptcy proceedings, civil cases, and debt collections. The lawmakers needed those criminals to join forces behind the city in the fight of its life. Besides, the U.S. embargo had driven merchants and planters to buy smuggled goods and slaves from the Laffites; why punish men of commerce? On reading the bill, Judge Hall advised the federal prosecutor that he had suspended his court proceedings until late February.

On December 16, General Jackson declared martial law in New Orleans. For a people with a lax attitude toward authority, the order was sobering: every person entering the city was to register at a military office or face arrest. No one could leave without the high command's written permission; no vessels or boats could depart without a passport. The city would go dark at nine in a strict curfew. Anyone on the street would be arrested on suspicion of spying. Few people wanted to test General Jackson's patience.

At about that time British vessels seized federal gunboats in Lake Borgne; British troops captured Jacques Villeré's plantation, ten miles below the city. Commandant Patterson, who had sacked the Laffite base at Grand Isle, confided to Jackson that he was short of men, and now gunboats as well. With eighty pirates in jail, Claiborne and one of his generals advised Jackson to support an amnesty and press the Baratarians into service on Patterson's short-staffed war boats and as soldiers on land. Jackson came around: he needed men who could fight.

Livingston's October letter to President Madison, seeking leniency for the Baratarians, sealed the deal. The translator at Jackson's side had become his confidant. Whatever Jean Laffite paid Livingston was worth its weight in stolen gold. The U.S. attorney general informed Claiborne that, with his permission, they would consider clemency appeals and recommend presidential pardons predicated on the Baratarians joining Jackson's troops in defense of the city and their good conduct thereafter.

When the pirates were released, Livingston, under Jackson's order, made them pledge allegiance to the United States and immediately mustered them into the militia. The Laffite brothers met with General Jackson in late December and received safe conduct passes to join the troops. No document on what they said has surfaced. One cannot imagine Andrew Jackson's piercing eyes as pools of pleasure in the moment; the general was at war and if the Laffites could help, well, get on with it.

Pirates, Black Soldiers, and Jackson

Planters sent slaves under military watch to dig trenches, shovel earthen mounds into shape, clear timber, and boost fortifications. Men of means were joining the effort. Among them, Henry Latrobe, twenty-one, was a son of the architect and master builder of Washington, D.C. In 1811, Benjamin Latrobe had sent his son, a newly minted architect himself and fluent in French, to New Orleans for a successful pitch to the city council to build a waterworks with a fifteen-year franchise. Henry went out to the front, overseeing 150 slaves building a defensive line south of the city at Chalmette.

"The citizens were preparing for battle as cheerfully as if it had been a party of pleasure," a Creole major and engineer in the Seventh Infantry noted, "each in his vernacular tongue singing songs of victory. . . . The several corps of militia were constantly exercising from morning till evening, and at all hours was heard the sound of the drums." The city was crowded with men waiting to fight. Upcountry soldiers tended to urinate in public, and stood naked washing themselves in the Mississippi, scandalizing ladies of society.

From the Acadian prairie and villages above the lake at Manchac, men with hunting rifles, swords, and knives headed for the city along with Choctaw and Chitimacha fighters, filling out a makeshift army of wildly different colors. Women organized first aid stations. The Ursuline sisters began prayers to Our Lady of Prompt Succor to protect the city from war.

As the free black soldiers gathered at the Place d'Armes, a mulatto boy, Jordan Noble, joined the Seventh Infantry Regiment as a drummer. The drummers sounded a moving backbone for the men, signaling commands with one rhythmic pattern for morning reveille, another for roll call, yet another for drill, and a steady staccato for marching into war. In the fall of 1813 the boy, his name then spelled Jourdan, and his mother, Judie (or Judith), were owned by James Brandt in Baton Rouge, who had a commercial warehouse. Jerry Brock, in an article drawn from a forthcoming biography of Noble, writes that Brandt sold mother and son for $550 to a French speculator in the slave trade, Jean G. Chaumette. He "then sold Judith and Jordan to Lieutenant John Noble of the 7th Regiment on June 2, 1814."

The difference in age between what Noble claimed to be during the war (14) and was noted on the 1813 bill of sale (seven) was credibly the result of several motives: the most obvious being an aggressive sales tactic as a younger slave would be considered capable of offering a longer valuable service.... Jordan, during his life, gave four different birth dates on different documents, the earliest being 1796 and the latest 1804, before settling on the year 1800 later in life.

Whatever his young age, Noble distinguished himself in the line of duty. Fighting began on the evening of December 23 as Patterson in Lake Borgne on the *Carolina* began shelling the British line moving out from the Villeré plantation. General Coffee led the Tennessee volunteers, followed by the Seventh Regiment with the slave drummer boy. "At eight o'clock, when the fog became particularly heavy, it was this boy's drum," writes Marcus Christian, "rattling away in the thick of battle, 'in the hottest hell of fire,' that helped to serve as one of the guideposts for the fierce-battling American troops." Savary moved forward with his battalion of black Creoles, which included his son Joseph, while a unit of French Creoles and a third force of Choctaw Indians powered toward the British, who had been setting up camp ten miles south of the city when the shelling from the ship began. After consulting with Coffee, Jackson made an arc with his troops to attack the British from the front; as the redcoats scrambled to return fire, the booming order "En main! En main!" (Take up your weapons!) galvanized the resolve of soldiers who had fought in France. Noble's drumming pushed into night darkness thick with fog and smoke from guns and cannons; the two sides barreled into each other in a wild scramble; many of the colored soldiers' guns jammed, forcing them to swing at the enemy with rifle butts like machetes.

Pierre Laffite served as a guide along Bayou St. John for Commandant Patterson, whose ships had destroyed the Grand Isle base; the older Laffite soon linked up as a guide for General Coffee, who advanced with 800 men through a cypress swamp, finding a path to the Villeré plantation where the British had landed.

The British began cannon fire, while Seventh Infantry troops advanced, followed by American artillery rounds. After two hours Jackson called his troops back. The surprise attack had secured "Jackson's troops' self-confidence, but also forged white, black, and red men, many of whom were raw militiamen with different cultures and languages, into an effective military weapon." Savary's troops had seven wounded.

On December 24, 1814, unbeknown to troops at Chalmette, the War of 1812 officially ended as American and British officials in Belgium signed the Treaty of Ghent, sealing what amounted to a draw, with all territories taken during the war reverting to their original holders. But it took weeks to send

Pirates, Black Soldiers, and Jackson

messages across the sea, and news of the treaty did not reach New Orleans until long after the fighting there was over.

Lt. Gen. Sir Edward Michael Pakenham arrived at base camp to shouts of approval from British troops who had been blindsided by the December 23 American attack. A hero of the war against Napoléon, Pakenham carried a secret proclamation naming him governor of Louisiana after the victory. The British began moving long guns and more soldiers off the ships and along bayous off Lake Borgne to their position at the edge of the Villeré plantation. Jackson ordered engineers to cut the levee below his plantation base closer to the city at Chalmette, creating a slow ooze that encircled the British front.

Over the week after Christmas, the Americans sent cannonballs and mortar fire onto the British position. Pakenham and his officers decided on a two-pronged attack, charging forward from base camp at the edge of the Villeré plantation with a second push across the Mississippi, taking the fight around to Jackson's base. The second prong—getting boats with troops and heavy weapons over the river—meant excruciating work, carving canals through the earth in the dead of winter in order to move the boats, men, and weapons, an effort that produced incredible fatigue among slaves digging a two-mile navigational route and drained British manpower too. Jackson learned about the plan from captured redcoats.

Pakenham had somewhere between 8,000 and 10,000 troops, most them well-trained; Jackson had about 4,000 men with no experience in the cohesion of an actual army, but the Americans had the advantage in heavy artillery. When British boats began the assault by crossing the river before dawn on January 8, 1815, Pakenham's planning failed to anticipate the muscular Mississippi current pushing against the men in the boats, forcing them to row harder and harder to keep on line, and pushing them away from their intended destination.

As dawn broke, Jackson from an upper window of the Macarty plantation had a panoramic view of thousands of troops, a sea of red slowly advancing over the mud. Jackson ordered three batteries to fire. The blazing force aimed low, burning through British soldiers in forward march as American ground troops advanced. Through the booming of artillery thunder and shrieking rockets, Jordan Noble kept drumming. Pakenham tried to rally his troops when his horse fell to a bullet that wounded the lieutenant general's knee; he scrambled for another horse but was shot dead by a musket ball. By eight in the morning the British, having lost their leader, had begun their retreat, carrying off some of their bleeding men, their snipers firing at Americans trying to mop up. The British suffered 2,037 casualties, including 291 killed, 1,262 wounded, and 484 missing, with many presumably taken prisoner. Jackson's army had 8 fatalities and 58 wounded or missing. Jordan Noble's sounding of taps at dusk signaled the end of the siege, and the war.

It took the British commander, Maj. Gen. John Lambert, ten days and nights to move his army of approximately 7,000 men down through the marshy terrain and bayous below the city toward the military vessels on the Gulf; they left behind two surgeons to care for scores of wounded men. Lambert arranged with Jackson for slave owners to access his camps under a white flag to retrieve "their stray sheep"—slaves who had defected.

On January 23, the streets, rooftops, and balconies were packed with onlookers as General Jackson walked through the Place d'Armes to the rolling applause and cheers, passing through a hastily erected archway of Corinthian columns, magnifying his image as the great conqueror, striding to St. Louis Cathedral as cannons boomed and young women in white gowns and blue veils outside the church, holding flags of various states, quickened the drama of his meeting with Bishop Louis William DuBourg. "Reverend Sir," said Jackson, "I receive with gratitude and pleasure the symbolic crown which piety has prepared; I receive it in the name of the brave men who have so effectually seconded my exertions in the preservation of their country."

The news from New Orleans did not reach Washington, D.C., until February 4, and it was thirteen days after that when the news reached America of the Treaty of Ghent, which had ended the war before Jackson and his army defeated the British at the Chalmette battle area. Down in New Orleans, still in the dark, Jackson insisted on maintaining the martial law order. That put him in conflict with the federal judge, Dominick Augustine Hall, who had cleared the way for the Barataria pirates to be released and in the meantime had issued an order releasing a legislator who had written an article criticizing the military authority under Jackson. Jackson had put him in jail. Now, with the war over, Hall acted on jurisprudence back to normal with a habeas corpus ruling for the man's release. Jackson ordered Hall's arrest and the judge to be put in jail. When official notification of the treaty reached New Orleans on March 15, Jackson ordered the release of both men. Judge Hall then ordered Jackson into court for being in contempt of his court. Jackson read a prepared statement on March 24. Judge Hall found him guilty and fined him $1,000. Jackson was a former attorney; he paid. The general spent several weeks enjoying time with his family amid the adulation of New Orleanians; the fine left a certain bitter aftertaste.

Jackson had given public praise to the colored battalions. A military band accompanied the black battalion led by Maj. Louis d'Aquin, a French baker who had fled the revolution in Haiti and was popular among the *gens de couleur libres*. Louis Hazeur was the lead musician of the band, the grandfather of the future jazz professor Lorenzo Tio Sr. and great-grandfather of Lorenzo Tio Jr., a jazz professor as well.

Lt. John Noble, who owned Jordan and his mother, and from whom the drummer boy got his surname, was severely wounded in the initial battle of December 23, 1814, along with Maj. Alexander White, according to Brock. Both men qualified for pensions and were classified as invalids. John Noble died three years later, after selling Judith and Jordan to White, who sold them to John Reed, a military musician who was later court-martialed and imprisoned. Just when Jordan Noble gained his freedom is, at this writing, unclear.

Many of the slaves who fought in the Battle of New Orleans did not receive the freedom they expected. As Gene Allen Smith writes in *The Slaves' Gamble*: "Ultimately, Jackson never fulfilled his promises to the slaves and only slowly fulfilled his obligations to the free blacks, further diminishing the status of both groups as the South moved toward a southern slave society based on cotton plantation agriculture."

The eighty or so Baratarian pirates drafted into Jackson's troops melted away after the war, pursuing opportunities elsewhere. The Laffite brothers "did provide several thousand musket flints to Andrew Jackson's army," writes William C. Davis, "and some of their followers did act as artillerymen in the battle, but their role was peripheral and hardly as decisive as the legend claims."

Jean Laffite left New Orleans for Galveston, seeking a new start, and secured privateering credentials from rebels in Colombia. Pierre spent several more years in New Orleans, skirting the law, embroiled in more problems. In 1821 he left for Mexico. Spanish warships were stalking him, and he may have been wounded. In early November, he went to bed with a high fever, never to rise. He was buried in the cemetery of a church convent in the Yucatán. Jean Laffite got into a firefight with Spanish warships off the Gulf of Honduras; he died of wounds on February 5, 1823, and was buried at sea, age forty-one.

For a city with such a slippery relationship to the law, it makes sense that Jean Laffite, the more daring pirate, would become an archetype of New Orleans history—the outlaw, flouting convention, shrouded in a romantic aura. William C. C. Davis demolishes much of the mythology embroidered over many generations around Jean Laffite, the symbol of a New Orleans mystique. That he made money selling people was subsumed into the image of a swashbuckling rebel and hero of the Battle of New Orleans. Jackson did utter some praise of him, but Jean Laffite was a guide in the backwaters below New Orleans in the fighting and hardly distinguished by military valor. The pirate is an image with staying power, however; the surname changed from Laffite to Lafitte as English supplanted French in popular use. The Jean Lafitte National Historical Park and Preserve is fifteen miles south of New Orleans. A town named Jean Lafitte on Bayou Barataria is twenty-two miles south of the city. A fishing town named Lafitte lies six miles farther south. The towns today are like islands slowly swallowed by rising seas and the staggering erosion of coastal cypress forests and wet-lands—an area today the size of Delaware lost over many decades to barge canals carved by the oil industry. Jean Lafitte is holding on.

7

The Builder and the Priest

The voices floated into his ears from a blinding fog. Before he could see New Orleans, he heard it on a passenger ship in the river, the docking delayed for bad visibility. It was dawn, January 12, 1819.

"A sound more strange than any that is heard anywhere else in the world," Benjamin Henry Boneval Latrobe wrote in his journal, "a more incessant, loud and various gabble of tongues of all tones than was ever heard at Babel . . . from the voices of the market people and their customers."

As the dense gray dissolved, he could see the outline of ships in a row below the Place d'Armes. Born in 1764 in Yorkshire, England, Latrobe had become a master builder in America; many ships flew the French tricolor "of Napoleon," whom he detested.

Standing in the Place d'Armes after disembarking, Latrobe saw two Choctaw women seated next to "a stark naked Indian girl, apparently 12 years old, with a monstrously swelled belly." His gaze ran along the levee, upriver and downriver, observing the early bustle of vendors, some white, "all hues of brown . . . all classes of faces, from round Yankees, to grisly & lean Spaniards, black negroes and negresses, filthy Indians half-naked, mulattoes, curly & straight-haired, quarteroons of all shades, long haired & frizzled, the women dressed in the most flaring yellow and scarlet gowns, the men capped & hatted."

Latrobe, fifty-four, traveled from Baltimore, where he had moved his family after a major project in Washington, D.C. In 1815 he became the chief government architect overseeing reconstruction of the fire-damaged Capitol, which he had helped build a decade earlier. A brilliant, driven, carefully mannered man, Latrobe nevertheless ran afoul of the black moods of President James Madison, who kept demanding faster results. In

September 1817, Latrobe reeled on learning that his son had died in New Orleans; the news triggered his explosion at Col. Samuel Lane—an irritating man, yet his immediate superior—whom he grabbed by the collar and called "a contemptible wretch."

Standing there, President Madison glared. "Do you know who I am, sir?"

"Yes, I do, and ask your pardon, but when I consider my birth, my family, my education, my talents, I am excusable for any outrage after the provocation I have received from that contemptible character." An overextended Latrobe resigned before he could be fired. The lost salary drove him into bankruptcy. He moved his family to Baltimore and traveled to New Orleans, where he would begin his next big project, building a steam-powered waterworks for a city sorely in need of it.

The market folk had arrayed their goods along the levee, some in stalls, others unfurled on dry palmetto leaves, "wild ducks, oysters, poultry of all kinds, fish, bananas, piles of oranges, sugar cane, sweet & Irish potatoes, corn in the Ear & husked, apples, carrots, and all sorts of other roots, eggs"—raw fixings for a feast in any corner of the world. Latrobe would eat well in New Orleans. But sorrow trailed him; his boy was buried here.

Henry Latrobe, an architect too, had died of yellow fever on September 3, 1817, just twenty-four, after a stay of six years, during which he arranged the contract for the waterworks, designed several distinguished houses, and served in the Battle of New Orleans. The waterworks, delayed by the 1815 battle, provided a five-year franchise for the Latrobe enterprise to furnish water to citizens and businesses for a fee.

Strangely, Henry's death is a mere flicker in his father's diary. Benjamin Latrobe, on paper, was not sentimental. The builder short-fused in Washington hustled hard on overlapping projects into which he often had to pack his own funds. The Roman Catholic cathedral he designed in Baltimore was being built as he reached New Orleans. The first professional architect and engineer in the United States, Latrobe had a writer's curiosity and the delicate touch of a seasoned artist as evinced in his drawings and paintings. His street scene *Market Folks, New Orleans* (1819), for example, depicts the dresses, hooded coats, and head scarves of colored and Indian vendors.

In 1793, the classically educated young Englishman was starting out in London when war with France stymied his business. In 1795, his wife, Lydia, died in childbirth, leaving him with two young children. Latrobe had a nervous breakdown. After getting himself together, he left Henry, three, and his older sister Lydia Sellon with relatives and sailed for Virginia, hoping to start anew.

On reaching Norfolk, a town battered in the Revolutionary War, "his charm, his musical knowledge, and his literary abilities won him almost immediate welcome," despite being an Englishman. He designed a state penitentiary. A trip to Philadelphia, the nation's capital, yielded an agreement to design and oversee construction of the Bank of Pennsylvania, a Greek Revival temple that the architect James Gallier would emulate many years later for New Orleans City Hall. In Philadelphia, Latrobe married Mary Hazlehurst, a witty, elegant patrician. She welcomed his two children from England; "from the first hour of their meeting, little Henry attached himself to her with peculiar fondness." Benjamin and Mary would have three children of their own.

Latrobe's many public works included the first water system in Philadelphia. Congested cities in the early 1800s faced a severe public health crisis as residents died in yellow fever epidemics. Philadelphia officials believed the epidemic stemmed from unclean water—a reasonable view, since mosquitoes spreading the blood-borne virus hatched in stagnant water. More accurate scientific findings about the insect lay far in the future; but cleaner water meant a healthier city, also helping to stave off cholera. Latrobe used steam pumps to power water from the Schuylkill River through hollowed-out oak trunks into a basin, then through a tunnel, and eventually to a reservoir before routing it to consumers.

In 1803 the U.S. capital moved to Washington; Latrobe followed. President Jefferson, who liked a learned mind, appointed him surveyor of public buildings. The position allowed for private contracts and provided a long run of stimulating employment—design work on the Capitol, the White House portico, the Navy Yard main gate, and St. John Episcopal Church, among other projects. Governor Claiborne met Latrobe during a visit to Washington and commissioned a tomb for his first wife, Eliza, and their daughter Cornelia, as well as a tomb for his brother-in-law Micajah Lewis.

The *basso-relievo* for Eliza was carved in marble by the sculptor Giuseppe Franzoni, whom Latrobe brought from Italy to work on the Capitol. The Claiborne relief features an angel like a liquid cloud above the woman in bed, a child clinging to her, a man kneeling at the foot of her bed, weeping. On shipping the piece to New Orleans, Latrobe wrote Claiborne in 1811 to say that "your feelings and affection and regret will receive solace.... My son Henry would be best able to direct the erection of the Monument."

Governor Claiborne won election to the U.S. Senate in 1817, but he never served in Washington. He died of a liver ailment on November 23, at forty-two, claimed by Louisiana once and for all.

Eliza Claiborne's tomb in St. Louis Cemetery was a precursor of the funerary architecture of neoclassical design that flourished in New Orleans across the generation after the Battle of New Orleans. As Andrew Jackson became a national hero because of the victory, New Orleans, for a time, was a symbol of America victorious. The general would ride his fame to the White House in 1828; the city like a petulant queen would revert to type, quarreling over identity issues and a racial paranoia that appalled Latrobe as he began dealings to get the waterworks on track.

Latrobe was a *flâneur*, from French, a walker in the city. His paths, notes, and conversations produced a major work about a city that would generate a substantial literary tradition of its own. *Impressions Respecting New Orleans: Diary & Sketches, 1818–1820*, is a probing look at the society. He found the Creoles elegant, effete, and obsessed with leisure; the Americans had come to make money. The "mixed" people—colored Creoles or mulattoes—haunted him.

Latrobe was dazzled by so many young ladies at a Carnival ball, "below the age of 24 or 25, more correct & beautiful features, more faces & figures for the sculpture, than I ever recollect to have seen together." The ball impressed him, too. A curious Latrobe went on Sunday to St. Louis Cathedral and found it packed with "all the beautiful girls in the place, & of 2 or 300 Quateroons, negroes, and mulattoes, & perhaps of 100 white males to hear high Mass." He heard the hunters' guns, booming out in the swamp.

Latrobe's most powerful passages report on slavery.

He was appalled when Mrs. Tremoulet, in whose boardinghouse he stayed, flew into a rage at the mulatto housekeeper ("famous also as a seamstress & for her good temper") for failure to make a bed. Mrs. Tremoulet had her tied naked to a bedpost and whipped the woman "till she bled," with Tremoulet's daughter watching, as if to learn.

"I shall leave the house as soon as convenient," wrote Latrobe.

In several short entries, Latrobe, normally keen to the exotic nature of the town, discovers a horror show of sadism. His new Irish landlady reveals that she saw through her fence the woman next door ordering a black man stripped nude and tied to a ladder; the Irish woman left for several hours till "the execution" was over.

Madam Lanusse is another of these Hellcats. Her husband is a very amiable man, president of the Bank of Louisiana, whom she had driven to seek a divorce, but the matter has been compromised lately. She actually did whip a negress to death, and treated another so badly that she died a short time afterwards. Mr. Nott, a principal merchant of this place, stated the facts to the Grand Jury, but it was hushed up, from respect to her husband.... The first wife of Bernard Marigny was a beast of the same kind.

Cruelty to slaves that the Spanish legal code sought to abolish surged back under planters' legislation of 1806. "What is more remarkable," the French traveler C. C. Robin wrote that year, "the Creole women are often much crueler than the men." Robin visited a plantation and saw a hole dug in the ground for a pregnant slave to lie, womb down, for the whipping. Accounts of similar barbarity so shocked Latrobe that at a Washington's birthday ball he saw the faces of women, "pale, languid & mild," and imagined each beauty, dancing and waving the whip, a fantasy of bloody violence that wrecked his evening.

Latrobe was an elitist; but an Enlightenment zeal for reason and justice marks his prose. It was not, perhaps, in his experience to assume sexual jealousy in Euro-Creole women toward colored Creole women. A generation earlier, the feathered hats of the *femme de couleur libre* had inflamed the insecurities of ladies in the big house, driving Governor Miró to order dark women to wear *tignons*, headwraps, instead. Latrobe recoiled from the spectacle of Creole beauties with "savage pleasure [as] those soft eyes can look on the torture of these slaves, inflicted by their orders, with satisfaction." We can assume that some ladies lashed the bodies of darker women in retribution for the double lives of Euro-Creole men, who for generations had slept with or sired the darker female targets of white womanly rage.

Latrobe's most famous passage recounts a visit to Congo Square, the former Place Congo. The field behind Rampart Street where slaves danced on Sundays had gone through several names as the space tightened with the expansion of Faubourg Tremé. In 1816 a traveling "Congo Circus" from Havana performed for white audiences, though the French name Place Congo was long in use.

One Sunday in late February 1819, Latrobe walking on St. Peter Street heard a thunder like horses trampling on the wooden floor of a mill. He got closer and saw "5 or 600 persons ... *blacks*. I did not observe a dozen yellow faces." The slaves had formed a series of concentric circles; he "examined" four of the human rings—"(but there were more of them)"—and saw in the center of each circle a smaller ring, "not ten feet in diameter." In the first ring two women were dancing.

They held each a coarse handkerchief extended by the corners in their hands, and *set* to each other in a miserably dull and slow figure, hardly moving their feet or bodies. The music consisted of two drums and a stringed instrument. An old man sat astride of a cylindrical drum about a foot in diameter and beat it with incredible quickness with the edge of his hand and fingers. The other drum was an open staved thing held between the knees and beaten in the same manner. They made an incredible noise. The most curious instrument however was a stringed instrument which no doubt was imported from Africa. On the top of the finger board was the rude figure of a Man in a sitting posture, and two pegs behind him to which the strings were fastened. The body was a Calabash. It was played upon by a very little old man, apparently 80 or 90 Years old. The women squalled out a burthen to the playing, at intervals, consisting of two notes, as the Negroes working in our cities respond to the Song of their leader. Most of the circles contained the same sort of dancers. One was larger, in which a ring of a dozen women walked, by way of dancing, round the music in the Center.

He notes a "square drum, looking like a stool," and a calabash "beaten by a woman with two short sticks." Latrobe thought the dances "brutally savage … dull & stupid." Peel away his pejorative view of Africans and Latrobe's descriptions, coupled with his drawings of instruments, are verbal snapshots of cultural memory.

"The drummer sitting astride his drum," writes Freddi Williams Evans in *Congo Square*, "originated among people of Kongo-Angola heritage." Ned Sublette adds, "Though he does not use the word, the stringed instrument Latrobe saw appears to be the first indication of a banjo in New Orleans. It's the most African-looking banjo to have been pictured in North America."

Latrobe also found that "the parade of funerals … is peculiar to New Orleans alone among all the American cities." He watched a fusion of African procession and Roman Catholic regalia as a black man marched with a military sword ahead of three boys in robes and pointed caps, "two carrying staves with candelabras in the form of urns at the top & the third in the center a large Silver cross." Farther along came "Father Anthony," as he approvingly called Père Antoine, and another priest "who seemed very merry at the ceremony of yesterday," followed by four pallbearers carrying a coffin adorned with white ribbons, then six "colored girls very well dressed in white with long veils," and the crowd behind with sixty-nine handheld candles, by Latrobe's count. Funeral parades were a form of freedom.

In May he saw a different burial rite, a twilight procession of 200 blacks, dressed in white—the African color for memorializing the spirit. Women carried candles. Edging into the cemetery, Latrobe saw a grave three feet deep, half filled in water, and a dozen skulls plus errant bones piled "like a heap of sticks." The procession of five priests followed three boys carrying "urns & crucifix on staves." The boys began to chant. As the priest prayed over the lowered coffin, the grave digger began dumping dirt, and "a great crowd of women pressed close to the grave, making very loud lamentations, and at the same instant one of the negro women, who seemed more particularly affected, threw herself into the grave upon the Coffin, & partly fell into the water as the coffin swam to one side." They hoisted the grieving woman. "The noise & laughter was general by the time the service was over"—slaves and freefolk webbed in harmony near the world of the dead.

St. Louis Cemetery at night, in an African custom of spiritual catharsis with Père Antoine presiding, was not an easy place for Benjamin Latrobe. The tomb he had designed for Governor Claiborne, nearly a decade after its installation, sat in the Protestant section of a cemetery grown congested since the original St. Peter Street graveyard closed for lack of space after the 1788 epidemics that followed the great fire. Opening the marble floor at the cathedral to bury members of the Illustrious Body was no longer practical. Moreover, St. Louis Cemetery on Rampart Street lay at a lower elevation than land along the levee, and the water level created problems as in the grave Latrobe saw. A shift began to the Spanish custom of oven-style brick vaults, similar to those in Cuba and the Latin Caribbean, with raised tombs adorned for wealthy people in the early nineteenth century. Funerary architecture from Paris became popular in New Orleans, too.

Latrobe describes the Claiborne tomb on a daylight stroll, his ruminations on death wandering across centuries and customs; yet not a word here on Henry, his son buried in that cemetery. The silence is striking. Two weeks before he sketched images of the brick "catacombs," Latrobe had walked the 1815 battleground in Chalmette with Vincent Nolte. A German-born cotton merchant and major financial figure in New Orleans, Nolte had been close to Henry, so close that he was paying forty dollars a month to help Henry's paramour, a colored Creole with whom Latrobe's son had four children. Shadow families were more common in New Orleans than in Baltimore or Washington.

Latrobe and "my friend," Vincent Nolte, walked the land where Henry and Vincent had fought with Jackson's troops; the architect drew sketches of the Macarty plantation house, jotting details to satisfy his sense of place and history. Nolte, a polished European, was forty then, fifteen years younger than Benjamin Latrobe, fourteen years older than Henry at his death. A calculating Nolte possibly felt it unwise to break such news of Henry that day, but a naturally curious Latrobe would have questions about his son and his life in these latitudes from so close a friend. How could Nolte, who was subsidizing Henry's family, *not* at some point tell him? Latrobe's diary does not hint at a father's grief over the loss that ignited his furor in Washington and cost him a good job. If Henry did write his father about his family, no such letter survives. Latrobe's silence may show a stoic's resolve—or anger at not being told. Benjamin Latrobe was a brilliant man who could handle a lot; but secrecy from the grave, and colored grandchildren? The fleeting references to Henry in so detailed a diary suggest an impasse too personal for written words.

· · · · · · · · · ·

THE CURTAIN CLOSES ON PÈRE ANTOINE

By the time of Latrobe's arrival, Protestant churches had taken root, but New Orleans was still heavily Catholic and Père Antoine a folk hero. The red-bearded Spanish friar built a hut behind the cathedral. Wearing his coarse robe and rope belt, he sat there, counseling many visitors, including Creole grandees. The penitential image of a hut, like a desert father of early Christianity, had its tint of irony. "In the truest sense he epitomized the character of his flock," writes Joseph G. Tregle Jr. "He moved through life with a supreme indifference to the niceties of ecclesiastical form or canon law and a tolerance for the weakness of his people which many more stern than he could accept as nothing short of an open invitation to sin. Sin seemed to concern Père Antoine hardly at all."

Governor Claiborne, assessing church attempts to oust him in 1805, had confided to Secretary of War Henry Dearborn: "We have a Spanish priest here who is a very dangerous man. He rebelled against his own church, and would even rebel, I am persuaded, against his own government whenever a fit occasion may serve." Claiborne had prescience, though it is unclear if he knew that Père Antoine had become a spy for Spain. In 1815, Pierre Laffite visited the hut, divulging details of revolutionary plans in Texas against Spanish colonies. As Cartagena ceased being a source for privateer credentials for plundering ships, Jean Laffite gave documents to Père Antoine on a plan in north Louisiana for embarkation to invade Tampico, a Mexican port on the Gulf. Père Antoine sent the papers to the viceroy in Havana.

When Latrobe met him, Père Antoine had enjoyed nearly two decades of control at the cathedral; he performed weddings of people who were divorced and Catholics wanting to marry Jews or Protestants; he presided at the funeral of a Masonic hall member. The Masonic movement was antipapist. Since the angry mob in 1809 had blocked Father Olivier, the delegate of Bishop Carroll and the Vatican, from getting keys to the cathedral, Olivier had stayed at the Ursuline convent, handling administrative duties, avoiding conflict with Père Antoine.

The Vatican tried again in 1815, appointing Bishop Louis DuBourg, who found the cathedral administration "scandalous"; he reported to Rome rumors of the housekeeper, a woman of color, and a mulatto altar boy who bore a resemblance to Père Antoine. Suspended by DuBourg, the priest retreated "to the swamps on the outskirts of the city." As Church historian Roger Baudier tells the story, "A mob formed and proceeded to the Capuchin's retreat, from which they brought him back to the city in triumph. The mob then proceeded to the Ursuline convent to demand from Father Dubourg [his] reenstatement.... So violent was the mood and the attitude of the populace so threatening that Father DuBourg was obliged to escape from the convent and make his way to the river." DuBourg established a diocese in St. Louis that included New Orleans, keeping his distance from Père Antoine.

New England Puritans considered New Orleans the "New Sodom" or the "City of Sin." But certain travelers were impressed by a Southern cathedral that welcomed all races. "From all that I can learn," wrote Alexander Hamilton, "the zeal of the Catholic priests is exemplary. They never forget that the most degraded of human forms is animated with a soul, as precious in the eye of religion as that of the Sovereign Pontiff." A Presbyterian minister, after thirty-five years in the city, wrote, "New Orleans is the most tolerant place in Christendom."

Studied in the cultivation of key people, Latrobe met "Father Anthony" and secured a commission to design a new tower for the cathedral. When an Irishwoman died in the boardinghouse where he had moved, her friends lacked the ten-dollar funeral fee. "I wrote to Father Anthony begging him to diminish the fees as much as possible, and received for an answer that if a dollar were paid to the Sexton he would pay the rest himself."

The bell tower contract helped Latrobe's finances, as did a hoist he designed for Vincent Nolte. He imported engine parts for the water system and advertised for timber logs to be used for piping. By late September 1819, Latrobe had decided on New Orleans as his new home, given the building opportunities. He headed back to Baltimore. After months of planning, Benjamin and Mary Latrobe began the long voyage downriver with their children, reaching New Orleans in early April 1820. Fearful that it would be a "vile hole" like Natchez, Mary, the Philadelphia patrician, was delighted at the balmy Place d'Armes; two waterworks barges pulled aside the vessel to collect their trunks, boxes, and valise and delivered them to the house her husband had bought just downriver. Refusing to wait for a carriage, Mary left the family, walking the mile and half, delighted to find the large rooms and walled garden with orange trees, jasmine, roses, figs, roses, and oleanders.

When the steam engine arrived from New York, the pace of Latrobe's work accelerated. By July, he had 5,000 feet of wooden pipe installed but awaited a main suction pipe. The city provided a chain gang to dig the trench. Mud from the summer rains made digging harder, and for a man of fifty-six overseeing crews was exhausting. When yellow fever took Latrobe it was sudden. He died on September 3, 1820, three years to the day after his son Henry.

Five months after her arrival, Mary Latrobe learned that her husband's available funds had gone into the waterworks. In her grief and worry, she was startled when a young mulatto women appeared at the door, introducing herself and Henry's three children. "I cannot express to you how shocked I was," Mary wrote a friend. "Custom in this place tolerates these connections with colored women." Henry's fourth child had died; he had bought his beloved a house, "and they receive $40 a Month paid regularly by Mr. Nolte."

Nolte's loyalty to Benjamin and Henry extended to Mary with gift of $100, the equivalent of nearly $2,000 today; but in acknowledging his support of Henry's family, Nolte faced the same dilemma as when he met Benjamin. How much to say of Henry? Did he tell the widow that her husband had learned of Henry's love, and children? Surviving family papers do not say.

"After his death, Latrobe's assets were frozen," writes Carolyn Goldsby Kolb. "Although the pipes had been laid, the water-works was still no more than a work in progress." To avert a sheriff's sale, the city bought the piping and machinery and had it running by 1823 but took a decade to build the reservoir. Although Latrobe's design was solid, absent his forceful presence, the scope and execution lagged. His son John, visiting New Orleans in 1834, noticed water leaking from pipes in a manner "much less efficient than ... under a proper management."

In 1824, President James Monroe invited General Lafayette to visit America all expenses paid. Born in 1757, Marie Joseph Paul Yves Roch Gilbert du Motier, the marquis de Lafayette, was the last living military leader of the American Revolution. He made a tour of the twenty-four states, a yearlong cavalcade celebrating American independence. The young Lafayette had fought with General Washington in 1776, forging close ties with him, Jefferson, and Hamilton. Lafayette returned to Paris and helped write the Declaration of the Rights of Man. Renouncing his title as a marquis, he pushed for a middle ground in the Revolution, but as the Jacobins turned on him, he fled to the Austrian Netherlands. Lafayette had spent five years in prison when Napoléon secured his freedom in 1797. By the time of Monroe's invitation, Lafayette was sixty-eight, a lion of history; he was also severely short of money, something a spectacular tour would bring.

New Orleans, in its evolution from French backwater to city of the Illustrious Body under a Spanish king, had early into its second century absorbed émigrés from Haiti and new French exiles after Napoléon Bonaparte's defeat. Jackson's victory in 1815 secured the city's American stature. Residents savored the city as a stage. New Orleans with the first opera house in the United States, African dances under the sun, Indian delegations in sinuous procession, and parades of church and military displayed itself as a crossroads of humanity, a universal place, despite the Creole gentry's view of arriviste Anglo-Americans as boors. If Lafayette was in America, of course he would visit New Orleans. The Illustrious Body was a forgotten term, but its descendants would welcome him in style.

In April 1825, when Lafayette's entourage came down the Mississippi, city officials had allocated $15,000 to provide the general a grand apartment in the Cabildo, replacing the wooden mantel pieces with marble. "Wealthy citizens lent furniture, carpets, window hangings, chandeliers, linens, china, and silver," writes Patricia Brady. The Place d'Armes, lit up by paper lanterns, was graced with a sixty-foot triumphal arch of wood canvas on a pedestal of green Italian marble, and pyramids of fire stood at the square's four corners. Amid the speeches, parties, and receptions, the military bands marched beneath his balcony; Lafayette was delighted by Choctaw Indians, a hundred strong, in feathers and war paint, prancing single file behind riflemen.

Père Antoine, in a cameo appearance, embraced Lafayette, by one account with tears trailing down his white beard, saying, "O my son, the good Lord has shown me great favor in allowing me to see and speak with the worthy apostle of Liberty." The priest praised an apostle of the Revolution that had decapitated its Catholic king, captured Church power, and waged war on his native Spain. Aching over Mexico's 1824 break from Spain, despite his espionage with the Laffites, the Capuchin monk at seventy-eight had outlasted his enemies in Rome and Baltimore, the better to enjoy his nimbus in the glow of Lafayette's celebrity.

When Père Antoine died at eighty-one on January 19, 1829, the city held three days of official mourning as the body lay in state at the cathedral. "His exemplary piety and his liberal ideas on religion and government made him the illustrious ornament of the religion he professed," observed the *New Orleans Bee*. "The memory of his virtues will be long embalmed in the grateful remembrance of the numerous poor who deplore his loss." Judge Edward Livingston adjourned his courtroom, stating that Père Antoine deserved sainthood. The Church would never canonize a cleric so unruly and unorthodox, but in a nod to reality it held a funeral befitting a head of state. Cannon fire opened the ceremony, four young men shouldered the coffin, flanked by eight honorary pallbearers in a solemn high Mass at St. Louis Cathedral while the most prominent citizens, politicians, diplomats, ecclesiastical officials, free blacks, and slaves looked on. As the coffin went down beneath the marble floor, the slow transition began from a Church in solidarity with slaves to one attached to white supremacy and the cause of the Confederacy.

Jean-Baptiste Le Moyne, Sieur de Bienville (1680–1767), founder
of New Orleans. Artist unknown. The portrait was done in Paris,
some time after 1743, when Bienville left New Orleans for the last
time. Very little is known of his last twenty-four years in Paris. Born
in Canada, Bienville and his brothers had titles of minor nobility
purchased from Louis XIV by their father, a French pioneer and
one of Montreal's wealthiest men. There is no known painting of
the Indian tattoos on Bienville's body. (Alcée Fortier, *A History of
Louisiana* [1904])

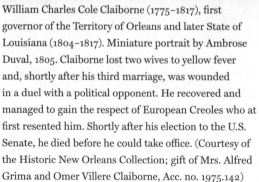

William Charles Cole Claiborne (1775–1817), first
governor of the Territory of Orleans and later State of
Louisiana (1804–1817). Miniature portrait by Ambrose
Duval, 1805. Claiborne lost two wives to yellow fever
and, shortly after his third marriage, was wounded
in a duel with a political opponent. He recovered and
managed to gain the respect of European Creoles who at
first resented him. Shortly after his election to the U.S.
Senate, he died before he could take office. (Courtesy of
the Historic New Orleans Collection; gift of Mrs. Alfred
Grima and Omer Villere Claiborne, Acc. no. 1975.142)

Vue d'Une Rue du Faubourg. View of a suburban street, ca. 1804. After the Great Fire of 1788, the faubourgs, or suburbs (villages-within-the-city), fanned out from the Vieux Carré, as plantation owners like Claude Tremé and Bernard de Marigny sold off land for streets and plots for housing. (Courtesy of the Historic New Orleans Collection, Acc. no. 1937.2.2)

Père Antoine, Antonio de Sedella (1748–1829). Arguably the most powerful Spaniard in New Orleans, other than the governors, from the late Spanish colonial era through the first quarter century of American life, Père Antoine was a monk of the Capuchins, an order affiliated with the Franciscans. He welcomed slaves and free persons of color to St. Louis Cathedral, had a huge popular following with European Creoles, and was involved in recurrent clashes with church officials for indifference to church law throughout his long tenure. For many years, he received visitors in a hut built behind the cathedral. (Courtesy of the Historic New Orleans Collection, Acc. no. 1982.43)

General Andrew Jackson (1767–1845), victorious leader at the
Battle of New Orleans, 1815. Jackson's defeat of the British made
him a national hero and provided a springboard to his 1828 election
as president of the United States. He made a triumphal return to
New Orleans late in life. In 1856, several years after his death, the
city erected a statue of the general on horseback opposite St. Louis
Cathedral in the Place d'Armes, or central plaza, and renamed it
Jackson Square. (Courtesy of the Historic New Orleans Collection,
Acc. no. 1950.28)

W. H. Brooke F.S.A.

Benjamin Henry Boneval Latrobe (1764–1820). Portrait attributed to Charles Willson Peale. The architect and engineer responsible for much of the work on the U.S. Capitol, Latrobe spent his last two years in New Orleans with a commission to build a waterworks, dying of yellow fever before the project was done. His journal, *Impressions Respecting New Orleans, Diary & Sketches, 1818–1820*, is a classic of New Orleans literature. (Courtesy of the Historic New Orleans Collection, Acc. no. 1974.25.27.225)

"Sale of Estates, Pictures and Slaves in the Rotunda, New Orleans, 1842." W. H. Brook. New Orleans was the largest slave market in America. People could dine well and sip wine in the St. Louis Hotel and watch human beings being sold. In 1811 Charles Deslondes spearheaded the largest slave revolt in American history, gathering rebels at plantations upriver from the city. The military put down the rebellion and decapitated many of the rebels. (Courtesy of the Historic New Orleans Collection, Acc. no. 1974.25.23.4)

Children carrying coffins during a yellow fever epidemic. New Orleans was hit with recurrent epidemics of yellow fever across the nineteenth century because of terrible drainage and poor water quality, which drew mosquitoes that spread the virus. (Courtesy of the Center for Louisiana Studies, University of Louisiana at Lafayette; from *History of the Yellow Fever Virus in New Orleans of 1853*, by Physicians of New Orleans [Philadelphia: Kenworthy 1854])

The yellow fever epidemic of 1853 was so severe that entire
families died within hours. The virus struck deepest in
poor tenements and areas with standing water, refuse, and
unsanitary conditions. (Courtesy of the Center for Louisiana
Studies, University of Louisiana at Lafayette; from *History of
the Yellow Fever Virus in New Orleans of 1853*, by Physicians
of New Orleans [Philadelphia: Kenworthy 1854])

FUNERAL OF THE LATE CAPTAIN CAILLOUX, FIRST LOUISIANA VOLUNTEERS (COLORED).—Sketched by a Native Guard.
[See Page 551.]

Funeral of André Cailloux, 1863. Funerals with military bands were commonplace in New Orleans from 1789 (with the memorial march for Carlos III, king of Spain) until the Civil War. The funeral for André Cailloux, an African American leader who fought for the Union with the Louisiana Native Guards, drew a huge crowd, primarily of black people. (*Harper's*)

Mistick Krewe of Comus, the oldest established Carnival organization in New Orleans, began parading in 1857. During Reconstruction, the 1873 parade, "The Missing Links to Darwin's Origins of the Species," featured costumes of scalding, often racist satire. The hyena represented Benjamin "Beast" Butler, the Union general who governed the city in the first year of occupation starting in 1862. (Comus 1873 Missing Links parade, Carnival Collection, Louisiana Research Collection, Tulane University)

Mistick Krewe of Comus, 1873 parade, featured a putdown of President Ulysses S. Grant as a tobacco grub. (Comus 1873 Missing Links parade, Carnival Collection, Louisiana Research Collection, Tulane University)

Jefferson Davis funeral, 1889. The former Confederate president fell
ill on a visit to one of his Mississippi plantations and hurried to New
Orleans by steamer. He died in the Garden District home of a friend,
Judge Charles E. Fenner. The December 11 funeral, one of the largest
in the city's history, cemented New Orleans as a bastion of the Lost
Cause mythology of the Civil War. (Courtesy of the Historic New
Orleans Collection, Acc. no. 1985.125.1)

FORMING THE PROCESSION

Rex parade, 1883. Founded in 1872, the Krewe of Rex rolls each
Mardi Gras morning, or Fat Tuesday, on St. Charles Avenue from
Uptown to Canal Street. The krewe selects a civic leader as its
annual king. The parade stops for Rex to toast the mayor at Gallier
Hall and then at a reviewing stand by the InterContinental Hotel
to toast his queen, a debutante of the season. Months of thematic
design and artistic work decorate the floats, drawn by tractors, with
maskers throwing beads and doubloons to people in the streets.
Rex's motto is Pro Bono Publico (For the Good of the Public), and it
has a foundation to support charitable causes. (*Harper's Magazine*;
courtesy of School of Design)

Contessa Entellina Society, the oldest Italian benevolent society in New Orleans, founded in 1886. Photograph at Jackson Square, 1926. Contessa Entellina is a town of Albanian origins in Palermo. (Courtesy of the American Italian Cultural Center, New Orleans)

Birthplace of Louis Armstrong. Jane Alley, 1901. The "Back o' Town" shack where Armstrong lived as a child was demolished decades later to make room for the municipal complex, housing City Hall and the civil district courts. (Courtesy of William Ransom Hogan Jazz Archive, Tulane University)

Louis Armstrong and Leon René (composer of "When It's Sleepy Time down South," one of Armstrong's hits), in 1938. Armstrong celebrated New Orleans throughout his life in his writings, song lyrics, and interviews; but the attempt by state and city officials to subvert school desegregation in the 1960s made him averse to return visits in his later years. He died in 1971 and was buried in New York. (Author's collection, gift of the late Leon René)

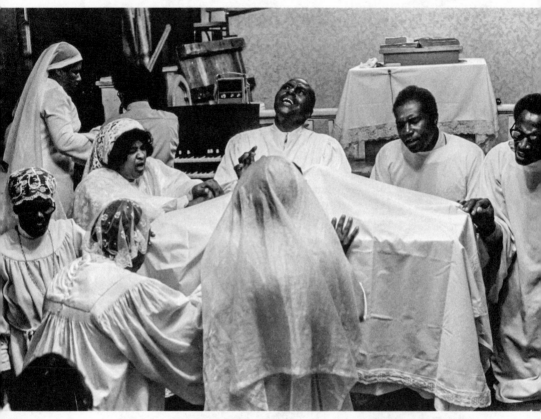

"Praying over the Body." The Spiritual Churches arose in 1920 after 40,000 rural African Americans arrived in the city. The earlier Holiness or Sanctified churches transplanted ecstatic worship and singing and dancing traditions that had a powerful influence on the emergent jazz idiom. (Photograph by Michael P. Smith, 1973, © the Historic New Orleans Collection, Acc. no. 2007.0103.2.62)

. . . .

The Burial Master

TIMES OF YELLOW FEVER AND WAR

Pierre Casanave was one of the most prominent men in the free black society. A colored Creole born about 1798 in Port-au-Prince, he was a child when the family arrived in New Orleans. His father became a grocer and cabinet-maker. An 1822 city directory lists young Pierre as an *ébéniste*, or furniture maker, a solid station in the caste between whites and slaves. An 1825 notice in the *New Orleans Argus* confirms that Casanave had established a shop at 82 Conti Street, between Royal and Bourbon, for "furniture made in the latest fashions and at moderate prices."

A store in prime real estate on Conti Street signaled prominently to white customers. By 1830, the city with a population of 46,082 was 43.7 percent white, its majority composed of slaves and *gens de couleur libres*. Casanave's father had died when Pierre married Rose Baraquin at St. Louis Cathedral on February 22, 1830. Her family was also from Haiti, and their wedding was noted in the *Argus*. His business as *ébéniste* had a growing clientele. Four years later, the *New Orleans City Directory* lists Casanave as operating a furniture warehouse.

Couples like the Casanaves typically came from close Catholic families. Between 1833 and 1839, Rose gave birth to four sons, Gadane, St. Felix, Pierre Jr., and François. In 1840 the four boys were baptized at St. Louis Cathedral. Two girls followed, Lumena in 1841 and Marguerite in 1842, then another son, Louis Nicolas, in 1844. The last three were baptized at St. Anthony Chapel on Rampart Street, just outside Faubourg Tremé, where the Casanaves settled.

Colored Creoles in the downtown faubourgs included a thriving artisan class of leatherworkers who made harnesses, shoes, and belts; tailors and dressmakers, some catering to the aristocracy; stonemasons, carpenters, brick makers, blacksmiths, and ironworkers who produced locks, hinges, and "the graceful lines of decorative balcony railings, fences and gates," writes Mary Gehman. At the margins of this free black culture, Quadroon Balls entranced and repulsed visitors, like Alexis de Tocqueville, who sat aghast at the "incredible laxity of morals" on display—white men of means openly courting fair-skinned dark mistresses.

Pressured by white ladies, city officials passed an 1828 ordinance prohibiting white men from attending "dressed or masked balls composed of men and women of color." It was rarely enforced. With balls at every rung of the social ladder, men of the Creole gentry who took mixed-race mistresses, some siring second families, were unlike Henry Latrobe, who was devoted to a woman he could not legally marry.

Plaçage was the French term for relationships that were illegal due to race, a woman of color "placed" in her home by a white man. Scorned by many, *plaçage* offered a certain degree of security to colored women, who outnumbered free black men. White fathers' assets, passed down in wills, gave support to common-law wives and dark children. Legal battles with white heirs in the antebellum era could be bitter, but "most often the mix-blooded heirs won in court," writes Joan Martin. "This type of support was greatly encouraged by the church."

The crueler extreme was "fancy girls" purchased at high bids at auctions by slave-owning men "to be their companions or simply their toys," writes Walter Johnson in *Soul by Soul*.

John Powell, a *Picayune* editor, "entertained his dinner guests at a house inhabited by his 'Quadroon mistress' and the couple's child ... [showing] a man who was at once civilized and sensational."

As men of rank took colored mistresses, the legislature feared free blacks and slaves would conspire in a revolution. Yet some free blacks owned slaves; they wanted wealth and stability. In a paradox of racial angst, lawmakers in the 1830s ordered free blacks to register with officials, banned new entry of free blacks, and ordered émigrés of the last five years to leave Louisiana; few did. Meanwhile, white men openly attended dances with quadroons (people one-fourth black) at the Globe Ball Room.

An 1834 state law disbanded the Battalion of Chosen Men of Color, ending the free black militia. In 1836, 855 free blacks paid taxes on nearly $2.5 million worth of property, "a total exceeding the value of black-owned property anywhere else in the United States."

From fine furniture, Pierre Casanave had branched out into building coffins. He was identified as an undertaker in an 1844 listing. In a city obsessed with death and music, such a move made financial sense. Benevolent societies of various ethnic groups guaranteed members a dignified funeral. Founded in 1829, La Sociedad Española de Beneficencia Mutua explained in a newspaper notice that the group

> numbers about 650 members, including representatives from all nations of Southern Europe and many from other climes. It is a benevolent society in the largest acceptation of the term. Its members, in case of sickness, are cared for by the society, their expenses are paid, their wants, of whatever nature they may be, are attended to. This is not all. A Spaniard, a Portuguese, an Italian, or foreigner arrives in this country without money and without friends; the Spanish Benevolent Society takes him by the hand, and herself, inspired by that charity which embraces all mankind in a universal brotherhood, teaches him that a man with neither friends nor money is, after all, a human being.

Benevolent societies included firemen and laborers in guilds. In a climate prone to epidemics, no breadwinner wanted to saddle his loved ones with the expense of a burial. Promoting self-reliance, the mutual aid societies held balls, suppers, and receptions after funerals.

In January 1836, fifteen free black men formed the Société d'Économie et d'Assistance Mutuelle at a building on Ursulines Street between Villere and Marais, in Faubourg Tremé, near the Casanave home. This solidarity stood in high relief against the Creole gentry's contempt for arriviste Anglo-Americans, an Old World view of boors from the New.

In 1836 the legislature carved out three municipalities, each with its own council and services, answerable to a single mayor, a wasteful move that retarded urban progress, notably work on the water system. The Vieux Carré, Tremé, and Marigny formed a largely French-speaking First Municipality. From Canal Street to Felicity Street in the emergent Garden District, where Anglo-Americans built mansions, composed the Second Municipality. The Third ran from Esplanade Avenue downriver to Chalmette, flanked by cypress swamps and Isleño villages on the water. The three-zone plan succumbed in 1852.

In spite of a balkanized officialdom, ordinary people were determined to live life well. "Thus, by 1829 even a second-rate ballroom employed an orchestra of fifteen musicians for its ordinary balls," writes Henry A. Kmen. People across the ragged metropolis spread their wings like the proverbial butterfly in winter, taking Mardi Gras beyond the province of the Creole gentry. However dismal the politics, people thrived on dancing, masks, and joie de vivre.

Pierre Casanave detected a certain value in the celebration impulse as it applied to his emergent livelihood as an undertaker; his aesthetic design would take several years to come together. His curiosity was commercial: how did one make money burying the dead? In 1844, he moved his business across Rampart into Faubourg Tremé, at Marais Street, between Bourbon and Conti. His white customers would venture a few blocks beyond the Vieux Carré, the old town, to a faubourg where French was widely spoken still. His store was a short walk from the Société d'Économie. Joining the Société was a natural move for Casanave; he had friends and neighbors among its members. Benevolent societies also held potential as a source of revenue for a man who made coffins and organized the program for burials. Wakes were typically held in people's homes, from which the funeral corteges walked or rode to the cemetery. A handsome coffin ennobled the life just passed and gave durable rest in the soil.

Casanave prospered as an undertaker in a time when New Orleans became the second-largest U.S. port, after New York. The city was also the nation's largest slave market, with a booming economy for exports in cotton, sugar, and human property.

Grueling dig work in the 1830s on New Basin Canal—from Lake Pontchartrain down to the city's western edge, turning on a long waterway to Rampart Street dock—was done by migrants from Ireland, toiling in the steamy muck, as slaves were property too valuable to risk for rent-out work. "Coinciding with the building of the New Basin Canal was a devastating cholera epidemic in New Orleans where approximately 5,000 people died," writes Laura D. Kelley. "The following year, 1833, saw another outbreak." Grim stories of canal toil and cholera fused in the popular memory, argues Kelley, who disputes publicized estimates by Irish groups of 8,000 to 20,000 deaths from the canal.

Whatever the human loss, the canal company turned profits, moving vessels and cargo, while the splintered city government failed to deal with stagnant water, waste drainage into the cypress swamp, and unpaved lanes where goats, hogs, horses, and cows meandered, some dying stuck in mud after torrential rain. People dumped refuse in the river. To recruit gravediggers during the 1832 cholera epidemic, three municipal cemeteries boosted pay from two dollars to six dollars per day.

As steamboats quickened commerce, cotton receipts in 1845–46 totaled

$33.7 million. In 1840 New Orleans had 1,881 stores, "the main reason that Louisiana had the highest per capita investment in retailing in the United States," writes Scott P. Marler. The port handled 500,000 tons of freight that year, a value of nearly $50 million. In 1849, 7,272 people came from Ireland. By 1850, New Orleans ranked fifth in population among U.S. cities with 116,000 inhabitants.

· · · · · · · · · ·

THE JESUITS RETURN

As the city increased its magnetic pull on European immigrants, the Society of Jesus in France sent four priests, a seminarian, and a religious brother in 1837, three-quarters of a century after their expulsion at the end of the French era, to restore the Jesuits' standing in a still heavily Catholic city. The order soon opened a college in Grand Coteau, on the Acadian prairie near Opelousas, and in 1847, with a loan from the Ursuline sisters, Father Jean Baptiste Maisounabe purchased land a block below Canal Street at Baronne and Common Streets for a church and college. Maisounabe died of yellow fever in 1848; later that year, the College of the Immaculate Conception began teaching students. Within four years, the enrollment had reached 160 young men, some as young as eleven, for a six-year curriculum. "The staple subjects were Latin, Greek and English with healthy doses of modern languages, mathematics, science, philosophy, and history. It combined high school and college," writes a Jesuit historian. "Many students dropped out along the way."

In 1904 the Jesuits purchased land that was part of an old plantation across from Audubon Park in Uptown and began building an academic complex. By 1912, when Loyola received its university charter from the state, the downtown school shifted to secondary-level students only, and in 1926, changing the name to Jesuit High School, it moved to a large new building in Mid-City on upper Carrollton Avenue.

With more European migrants, hotels began replacing black workers with waiters, porters, and staff from Ireland and Germany. Meanwhile, as revenues surged for merchants, bankers, shippers, and planters, the captains of commerce yawned at the idea of a manufacturing base to compete with an industrializing Northeast. Slave sales undergirded the economy, human collateral on the balance sheets. The elite's myopia extended to a civic ethos for a more livable city. Out of sight from the Creole balconies and verandas of the Garden District stood cheap riverfront lodgings and tenements in which "a family might use a single room to raise together children, dogs and fowl; privies were seldom cleaned, and streets and levees often used in their stead."

Public cynicism toward politics grew like mushrooms after summer rain; but people rallied for the celebrations of the city as place. In 1840, seventy-two-year-old Andrew Jackson, the former president, came downriver for a reception over several days, commemorating the 1815 victory. "As the procession passed along Canal Street, a dense mass of citizens thronged each side," wrote the *Daily Picayune*, "ladies waving their handkerchiefs, while the silver-headed warrior bowed in acknowledgment of their salutations." He died four years later. In 1856, the city lodged an equestrian statue of the general in the center of the Place d'Armes and renamed it Jackson Square.

· · · · · · · · · ·

THE YELLOW FEVER SCOURGE

Street-cleaning work was patronage fat, the contractors' results rarely checked. In 1853, the City Council had yet to empanel a board of health, as statute required they do each spring. When deaths from yellow fever began in early June, the council moved to impeach the street commissioner. By late June, as medical authorities reported more yellow fever deaths, the *Crescent* pronounced yellow fever "an obsolete idea in New Orleans." By July 16, with 204 deaths attributed to the disease in the preceding week, the *Orleanian* reported "no prevalent diseases or epidemics." But people saw people dying. "When thousands of people were in full flight from the city," wrote the medical historian John Duffy, "the newspapers still denied or discounted the significance of the mounting yellow fever toll."

Many blamed the outbreak on shipping and migrants laden with germs. "Some physicians believed that heat, moisture, and certain unhealthy shipboard conditions spawned the fever," writes Benjamin H. Trask. Others "argued only that fever germs or fomites were generated by the city's own cesspools before infected vessels arrived. Despite notable theories to the contrary, the finger pointing at ships and their occupants was regular practice."

In July of that deadly 1853, the Société d'Économie et d'Assistance Mutuelle purchased a lot across Ursuline Street from its original building with plans for a large hall. Casanave would oversee the final stages of construction as president.

On July 25, Mayor A. D. Crossman summoned the aldermen and assistant aldermen, urging them to empanel a board of health with emergency funds. After delays, with nearly 100 people a day dying from the fever, the aldermen approved $10,000 for the health board and adjourned for summer, allowing the aldermen to join a frightened exodus to Grand Isle, the Gulf Coast, or across Lake Pontchartrain.

The Sisters of Charity, who ran Charity Hospital, worked around the clock as beds filled with people drenched, writhing, groaning, and spitting up black bile. The dead were toted out quickly to make room for the waiting sick. Jammed hospitals let the sick and dying sleep in halls; overworked doctors (a few of whom would die) dispensed quinine, opium, or liquor to sedate the most severely afflicted patients. In the last week of July, 692 people died. Makeshift infirmaries opened, "even the workhouse, the city insane asylum, the parish prison, and the notorious Globe Ball Room. Nurses and nuns in charge of the sick fell victim to the fever," writes Robert C. Reinders. "At least fifteen clergymen lost their lives [to] the fever."

In August 1853 alone, 4,844 people died, a staggering 4.3 percent of the population. With only 50,000 people remaining in the city, the *New York Times* estimated mortality "at the rate of 7,950 deaths a month, or one out of every six inhabitants." Mosquitoes festering in filthy water spread the contagion like an invisible army. Buggy hearses trundled along the streets, some ragged and forlorn, others to bands playing dirges as people followed in carriages, the processions halting to make way for doctors' coaches. In the poorest neighborhoods, entire families died in a space of hours. The "full horror and virulence" lay in "these miserable shanties," reported a *Harper's New Monthly Magazine* writer, "sleeping a half dozen in one room without ventilation.... Here you will see the living babe sucking death from the yellow breast of its dead mother."

Pierre Casanave's decision to learn embalming responded to fears of "the odors of rotting corpses, exposed to the heat of the sun, swollen with corruption, bursting their coffin lids," as the *Daily Crescent* wrote. "What a feast of horrors! Corpses piled in pyramids!"

Musicians willing to march in funerals risked their lives, joining mourners, equally at risk, in a ritual of basic human solidarity, giving the dead their due; the corteges entered bulging cemeteries, the sweat-lathered gravediggers strapped into nose bags with camphor and spices to blunt the stench and keep from going mad. Little wonder the bands turned to cheerful melodies heading back to the city of life. The *Daily Picayune* objected to this in late August of that annus horribilis:

In times of an epidemic, such as now afflicts our devoted city, we are opposed to music at funerals, and here raise our voice against the practice. ... We would ask, what benefit is all this parade and show of lamentation on the loved one, whose remains his friends accompany to the "house appointed for all living"? No answer is needed. We do not pretend to imagine that they think it benefits him. Then, as the sound of the mournful dirge, as they slowly and sadly bear their companion away, or of the gay and lightsome air as they return from his grave, may have a fatal effect on the nerves of the sick, whose homes are passed in every square, if not in every house, we respectfully suggest to our noble military companies, our gallant firemen, charitable and other associations, to dispense with their bands of music at funerals—at least while the epidemic lasts.

But as Casanave well knew, the music was for the living, to cheer their spirits and foster their hope. "The high point of the funeral was the procession, which by the fifties, due in part to the influence of a free Negro undertaker, Pierre Casanave, had become extremely elaborate and ceremonial," writes Reinders in *End of an Era*. "The hearse, a large bulky conveyance, ornately carved and draped, was drawn by caparisoned horses—undertakers also operated livery stables."

· · · · · · · · · ·

MOREAU GOTTSCHALK COMES HOME

However discordant life became in a city so ill-governed and prone to epidemics, people thrived on cultural activity for exaltations of the human spirit. The Creole gentry, refined Anglo-Americans, and certain *gens de couleur* savored the European high tradition at plays, operas, and classical music performances. The return of a favored son would soothe an urban elite demoralized by the yellow fever scourge.

In late February 1855, the illustrious pianist and composer Louis Moreau Gottschalk returned to his native city after thirteen years in Paris and concert itineraries in various countries. Twenty-six, lionized in the press, Moreau, as he was known, nevertheless found himself "flat broke and without a piano to boot," notes the biographer S. Frederick Starr.

Born in 1829 to a London transplant and a mother from Saint-Domingue, Moreau's early years in New Orleans and a brief time on Rampart Street near Congo Square prompted scholarly speculations on slave music as an influence on the elegant percussive rhythm in his style in *Bamboula*, among other notable compositions. Starr writes that Moreau as a child heard the lullabies and folkloric songs of Saint-Domingue from his Haitian grandmother and African American nurse, Sally. "His sisters sang them and he learned to play them on the piano."

　　　　　　The Burial Master

His father sent the youth to Paris to study piano; at sixteen he gave a concert. Chopin was in the audience and went backstage afterward to say: "Give me your hand, my child; I predict that you will become the king of pianists." As he became professionally established, he had to work extra hard generating commissions and concerts to support his mother and six siblings, who moved to Paris, depending on him. By the time of his return to New Orleans, Moreau Gottschalk was a legendary artist, trailed by tales of escapades with women and perpetually short of money. Plunging into recitals and concerts to sell tickets, he premiered *The Last Hope*, which stirred a woman in the audience to write that she "felt ashamed of myself for crying," only to notice "that nearly everybody else was crying also." A high point, it might be called, of his return, and well advertised in the press, found him inside the wicker gondola of a hot air balloon on Palm Sunday, holding a small keyboard instrument called a harmonicon. A brass band entertained the crowd, and then fell silent, writes Starr.

> Once aloft, Gottschalk found inspiration in the circular horizon and shifting light. Then, as the Gulf of Mexico came into view, Moreau improvised ecstatically on the harmonicon. . . . The resulting composition, *Pensée poétique*, is a lyrical reverie that modulates from minor to major in such a way as to suggest the surmounting of earth-bound concerns.

The next night he gave a well-received concert, after which he fell ill; he spent six weeks in bed before heading back on the road.

. . . .

PREPARATIONS FOR THE DEAD

The horrors that people saw, heard, or read about during the worst of the yellow fever epidemic had an impact on Pierre Casanave. He took care to provide buggy hearses with a certain ornamental beauty and arranged for musicians to escort the burial processions. He did not believe he was exposing himself to the lethal disease by preparing the dead for burial. We know this from the dramatic turn in his newspaper advertisements in 1856. From the *New Orleans Daily Creole*:

Embalming the Dead.
P. Casanave,
Undertaker,
    Having purchased a right from Dr. Holmes, of New York city, of EM-

BALMING THE DEAD, will attend promptly to all orders, by day or night. The process is simple, and is done with no inconvenience or exposure. Bodies embalmed by [the undertaker] are warranted to keep free from decomposition and can be taken to any part of the world without exhaling the slightest odor, in [any] season of the year. Bodies in an advanced state of decomposition restored to a perfect state of preservation.

Full particulars in pamphlets will be given to those who may apply.

N.B.—Deceased ministers, physicians and lawyers will be embalmed free of charge.

Casanave knew that the procedure was an emotional salve to grim realities of the yellow fever; a corpse presentable for the parlor, living room, or benevolent society hall was a worthwhile expense to preserve a ritual harmony for the deceased. The "Dr. [Thomas S.] Holmes" he referenced was a pioneer of embalming in America. Expelled from Columbia medical school in the 1830s for conducting professional experiments at home, Holmes got work as an examiner in the city coroner's office, calling himself "Doctor" and experimenting with chemicals to preserve cadavers. In whatever fashion the two men met or communicated, Casanave milked it in his marketing.

In 1857, Casanave was president of the Société d'Économie when it opened the "large two-story building that towered over the neighborhood of small single and double shotgun houses," writes Fatima Shaik, whose forthcoming book on Economy Hall draws in part on documents preserved by her family. "It had a large ballroom, an auditorium, and several meeting halls. There was a separate kitchen building and a fence at the front of the property. On the hall itself was a copper cornice and a beehive for decoration, which was the symbol of the organization. It was the site of banquets, dances and political rallies from the time it opened.... The Economic Society's minutes are kept in French until the second decade of the 20th century."

Casanave made a major move on April 14, 1859, with the purchase of Pigneguy's Stables at 424–426 Bourbon Street from Virginie Flietas, the widow of Louis A. Pigneguy; she had remarried a Parisian. The lot on the corner of St. Louis Street was excellent real estate; Casanave paid $8,475. He opened a mortuary with horse-drawn hearses in the heart of the Vieux Carré, hiring bands for the burial processions.

In December 1859, Casanave filed a criminal affidavit against one Joseph Grulick for attempting to steal 400 pounds of lead from the front of his Marais Street premises. "The lead was carried off in a wheelbarrow," reported the *Daily Picayune*, "but the great weight was too much for the old vehicle, and it broke down. Grulick was arrested in the act of picking up the lead. His companion made his escape."

The bumbling white thief is laughable. More striking is Casanave's confidence in reporting a crime to the justice system at the end of a decade that saw setbacks to the rights of free blacks. In the 1850s policemen spied on St. James African Methodist Episcopal Church and five times arrested the pastor for allowing slaves to attend services. Certain Masonic lodges welcomed slaves; in 1857 police arrested thirty blacks, free and enslaved, at a ceremony held in Orleans Ballroom. A magistrate charged them with unlawful assembly, ordering twenty-five-dollar fines for freemen and beatings for the slaves. The legislature abolished slave emancipations in 1857. In 1858, the city closed St. James AME Church for unlawful assembly and seized the property. As several newspapers endorsed the expulsion of free blacks, 150 people of color emigrated to Haiti.

Economy Hall in the 1850s became a meeting place for members allied with AME ministers "for political and social quality," writes Fatima Shaik. As a former Economy Hall president involved in financing its construction, Pierre Casanave straddled the racial chasm. "In our own city a new inventor has sprung up—Mr. Casanave—who claims to have discovered a means by which decay can be prevented," the *Crescent* (no champion of black freedom) announced in April 1856. "We saw yesterday at his establishment, No. 37 Marais street, the body of a gentleman who had died on the 6th of April, as shown by a certificate of Dr. Cenas, and it was as fresh and clean as though but a day old."

It is a safe bet that the "gentleman" embalmed was white. A conservative daily was unlikely to use that word for a black man; Casanave needed a white dead man to generate publicity. A colored undertaker showing white journalists a well-preserved corpse held a shape of things to come—the massive loss of life in the Civil War, which would see Thomas Holmes of Washington, D.C., embalm "more than four thousand soldiers at a price of one hundred dollars each," writes Drew Gilpin Faust. "The war made him a wealthy man."

Elected president in 1860, Abraham Lincoln held the Republican view that the South's slave-labor system was doomed, that its economy had to diversify, and that slavery should not expand into other states. Lincoln also believed that the Constitution did not give him the power to end slavery. The *Charleston Mercury* echoed rising Southern sentiment, stating that Lincoln's election foreshadowed "the extinction of slavery." The secession of

Southern states came in a chain reaction, and it was uncertain how Lincoln would respond.

In Louisiana, with no popular referendum as required by the state constitution, Governor Thomas Moore, a slave owner, summoned a special session of the General Assembly to call a convention on whether to leave the Union. In a three-week period the two sides—cooperationists (wanting more time, and a convention of all Southern states to decide) and secessionists, ready to leave immediately—canvassed people through a popular vote across the state. "It is impossible to learn whether a majority of delegates favored secession," the historian Roger W. Shugg wrote in 1939, after researching the available records.

> Gossip was rife that the Co-Operationists had actually carried the state by more than three hundred votes; and the convention did not quiet these rumors by refusing to make the returns public.
>
> Long and loud were the demands of the *Picayune* for their publication. Not until the convention had finished its business, three months after resolving on secession, was a tabulation of parish votes released through a party organ. . . . These belated returns were not above suspicion.

The delegates in Baton Rouge voted 113 to 17 to secede—a tiny number of men putting tens of thousands of whites who had no slaves on a road to military service. On March 21, Louisiana joined the Confederate States of America.

This had an immediate impact on Capt. Pierre Gustave Toutant Beauregard, the engineer in charge of federal projects in Louisiana. Born in 1818, Beauregard came from a long Creole line at a St. Bernard Parish plantation; he learned English at eleven and entered West Point at sixteen. As an engineer in the Mexican-American War, he served in Gen. Winfield Scott's army with a young Robert E. Lee, making the triumphal 1848 march into Mexico City covered in mud with minor bullet wounds. With a dark mustache, chiseled features, and high sense of self-worth, Beauregard after the secession vote left New Orleans for Montgomery, Alabama, to meet with Jefferson Davis, the newly selected president of the Confederate States of America, formerly a U.S. senator from Mississippi. Davis, who had fought with Beauregard in Mexico, dispatched him to Charleston, where he oversaw the firing on Fort Sumter on an island of the city harbor. Beauregard became a legend for the salvo that began the Civil War, driving Federal forces out of the fort.

In New Orleans, authorities called for white men to the join the military. The city had had an estimated 49,000 white men of military age, of whom 20,000 fought for the Confederacy, according to Howard Hunter. Of that group, about 5,500 were foreign-born. The city had absorbed 10,000 more French migrants in the last decade amid the stream of Irish and German émigrés; many had little allegiance to a slave economy.

As anxieties flared among working-class whites, a black militia called the Louisiana Native Guards organized 1,500 volunteers to fight for the state. Jordan Noble, the drummer boy of 1815, had since fought in Mexico and marched annually in parades commemorating the Battle of New Orleans. Many men came from benevolent societies and Masonic lodges. The South revolted because of slavery. Alexander H. Stephens, the vice president of the Confederate States of America, declared on March 21, 1861, at Macon, that the Confederacy's "foundations are laid, and its cornerstone rests, upon the great truth that the negro is not equal to the white man; that slavery sub-ordination to the superior race is his natural and normal condition. This, our new government, is the first, in the history of the world, based upon this great physical, philosophical, and moral truth."

Why would free Negroes volunteer for that cause?

New Orleans had the South's largest free black community with a level of wealth, education, and social standing that "set it apart not only from the slaves but free persons of color elsewhere," writes Eric Foner. What was their choice? Fight for their assets to prove loyalty and avoid seizure by the state? Wait, passively, to see if a victorious South enslaved them? Or gamble, sup-porting the Union and risking prosecution for treason? The legislature's draconian laws of the 1850s induced them to prove themselves in battle and try to reverse the erosion of their liberties. The options were reduced by Louisiana authorities: flush with hubris as the war began, they did not want black soldiers.

Casanave's son St. Felix was working with him by 1861 when he placed an ad in the *Times-Picayune*. "The highest cash price paid for Second-hand Furniture," presumably to recycle in building coffins.

Pierre Casanave had a certain safety in providing services white people would need in time of war. At sixty-three he was too old to become a soldier; he was not an out-front activist; but he had allegiances.

André Cailloux, in contrast, joined the Native Guards with zeal. Born a slave in 1825 on a downriver plantation, he was manumitted at twenty-one by the family who had previously sold his mother. A free man in the city, Cailloux married, had children, and proudly took a place in free black society. "Cailloux was one of 156 Afro-Creole cigar makers in New Orleans, the third largest group of artisans after carpenters and masons," writes Stephen J. Ochs. In 1849 Cailloux bought a slave, his mother, in order to emancipate her.

In 1861 the Order Company elected Cailloux first lieutenant. His company took its name from the Friends of Order, a mutual aid society. Economy Company, led by his friend Henry Louis Rey, took its name from Economy Hall, of which Rey's father-in-law had been a founder. Other black units elected officers from their mutual aid societies; the soldiers had to purchase uniforms and weapons for drill exercises at Congo Square, holding parties afterward with singing and dancing.

Shunning them, the legislature in January 1862 specified only "free white males capable of bearing arms." That folly had a mirror at the apex of the Confederate States. In Richmond, President Jefferson Davis, a man of Olympian self-confidence, frowned on a huge force in New Orleans. A war unfolding in several regions needed the smart allocation of assets. Gen. Mansfield Lovell, commanding officer in New Orleans, was a West Point graduate and native Marylander who had resigned as New York deputy street commissioner to join the Confederacy. "The new major general arrived in early October and was appalled at the unpreparedness," writes Shelby Foote. After recruiting, training, and arming 30,000 volunteers to defend the port he deemed strategic, Lovell had to stomach the War Department's diverting 27,000 of his men and eight gunboats upriver to Shiloh and Memphis.

In late March, Union flag-officer David G. Farragut guided a fleet of steam sloops, fourteen gunboats, and nineteen mortar schooners up the Mississippi from a staging zone in the Gulf of Mexico, followed by vessels bearing Gen. Benjamin Butler and 15,000 soldiers. New Orleans had 3,000 short-term militiamen, two warships being built, and in the outlying riverfront forts some 1,100 men, many of them foreigners forced into duty at bayonet point to man the forts.

On March 24, 1862, as the Federal flotilla advanced, a desperate Governor Thomas reinstated the Native Guards to boost the city's defenses. General Lovell was moving his soldiers and matériel out of the city. The mayor told the black soldiers to disband and hide their weapons. Economy Hall became a storage unit for Native Guard muskets. Casanave surely knew this, though if pressed by Union authorities he could say that the men were carrying out Lovell's orders.

Capt. Henry Louis Rey of the Economy Society was close to Casanave. Born in 1831, Rey was the scion of a prominent black Creole family. His father, Barthélemy Rey, a benefactor of Sisters of the Holy Family Convent, financed a stained-glass window in St. Augustine Church in Tremé upon the church's completion in 1842. Pierre Casanave and his family paid for a pew in the church's colored section. Henry Rey was exceptionally close to his parents; his mother, Rose Agnes, had visions of her deceased children. When Barthélemy died in 1845, Henry was furious at the parish priest for draining family coffers to cover a lavish funeral. He experienced visions of his father, and in his alienation from the church found himself in 1857 with a coterie of spiritualists seated for séances, black Creoles, rarely more than seven at a time. The Cercle Harmonique invoked spirits of the dead, whose words they carefully took down. Henry Rey on jotting words grew fatigued until his father's voice came to him, *You are not tired.* The ledger-like books of this remarkable group are preserved in a library archive at the University of New Orleans. Mostly Catholic by background, several from slave-owning families, these Creoles hungered for French ideals of liberty and words of transcendence amid the racial madness of a city headed for war.

"In Rey's early years as a Spiritualist, Père Antoine was one of the most frequent spirits to visit," writes Emily Suzanne Clark in *A Luminous Brotherhood.* "Sedella promised that those who sought the truth would find it and that 'we [the spirits] are with those who are with us.' Père Antoine described a benevolent Creator of 'magnificent works' whose 'infinite wisdom created the world and its laws.' In contrast, the God of non-Spiritualists was the result of human materialism projected onto a deity and thus, an 'unjust and cruel' God. Only Spiritualists had a proper and correct understanding of a wise, loving, and republican God."

When Henry Rey's widowed mother-in-law died in December 1860, her youngest son, eleven, became an orphan. Pierre Casanave was one of five men legally designated to approve Rey as the boy's guardian. Among those French-speaking black Catholics, Rey and Casanave lived within walking distance of Economy Hall.

The Union shelling of low-lying forts on the Mississippi began on April 1, 1862; General Lovell sent twelve gunboats and tugs pushing out rafts with burning pitch and pine, setting off spectacular fireworks but inflicting little damage. Hard river currents slowed the Federal incursion. As fear roiled the city, Mayor John T. Monroe pleaded with Lovell to evacuate citizens. Lovell's job was to move his troops north. For the first time in its history, New Orleans prepared for an enemy invasion.

When Gen. Benjamin Butler led Union troops into New Orleans on May 1, he found a sullen populace, the port economy shattered, markets short of food, and fugitive slaves crowding into the city. As a prewar Massachusetts lawyer, Butler had sued textile mills on behalf of working women for better wages; as a wily political operator, he supported Senator Jefferson Davis before the latter became president of the Confederacy. Lacking previous military experience, Butler had connections in Washington and vaulted into the Union Army as brigadier general. Butler sized up the Confederacy as a case of landed wealth milking the slaves and white poor. He responded to a destitute New Orleans "by setting up a welfare state," writes Howard G. Hunter. Butler's father had died of yellow fever; he knew the city's reputation in that regard and recoiled from so many pools of stagnant water. His tax on businesses and individuals "allowed the military government to employ 2,000 men at 50 cents a day cleaning up a city strewn with filth and dead animal carcasses." Butler "put on relief 11,000 families, most of whom were Irish and German."

Corpulent, cross-eyed, and balding with long stringy hair, Butler looked older than forty-four. When soldiers complained of white women dousing them from balconies with chamber pots and spitting on them, he issued an order stating that any woman showing "contempt for any officer or soldier of the United States ... shall be regarded and held liable to be treated as a woman of the town plying her avocation"—a prostitute. Volleys of scornful press boomed from as far as England. People called him "Beast." But the behavior stopped. He canceled a Catholic church's call for a day of fasting in honor of Jefferson Davis; he shuttered a Catholic paper and the *Crescent* for supporting the Confederacy; other papers published under mild censorship.

With the city under martial law, Butler ordered the surrender of weapons. To discuss that, Capt. Henry Rey was among four leaders of the Native Guards who met with Butler in July 1862. "A very intelligent looking set of men they were," Butler would write. Quizzing them on their prior allegiance to the Confederacy, he was satisfied by their logic of self-preservation. Butler needed more troops. Rey returned on August 15, pledging his men's loyalty. On August 24, Butler issued an appeal for men of color to join the Union Army. As hundreds of black soldiers gathered at a local camp, Captain Rey wrote to *L'Union*, the voice of the black Creole community: "In parade, you will see a thousand white bayonets gleaming in the sun, held by black, yellow and white hands." In a clever interpretation of the Union's right to confiscate property of Confederate officials or sympathizers, Butler began drafting slaves. He managed the city comparatively well, but, overtaken by his inexperience as a military commander, he left in late December 1862. Gen. Nathaniel Banks took his place.

In March 1863 several regiments of the Native Guards were moving northwest toward Port Hudson, a Confederate stronghold south of Baton Rouge. At this point, the careers of André Cailloux and Henry Rey diverged sharply. Cailloux had proved himself an able recruiter. "Polished in manners, bilingual, athletic, daring, a good horseman and boxer, he was, according to contemporaries, a born leader," writes Stephen J. Ochs. With loyal troops, Cailloux was on a roll.

Not so Henry Rey. In a regiment with low morale, he was depressed from "the drudgery of garrison duty and tedious repair work," writes his biographer, Melissa Daggett. Blacks facing six months' back pay had "obsolete muskets, second-hand uniforms and damaged backpacks.... The hardest pill to swallow was the prejudice and strident racism that the black soldiers had endured for six long months."

Rey and several black officers submitted resignations. On April 9, 1863, he was honorably discharged for medical reasons, "syphilitic rheumatism and sore throat," an ironic diagnosis in the cause of honor. A disillusioned Rey headed back to New Orleans as Cailloux bolstered his men in advance of Port Hudson. Whether the friends spoke before Rey left, we do not know. As dreams of military glory faded, Rey reunited with the Cercle Harmonique.

On the morning of May 27, 1863, Cailloux's troops near Baton Rouge moved out of a willow forest toward a moat beneath a bluff held by Rebel troops. In the hail of gunfire, a bullet shattered Cailloux's left arm, which dangled as he urged his men to press on, charging the ditch when a shell smashed his head. Another officer died; some three dozen Native Guardsmen trying to ford the backwater died in a storm of bullets. The company retreated, one man carrying a piece of Cailloux's skull. In a truce for both sides to retrieve their dead, Union soldiers hauled back the remains of white casualties; General Banks left the black dead scattered on the field in an apparent "calculation that the stench of their decomposing bodies would make life more miserable and unhealthy for the defenders," writes Stephen J. Ochs.

Reports of Cailloux's death made him a martyr. *Harper's Weekly* would call him "one of the bravest soldiers in our country's service, though a colored man." As the bloated body decayed in the heat and rain, his spirit spoke to a bereaved Henry Rey in New Orleans. "I have left your world a lover of liberty, fighting for my brothers; I have won the same in the spirit world, for God has rewarded me," the channeled voice told the Cercle Harmonique. "Dear friends in the battles, my spirit will be among you.... I will be your torch bearer."

A long poem eulogizing Cailloux appeared on July 17 in *L'Union*. "Those noble dead in the abode of glory! Always follow Cailloux!"

General Banks's disregard for the remains was not widely known as he began purging black officers, trying to nudge white public opinion toward the Union. When Port Hudson fell forty-one days after Cailloux's death, the uniform shards and bone fragments finally went back to the city and what must have been a grim task for Pierre Casanave. His continued advertisements in the press for embalming signaled to Confederate families a sensitive hand for their fallen sons. Business was business. But Casanave was a builder of Economy Hall and an avuncular figure to Henry Rey, whose good friend had died defending the Union. What did the burial master think of the denigration of those scant remains as the colored elite made preparations for the march? Did Casanave foresee the white rage after a funeral whose size would far exceed that of any black man previously buried in New Orleans, and whose music (of which the *Picayune* so disapproved) would be taken to another level? Did he give a damn?

On July 25, the coffin draped in the Union flag lay in state at the Friends of Order hall with Cailloux's sword, belt, soldier's coat, and cap atop the flag. Hundreds of people filed through the candlelit room, day after day, paying their respects. On July 29, the service began with a eulogy by Rev. Claude Paschal Maistre, a Frenchman who had clashed over his parish finances and abolitionist stance with Archbishop Jean-Marie Odin. Odin, also French, had spent years cultivating political leaders to cement trust in his office, and in a hierarchy loyal to Rome. Odin championed the white South in an 1862 pastoral letter. Amid New Orleans priests who blessed Confederate regimental flags, some donating church bells for use as cannon parts, Maistre stood a pariah.

White musicians of the Forty-Second Massachusetts Regiment began a dirge with a phalanx of soldiers including captains of Cailloux's Friends of Order, who carried the casket into the morning air, onto an Esplanade Avenue lined by thousands of people, many waving Union flags. The casket was followed by two black companies of the Sixth Louisiana Regiment; a carriage bearing Cailloux's widow and four children; as well as members of Economy Hall, the Arts and Mechanics Association, the Artisans Brotherhood, the God Protect Us Society, the Children of Moses, and a litany of other societies named for saints. It was an African American funeral on the scale of those for white generals and politicians, in a city where military parades historically symbolized white might. Moving through downtown streets and across Congo Square, the cortege reached St. Louis Cemetery Number Two, the place of burial.

Such a procession for a man of color surely gave some satisfaction to Pierre Casanave; several weeks later, a full page inside *Harper's Weekly* captured the scope of the march in a lifelike drawing with eight musicians leading the horse-drawn carriage.

· · · · · · · · · ·

WAR, DEFEAT, AND THE POWER OF MYTH

When the war ended in 1865, Congo Square filled with people rejoicing, free at last. As defeated soldiers from New Orleans returned to a city that had been well-governed by the occupation generals, many more men released from Confederate service avoided towns and cities that had been damaged and went to New Orleans precisely because it was intact. The real war in New Orleans began after the war.

On April 21, 1865, a mass meeting at Congo Square sent up wails of sorrow for the death of Abraham Lincoln. The conquered city became a free zone for former slaves. But the transition to a peacetime economy ran headlong into the identity crusade of the defeated South, determined to achieve what the Confederacy had failed to do. Slavery was done; white supremacy lived to fight on.

Ironically, for all of the Creole gentry's sense of entitlement and Beauregard's notable military record in the war, New Orleans had never been a Confederate stronghold. The port culture, black folkways, and melding of Mediterranean and African culinary practices made for more of an international city. The continuing stream of French migrants held a greater allegiance to republican values than to Jefferson Davis; the Irish who had fled the great famine, the rooted black Creoles, and Latin peoples formed a crossroads of humanity unique to the South. Economy Hall became a meeting place for blacks leaning to allegiance with Republican Party radicals pushing for greater equality.

Racial tensions reached a fever pitch at a constitutional convention on July 30, 1866, in Mechanics Hall, with delegates supporting black suffrage. Mayor Monroe deemed it an illegal gathering and ordered it shut down. The police shot, clubbed, and slaughtered thirty-four blacks and three whites, leaving scores of people wounded. An outspoken abolitionist, the dentist Anthony Dostie was shot, stabbed, beaten, jailed, and released, dying six days later. The massacre triggered a congressional investigation and Reconstruction legislation in the South geared to create a base of black voters. The idea of a rebuilding South also offered lucrative prospects to Northerners with money.

Cercle Harmonique séances gave Henry Rey and his small group a cocoon of hope during the violence of postwar politics. Echoing Cailloux's spirit voice came that of a new martyr, Dostie, telling the believers his words for his murderers: "God is to be your judge, but Dostie will be the one who will ask him forgiveness for your great Sin."

We can read into the language of these séances the psychological motivations of the circle, a projection of justice and interracial harmony; the reality lies in the members' belief, just as the faithful of mainstream religion adhere to rituals, praying for hope and sustenance. The more striking story is how the black Creole members maintained their hope in a bloody time of justice trampled, as the spirits of people killed kept sending them words of uplift.

Pierre Casanave died on December 1, 1866, before the worst of the backlash against Reconstruction. The modest obituaries give no hint of a ceremonial parade. Two sons took over the mortuary business. The culture of spectacle that so influenced Casanave in orchestrating funerals shifted radically in the few years after his death.

· · · · · · · · · ·

MEMORY AND DESIRE

Oscar J. Dunn was a leading light of the new African American politics. A plasterer and violinist before the war, Dunn opened an employment agency for newly freed slaves and became an advocate for black land ownership and equal protection laws under the Fourteenth Amendment; he also guided a school desegregation plan that saw black and white youngsters in classes through the early 1870s. In 1868 he accepted Henry Clay Warmoth's invitation to run on the Republican ticket as his lieutenant governor. Dunn was forty-two, Warmoth twenty-six. The Illinois-born lawyer was a Union veteran appointed a regional judge in New Orleans in 1864 by General Banks and used his postwar practice as a political springboard. Warmoth had "blind ambition and social aplomb," writes Justin A. Nystrom. "He never missed a party and never passed up opportunities to meet influential men or to flirt with their wives and daughters." With the newly enfranchised black votes, and many Confederate veterans ineligible under the 1868 constitution for not pledging support to a new order, Warmoth and Dunn were elected.

By early 1871 Dunn had grown disillusioned with Warmoth, a dealmaker trying to pull in hardline Democrats and appease Republicans feuding over federal patronage. A pliant legislature gave Warmoth control of the Metropolitan Police; new laws allowed him to appoint state officials who would thereby avoid elections, owing loyalty to him. The House Speaker (a Warmoth appointee) approached Dunn about taking over if they impeached the governor. In August of that year the U.S. marshal used Gatling guns to prevent Warmoth and his faction from entering the Custom House for the Republican convention. When Dunn suddenly died in November, many people suspected he had been poisoned. Another massive funeral, with Warmoth a pallbearer, registered the agony of African Americans in a new world.

Two and a half weeks after his death, Dunn's voice appeared at Henry Rey's séance table, writes Emily Suzanne Clark, "and he seemed to speak directly to the tension among the city's black and Republican population."

"For the sake of harmony, and freedom for all, don't shatter to pieces the great Work already done," said Dunn's spirit. "Dividing a house is ruinous to all." The martyred Dostie entreated them to unite for "power to secure victory"—a Republican victory.

Politics descended into madness. In early 1872, the U.S. marshal, in league with Warmoth's Republican opponents at the Custom House, arrested Warmoth and eighteen lawmakers. His enemies set up a rival legislature at the Gem Saloon and sent their loyal militia to seize lawmakers and transport them to the Gem to achieve a quorum, an absurdist drama that ended with a lawmaker shot to death. Securing bail, Warmoth sent the Metropolitan Police to arrest the ringleaders. He convened an emergency session of the legislature and installed a black ally, Pinckney Benton Stewart Pinchback, as lieutenant governor to fill the vacancy left by Dunn. The Custom House Republican faction pressured the state senate to impeach Warmoth; Pinchback became governor for thirty-six days. In 1872, Republican William J. Kellogg won the governorship in an election "so shot through with fraud that no one ever had any idea of who actually won," writes historian Joe Gray Taylor. Refusing to concede, the Democrat John McEnery took an oath of office just as the Republican Kellogg did. Kellogg assumed his office in the Mechanics Institute, McEnery in the Odd Fellows' Hall.

Against this background, Carnival season in 1873 had a supercharged pageantry, as people across the society acted out dreams and retribution fantasies. The Mistick Krewe of Comus paraded a political allegory. Founded in 1857 by Anglo-American businessmen outside old Creole society, Comus was known for parades of costume beauty and lavish balls; the celebrations had gone dark during the war. Seething resentments toward Republican rule fused into the 1873 Comus parade, "The Missing Links to Darwin's *Origins of the Species.*" Illustrations of the costumes are pictorial gems. A masker in the guise of the rattlesnake portrayed Warmoth. "Each Link was attended by a squire masked and costumed as an Ass," writes Henri Schindler. While satire did not mark the features of every link, many of them bore unmistakable resemblances to political figures of the day. "Snail, Leech, and Gorilla were members of the Louisiana Legislature; the Hyena stooped with booty was General Butler, and Tobacco Grub was the face of President Ulysses S. Grant."

The artists' illustrations of the costumes have an undeniable beauty; they are eerie, too, as symbols of a psyche in polite society animated by vengeance. "The racism that informed the satire of Darwin's work has never been exceeded either," writes James Gill. "Supposed lord of all creation was a banjo-playing gorilla, who was seated on a throne in the tableau."

The patrician Pickwick Club membership overlapped in Comus. Gubernatorial pretender McEnery was in the Pickwick Club. On Ash Wednesday he sent his militia to attack the Metropolitan Police station at the Cabildo. Governor Kellogg made a desperate plea to the commander of federal troops in the city, who drove McEnery's forces to surrender. Kellogg's police shut down the rival legislature as McEnery fled town.

The Pickwick and Comus members coalesced with men in the elite Boston Club and the Krewe of Rex, closing ranks in the Crescent City White League—Democratic Party militants for white supremacy, determined to drive out Republican carpetbaggers. The White League opened fire on September 14, 1874, in an insurrection against the Metropolitan Police, at a cost of twenty-nine lives. The attack briefly ousted Governor Kellogg.

None of the White League militants was prosecuted, though they had crippled the Metropolitan Police as a paramilitary force. President Ulysses S. Grant sent federal troops to reinstate Kellogg. The White League revolt "served as a defining moment for a generation of elite, young men in New Orleans," writes Nystrom.

In 1877 federal forces withdrew from the South, ending Reconstruction. The goals of a more just society collided with a violence across the South that our age would call terrorism—whites used lynching to strike fear in blacks, gradually purging African Americans from voting rolls in rebuilding a white base of control.

The gun battles over political power in New Orleans occurred amid a brief, successful experiment in school desegregation envisioned by Oscar Dunn, which ended after Reconstruction. The vigilante tactics to win the war-after-the-war needed a rationalization of some kind. The New Orleans aristocracy enshrined the Civil War mythology of the Lost Cause that was gathering strength across the South. Carnival balls celebrated lords and ladies of the realm, a world of chivalry with good darkies, all so misunderstood in the industrialized North. As statues and monuments celebrating the Lost Cause went up, the truth of the city became an improvisational memory drama, staged on the streets.

· · · · · · · · · ·

CODA

Henry Rey did well in the early postwar years. Starting in 1868 he served a two-year term in the legislature, and on April 13, 1870, he was appointed as assessor of the city's Third District, a sinecure seemingly linked to his friendship with Governor Warmoth, before the latter's impeachment. He lost the position two years later but remained active as a Republican.

Pierre Casanave's spirit appeared in a Cercle Harmonique séance in May 1874. "There are many secrets revealed here," said the voice in the words transcribed. "I have to reconcile with many Beings here. I'm not ready to forgive them all. It is repugnant to me to take the first steps towards others. I have a lot to do here to accomplish a period that will bring the hour that will sound my grand march."

"I suffer here."

9

The Time of Jazz

Jazz is a music; jazz is a language. Jazz begins as a story of the city in church and parades, a performance narrative countering that of the Lost Cause. From African American pews and parades came an ensemble style, "playing the melody with a beat," writes Bill Russell, "sung by the various instruments with a beautiful, vocal-like warmth ... [and] moderate, relaxed tempos to which people can dance or march, even in a hot climate." The music traveled far before the official city awakened to the life force that generated the "sound" of New Orleans style.

Rural churches released a memory stream in the ring shouts, dancing, and ecstatic worship among many of the 40,000 black folk who fled Louisiana plantation poverty between 1880 and 1910 for dreams in the shambling metropolis. The flowing spirituality in small New Orleans churches hit a countercurrent in the jaunty rags played in taverns, dancehalls, parks, and brass band parades.

Family structure, too, was central to early jazz. Dozens of jazzmen came from families with music-making elders, siblings, or cousins, often with a piano at home. George "Pops" Foster, a bass player born in 1892 and raised on an upriver plantation near Donaldsonville, recalled, "Before we came down to New Orleans we had a three-piece family band."

> My sister played mandolin, my brother played guitar, and I played the cello. I started learning music when I was seven. I'd stand on a box and play the cello like a bass with a bow.... The people who my mother worked for were the McCalls. They were the cause of my playing music. The mother played piano and she would see that we rehearsed on certain days. They used to give a dance—they called 'em "balls"—they'd get one

big room and ask 25 cents at the door and 15 cents if you'd buy the ticket beforehand.

Jazz rose from other wellsprings, notably the ragtime style of well-trained black Creoles like John Robichaux, a drummer and violinist born in 1866 in the town of Thibodaux. He moved to the city in 1891 and by century's turn led the John Robichaux Dance Orchestra. They played quadrilles and waltzes at the New Orleans Country Club, with some variation for colored Creoles at Economy Hall in Tremé, among other venues. Robichaux took players to the city's southwestern fringes, in Carrollton, at Lincoln Park, where African Americans thrilled to a hot air balloonist. Park manager Buddy Bartley, a waiter and promoter with a minor rap sheet, "rode a smoke-filled balloon up to the sky and then on cue from a shotgun blast fired from the ground, parachuted out," writes John McCusker. "Sometimes he landed in the park." Strong winds once sent Bartley into Lake Pontchartrain. Another time his crash-dive hit a chimney, "and what a mess he was," said the trombonist Kid Ory.

Robichaux mixed rags and vaudeville music in his Lincoln Park shows. He found a bravura rival in Buddy Bolden, "one fine-lookin' brownskin man, tall and slender and a terror with the ladies," said the trumpeter Bunk Johnson. Bolden played in Johnson Park, which opened for baseball opposite Lincoln Park, in 1902; he would jut his horn through the Johnson fence and release a hot rolling wave to "call my children home," pulling fans from Robichaux.

"Buddy Bolden is the first man who played blues for dancing," stated Papa John Joseph, an influential early bass player who came from a musical family upriver in St. James Parish. Bolden played cornet, forerunner of the trumpet. Leading small bands, Bolden fused rags, passages improvising around a melody, with a hot moaning blues in simulation of sounds from rowdy bars in the "tango belt," above Canal Street, just outside the Storyville bordello district, in lower Tremé. With an intuitive grasp of how to make people move, Bolden mixed church songs, like "Oh What a Friend We Have in Jesus," with the erotic heat in songs like "Make Me a Pallet on the Floor."

Make me a pallet
   on the floor
Make it soft
   Make it low
So your sweet man
   Will never know.

Born in 1877, Charles Joseph Bolden spent his formative years at 2309 First Street, a working-class area well back from St. Charles Avenue on a street grid paved over the once-forested back swamp between Uptown and Canal Street. The city's primordial pattern of plantations-into-neighborhoods had avoided interior swamps. A massive drainage project in the 1890s began clearing land on both sides of New Basin Canal. The Bolden home on First Street sat in a core called "Back o' Town," its origins in the shacks and slave cabins on the fringes of the swamp, set behind the antebellum townhouses and homes of the wealthy. Rich whites coveted the Greek Revival mansions built in the 1850s in the Garden District, the area with large lawns and gracious oaks that lay below Canal Street between the river and St. Charles Avenue. As the city developed upriver, Victorian cottages and duplexes became popular, while buildings along the fringes of the old back swamp were split into tenements. "Destitute and excluded, most freedmen had little choice but to settle in the ragged back-of-town, where urban development petered into amorphous low-density shantytowns," writes Richard Campanella.

City government tried to ignore the poverty. "There is no way of concealing filth," the *Daily Picayune* opined in 1891, "exposed to view in the streets and every stranger sees it." Black infant mortality was 45 percent. Life expectancy was forty-six for whites, thirty-six for blacks. Bolden's sister died of encephalitis at five, his father of pneumonia at thirty-two. In response to the misery, a reform coalition, the Women's League for Sanitation and Drainage, campaigned for the assessment of property taxes to pay for infrastructure repair. Drainage cleared a swath behind houses along Bayou St. John, the cypress swamp north of Tremé and Marigny, that allowed growth toward Lake Pontchartrain. Elysian Fields Avenue ran through the burgeoning streets of Gentilly Woods.

The music fanned out as the city grew. West End was a venue on the shores of Lake Pontchartrain. The Milneburg resort had piers, slips, houses on stilts called "camps," pavilions, restaurants, and dances. Paul Barbarin, an influential drummer born in 1899, spent his early years in Tremé. In 1908 he began taking "Smoky Mary" on the Pontchartrain Railroad to Milneburg with his aunt and sister, visiting friends with camps. Barbarin, who composed "Bourbon Street Parade," recalled Milneburg in an unfinished memoir:

Imagine the bright summer sunshine, the blue lake, the camps white, green, yellow, every color of paint. Decoration Day, July Fourth, flags flying all over. Some porches hung with paper lanterns. The white summer dresses, many colored parasols. The gold lettering on the brewery truck and the harness shining and the brass shining. Each horse as big as an elephant to a ten year old kid. . . . About five or six bands playing five or six tunes and not over one hundred yards apart. Laughing men, rolling a half keg of beer along the boardwalk to a camp. Hot dogs, oysters, crawfish, green crabs and fat lake trout. Everybody eating, singing, making music and laughing.

Barbarin's memory is one strand in a narrative web of early jazz—story lines about the city. The music hummed with place-name melodies and lyrics of a culture celebrating its arrival and becoming. Jelly Roll Morton's "Milenburg Joys," recorded in 1923 in Chicago with a white band, the New Orleans Rhythm Kings, pays homage to the city he left in 1907. (Note how Milneburg becomes Mile*n*burg.)

Rock my soul with the Milenburg joys
Play 'em, Mama, don't refuse
Separate me from these weary blues.

All night long, with that dixieland strain,
Play it down, then do it again,
Every time I hear that tune,
Luck says I'll be with you soon.

That's why I've got
Those Milenburg joys.

The music held a floating mirror to the city's social mosaic.

The shotgun house on First Street where Bolden came of age in the 1890s sat in a melting pot of Irish, Germans, Italians, and African Americans: carpenters, plasterers, teachers, longshoremen, shop owners, and porters living within a block of a Hebrew cemetery. Dryades Street, which ran through the urban core in rough parallel to St. Charles Avenue, had Jewish émigrés with tailor shops and stores. Hitting stride about 1898, Bolden drew intonations for his new sound "from the 'Holy Roller' Baptist Church on Jackson Avenue and Franklin," recalled Kid Ory. "I know he used to go to that church but not for religion; he went there to get ideas for his music."

Kid Ory was one of the great early jazzmen. Born in 1886 to a black mother and a white father in St. John the Baptist Parish, upriver, the boy grew up in the slow life of a plantation culture. He thrilled to the sight of Bolden's band, pulling into LaPlace on whistle-stops. Raised a Catholic,

Ory used "Holy Roller" as a generic term for Holiness or Sanctified sects. He moved to the city in 1907, and, after summoning his Woodland band to join him, used an entrepreneur's flair in promoting them on a rented furniture wagon that clattered through town. His blues trombone was called "tailgate" because he stood at the end of the wagon, swinging the slide of the 'bone like a tail at the gate.

Bolden used a cup to muffle the "moan in his cornet that went all the way through you," the drummer Bill Matthews recalled, "like a Baptist preacher." Donald J. Marquis's milestone biography, *In Search of Buddy Bolden*, spotlights the upstart churches, of which the city had about fifty in 1900, that welcomed rural migrants. "The ministers, sometimes unordained and illiterate," writes Marquis, would "stir the congregation with the words and to evoke a rhythmic response that could lead individuals in a trance-like state ... [and] a kind of jumping called the 'shouts.'" Neighbors sometimes called the cops about the noise.

Bolden's horn made people dance as preachers got them gyrating in church, but he never recorded. "Traditionally, the highest praise given a blues musician," writes Albert Murray in *Stomping the Blues*, "has been the declaration that he can make a dance hall rock and roll like a down-home church during revival time. But then many of the elements of blues music seem to have been derived from downhome church in the first place."

One Bolden venue, Union Sons Hall, owned by a colored relief association at the corner of Perdido and South Rampart Streets, held Saturday night dances that ran till 5:00 A.M. "On Sunday mornings," reports Marquis, "the hall served as the First Lincoln Baptist Church."

The club had a nickname, "Funky Butt Hall," from a satirical rag Bolden popularized with the refrain: "I thought I heard Buddy Bolden say / Funky butt, funky butt / take it away." Marquis traces the origins of Bolden's signature song (alternately called "Buddy Bolden's Stomp," "Funky Butt," or "Buddy Bolden's Blues") to a ballad with parodies "sung in towns up and down the Mississippi," likely carried by men working the boats. Many sang this older version:

I thought I heer'd Abe Lincoln shout,
Rebels close down them plantations and let all the niggers out.
I'm positively sure I heer'd Mr. Lincoln shout ...
You gonna lose this war, git on your knees and pray.

In 1940, Jelly Roll Morton recorded "Buddy Bolden's Blues," a cutting satire that aligns Bolden, complaining of foul smells in a rough-house club, with Judge J. J. Fogarty, a man notorious for meting out jail time to working folk and musicians hauled in for marginal offenses.

> I thought I heard Buddy Bolden say,
> You're nasty, you're dirty, take it away …
> I thought I heard Buddy Bolden shout,
> Open up that window and let the bad air out.
> Open up that window and let the foul air out.
> Thought I heard Judge Fogarty say,
> Thirty days in the market, take him away.
> Give him a broom to sweep with, take him away.

"The police put you in jail if they heard you singing that song," recalled Sidney Bechet. As a boy, the supreme clarinetist and soprano saxophonist saw Bolden in a cutting contest with the Imperial Band, "singing his theme song, people started singing, policemen began whipping heads." The power of music unsettled the guardians of the racial fortress.

"Bolden's ragged and raucous music stood in stark contrast to the more traditional quadrilles, waltzes and marches of New Orleans Creoles," writes Ted Gioia in *The History of Jazz*. "Ragtime," or "the music," sent syncopated melodies into clubs, society and concert halls, as well as into the streets of a parading culture. Jazz rose from working-class roots to popularity with white dancers in gowns and tuxedos as orchestras like Robichaux's stretched from ragtime and show tunes to touches of the blues heat. As brass bands spread in late nineteenth-century America, the marching brass with drums and woodwinds flourished in towns near New Orleans— Mandeville, Houma, Thibodaux, Donaldsonville, the list goes on. White bands, black bands, rarely mixed, played funerals for prominent people and lesser-known members of benevolent societies in the 1890s. The repertoire rapidly evolved in New Orleans.

Bolden's song bag retrieved "Go Down, Moses," and a metaphorical cry to slave masters: "tell old Pharaoh / to let my people go." It was one of the few slave songs absorbed by the brass bands in moving to a better time. Parades back from the graveyard rang in hope with "Just a Little While to Stay Here" or "Lord Lord Lord" and a booming bass drum:

> You fed me when I was hungry and
> You warmed me when I was cold
> You gave me drink when I was thirsty
> Lord Lord Lord you really been good to me

People behind the bands sang with gusto, dancing in what Joseph Roach calls "a performance of memory." The bands found an anthem, "When the Saints Go Marching In," for the graveyard-exiting second line—joy for the soul's reward, dancing a release from life's daily grind. The lyrics of "The Saints" were pared down over time behind a refrain—"Oh when the saints / Go marching in / Oh, I want to be in that number / When the saints go marching in." Imagery of the beloved dead in celestial procession appealed to whites, too. The lyrics had come a long way in black churches, sung as a slow-tempo hymn or as a rousing crusade:

Oh, when the drums begin to bang
Oh, when the drums begin to bang

[refrain: When the saints go marching in]

Oh, when the stars fall from the sky
Oh, when the stars fall from the sky

[refrain]

Oh, when the moon turns red with blood
Oh, when the moon turns red with blood

[refrain]

Oh, when the trumpet sounds its call
Oh, when the trumpet sounds its call

[refrain]

Oh, when the horsemen begin to ride
Oh, when the horsemen begin to ride

[refrain]

Oh, when the fire begins to blaze
Oh, when the fire begins to blaze
... I want to be in that number
When the saints go marching in.

The bleeding moon, war trumpets, horsemen, and fire echo the Book of Revelation, the New Testament scripture on the Lord's battle over evil. James H. Cone writes that black spirituals had a message: "Slavery contradicts God, and God will therefore liberate black people." In "Wading in the Water," repetitions of the title line signal water throwing bloodhounds off the scent, the maroon finding freedom. Parading carried memories of this quest. Brass bands popularized lyrics celebrating a new horizon. Louis Armstrong's 1938 recording of an up-tempo "When the Saints Go Marching In" was quickly adopted by brass bands; few singers tried to emulate the satirical set-piece opening, "Reverend Satchmo" calling out his trombonist like a preacher to the choir. The band uncorks a swinging melody, with no hint of apocalypse, only a surge of sweetness and hope.

Born to fifteen-year-old May Ann Albert and her boyfriend, Willie Armstrong, on August 4, 1901, Louis grew up in Back o' Town poverty. He lived first with his paternal grandparents, then his mother and little sister, in a shack that was razed years later to make room for the municipal complex. "In that one block between Gravier and Perdido Streets more people were crowded than you ever saw in your life," he wrote in his 1954 classic, *Satchmo: My Life in New Orleans.*

There were churchpeople, gamblers, hustlers, cheap pimps, prostitutes and lots of children. There were bars, honky-tonks and saloons and lots of women walking the streets for tricks to take to their "pads." Whether my mother did any hustling, I cannot say. If she did, she certainly kept it out of my sight. One thing is certain: everybody from the churchfolk to the lowest roughneck treated her with the greatest respect. She was glad to say hello to everybody and she always held her head up.

May Ann took the children to a church where people danced as saints on salvation's path. "It all came from the Old 'Sanctified' Churches," wrote Armstrong, a grade-school dropout, in a 1967 letter on his trusty typewriter. "The whole Congregation would be *Wailing*—Singing like mad and sound so beautiful. I being a little boy would 'Dig' Everything when those Sisters would get so carried away while Rev (the preacher) would be right in the middle of his sermon."

"May Ann made a choice,'" writes Thomas Brothers in *Louis Armstrong's New Orleans.* Born in an upriver town, she joined thousands of first-generation free folk in the city. Abandoned by Willie, she survived. For church, she chose "*her* tradition ... closest to the ring shouts of slavery, the one that featured communal focus on a direct experience of the Holy Spirit, the one that cultivated vigorous rhythms that made your body move and deeply felt melody that made your heart pour out."

"When I was in church and when I was 'second lining' ... following the brass bands in parades," Armstrong wrote, "I started to listen carefully to the different instruments, noticing the things they played and how they played them." The memoirs and oral histories of early jazzmen reveal great attention to the past. They knew they were creating something unique. Their reflections riff on the rites and pageantry of a town that, for all of its poverty and repression, furnished the stage for a rocking human comedy. Wakes were in people's homes; the deceased on a front room "cooling board," a table or makeshift platform. "In New Orleans, we would often wonder where a dead person was located," Jelly Roll Morton (born Ferdinand LaMothe in 1885) recalled in 1938. Seated at a Library of Congress piano, Jelly unfurled life episodes for Alan Lomax. He had a boyhood quartet "for the purpose of finding someone that was dead, because the minute we'd walk in, we'd be right in the kitchen."

Plenty ham sandwiches and cheese sandwiches slabbered all over with mustard, and plenty of whiskey and plenty of beer. Of course, the dead man would be laid out in the front and he'd be by himself most of the time and couldn't hear nothing we would be saying at all. He was dead and there was no reason for him to be with us living people. And very often the lady of the house would be back there with us having a good time, too, because she would be glad he was gone.

Then we would stand up and begin—
Nearer my God to thee
Very slow and with beautiful harmony, thinking about that ham—
Nearer to thee
Plenty of whiskey in the flask and all kinds of crazy ideas in the harmony which made it impossible for anybody to jump in and sing. We'd be sad, too, terribly sad.

Jazz grew as the African genius for polyrhythm and improvisation embraced European instrumentation and melody. Bolden was like many poor, darker players of the Uptown inner city; he learned melodies by ear, improvising on what he heard. The classically trained black Creoles, like Jelly, congregated more in Downtown wards, adapting to a powerful blues stream of the musically unlettered. "A fiddler is *not* a violinist, but a violinist can be a fiddler," Paul Dominguez famously told Lomax. "If I wanted to make a living, I had to be rowdy like that other group. I had to jazz it or rag it or any other damn thing."

"Bolden cause all that," Paul said bitterly. "He cause these younger Creoles ... to have a different style altogether from old heads like Tio and

Perez. I don't know how they do it." Paul's anger was mixed with admiration. "But goddamn they'll do it. Can't tell you what's there on paper, but just play the hell out of it."

The clarinetist Lorenzo Tio was a renowned teacher. The cornetist Manuel Perez, "a titan of early jazz," led the Onward Brass Band, a group that mesmerized young Kid Ory in the town of Reserve, where Onward formed. Several years later, in the city, Perez guided the Onward as an illustrious brass band into the 1920s.

· · · · · · · · · ·

AN IRONIC REVOLUTIONARY

Bolden was ten when the precursor stamped his fingerprints on the emerging art form. About 1887, James Brown Humphrey began making weekly train trips to plantations as far as twenty-five miles down the Mississippi. Dapper in a swallowtail coat, "Professor" Humphrey courted planters to pay for his services on some nineteen large farms. He taught fieldworkers and house servants to whom the landowners provided instruments in hopes of securing a low-wage labor force, keeping their servants happy. Humphrey was an ironic revolutionary. By training musicians, he enabled them to leave plantation life and pursue careers in the city.

Born in 1859 in Sellers, an upriver village later subsumed into Norco, Humphrey had fair skin and red hair, the son of a black mother and a white father who provided support as the boy made his way. Married at nineteen, Humphrey had four children; three trained as classical musicians. Humphrey the multi-instrumentalist performed in the Bloom Philharmonic Orchestra, which catered to black Creoles. His teaching had extraordinary reach. The jazz scholar Karl Koenig has chronicled how Humphrey formed bands at the plantations named Magnolia, Deer Range, and in the towns of St. Sophie, Ironton, Jesuit Bend, and Oakville. Humphrey launched the Onward Brass Band in Reserve; after the Onward moved into the city, Manuel Perez added the cornetist Joe "King" Oliver, who became a father figure to Louis Armstrong.

"Jim Humphrey would bring a new piece each week written out," recalled the bandleader Bebe Ridgley, an early pupil. "The brass band hadn't started dance music at that time." Humphrey trained his charges to read parts and play melodies for marching. He wrote syncopated rhythms as musical exercises. "These rhythms were characteristic of early jazz phrasing," notes

Koenig, "something that did not appear in the music of the march or even constantly in early ragtime. But, when added to ragtime, this syncopated reeling was an early example of what we call 'swinging' a piece of music."

Taking students into the city, where parade groups needed marching units during Labor Day and Carnival season, Humphrey exposed rural African Americans to the grandeur in city life. Throngs in the streets watched them parade, with even white people applauding.

"One of the surest signs of prosperity is to see one purchasing property. Among those buying lots in the 6th district are Professor J. B. Humphrey," the black *Weekly Pelican* noted in September 1887.

"Grandfather made his money in real estate," the clarinetist Willie Humphrey (1900–1994) told Koenig. Professor Humphrey bought in Uptown black neighborhoods. "He had a garden for much of his food and I think teaching music was a labor of love." Teaching may have been love's labor for Humphrey in later years, but the pace of his train-riding twenties provided money for him to buy real estate.

One of Humphrey's valued clients was Henry Clay Warmoth. Since his 1873 impeachment as governor, Warmoth had been trailed by the image of a carpetbagger. A wealthy man, he bought Magnolia Plantation at Pointe-à-La-Hache; Mark Twain and Horace Greeley had been guests of previous owners. Warmoth and Humphrey probably met in 1887. Did the fair-complexioned young professor with a derby hat know of Warmoth's five-day incarceration in 1874 for stabbing a newspaper owner in self-defense? Did Humphrey care? In Warmoth, seventeen years older, his walrus mustache streaked gray, the twenty-seven-year-old musician found a man more enlightened than most whites. He paid for musicians' uniforms, orange coats, and black pants of the Eclipse Brass Band, as it became known. They played in the plantation's church. As Benjamin Turner, who grew up there, recalled, the band would parade behind a U.S. flag and

> would march all around the quarters. They had streets and everything at Magnolia.... The band played for the trains, came once in the morning and then again at night. They marched on the big wharf from the warehouse to the river ...
>
> People got baptized at Woodland church and come back and have their party at Magnolia. Big hall in the warehouse building, in front of the building was supply store. They would have the party and dance in the hall back of the store.... Yeah, they went to New Orleans and played in the parades. Labor day was one of them. The governor was proud of them.

In his 1930 memoir, Warmoth wrote that whites "generally showed a tender love for their black slaves." Did he truly believe this? He had seen Reconstruction violence. "We must encourage the negro in his political and civil rights; educate, encourage, and show him friendship by justice, human charity, and brotherhood.... The American negro has waded through a sea of blood to his Promised land." In 1888 Warmoth tried a comeback for governor; he lost to former Confederate general Francis T. Nicholls in a landslide—136,746 votes to 51,993.

Warmoth's "sea of blood" metaphor was apt. Between 1882 and 1903, as the *Chicago Tribune* reported, 232 blacks were lynched in Louisiana. "More often than not, serious acts of violence against Negroes in Louisiana were committed by men of some substance in the white community," wrote the historian William Ivy Hair. "But almost never did conservatives publicly criticize the many lynchings in which the black victims had been accused of some crime. Often they praised such events."

The violent double-standard of law in Louisiana (and other states) failed to dim the African American brass bands' elation in the pride of arrival, a presence in the city as they slowly reworked a white military repertoire. In 1881, the black *Weekly Pelican* described the Excelsior Brass Band (which Humphrey helped launch) in Prussian-modeled uniforms, "dark blue helmet hats, ribbed with burnished brass, corded in white, with long horse hair plumes, long military coats, three rows of brass buttons ... epaulets, pants of dark navy blue cloth with white stripes ... heralded with murmurs of admiration."

The *Pelican* ran many notices of the Excelsior, Onward, and other brass bands performing for benevolent societies, fraternal groups, and churches. Brass bands and churches provided a foundation for the movement and songs of early jazz.

....

THE DOMINANT NARRATIVE

The rising African American identity was initially no match for a white redemption narrative. As black people danced in the sunrise of jazz, the official city gazed backward, seeking salvation in a sanitized Confederate past. The psychology of power meant softening the cult of lynching, or rationalizing the armed attacks by members of the Boston and Pickwick Clubs in the 1874 White League insurrection, to spin a story of Southern salvation. The White League assault became "the Battle of Liberty Place." St. Louis Cathedral, no longer so welcoming to blacks as under the long-buried Père

Antoine, held Masses for White League veterans on the anniversary from 1877 until 1882. A procession to the graves of a fallen militant and the laying of a wreath, as if to a martyr, had the trappings of a pilgrimage. "The high point of the anniversary was the military pageantry performed by the units of the State militia, which by now was simply the White League in official garb ... to a point near the river for a 21-gun salute," writes Lawrence N. Powell. "Crowds surged through balconied streets festooned with banners and bunting." Celebrations lit the night.

As Howard Hunter writes, "While Northern publications depicted September 14 as a carryover of the old Confederacy—the cover of *Harper's Weekly*, for example, illustrated a man in a Confederate uniform firing a cannon on Canal Street bearing a banner with 'Fort Sumter 1861 and New Orleans 1874'—local participants denied the connection."

The "reinvented tradition" was a whitewash of history. Just as the Civil War had never been about slavery, so was White League terrorism a feat of proportional justice. The neo-Confederate mentality used a bloody brush to paper over the realities of a multiracial city. "Creole came to be a term that applied exclusively to whites, the origins of New Orleans, singularly French, and the contributions of Africans negligible," continues Hunter.

George Washington Cable bucked the tide in "The Freedman's Case in Equity," a lengthy *Century Magazine* essay from January 1885. (The issue included an excerpt from his friend Mark Twain's *Huckleberry Finn*.) Cable argued that the South should provide "universal justice and equity" for the former slaves to build a better society. Appealing to Southern honor, Cable called for a color-blind legal system. "I have seen the two races sitting in the same public high school and grammar school rooms, reciting in the same classes, and taking recess on the same grounds," he wrote of the brief time of New Orleans desegregation, "although the fiercest enemies of the system swarmed about it on every side."

Cable was on a lecture tour with Twain when the article provoked an angry response, including editorials in the New Orleans press. The *Century* asked *Atlanta Constitution* editor Henry W. Grady to reply for the opposition. A champion of Northern investment in the South, Grady advocated white supremacy by peaceful means. But how could the law guarantee that? Cable's reply was so long that the editors waited several issues to publish "The Silent South." A defensive Cable, insisting that he had the tacit support of a large Southern audience, wrote paradoxically: "Social relations must not impose upon civil rights nor civil rights impose on social relations. We must have peace. But for peace to be stable we must have justice." As lynch mobs roamed, how could civil rights *not* impose on social relations? Still, Cable's voice was braver than most.

In New Orleans, a huge white-unity event happened by accident. Jefferson Davis, the eighty-one-year-old former president of the Confederacy, fell ill while visiting one of his plantations in Vicksburg. He hurried to New Orleans by steamer and died in a friend's Garden District home on December 6, 1889. As church bells tolled, federal offices lowered no flags for a man the Northern press deemed a traitor. Davis's two years in prison after the war mattered not to his base. White horses pulled the black hearse bearing the deceased to Gallier Hall, the Greek Revival temple downtown at Lafayette Square, its columns wreathed in ivy, the flowers shaped as guns and swords, the open coffin draped in a Confederate flag.

Had Davis died at home near Biloxi, New Orleans would have been another Southern city holding a major commemoration, rather than *the* stage for Lost Cause ascendancy. Thousands of Confederate veterans and partisans filled the hotels, ate at Antoine's and Tujague's, and attended the December 11 procession, greater than any Carnival event. For the South they marched—riflemen, military brass bands, forty-eight honorary pallbearers, fourteen former Confederate generals, eight Southern governors, "judges, justices, tax collectors, state engineers, members of the Board of Health, state senators and representatives, members of the Chamber of Commerce, Assistant Postmaster Henry Rensaw, Mayor Shakspeare, and other city officials." The Società Italiana del Tira al Bersiaglio and benevolent groups followed the caisson pulled by six black horses out to the cemetery in Metairie across the city line. Two years later, the Davis family held a reburial in Richmond.

"The Lost Cause had its icons, including pervasive images of Robert E. Lee, Jefferson Davis, and Stonewall Jackson," writes Charles Reagan Wilson. "Southerners were a Chosen People, but they were also a Tragic People," holding rituals to honor "a civil religion, which saw religious significance in the Confederate nationalist experience."

Reverend Benjamin Palmer, the city's preeminent Presbyterian pastor, had preached of the war as sacred cause, espousing slaveholders' paternal duty to a servile people. "Can a cause be lost which has passed through such a baptism as ours?" he asked years later. "Principles never die ... and if they seem to perish it is only to experience a resurrection in the future." The city would name a park and an Uptown avenue after Palmer.

As white supremacy in the 1890s purged African Americans from voting rolls, the new music pared down marching band parts in a tighter style for dancing in clubs and halls, letting the blues stream flow. The music soared as African Americans massed for funeral parades. Despite the prewar history of cops spying on black churches, a heavy-handed police department was wary of breaking up rituals for the dead with such large numbers of people.

Jazz was a merger of the sacred and profane, the mournful songs in pews distilled into dirges for marches by many of the musicians who at night played hot music with dancing syncopations on the sawdust-spattered floors of cabarets, some with bordello bedding upstairs.

African American funerals moved through the city's streets like a spiritual army, a coming together of the ring and the line. The circles of danced memory, from Congo Square into small churches, opened into second liners dancing behind the linear procession of musicians who were loosening the military spine of parades, blending blues into sacred harmonies of sorrow, and, after the burial, swinging out in counter-rhythm to the gyrations of people following the band.

The rhythm section of late nineteenth-century brass bands was the springboard for jazz rhythms fashioned into dance music on bandstands. As the memory line from slavery embraced more joyous hymns, like "By and By," "What A Friend We Have in Jesus," and "The Saints," funeral parades carried a message—*freedom rising*. African Americans dancing in the streets like a satirical chorus to the bands challenged white sensibilities. In 1890, New Lusitanos Benevolent Association (founded 1858, its membership French Creoles and wealthy Anglo-Americans) decided to hire carriages in lieu of a thirty-dollar band fee. Why ditch the band? With a society tomb in the Girod Street Cemetery, the New Lusitanos board faced "considerable opposition," noted the *Daily States*:

> Music is simply vainglorious ostentation, of no benefit to anybody. It is considered by many to be *a mockery because of the marked contrast between the tunes played before and after.* When the funeral cortege is slowly moving along the band plays a "Dead March" and at the grave gives the impressive bars of the hymn, "Nearer My God To Thee," but on returning from the cemetery it strikes up "Yankee Doodle" or "Little Annie Rooney." Thus showing very little respect for the memory of the dead.

Deriding "vainglorious ostentation" in a city of music that varied from the French Opera House to Carnival balls, parades, and Milneburg suggests a bitter editorialist (probably the bellicose editor, Henry James Hearsey).

If "Yankee Doodle" dishonored the dead, why not a song-change? By 1890, the tradition of white funerals with music faced African American street dancing as a threat to conformity. "Reform in Funerals" is the headline of a follow-up *Daily States* article on the move by "benevolent societies to abolish the custom of brass bands at funerals." Why halt the tradition for Italian, Spanish, German, French, and other burial societies whose members had marched in the Jefferson Davis funeral a year before? Claiming a need for more dignity, the article heaps blame on unseemly people.

> Five years from today the *hideous brass band* and long lines of vari dressed and tired men traveling through mud and slush at funerals will no longer be seen.
>
> There is room for reform in the method of attending and conducting funerals and in the dispensation of the brass band attachment to the funeral of every humble member of some obscure society or club or company.

The blame extends to "every humble member of some obscure society"— black folks. The more likely reason to propose ending this tradition, which dated at least to the 1789 funeral for Carlos III, lies in the "long lines of vari dressed and tired men"—meaning African Americans, changing the style of funeral parading in open view. Funerals for white groups did not halt overnight; but black street dancers and changes in the music meant open streets for all. An 1890 *Picayune* report on a Magazine Street parade, between the Garden District and Irish Channel, faulted "young white hoodlums" for

> a small-sized riot ... between a crowd of Negroes and whites, during which rocks, bricks and clubs were freely used, and several persons were slightly injured.... It appears that a colored procession headed by the Onward Brass Band was marching out Washington Street. They intended serenading a colored woman, Mrs. Johnson, mother of one of the members. The usual crowd of Negroes who follow up parades of this kind were on hand in force and took charge of the sidewalk as is their custom.

The "usual crowd of Negroes" signals that second liners following a band were not only a known reality but threatening in "their custom" of taking over a sidewalk. "A force of young white men ... pelted them with rocks ... a signal for a general battle on all sides."

Looking back in his later years on the street dancers of his youth, Louis Armstrong wrote: "Anybody can be a Second Liner, whether they are

Raggedy or dressed up.... They seem to have more fun than anybody. (They will start a free for all fight any minute—with broom handles, baseball bats, pistols, knives, razors, brickbats, etc.)" That pivot between having fun and fighting suggests a demand for open streets, no pushback from whites, even if the free-for-all erupts from an internal clash. The Masked Indian gangs—black men, parading in feather suits at Mardi Gras—advanced a chant line: *Don't bow down.* For descendants of slaves, parading stood for freedom. Armstrong recalled a baseball game in Algiers. When the Onward Brass Band playing "When the Saints Go Marching In" came along, the game halted and people "followed the parade ... Everybody were so busy "Swingin' + Dancing' they almost missed their ferry boat back to N.O."

Armstrong's verbal shift from violence to baseball-lovers leaving their seats to parade is a freeze frame on this tiny cosmos. The second liners' propensity to fight spotlights the memory of Congo Square dancers, in symbolic rebellion, vaulting across the decades to controlling the streets, if only for a few hours. Second liners fought for the same reasons other poor people fought. They were also breaking cultural boundaries with their unleashed body language.

The African American cultural stream gained momentum in the 1880s as their parading claimed a role and a place in city life. The Longshoreman's Protective Union Benevolent Association on its fifteenth anniversary marched nearly five miles in the heat of early summer 1887, "Erato to Carondelet, to Canal, north side of Canal to Camp to Calliope to Dryades, to Philip, to St. Denis, to St. Charles, to Louisiana Avenue to Tchoupitoulas to Upperline to Orange Grover [for] the installation and other exercises," reported the *Weekly Pelican.* The Onward Brass Band, carrying thirteen pieces, followed the grand marshals, while behind the band in carriages sat the president and secretary, followed by "a handsomely dressed and as well behaved a body of men as ever paraded the streets of the city."

The rise of black parading sent a signal of changing times to the established tradition. Jack Laine, born in 1873, was a pioneering white drummer who got his start in 1889 and led the Reliance, a band that put Irish, German, and Sicilian players into the mix. Laine claimed that burial parades for whites "ended at about the same time he went to play for the [World] Exposition in St. Louis, which was in 1904," reports jazz scholar Jack Stewart. Stewart contends that a "devastating blow" to the musical funerals for whites came with a 1903 declaration by Pope Pius X in a *moto proprio* (by his own hand) titled "On Sacred Music": "It is strictly forbidden for bands to play in church; and only in some special case, with the consent of the [bishop], will it be allowed to admit a limited choice of wind instruments, provided the composition and accompaniment to be executed be written in a grave, fitting style and entirely similar to that proper to the organ."

The pope wanted the faithful more deeply involved in sacred music, particularly Gregorian chant, rather than in music as entertainment. As Catholic churches fell into line, black Creole musicians from Catholic families played funerals in other churches as the burial tradition spread. Nevertheless, the Holy Ghost parish in the central city sponsored a brass band in the 1920s. "We played up there where the organ sits, played the hymns for religious concerts," recalled alto saxophonist Harold "Duke" Dejan, future leader of the Olympia Brass Band.

Sicilians in the Meld

Jazz flowered in a melting pot thickened by the arrival of 69,937 Italians, mostly from Sicily, at the Port of New Orleans between 1898 and 1929. Unified only in 1861, Italy was still a predominantly agricultural country. The island of Sicily in the south, a peasant society beleaguered by crop disease, deforestation, and criminal overlords, generated a huge diaspora. As African Americans left plantation towns for the city, Louisiana planters sent agents to entice Sicilians with farm jobs. New Orleans by 1900 had 21,000 Italians among its 287,104 inhabitants, and 90,000 blacks. Within nine years, the number of Italians doubled. A culture of close families, loyal to the Church and one another, gave birth to a Sicilian ghetto in the Vieux Carré backstreets.

By 1912, at least a dozen pasta factories were operating in the oldest neighborhood. The melding of seafood and pasta dishes enlivened Creole cuisine, an ever-adaptive foodway spread by the popularity of Tujague's on Decatur Street and Uptown restaurants like Pascal Manale's on the corner of Napoleon Avenue and Dryades Street.

Sicilian families settled in the Seventh Ward, Back o' Town, and Tremé, where the flamboyant singer-bandleader Louis Prima, born in 1910, grew up near Paul Barbarin's childhood home. "The smells of the food and sounds of the music wafted across shared porches and balconies," writes Anna Harwell Celenza. St. Mary Parish, on Decatur Street, built on the site of the earliest Ursuline convent, held Sicilian holy day processions. On St. Joseph's Day (March 19), families lined the altar with decorated baskets of oranges, ham, sugarcane, yams, and fragrant sweets soon distributed to the needy. On the same night, another tradition arose, Masking Indians, blacks in many-feathered costumes, parading along backstreets with thrumming tambourines and bravura chants.

Irish and German ward bosses of the Ring, a Democratic machine, recruited Sicilian dockworkers. The Ring turned the police into a patronage hive, with heavy-handed tactics toward African Americans, yet also causing private citizens who could afford it to hire private patrols. City governance crawled along like a skeletal sailor searching for a fruited plain. Instead of electrified trolley lines, mules pulled streetcars; antique gas lamps lit muddy streets that needed paving; stench rose from gutters; the port needed capital improvements. The big money, concentrated Uptown, and around long enough to be considered old, recoiled from higher taxes in a city hobbled by corruption. As French Creoles clung to dreams of grandeur, bordellos and concert saloons sprouted in their beloved Vieux Carré. High-kicking women wore body stockings and "in some cases," writes Alecia P. Long, "actually simulated sexual acts onstage or in backlit silhouettes." For undereducated women, black and white, facing poor pay as maids or factory workers, sex work paid.

In 1888, the patrician-backed Young Men's Democratic Association (YMDA) fielded a slate against the Ring. Declaring war on corruption, the YMDA put armed men at the polls, helping elect Joseph A. Shakspeare as mayor. Hostile to blacks and migrants, shaped by a Southern idea of Christianity that equated status with virtue, the YMDA wanted control. Shakspeare in a previous term had reduced city debt by selling rights for the Carrollton Railroad. For police chief, he chose David C. Hennessy, thirty years old and ruggedly handsome, with a handlebar mustache. "Brothel and casino operators had paid protection money to the Ring," writes Justin A. Nystrom. "Shakspeare placed Hennessy in charge of collecting these taxes" on vice.

Hennessy's family had fled Ireland in the 1840s famine. His father, a policeman, was killed in a bar fight; Hennessy at twelve started work as a police messenger. In 1881, as a young detective, he made headlines for arresting a Mafioso seeking seclusion in Louisiana; the mobster was soon deported to Italy. Hennessy lost his job after shooting to death a rival detective; a jury later cleared him on grounds of self-defense. Working as a private detective in the meantime, Hennessy befriended the three Provenzano brothers, who controlled dockworkers unloading fruit. He was pals with Tom Anderson, a card player angling for a stake in the saloon business. Hennessy, Anderson, and the Provenzanos belonged to the Red Light Social Club, its name an jaded satire of the elite Boston and Pickwick Clubs. "It ill becomes the head of the police force to be so mixed up with an organization," fumed *The Mascot*, "the members of which expect and do profit by their connection with the public women of the town."

In the shadowland between cops and criminals, Hennessy never faced allegations of bribery or links to prostitution. At the Red Light Club he rubbed elbows with Joseph Macheca. An adopted son of the Maltese founder of the Macheca steamship company, Joe as a twenty-four-year-old in 1868 led the Innocents, a white-caped gang that tried to undermine Grant's presidential campaign in Louisiana by assaulting blacks and "reputedly left a trail of bodies behind them every time they paraded," writes Tom Smith in *The Crescent City Lynchings*. In 1874, Macheca fought for the White League. A partner in Macheca Brothers, a fruit-importing business, he was by 1890 a mustachioed widower who sported "a large diamond stickpin in his cravat and lived with five of his six grown children on Bourbon Street."

Many Sicilians relied on a transplanted system of *padroni*, men who "found jobs for immigrants," notes a history of Louisiana Italians.

> They may have, on their own or with financial backing by employers, prepaid the immigrants' passage, found the laborers their jobs, collected their wages, written their letters, acted as their bankers, provided them with room and board, and served as their go-between in dealing with employers. Upon their arrival in the United States, the largely illiterate, non-English speaking immigrants were initially so dependent on the *padroni* they were easy prey for those among them who were unscrupulous. ... Often the employer would pay the *padrone* instead of the worker.

Even after breadwinners secured some autonomy, the *padrone* as a job boss held great power. In the mid-1880s, a rival clan, the Matrangas, undercut Provenzano control, leaving workers hostile over lower pay. Sicilians with close families and a strong work ethic were restitching folkways of village life. The African American idiom forged of blues and church song attracted young Sicilians to a common terrain, as Bruce Boyd Raeburn has written, a sound that beckoned Jews, Irish, Germans, and others to the instrumental voices improvising.

Democratic-Conservative politicians insured that laws to purge African American voters protected Sicilians, who represented ballots to control. A tough man for a tough town, Hennessy brought the Matrangas and Provenzanos to the table for talks at the Red Light Club.

On March 5, 1890, two Matranga brothers and five workers were ambushed after work. Two Provenzano brothers and four men close to them were arrested, tried, and convicted; but as they sat in prison, a pair of Ring-allied defense lawyers delivered ten affidavits to the court from police officers, reporters, and residents near the crime scene, questioning whether the ambushed men had lied under oath in saying that they had seen the faces of the shooters. The judge reviewed the information, inspected the crime scene, vacated the verdict, and ordered a new trial. Hennessy, who helped prosecute the Provenzanos, reversed course and began investigating the Matrangas for criminal ties to Italy.

On the night of October 15, 1890, Hennessy was walking home when he went down in a fusillade of shotguns; he managed to return fire but was severely wounded when police arrived, along with his friend Billy O'Connor, a private detective. "Who gave it to you, Dave?" he said. "Dagos," whispered Hennessy. Taken to Charity Hospital, the chief greeted well-wishers until his body failed. He identified no shooter.

Hennessy's assassination hit New Orleans like a bomb. The word *mafia* first surfaced in the local press. Appalled patricians found in Henry James Hearsey, the hard-drinking editor of the *Daily States*, a Lost Cause champion itching for a fight. "Florid-faced and goateed," wrote William Ivy Hair, "he seemed like an out-of-date burlesque of Southern manners. Yet his ability to mold public opinion was no laughing matter." With the pivotal witness dead, Hearsey called for war: "No community can exist with murder associations in their midst. These associations must perish or the community itself must perish."

Ten months after the majestic Jefferson Davis funeral, the march for Hennessy passed sullen people in a drizzle to a low, thudding drumbeat. A black horse, riderless, pranced before two carriages of priests; then came the casket escorted by teams of police with white crepe armbands, followed by dozens of carriages with detectives and their families, African American civic leaders, lawyers, judges, sheriffs, court employees, and the Democratic Party kingpin James D. Houston, who had been acquitted in the shooting death of the man who killed Hennessy's father. People in the rain watched policemen carry the coffin up the stairs beneath the Greek Revival pillars to lie in state at Gallier Hall. After Mass, the line of dignitaries and organizations had little of the elegiac glory surrounding Jefferson Davis as history's lion. Hostility toward Sicilians seethed during the dragnet that sought to catch Hennessy's killer.

At two in the morning after Hennessy's death, Joe Macheca with a clutch of drunken Italian pals showed up at Fanny Decker's Burgundy Street bordello. Decker gave them a parlor and as the bill ran up on wine, the madam made cathouse chitchat, saying what a shame it was about Dave. "Yes," replied Macheca, plastered. "These are all Dave's enemies." A courtesan recalled Macheca muttering, "I'm glad he's shot."

Macheca was not among the four men in custody when Shakspeare denounced "despicable assassins. . . . The wretches who committed this foul deed are the mere hirelings and instruments of others higher and more powerful than they." He called for a committee to investigate secret Italian societies. An alderman advocated the "total annihilation of such hell-born associations." The police sweep continued, arresting members of the Provenzano and Matranga clans, as well as Joe Macheca.

Heeding the mayor, the Committee of Fifty formed with core members from the Boston and Pickwick Clubs; they were in a quandary of their own making. The entire legal apparatus had washed its hands of White League vigilantism by certain committeemen. What *was* justice? With reports that the detective Dominic O'Malley (who got his start as a snitch for Internal Revenue agents) was working for the defense, the Olympian committee wrote to demand that he withdraw from "the Italian vendetta cases, either personally or through your employees . . . [and] keep away from the Parish Prison, the Criminal District Court and the recorder's courts while these cases are on trial or under investigation." O'Malley scoffed in reply.

The Provenzanos were acquitted at trial.

As blame turned to the Matrangas, the committee raised funds to bolster the city investigation. February 1892 saw nineteen Sicilians indicted, including fruit sellers, a shoemaker, peddlers, Macheca, and Charles Matranga. For such a trial today, the judge would surely order a change of venue owing to overheated press coverage. The district attorney secured an order to hold two trials for so many defendants. As the trial began for nine men, Hearsey thundered in the *Daily States*: "The vendetta—the highest law of their own lands—is in most instances the only thing [Sicilians] bring with them to the country of their adoption. . . . To the ward boss then this lot of cattle becomes very valuable."

Trial transcripts have not survived. "The evidence presented in court was extremely feeble to judge from newspaper accounts," writes James Gill. Defense lawyers presented alibis to cast reasonable doubt. Fanny Decker's testimony about Macheca's nocturnal visit offered no smoking gun. Macheca, Matranga, and four others were acquitted; on the three other men, jurors split: a mistrial. With a separate charge pending, of "laying in wait," all nine went back to the prison shadowing Congo Square, the major defendants anticipating a swift release with appeals on the thin remaining charge after their acquittal on others.

"Rise in your might, people of New Orleans!" roared the *Daily States*, charging that jurors had been bribed. No such fact emerged; the prosecution had relied on an inept investigation. On March 14, 1891, 8,000 people massed at a midmorning rally at the Henry Clay statue on the Canal Street median, including Committee of Fifty leaders. "Talk is idle!" declared William Parkerson, who had been Shakspeare's campaign manager. "*Action* must be the thing now!"

"The law has proven a farce and mockery," cried Walter Denegre, a future Rex. "Not since the 14th day of September, 1874, have we seen such a determined looking set of men," he declared in reference to the White League insurrection. He accused the detective O'Malley of bribing jury members. Lawyer-journalist John Curd Wickcliffe rose to add, "Within the walls of the parish prison are confined a number of men declared innocent by a jury of the murder of Chief Hennessy. Are those men to go *free*?"

As the gun-wielding mob followed them up Canal Street toward the prison, the Italian consul, Pascal Corte, pleaded in vain with Governor Nicholls and Shakspeare to intervene. The mob poured into the prison like lava down a volcano. Guards scattered, leaving open passageways for the Sicilians to seek hiding elsewhere in prison. The warden pleaded with the mob not to fire at will. Macheca clubbed through an interior gate before the bullet hit his head. Eight other Sicilians were shot or beaten to death; the mob hung two men outside. Matranga escaped violence, Parkerson, who accepted Matranga's acquittal, quelling the attackers. Eleven men were slaughtered.

White newspapers defended the lynchings; the city Stock Exchange and Board of Trade passed approving resolutions. No one was indicted. The district attorney refused to indict O'Malley for jury tampering. Italy recalled its ambassador. The U.S. government eventually paid $24,330 in reparations to the families of three men who had held Italian citizenship.

Three of the dead were quietly buried in a potter's field. Another, after a discrete service at the home, entered the Tiro al Bersaglio tomb in Metairie Cemetery. People were afraid. In contrast, as Tom Smith writes, the St. Louis Cathedral service for Joseph Macheca and his friend Jim Caruso had "the grand choir sing for their families." Caruso's brother sobbed on the dead man's chest. Macheca's fellow volunteers in Pelican Fire Company No. 4 avoided the church, presumably in fear. Among the pallbearers, Judge Anthony Sambola "helped carry Macheca's gold-and-silver trimmed coffin to a St. Louis Cemetery Number 1 crypt, mulling over the fact that potential jurors who had claimed to oppose capital punishment and were thus excused from sitting in judgment upon Macheca were among those who killed him."

Five and a half months after the massacre, on September 1, 1891, White League veterans, including Shakspeare and Committee of Fifty members, gathered at the Canal Street statue of Henry Clay for the installation of an obelisk, honoring the 1874 "Battle of Liberty Place." U.S. senator Benjamin F. Jonas, a Confederate veteran, said that the 1874 uprising "had no relation to the war of secession." Nor indeed, to the massacre of Sicilians. But the linkage in vigilante rule is clear.

The fantasy of democratic governance fell in line with the Lost Cause mythology, the idea that men of high social rank would intervene when the legal system faltered, using force as necessary. Justice as an objective standard was a dream that would take decades to realize.

Cultures rely on storytelling, art, and ritual drama to form an identity, a bridge between memory and hope. Sicily had a funeral band tradition; but in traumatic aftershocks to the 1891 massacre, the cultural memory surfaced not in burial pageants but in a tunneling process that found light for Italian musicians in healthy numbers, playing in Jack Laine's and other brass bands, while ragtime spread across map-of-the-world neighborhoods. George Paoletti, born in 1867, a cornetist at the French Opera House, was long associated with the Società Italiana del Tiro al Bersaglio, a burial society that doubled as a gun and hunting club. As syncopated rags seasoned the fin de siècle city, German bands marched in the Irish Channel, and Sicilian and Jewish musicians absorbed black polyrhythms. Jazz, an African American idiom, seeped into enclaves "much older than the segregation laws of the 1890s," writes Bruce Boyd Raeburn. Legislation that restricted black seating in streetcars barred neighbors from sitting together. "What united people of diverse backgrounds within these neighborhoods was the vernacular cultural identity that defined their social lives and festival traditions ... in language, foodways and music." Raeburn adds:

Many of these Italian-American musicians were stalwarts of the Reliance bands, including Lawrence Veca (cornet), brothers Manuel and Leonce Mello (cornet and trombone), Nick LaRocca (cornet), Anthony Sbarbaro (drums), Vincent and Joe Barocco (alto horn and tuba, but not related), Manuel Belasco (baritone horn), as well as Johnny Lala (cornet), Tony Schiro (Luke's older brother, guitar), Arnold "Deacon" Loyacano (piano, bass, tuba, guitar, and drums), and his brothers John "Bud" (bass and tuba) and Joe "Hook" Loyacano (trombone, bass and tuba).

As exchanges in music and cooking bubbled through the melting pot, the state's Separate Car Act spurred eighteen black Creoles, the Comité des Citoyens, into action. Their meetings began in 1890 at the office of the *Crusader*, attorney Louis Martinet's paper that called down injustice. Martinet had been a school board member in the window of desegregation during the 1870s. Lawyer, poet, and *Crusader* contributor Rodolphe Desdunes was a Custom House clerk. C. C. Antoine had served a term as lieutenant governor. Most of the committee members lived within walking distance of one another in the Vieux Carré, Marigny, or Tremé, mixed-race men "fluent in French and English, Roman Catholic, professional rather than laboring," writes Keith Weldon Medley. Once privileged *gens de couleur libres*, they realized that "even one drop of African heritage could instantly place one in a permanent and irrevocable state of second-class citizenship."

Homer Plessy, a shoemaker and clerk, agreed to be the plaintiff in testing the car law, which the railroad company considered a barrier to commerce. The Comité recruited Albion W. Tourgée, an Ohio native, Union veteran, former judge, and crusading novelist for the inevitable appeal. After boarding a city train bound for Covington across Lake Pontchartrain, Plessy refused to give up his seat and was escorted off the train. The lawsuit argued that his equal rights protection, under the Fourteenth Amendment, had been violated. New Orleans judge John H. Ferguson dismissed the suit. Tourgée guided *Plessy v. Ferguson* up the appellate ladder. His Supreme Court brief was eloquent: "Justice is pictured blind and her daughter, the Law, ought at least to be color-blind." In 1896, however, the high court signaled a Northern mood in washing its hands of Southern racial issues, ruling eight to one in *Plessy v. Ferguson* for the state. The famous dissent by Justice John Marshall Harlan, a former Kentucky slaveholder jolted by Reconstruction lawlessness, is among the most oft-quoted statements in U.S. legal history. "Our Constitution is color-blind, and neither knows nor tolerates classes among citizens," wrote Harlan, echoing Tourgée. "The law regards man as man, and takes no account of his surroundings or of his color when his civil rights as guaranteed by the supreme law of the land are involved."

Harlan's idealistic dissent hardly softened the cut to Plessy and his allies. The *Crusader* closed two years later; the Comité dispersed. In *Our People and Our History*, Desdunes, the man of letters, was rueful: "Our defeat sanctioned the odious principle of *segregation of the races*."

As Ring bosses greased police, the aristocracy disdained the riffraff and reveled in Carnival. The city of music with its rainbow of peoples became a winter vacation spot. Fine restaurants, Old World ambience, and Mardi Gras, magnified by Rex (a king!), formed a patina to cover the racial paranoia. "This quaint and sunny old city, lying half asleep, blinking, as it were, under her luminous skies, luxuriously lounging on the elbow of the great yellow river," rhapsodized *The 1897 Picayune's Guide to the City of New Orleans*, beckoning suitors. "Her very name is a souvenir of gayeties; her breath is as sweet as a willow copse in June, and something about her always makes one think of the opera and the 'bal masque,' the carnival, the palm-leaf fan, the omelette souffle and the rose."

The souvenir of gayeties had dozens of real women selling time in their bodies. Prostitution was rampant in many late nineteenth-century American cities. French Quarter residents and business owners railed against low-rent cribs and bawdy saloons, a sign of decay in the Vieux Carré since the seat of government had vacated the Cabildo in the 1850s for Gallier Hall, across Canal Street. Thus, in 1897, a patrician alderman, Sidney Story, pushed an ordinance that made it unlawful for "any prostitute or woman notoriously abandoned to lewdness" to function outside a sixteen-square block area in lower Tremé. The city did not legalize prostitution but rather clustered it with a wink and legal yawn in order to protect property values and smoother society in other parts of town. The "District"—bordered by Basin, Customhouse, Robertson, and St. Louis Streets—stood across the Basin canal from Congo Square and the site of Parish Prison, which the city had demolished in 1895. Lumber merchant George L'Hote and the black Union Chapel Methodist Episcopal Church, who were neighbors, sued the city to halt the ordinance; they failed.

Embedded with the Ring, Tom Anderson moved fast, buying property in the District. Anderson's Annex stood opposite the Basin Street depot, where men stepped off the train to free copies of the *Blue Book*, a pamphlet whose title satirized the social register, promoting opulent bordellos with ads for perfume, apparel, soap, liquor, and antidotes to venereal disease. The District, writes Alecia P. Long, was "one of the few places in turn-of-the-century New Orleans where men and women of all classes, races and ethnicities mingled so intimately, casually and continuously in the pursuit of sex and leisure activity."

Mansions on Basin Street built before the District was concocted became bordellos catering to rich white men. Josie Arlington and Hilma Burt, big-ticket madams, bought *Blue Book* ads "that depict the fussy, over-decorated domestic interiors typical of middle and upper middle class late Victo-

Sicilians in the Meld

rian houses—except few residences contained mirrored ballrooms," notes Pamela D. Arcenaux. Mayor Paul Capdeville, backed by the Ring, shared an agenda with blue-blood Democrats who wanted vice segregated, out of sight, out of mind; Ring potentates rubbed their palms, moist for cash to come. As cops forced hookers into the District, property values soared in "Storyville," a name Story detested. Money rolled in liquor sales and a carousel of jobs, like B-girls paid for how many drinks they sold. "You think, it is pretty low in weaning a dollar bill out of some fellow who thinks he knows it all," a table girl told an *Item* reporter. "But, what we get don't pay us for the stabs at the heart . . . the beasts we meet. And the money comes to us cleaner than it does to a lot of the people in this town who bark at us a lot."

Black musicians gained venues amid the brawls, petty crime, and occasional homicide. White women held a slight majority in the fast trade. Anderson, as power broker and the District's de facto mayor, served sixteen years in the legislature. Storyville resurrected the city's French image as "the devil's empire" and its antebellum reputation as the Great Southern Babylon (which vied with its identity as "Queen City of the South"). Segregation laws, openly disdained in *Blue Book* ads, designated certain houses with an O, for octoroon, a woman one-eighth black. "Storyville served a fantasy of the Old South patriarchy, mimicking the slave pens of antebellum times," writes Emily Epstein Landau. Women "entertained and flirted in the parlors downstairs but their real business was upstairs." Octoroons harked back to "fancy girls" sold as slaves, the bordello providing "absolute power over another human being—if only for an evening." Countess Willie Piazza, proprietress of one of the larger mansions, advertised "the most handsome and intelligent octoroons. You should see them, they are all entertainers."

Lulu White, the "Octoroon Queen," ran Mahogany Hall, four stories, thick with marble. "The girls would come down dressed in the finest of evening gowns, just like they were going to the opera," recalled the pianist Clarence Williams, a future song publisher. Piano players unfurled rags and slow blues as soundtrack for the bodies bouncing in beds in private rooms. The piano professor's base pay, a dollar a night, mushroomed to fifty or sixty bucks in tips.

"One thing that always puzzled me was that the prostitutes from the District would go to church and take flowers to put on the altar," the trumpeter Lee Collins recalled. "Maybe they had not altogether forgot the way they were brought up. Some of the girls that worked in the District came from fine old Creole families. Lots of them never went back again."

Ferdinand LaMothe was about seventeen when he began playing piano at Mahogany Hall in 1902. His mother had died, he detested the stepfather, and despite his closeness to grandmothers and an aunt, the musical prodigy felt the gravitational pull to another world. With training on several instruments, and an early interest in opera, his style was a sponge for the blues. Playing "Hot Time in the Old Town Tonight" his first night in a tenderloin bar brought a rainfall of bills from the hothouse flowers. Evicted by his Catholic grandmother for spending time in the District, he plunged into the demimonde. To avoid being called "Frenchy," he renamed himself Jelly Roll Morton; the female anatomical allusion tracked another nickname, Winding Boy, slang for a winder, a long-distance body-soother between the sheets. In discovering his artistic reach, Jelly imbued Scott Joplin standards like "Maple Leaf Rag" with shifting melodic colors, developing a stylistic attack as if his fingers contained an orchestra.

"Champagne flowed more than water," he wrote in a 1938 letter, recalling the mansions, and women "bedecked with diamonds from their waistline to their head, the sparkling gems sometimes found their way to the shoes for buckles and garters of the lavish, big hearted free spending madams." Jelly sported a front tooth capped by a gold crown and a half-carat diamond. Never short on braggadocio, he told Alan Lomax years later that he invented jazz in 1902.

Among those Jelly met, Joe Oliver was a sensation on cornet. A minister's son who played in the Onward Brass Band for funerals and the second-line clubs, he galvanized District cabarets with melodic embellishments to thrill the working girls who partied late with pimps and bottom-feeders. Louis Armstrong recalled, as a boy, carting coal to the shack of a prostitute near Pete Lala's club: "I'd just stand there in that lady's crib listening to King Oliver. And I'm all in a daze."

As Storyville harvested improvisations of ragtime and blues, the African American identity-narrative branched out. Funeral pageants fashioned a march of the Saints, declaring that life mattered regardless of the deceased's social rung. "Most of the funerals I used to play were for the gamblers and hustlers," recalled Kid Ory. "They used to support my dances, and when a friend would die—they wouldn't give him a dollar when he was hungry, but they would put up five dollars to bury him. The biggest funeral I played was for a boy named Kirk ... the hottest pimp in Storyville. Diamonds in his garters and all over his mouth. So many people came out, you would think it was the President of the United States that was dead. We had three bands that day. When you had three bands, you were in big business."

With a nod to the District, second liners embraced an up-tempo anthem for a soul cut loose, "Didn't He Ramble." Spawned as a British drinking ditty about a bounding ram, the tune carried across the Atlantic and down the Mississippi, the bands replacing the ram with a hustler who could have been a casualty in Storyville.

> His feet was in the market
> His head was in the street
> A lady come passing by,
> Said, "Look at the market meat!"
> Oh, didn't he ram-ble?
> Oh, didn't he ram-ble?
> Rammm-bulllll
> He rambled all around
> In and out of the town
> He rambled till the butcher cut him down

· · · · · · · · · ·

ROBERT CHARLES

The image of a man cut down by a butcher was real enough in the tough port city, particularly after the blood storm surrounding Robert Charles. Born in 1865 in Mississippi, Charles grew up in a sharecropping family. During the 1883 elections, marauding whites bent on keeping blacks from voting forced his family to hide in the Copiah County woods. Several years later, after an altercation with a white railroad flagman in which each shot at the other but neither was wounded, he left Mississippi, knowing his days there would be numbered.

Charles had strong political convictions. In New Orleans, working as a day laborer, he canvassed for the International Migration Society, a group seeking blacks who wished to leave for Africa. He put down money for a ticket to Liberia just after Louisiana's 1896 election, in which white-supremacist Democrats regained power. The 1898 state constitution furthered a purge of African American voters.

In the midsummer of 1900, unemployed and on the edge, Charles was sharing a room with another man in Back o' Town, not far from Buddy Bolden's home. One night they were sitting outside a house on Dryades Street when three black women, suspicious of them, alerted police. Police officers arrived, demanding to know what they were doing. Tensions flared. Patrolman August T. Mora went after Charles with a billy club, Charles pulled a pistol and shot him in the hip. Mora returned fire, Charles fled with a wound to the thigh. "The only evidence that Charles was a desperate man lay in the fact that he had refused to be beaten over the head by Officer Mora," the black journalist Ida B. Wells-Barnett, author of *On Lynching*, wrote from Chicago, in a polemical narrative citing local press accounts. "Charles resisted an absolutely unlawful attack, and a gun fight followed."

The police took his roommate, Lenard Pierce, into custody. Pierce co-operated. Shooting a cop was sure to bring more after Charles. Why didn't he leave town? At three in the morning on July 24, a police wagon pulled up at the yard outside his room. "Open up in there!" rang the voice of a captain, approaching with two officers. Nudging the door open, Charles stood in darkness and shot Capt. John T. Day in the chest with a rifle. In a bewildering moment for police unused to black men firing on them, the two cops froze. Charles put several bullets into the dead captain and shot another policeman in the head. The third one fled. The police wagon retreated to call for reinforcements.

When the sun rose Charles was gone. "Hundreds of policemen were about; each corner was guarded by a squad, commanded either by a sergeant or a corporal, and every man had the word to shoot the Negro as soon as he was sighted," reported the *Picayune*. "He was a desperate black and would be given no chance to take more life."

After ransacking his room, the police launched a manhunt, stopping streetcars and ferry boats and going house-to-house. Race-baiting editorials by Hearsey in the *Times Democrat* whipped up furor to match the public fear. "A mob of some two thousand whites formed in Lee Circle, at the foot of the towering monument to the Confederate general," writes Gary Krist. It was a "scene hauntingly reminiscent" of the rally after "the Hennessy acquittals just nine years earlier." Speakers urged them to fight, "to save the good name of New Orleans by punishing a black population that was clearly sheltering the murderous fiend in their midst." The mob rampaged across Canal Street and tore through Storyville, causing musicians and anyone black to run for their lives. Buddy Bolden left his watch hanging on a bandstand wall and escaped through a back alley with two musicians, spending the night in a friend's house. Three African Americans were murdered by the mob and six were critically wounded. Several whites were shot and beaten in the mayhem. The following night, with a volunteer special police contingent fanning out at the mayor's behest, the mob retreated, after two more blacks were killed and fifteen wounded. "The fact that colored men and women had been made the victims of brutal mobs, chased through the streets, killed upon the highways and butchered in their homes, did not call the best element in New Orleans to active exertion in behalf of law and order," wrote Ida B. Wells-Barnett, outraged in Chicago.

As the violence raged, Robert Charles waited in the empty annex of a

Central City apartment about a mile from his own. When the police came, Charles hid in a closet. A sergeant approached a water bucket outside the door. Charles shot him in the chest, and hit a corporal just behind him, raising to four the number of police he had killed. Trundling up to a second-floor room, he bashed through a wall to an adjacent flat in the wooden duplex. Police called for more men; white vigilantes crowded into the tenement courtyard. From his upper window, Charles killed a nineteen-year-old man, an onlooker. The crowd swelled to several thousand; men with guns on rooftops began firing at Charles's perch. Charles kept shooting, wounding nineteen people. A police captain had an old mattress doused with kerosene and tossed on the stairwell. As Charles paced upstairs, darting and shooting, the smoke drove him out. A medical student hit him with the first shot followed by a volley from other guns; men dumped the body on the stoop, shooting it over and over in a release of fury. The mob roared through city streets, killing two bystanders and burning down the Lafon School, founded by the colored Creole philanthropist Thomy Lafon.

"In the frenzy of the moment, when nearly a dozen men lay dead, the victims of his unerring and death-dealing aim, it was natural for a prejudiced press and for citizens in private life to denounce him as a desperado and a murderer," wrote Wells-Barnett. "But sea depths are not measured when the ocean rages, nor can absolute justice be determined while public opinion is lashed into fury." Citing the trunk of books found in his room, copies of *Voice of Missions* (the paper for the society for African repatriation), and letters she received from people who knew him, the black journalist challenged the "desperado" image. "His work for many years had been with Christian people, circulating emigration pamphlets and active as agent for a mission publication. Men who knew him say that he was a law-abiding, quiet, industrious, peaceable man. So he lived and so he would have died had not he raised his hand to resent unprovoked assault and unlawful arrest that fateful Monday night. That made him an outlaw, and being a man of courage he decided to die with his face to the foe."

In calling him "the hero of New Orleans," Wells-Barnett was speculative, casting Charles as a one-man backlash against the widespread lynchings which she cites. Yet it is reasonable to assume that despite the crushing loss of life from the riots, any number of African Americans admired Charles for fighting back. Jelly Roll Morton, who lived near Charles's place, told Alan Lomax in 1938, "They had a song out on Robert Charles, like many other songs and like many other, er, bad men that always had some kind of a song and somebody originated it on 'em. But this song was squashed very easily by the [police] department. And not only by the department, by any of the surrounding people that ever heard the song. Due to the fact that it was a trouble breeder and it never did get very far. I used to know the song, but I found it was best for me to forget it. And that I did, in order to go along with the world on the peaceful side."

. . . .

BOLDEN'S DENOUEMENT

Buddy Bolden lost out in 1906. At twenty-eight, the hard-drinking musical pioneer began having psychotic episodes that frightened his wife and family. On March 23, after a bed-ridden weekend, he thought his mother-in-law was lurking with a lethal drug; he smashed her in the head with a water pitcher and got hauled in by police at the family's request, until he regained some normalcy. He grew so erratic that trombonist Frankie Duson seized control of his group, renamed it the Eagle Band, and told him, "We don't need you anymore." Nevertheless, Bolden went out in a 1906 Labor Day parade with bands for the colored societies, in carriages and floats before a reviewing stand of city council members, an acknowledgment of the culture in some fashion. In ninety-degree heat that day Bolden peeled out of the parade, fogged in confusion, and watched the bands march on.

On March 13, 1907, his mother had him booked for an eruption a third time, at the local precinct. An April 4 coroner's report on Charles Bolden, at the House of Detention, noted, "CAUSE OF INSANITY: Alcohol." Enough stories of his boozing suggest Bolden was an alcoholic; but the wild delusional swings point to a deeper source. On June 5, 1907, with his family's consent, the music pioneer, twenty-nine, went to a state asylum in rural Jackson, Louisiana, thirty-four miles above Baton Rouge, never to return. A 1925 psychiatric evaluation states, "Paranoid delusions, also grandiose. Auditory hallucinations and visual. . . . Picks things off the wall. Tears his clothes." The diagnosis, "dementia praecox, paranoid type," is akin to paranoid schizophrenia today.

In 1926, a physician wrote his mother: "He continues to get along nicely. While on the ward he insists on going about touching each post, and is not satisfied until he has accomplished this at least once." What did the posts mean? Was the routine of touching them a ritual of remembering who he once had been? He died on November 4, 1931, at fifty-four. The pine-box coffin came back for burial at Holt Cemetery, the city's poorest graveyard, where Robert Charles had been buried in 1900. Bolden's resting place had no headstone either, or musicians playing dirges. Buddy Bolden is a tragic figure, the blazing star of a new art form and culture rising, cut down by mental demons in his prime.

· · · · · · · · · ·

THE DIASPORA AND THE STORY

The city became a healthier place in 1909 with completion of the sewerage system, four years after the last yellow fever epidemic. The music rolled on like a sweet river through colored dancehalls, society picnics, Milneburg pavilions, church parades, funerals, Storyville, and varied white venues that provided gigs to Sicilian, Jewish, and Irish musicians, too. African American bands played often for white events, but segregation laws meant that musicians rarely played in mixed ensembles. "None of the white bands ever had a really good rhythm section," the cornetist Johnny Wiggs opined to the early jazz chronicler Bill Russell. "A colored New Orleans rhythm section sounds like a great big basket of cotton, so soft and caressing, so liquid, yet it still can whip people up into a frenzy.... When you hear it, grab it. It makes you want to dance and get your horn out and play."

The year after Bolden left, Kid Ory rose with entrepreneurial flair and cut out the middle-man in renting dancehalls for concerts; his bands played on wagons advertising the events. Ory helped move "jass" into a developmental phase, sharpening the focus of the ensemble style as musicians distinguished between "ragtime," with its tied-to-the-beat structure, and "hot" or "ratty" blues-pulsed improvisations.

An astonishing range of talent gathered in the city's crossroads of humanity, a Creole culture of adaptive folkways that seeded culinary and art traditions, too. As Canal Street became a marquee thoroughfare and Uptown streets featured handsome gardens, the governing mentality shrugged at poverty, providing a single public high school for all the blacks in New Orleans who did not attend Catholic school. Some bandleaders earned a living at music; most musicians had day jobs. But careers in entertainment led down a dead-end street. They began leaving, dozens of musicians, well into the 1930s.

Jelly Roll Morton was among the earliest to leave, in 1907, passing through Harlem, St. Louis, Los Angeles, and then Chicago. When gigs ran slack, he hustled as a pimp, pool shark, and bouncer. In the 1920s, Jelly surged as a composer and recording artist as jazz swept Chicago. His band, the Red Hot Peppers, had Crescent City transplants: banjoist Johnny St. Cyr, clarinetist Johnny Dodds, brother Baby Dodds on drums, Ory on trombone, and clarinetist Omar Simeon. They made gems like "Dead Man Blues," "Black Bottom Stomp," "King Porter Stomp," and a grand mosaic, "Jungle Blues." Like a symphonic conductor, Morton blended each instrument as an improvisational voice, his strong left hand layering in "the Spanish Tinge," giving shape to New Orleans Style.

"Nothing so rhythmically free had ever been heard on a piano," write Morton's biographers, Howard Reich and William Grimes. "With the completion of 'New Orleans Blues,' the flood gates opened. . . . Morton began creating (though not writing) compositions that bristled with dual themes played at once, harmonies of extraordinary richness and passing dissonance, and rhythms that surged forward with a ferocity that foreshadowed the swing era to come."

In 1908, Louis Armstrong gravitated to the South Rampart Street home of the Karnofsky family, Lithuanian Jews who worked as peddlers. Working on their coal cart, sharing family meals, absorbing lessons (to say "this" instead of "dis," etc.), he borrowed five dollars to buy his first cornet; he was seven. Armstrong praised the Karnofskys lavishly in a late-life essay, stating, "If it wasn't for the nice *Jewish* people we would have starved many a time. I will love the *Jewish* people, *all* my life."

Home was still the shack a few blocks away with his mother, May Ann, and his younger sister, Beatrice, known as Mama Lucy. On New Year's Eve 1912, he was arrested for shooting a pistol, celebrating in the streets. The court sent him to the Colored Waif's Home, set on a pasture beyond Bayou Road at the city's edge, by the cemetery where Bolden would go. Capt. Joseph Jones, the home's African American founder, and a former soldier, was "a hardheaded idealist who believed that children who got into trouble belonged not in jail, where they would be at the mercy of older criminals," writes Armstrong biographer Terry Teachout, "but in the hands of reformers determined to give them a chance to change their lives." Armstrong had at least two substantial stays at the Home before mid-adolescence. The daily order, nurture, and discipline helped him, as he recalled years later. The Home had a schoolroom, mess hall, and chapel with a dormitory upstairs. The regimen included cleaning chores, learning carpentry, gardening—and music. Twice a week they marched with wooden guns and wooden drums. Band instructor Peter Davis invested serious time in the boys; he saw Armstrong's talent. "We used to go fishing behind the home," Deacon Frank Lastie recalled. Louis blew "taps on a bugle to let us know it was time."

Armstrong marched with the Waif's Home band in a 1915 May parade that featured Kid Ory's group. A year later, after leaving the Home, he sidled up to Ory, who hired him several times. Armstrong coaxed Joe Oliver, who became a father figure, to give him cornet lessons; his wife, Stella, fed the boy red beans and rice. In 1917, Armstrong was playing cornet with Oliver in Ory's band when the U.S. Department of War ordered Storyville closed as a threat to the health of navy sailors stationed in New Orleans. Women scattered, some to the French Quarter. In the 1930s, madams bought their bedding, chairs, and sofas at a hefty markup from Mayor Bob Maestri's furniture store.

Joe Oliver moved to Chicago in 1918 at the suggestion of drummer Paul Barbarin, who had already left. The wartime economy was crimping New Orleans musicians before the District closed. Ory took work in construction for a brief period; he ran into conflicts with club owners. "Louis was with me when Pete Lala and I were running dances together at his place on Claiborne," Ory said. "Then Pete Lala got mad when I didn't cut him in on the dances at the Economy Hall and the Co-Operators Hall. So he got about fifty cops to go around, run my customers away. I felt like I was going to lose my health.... I didn't like the climate."

On February 26, 1917, the Victor Talking Machine Company in New York recorded the Original Dixieland Jazz Band's "Livery Stable Blues," which sold a million records. The five white New Orleans musicians, sporting tuxedos, cut a fine promotional image—the leader, cornetist Nick LaRocca; clarinetist Larry Shields; drummer Tony Sbarbaro; trombonist Eddie Edwards; and the pianist, Henry Ragas. Billed as the originators of jazz, which they were not, the Original Dixieland Jazz Band became an overnight sensation. Jazz entered the vocabulary of America, and soon the world. The debut by a white band was doubly ironic. The buoyant tempo and Shields's rich filigrees on the clarinet swirl around LaRocca's bursting cornet on "Livery Stable Blues." More ragtime than improvisational, the tune simulates the bray and peck of barnyard animals; it is not blues. The African American pioneers back home listened, comparing technique and stylistic attack—another sign that a shot at the better life required leaving town.

The role of white musicians in the rise of jazz has vexed many fans and historians. "Livery Stable Blues" came five years *before* the three New Orleans geniuses—Louis, Jelly, and Sidney Bechet—began recording, after each of them reached Chicago. *Dixieland* is a commercial term meaning New Orleans jazz played by whites. Some black musicians would use the term as synonymous with New Orleans. The ODJB songs, rarely heard today, do not come close to the aesthetic standard of Armstrong's 1926 Hot Five recordings, or the early output of Bechet and Morton. Nevertheless, sixteen years after the Parish Prison lynchings, a band led by a Sicilian musician put jazz on the map.

Born in 1889, Dominick James "Nick" LaRocca was a son of Sicilian migrants who grew up on Magazine Street in the blue-collar Irish Channel, watching white bands play parades and political rallies. LaRocca borrowed his father's cornet to practice. His father, Giarolamo, a shoemaker who played clarinet on the side, destroyed the horn. "Musicians are like gypsies," he fumed. "They wander around the country, they are always penniless." Then daddy destroyed his second horn. Undaunted, Nick LaRocca got a horn for keeps and kept playing.

The most gifted musician in the ODJB was Larry Shields, the clarinetist who grew up two doors from Bolden's house. Born in 1893, Shields as a boy listened to Bolden play on his front porch; he stood outside Nolte's Hall a few blocks away, barred entry because of his age and race, listening to the meteoric clarinetist Johnny Dodds. Shields and LaRocca left in the early jazz diaspora and reunited in Chicago in 1916, playing with Stein's Dixie Jass Band (under drummer Johnny Stein). Trombonist Eddie Edwards got into a beef with Stein over money and slugged his nose. The band regrouped under LaRocca as the Original Dixieland Jass Band. The mob controlled certain Chicago venues; LaRocca ran afoul of a mobster, so the band split for New York. Playing at Resenweber's Restaurant, they fired up the well-dressed dancers, ditched the two s's and became Original Dixieland Jazz Band—*jazz* now minted for cultural commerce. Two other songs they carried, "Tiger Rag" and "Clarinet Marmalade," became standards back home. The band was about to sail for London in 1919 when Ragas, the piano player, died in the influenza epidemic. With new personnel they finally sailed and kept going until 1925, when LaRocca had a nervous breakdown.

From such Olympian heights, LaRocca in the years after his recovery abandoned music and became a home builder. The band had a brief comeback but never hit it big. Embittered in his later years, LaRocca claimed that *he* invented jazz and black musicians had no part in it. The thinly veiled racism eroded his credibility. Tony Sbarbaro enjoyed a long drumming career. Larry Shields, whose fortunes dwindled in the Great Depression, make a comeback in the 1940s.

When Louis Armstrong left New Orleans in 1922, the great talent of early jazz joined his mentor, Joe "King" Oliver, in Chicago. As his prolific recordings made Armstrong a celebrity, he moved to New York and traveled the world. Many of his songs, interviews, and writings memorialized his native city. As other black exiles reaped rewards, they broadened the memory narrative of African American culture in its arrival and becoming through the music. Spencer Williams, a songwriter who lived several years in his aunt Lulu White's bordello, composed "Mahogany Hall Stomp" and elevated Storyville to clouds of myth with "Basin Street Blues."

> Won't you come along with me
> To the Mississippi
> We'll take a boat to the land of dreams
> Steam down the river, down to New Orleans
>
> The band's there to meet us
> Old friends there to greet us
> Where all the light and dark folk meet
> Heaven on earth,
> They call it Basin Street

"Where all the light and dark folk meet" is euphemism for the sex trade between white men and women dark and light. Much later, Louis Prima's bouncy version dilutes the line to "where all the boys and good folks meet," as if at a picnic. The image of a steamboat down the river "to the land of dreams" gave the city a rare marketing image, which took decades to sink in. Instead, in 1918 the voice of the officious city intoned in "Jass and Jassism," a *Times-Picayune* editorial. Ignoring the double-*z* spelling that by then was in national use, the emergent newspaper adopted a condescending tone. No longer a woman beckoning at the yellow river, the voice of morality borrowed from John 14:2 ("In my father's house are many mansions") to denounce a legacy of Storyville, conveniently ignoring that the District was a legal creation of the city: "Jass music is the indecent story syncopated and counter-pointed ... listened to blushingly, behind closed doors and drawn curtains, but, like all vice, it grew bolder until it dared decent surroundings.

"There are many mansions in the house of music. There is first the great assembly hall of melody—where most of us take our seats at some time in our lives—but a lesser number pass on to inner sanctuaries of harmony." Torturing the metaphor, the editorialist derides the basement as a "servants' hall of rhythms," where one finds "the thumpty-tumpty of the negro banjo, and, in fact, the native dances of a world" along with ragtime, for those "who love to fairly wallow in noise.

"In the matter of jass it has been widely suggested that this particular form of musical vice had its birth in this city ... from doubtful surroundings in our slums. We do not recognize the honor of parenthood, but with such a story in circulation it behooves us to be last to accept the atrocity in polite society, and where it has crept in we should make it a point of civic honor to suppress it."

As the newspaper harrumphed its defense of civilization, Kid Ory's band was playing Saturday nights at the New Orleans Country Club. It was 1918. Blue bloods dancing to jazz! Men of the Rex and Comus societies, and their wives, down in the basement "servants' hall of rhythms." Ory surely supplied more blues heat than the Robichaux band. After generations of ruthless treatment of African Americans, jazz, laden with songs of sex and love, had infiltrated the big house.

A year later Ory packed off to Los Angeles. Six years later, from Chicago, Armstrong and King Oliver contacted him, seeking him for recording sessions. And so Ory moved again, taking the rich tailgate trombone style into Hot Five sessions that yielded classics like "Muskrat Ramble," "Struttin' with Some Barbecue," "Ory's Creole Trombone," and "Heebie Jeebies," in which Armstrong bursts into joyous scat singing, songs soon played by New Orleans musicians who stayed home in the Depression of the 1930s, songs in play ever since.

....

Mother Catherine and the
Lower Ninth Ward

In the 1920s, Canal Street had a cosmopolitan appeal for New Orleanians who relished "going downtown." Streetcars trundled along the broad median, paved in red-and-white terrazzo marble, and on sidewalks in front of the Maison Blanche department store, hotels, offices, the Boston Club, restaurants, and Werlein's, which sold instruments and sheet music. The Canal streetcar ran several miles west to the city limit at New Basin Canal, by Halfway House Restaurant, a dancehall where the track turned out to the lake and reached West End. At Spanish Fort, the Tranchina's Restaurant dance floor had potted palms, paper lanterns, and Creole composer Armand J. Piron and His Society Orchestra in tuxedoes.

As Prohibition took hold in the United States, New Orleans was a key port for liquor smuggled out of Cuba, the Bahamas, and British Honduras. Ships unloaded cargo in the marshes and bayous of St. Bernard Parish, on the coast of Lakes Borgne and Pontchartrain, with armed guards alert to federal agents. Liquor remained plentiful as the city hummed along. Crime and police corruption were major problems.

The French Quarter, down on its heels, losing French Creoles to Sicilians and blacks, attracted artists to cheap apartments with balconies and Spanish patios. The novelist Sherwood Anderson lived at Jackson Square and befriended a young William Faulkner, who wrote in a Pirates' Alley flat behind St. Louis Cathedral before heading home to Mississippi, where his epic output began. As John Shelton Reed writes in *Dixie Bohemia*, white artists and literati barely interacted with blacks, so strong was the vise of segregation law.

The city spanned about twelve miles along the Mississippi's curl with ferry service to the Algiers neighborhood on the west bank. The 198.1 square mile urban area was huge for a population of 387,408, with undeveloped areas, thick in tropical growth, reptiles, and rodents. The engineer Albert Baldwin Wood, a Tulane graduate, invented the screw pump with a hydraulic system for drainage and clearing swamp. As the city developed north, toward the lake, the Ninth Ward grew downriver as Claiborne Avenue ran from Uptown all the way to the outback, where it became a thinner trail. By the 1890s the Ninth had 17,000 residents.

"Within the city limits are the best fishing and duckhunting resorts in the South," an 1895 city guidebook crowed, "and there are probably sections of the Ninth Ward which have never been visited by man, and as unknown as the centre of Africa." In 1821 Ursuline sisters penetrated that heart of darkness, building a beautiful convent and school with a wraparound porch at a bend in the river; they added a French mansard roof in the 1850s. The sisters "worshiped, taught girls, welcomed visitors, aged and died among the oaks and gardens of their Old World–style nunnery," writes Richard Campanella. The original French Quarter convent, the oldest building in the Mississippi Valley, became a bishop's residence and is today a museum.

The Mississippi was a demanding god. New Orleans Levee Board engineers detected erosion from shifting currents in the protective embankment along the Ninth Ward. In 1912, the city persuaded the Ursulines to sell; they moved Uptown to a new convent and school. The city demolished the riverfront facility to accommodate the levee upgrade. The Dock Board subsequently dug a link between the river and the lake. Completed in 1923, the Inner Harbor Navigational Canal—"Industrial Canal"—bisected the sprawling Ninth, which beyond New Orleans was a little-known appendage of the city for decades to come.

Nevertheless, the Lower Nine grew as blacks, Sicilians, and other ethnic whites found housing near St. Claude Avenue, which ran all the way down to St. Bernard Parish. Several large houses rose on high ground by the levee, but the Lower Nine had mostly smaller houses. Men hunted rabbits and squirrels in fields of palmetto, crepe myrtle, and oak.

On a fall day in 1928, Zora Neale Hurston crossed the only bridge, following St. Claude, turned north at Flood Street, and drove a mile and a half before walking the final yards to her destination. The Manger, which covered two blocks, was surrounded by high wooden walls with a Greek cross atop the chapel. At the top of a large tent inside the fence hung a U.S. flag. The gate had a bell, and a sign: *Mother Seal is a holy spirit and must not be disturbed.*

Hurston's literary fame lay several years ahead. She was thirty-seven, a quicksilver mind whose writings and flair had impressed Langston Hughes and other Harlem Renaissance figures. With a degree in "the spyglass of anthropology" from Barnard College of Columbia University under her mentor, the renowned Franz Boas, she was out gathering folklore with a white benefactress's support.

Born in 1891, the fifth of eight children, and raised in a roomy house on five acres in all-black Eatonville, Florida, Zora adored her mother, Lucy, and despite his infidelity had a certain awe for her father, John, a brawny carpenter-preacher. Village folkways seeded her imagination.

In 1928, Hurston rented a room in Algiers. Immersed in a voodoo cult, she spent three days lying naked on her stomach across a snakeskin for initiation as a priestess. The episode enriched *Mules and Men*, her breakout 1935 nonfiction book. Hurston's time at the Manger quaked with memory.

Lucy Hurston had encouraged her reading, telling Zora and her siblings to "jump at de sun"—seek their dreams. She was traumatized at thirteen when Lucy died. "That hour began my wanderings," she wrote, "not so much in time as in spirit." John, her father, sent Zora to a Baptist school in Jacksonville and promptly married twenty-year-old Mattie Moge. Miserable and homesick, Zora left school when her father failed to send support. Lucy in her memory was "the archetypal Good Mother," writes the biographer Valerie Boyd, and Mattie "the epitome of the Evil Stepmother." Making her way home, she found neglected younger siblings, her father cowed by Mattie. She left in despair, living first with friends, scraping along with menial jobs from 1906 to 1911, reading as she could. At twenty, Zora went home again and beat Mattie "in a savage smelting of outrage, desperation, and grief," writes Boyd. A neighbor trying to intervene dodged a hatchet hurled by the enraged daughter.

Zora bounced through low-paying jobs until hiring on as the maid to an actress in a Gilbert and Sullivan traveling troupe. She quit, in Baltimore, in 1917, and deducted a decade from her twenty-six years to qualify for free tuition to earn a high school degree. She advanced to Howard University, began publishing stories, and thrived in the Harlem Renaissance while on scholarship at Barnard.

An acolyte led Hurston into the chapel of the Manger, telling her to pray until Mother Catherine summoned her. An agnostic, Hurston observed "a place of barbaric splendor, of banners, of embroideries, of images bought and created by Mother Catherine herself; of an altar glittering with polished brass." She counted 365 kerosene lamps. The walls and ceiling, painted red, white, and blue, had a snake design. "The African loves to depict the grace of reptiles," she noted wryly.

Admitted to the tent with many benches, Hurston saw ten musical instruments and a piano on the stage, along with tables, chairs, rockers, a big coffee urn—and Mother Catherine's bed. "Catherine of Russia could not have been more impressive upon her throne than was this black Catherine sitting upon an ordinary chair at the edge of the platform," wrote Hurston, discarding an anthropologist's neutrality. "She might have been the matriarchal ruler of some nomad tribe as she sat there with the blue band about her head like a coronet; a white robe and gorgeous red cape falling away from her broad shoulders, and a box of shaker salt in her hand like a rod of office." Then come the lines of Hurston's spiritual craving.

And so it seemed perfectly natural for me to get to my knees upon the gravel floor, and when she signalled me to extend my right hand, palm up for the dab of blessed salt, I hurried to obey *because she made me feel that way*. She laid her hand upon my head.

"Daughter, why have you come here?"

"Mother, I come seeking knowledge."

"Thank God. Do y'all hear her? She come here lookin for wisdom. Eat de salt, daughter, and get you mind wit God and me. You shall know what you come to find out. I feel you. I felt you while you was sittin in the chapel. Bring her a veil." [Emphasis added]

Mother Catherine was forty-one, only four years older than Hurston; the weight from years of sorrow hung heavy on the priestess, whereas "Daughter," with a clear Creole brow, appeared young enough to possibly be one. Hurston did not say she planned to write about the Manger, revealing it later in the two-week stay. Mother Catherine approved.

By 1928, the Manger had been going six years, harboring pregnant girls, homeless youth, and abused women with their kids. "We are happy living together as Virgin children in here with me and Virgin women," reads a line from the 1929 will that Mother Catherine dictated and signed with an X, "as [she] was unable to write," the typist noted. Born in 1887 in Hustonville [presumably Houstonville], Kentucky, her given name Nanny Cowans, she was raised in Lexington; she lists relatives. "I came here at the age of 16"—nothing on how, why, or with whom. The name in the will is Mother Catherine Seal; the name on the death certificate is "Seals," the name used by the press and her followers, in reference to the seven seals of revelation.

"Mother Catherine's religion is matriarchal," Hurston wrote. "Only God and the mother count. Childbirth is the most important element in the creed.... *There is no sinful birth."*

During the services, parrots squawked in cages, toddlers crawled on-stage, and canary birds trilled. Hurston registers detachment *and* approval at the exotic milieu, a throwback to her youth in the Florida village, seeing a donkey, sheep, hens, and a goat wander the grounds as peacefully as if on a farm. "Mother Catherine's concept of the divinity of Christ is that Joseph was his foster father as all men are foster fathers, in that all children are of God and all fathers merely the means." Hurston reported this sermon by Mother Catherine:

> God tells me to tell you (invariable opening) that he hold the world in the middle of His hand.
>
> There is no hell beneath this earth. God wouldn't build a hell to burn his breath.
>
> There is no heaven beyond dat blue globe. There is a between-world between this brown earth and the blue above. So says the beautiful spirit....
>
> It is right that a woman should lead. A woman is what God made in the beginning and out of that womb was born Time, and all that fills up space. So says the beautiful spirit.
>
> Some are weak to do wisdom things, but strong to do wicked things.
>
> He could have been born in the biggest White House in the world.
>
> But the reason He didn't is that he knowed a falling race was coming what couldn't get no great White House, so He got born so my people could all reach.
>
> It is not for people to know the whence.
>
> Don't teach what the apostles and prophets say. Go to the tree and get the pure sap and find out whether they were right.
>
> No man has seen spirit—men can see what spirit does, but no man can see spirit.

Catherine's cosmology was akin to the Great Mother cults, much older than Judeo-Christian traditions, which celebrate the cycle of seasons re-newing the earth. The spirit resides not in the Word, but in creation. The miracle of nature, life given bodily through woman, has a spirituality of mercy and abundance that Catherine melded with Sweet Jesus. The Man-ger was a unique outgrowth of the Spiritual churches, a movement similar to the Sanctified or Holiness sects for the dancing and ecstatic worship, with music in church, but with a very different taproot.

Nineteenth-century Spiritualism arose in the Northeast and Midwest, a largely white movement of séances, communing with the dead as the Creoles' Cercle Harmonique had once done in New Orleans. Many mediums were women. In 1918 a Spiritualism strain reached New Orleans in the person of Leafy Anderson, a charismatic woman of mixed African and Indian bloodline who rented space for services at Longshoremen's Hall above Canal Street on Jackson Avenue. Born in Louisiana about 1887, Leafy Anderson moved to Chicago, joining the Eternal Life Christian Spiritualist Church. Leaving behind a bad marriage, she drew crowds in New Orleans by invoking the spirit of Black Hawk, who led Sauk and Fox warriors in a losing 1832 war against whites in Illinois. After a stretch in prison, Black Hawk was escorted by a young Jefferson Davis to the White House. President Andrew Jackson urged him to retire in peace. On a tour of East Coast cities to see why he should no longer fight, Black Hawk became a celebrity in news coverage, dictating an autobiography in retirement. Perhaps Leafy Anderson read the book. Just how she encountered Black Hawk's spirit is less important than why they hit it off so well. Wearing a yellow and gold robe with a shawl bearing Black Hawk's image, Leafy Anderson's spirit-summoning was a ritual drama. Jesus was one figure in a pantheon of saints borrowed from Roman Catholicism. She held out St. Michael the Archangel, Queen Esther of the Old Testament, and Black Hawk as protective spirits for poor folk. Black Hawk appealed to African-blooded people whose family lines melded with those of Native Americans. In 1922, she purchased a three-story clapboard building in Central City, Uptown, and began her church. A 1926 notice in the black *Louisiana Weekly* announces an autobiographical performance: "'The Life of Mrs. Leafy Anderson—Mortal and Immortal,' in three parts— the Woman, the Medium and the Mother. . . . The play opened with a night scene in Chicago, then the home life of Mrs. Anderson was shown, her call to spiritualism, and her works. Mrs. Anderson played the leading role."

"Mother Anderson's followers are not allowed to call the name of Jesus," noted Zora Neale Hurston on a 1928 visit to the church, several months after Leafy Anderson's death. "Jesus as a man was not important—he was merely the earthly body of a nameless 'Spirit' by which name the deity is always addressed."

Leafy Anderson trained ministers, mostly women, a few whites among them; they spread the Spiritual churches with Catholic trappings in the robes, altars, and feast days, a black Protestant gospel of liberation, and "in the spirit" possessions of an African ritual psyche. While many preachers denounced jazz and blues, Leafy Anderson invited Chris Kelly, a plantation-born cornet player taught by Professor Humphrey, to perform in church. The balladeer Danny Barker wrote, "Chris Kelly played for those blues-loving, real primitive cane-cutting people"—the people Anderson welcomed.

The press covered Mother Catherine as an exotic public figure in a fairly respectful tone, given the pejorative racial attitudes. Little was reported on Leafy Anderson. More details come from Louisiana Writers' Program (LWP) reports under the federal Works Progress Administration in the late 1930s. Both women were deceased when LWP researchers interviewed their followers. (Hurston supervised the Negro unit of the Florida Writers' Project.) The LWP writers, black and white, had a more condescending slant on Spiritual churches than the reporters who covered Mother Catherine. Working in the Great Depression, LWP writers were skeptical of hucksters and mindful of Brother Isaiah (John Cudney). The white man with a snowy beard had a houseboat at the Audubon Park levee in 1920. After press reports of his reputed healing powers, crowds swamped his "Camp of Saints." Isaiah lay on healing hands without washing his own. Ministers and physicians spoke against him. Soon people who said he had cured them recanted. Isaiah fled to Biloxi, a sister claiming that he had fleeced her of $2,000. Coverage of his 1934 death in California noted forty graveside followers awaiting his resurrection.

Brother Isaiah was at his zenith when Nanny Cowans Jenkins, an overweight cook and laundress, childless, twice-divorced, beaten by her third husband, limped out to the levee camp in desperation. "He told me he was not healing colored folks that day, and I was so sick I fainted," she later told a reporter. She prayed: "Ain't you brought us out of the house of bondage, jes' like you brought de Israelites?"

"And I promised Sweet Jesus right then, if he would teach me how to heal, I would help everybody. I don't care what kind they are. . . . About a month later I got up and walked. The people 'round my house heard about it and I began to heal them."

Catherine's awakening happened as Leafy Anderson was gaining attention, defying conventions of faith and gender. Both women were thirty-three in 1920. Leafy could read, write, handle money, and gave rooftop parties with jazzmen who played in her church. "We were all supposed to wear white in class," Bessie S. Johnson, a Spiritual Church archbishop, told the photojournalist Michael P. Smith for his 1984 book, *Spirit World*. "Catherine came into class one day wearing a 'middy' blouse against a red collar, which was against the laws and they had a little misunderstanding. Then Mother Catherine left." The self-discovered healer who believed in "Sweet Jesus" provoked her own departure; in a Great Mother role she probably had problems with Black Hawk, too.

Spiritual churches dropped the "-ist" in a loose structure, echoing the line, "God is a spirit and they that worship him must worship him in spirit and in truth" (John 4:24). A line of female bishops emerged from Anderson's disciples. Mother Catherine's healing drew crowds on Jackson Avenue. In 1922, she paid $1,100 for the Lower Ninth Ward tract and $3,000 more to build the Manger. In October 1924, a neighbor called the cops over the tent music, an "African devil dance ... [they] hum, moan, shout, scream, beat a drum, use tambourines, strike bells and gongs, strum a guitar, clap their hands." No arrests were made. One month later, a journalist found "automobiles wending their way ... to see Mother Catherine whose colored disciples frequent the 'end' of the city." Women in white gowns "in tunic fashion and a veil," and men with sleeve bands, "their beards grown in the fashion of the disciples," attended to her. "Almost every day at her strange services may be seen some white persons, some of whom arrive in luxurious automobiles. Stories of valued gifts, rich lamps and rare relics, made to the tabernacle by wealthy white persons, are whispered in tones of awe."

"I never saw any miraculous cures," an admirer, one Mrs. Fuccich, said in an LWP interview. "I was told about a little Italian girl who was unable to walk, and Mother Catherine cured her. . . . The parents gave Mother Catherine $500."

The girl in question was Gloria Rosselli, a retired pianist, age seventy when we spoke in 1996. She said she had been born with osteoporosis, or rickets, a condition of weakened bones that more typically afflicts the elderly. She was two and unable to walk when her family brought her to Mother Catherine at the Manger. "My grandmother gave her five hundred dollars. They all went. It seemed like she lived in a tent if I remember right. She said, 'Put this child out in the heat of the day, give her cod liver oil till it's coming out of her ears.' That must have been her cure besides prayer. It was God first and then cod liver oil. I believe in miracles. I walked. I became a musician."

"That was exactly what the kid needed," said Jacalyn M. Duffin, the author of *Medical Miracles*. A physician who has studied Vatican archives on cures attributed to saints, Duffin responded to accounts of Mother Catherine's healing that I sent. "Cod liver oil comes from codfish and is full of Vitamin D. You get rickets when you don't have Vitamin D and don't get enough sunshine, which is hard to imagine in New Orleans. It could have been a dietary insufficiency. People with a good diet who don't get any sun can also get rickets. Mother Catherine's use of cod liver oil is consistent with why doctors prescribe Vitamin D."

If some of her healing acts are consistent with scientific naturalism, other "miracles" leave a trail of mystery. Several people told the LWP writers that she caused the lame to walk by whipping them with a wet towel and calling out demons to leave their bodies.

A ten-piece band played several times a week in the crowded tent services. Donors pinned bills to Mother Catherine's veil as if she were a bride. We have no data on how many people lived at the Manger in the peak years before 1930; large crowds rocking to an orchestra suggest a de facto community center with a floating residential population. People met privately with her for healing or counsel. She took in and fed any pregnant teenager, woman, or child. Many women had fled brutal men.

· · · · · · · · · ·

THE CAGNOLATTIS AND THE JOHNSONS

A photograph outside the tent shows people in white gowns surrounding Catherine. "Ernie Cagnolatti played the Angel Gabriel," the musician and memoirist Danny Barker wrote on the lower edge.

"E. Cagnolatti," eighteen, was a signatory to Mother Catherine's 1929 will. As the Angel Gabriel, the white-robed Ernie, suspended by a wire, played trumpet; he also took music lessons outside the Manger and from playing in Catherine's band went on to become a well-recorded jazzman with Paul Barbarin, the Eureka, Preservation Hall, and other bands. Ernie Cagnolatti's story opens a wider lens on Mother Catherine.

The ancestral Ernie Antoine Cagnolatti (1815–94) was the son of an emigrant from Milan who had a plantation below New Orleans. Cagnolatti and a slave, Lucy, had a son, Antoine (1835–84), designated as "mulatto." Antoine's son, Leonce Cagnolatti (1877–1958) was, in a 1913 family photograph, a muscular colored Creole with a sweeping black mustache and radiant smile; he had a grocery store across Lake Pontchartrain in Madisonville, a fishing village, where Ernie was born in 1911. At five, inspired by his oldest brother, he began playing drums.

Leonce Cagnolatti and his wife, Anna Shelby, had eight children. Ernie Joseph was the seventh. "The 'black' Cagnolattis were virtually invisible to their 'white' counterparts," writes Bruce Boyd Raeburn, "but it is clear that Leonce monitored the activities of his illustrious white relatives." Leonce named his eldest son Klebert, after Jerome Klebert Gaudet, a planter and state senator. The family spelled it Claibere.

Leonce lost a hand in a sawmill accident. In 1920, as Prohibition began, he got involved in bootlegging and left home. Ernie, nine, lived briefly in New Orleans with the family of his brother Claibere, who was twenty-five, a carpenter and drummer.

"My grandmother needed help with her eight children," writes Ann Cagnolatti, Ernie's daughter, in a family history. Born in 1939, Ann Cagnolatti gave more information in interviews. When her grandmother took Ernie and two older siblings to the Manger, their center of gravity shifted. "Word was getting out. Families were coming to her for help. Daddy grew up in the Manger, where he met my mother, Ruth."

Ruth Johnson was the youngest of fourteen from a Baton Rouge family so traumatized that "the oldest son pulled a gun on his daddy and threatened to kill him if he hit his mother one more time." The mother, Eliza Johnson, "left with what she had on her back and her baby girls, Ruth and Elizabeth, running behind her without shoes," explains Ann. "She brought them to New Orleans. They went to one of the brothers; he was married."

Ruth Johnson—Ann Cagnolatti's mother—had a grade-school education. She was about sixteen when she went with her mother, Eliza, to live in the Manger. Eliza Johnson, Anna Cagnolatti, and their children were involved with Mother Catherine for nearly a decade.

The Manger had its raw moments. Catherine renounced sex with her husband, George Jenkins, who spent some time at the compound. When he made advances on women, she cried, "There is sin in this house!" George pulled a gun, states Ann Cagnolatti, citing her mother, Ruth, as a witness: "My godfather got shot, John Pierre—we called him Uncle Cedric." A November 20, 1925, police arrest report on Jenkins identifies John Pierre and Marie Cummings as wounded. The event probably caused Catherine to have guards frisk visitors. Jenkins died in 1927 at the same state mental hospital housing Buddy Bolden.

Pierre survived the wound and married Elizabeth Johnson, Ruth's nearest sister in the sibling line. He played violin in the Manger band. As Eliza's older children visited the Manger, her son Paul fell in love and married Claudia Cagnolatti, Ernie's older sister. Three of the eight Cagnolattis met their spouses in the Manger. Both families, the Cagnolattis and Johnsons, revolved around the Manger across the 1930s through siblings, cousins, in-laws, and friends.

Mother Catherine's 1929 will refers obliquely to two natural children—daughters she lost in infancy, as a teenage mother. "The oldest one I have now standing with me is Eliza Johnson and one child, Ruth Johnson." Ruth, then twenty-three, had arrived as a teenager, trailed by memories of her father's violence, watching her mother rise from destitution to some substance as a religious woman. Two other named witnesses are Paul Johnson, one of Eliza's older sons, and his wife, Claudia, a daughter of Anna Cagnolatti.

Ernie Cagnolatti was a mite, just shy of five feet as a grown man; he attended Macarty School near the compound. His education ended in eighth grade, like most black boys in New Orleans of his generation. Taking trumpet lessons with jazz professor Arnold Metoyer, Ernie was getting gigs as he played in the Manger's band. For "Cag" and Ruth, the Manger must have been a wonderland under the benevolent Mother who walked barefoot amid the animals, preaching, healing, and governing the men who did repairs and guarded the women.

Eliza Johnson lived nearly two decades in the Manger. It is unclear how long (or how often) Anna Cagnolatti stayed after her reunion with Leonce. In the late twenties, Leonce had a pool hall/grocery store fronting a bootleg liquor operation in Tremé. Anna sewed cheesecloth robes for women and girls in the Manger; Leonce brought groceries. "Grandpa was told by Mother Catherine to stop [bootlegging], he had made enough money," writes Ann. Her warning was prescient.

When the Feds raided the house my grandmother [Anna] was sitting on a barrel of 100% pure alcohol and hundreds of thousands of dollars around her waist. They were about to get away with their operation when the feds went to the side of the house where they found a ladder leading to the roof top room where all of the barrels and intricate operations of the illegal business was held. Uncle Wilbert left the ladder out.... Grandpa did not go to jail because grandma gave up all the money and all the supplies to keep him out of jail. I figure whoever raided him, they kept it for themselves, or his nephew made quite a deal for him[self]. I never found out how he got out of it.

Ernie Cagnolatti met Ruth Johnson in 1926. Five years older than Cag, she was playing trombone in the Manger's band. Cag probably stayed there, given his mother's ties to the community and his daddy's bootleg operation in Tremé. The chemistry between Ernie and Ruth ripened under Mother Catherine, a trombonist herself. The band was a magnet for kith and kin in the Lower Ninth Ward.

Frank Lastie (1902–93) played the drums. After living at the Colored Waif's Home with Louis Armstrong a decade earlier, Lastie worked at bordellos, went to Chicago as a hustler, and returned to a life-altering encounter with Mother Catherine. She baptized him in 1928. Devoted to the Manger, he gained her trust. "The people she healed through the power of prayer. I've never seen things like that in all the days of my life!" In later years Deacon Lastie led his own Guarding Star Spiritual Church in the Lower Nine. Three of his sons (Melvin, a trumpeter; David, a saxophonist; and Walter, a drummer) rose from playing in church to careers in jazz and rhythm-and-blues. Two grandsons are third-generation drummers; Joseph Lastie Jr., long affiliated with Preservation Hall; and Herlin Riley, a stellar recording artist after extensive work with Wynton Marsalis and Ahmad Jamal.

The Manger band had a sweet-playing alto saxophonist in Harold "Duke" Dejan (1909–2002). He would go on to lead the fabled Olympia Brass Band for nearly four decades, starting in 1958. Dejan was a teenager when his father hauled him in to see Mother Catherine after he punched a boy in the eye. "They couldn't set the eye straight, so [the family] went to Mother Catherine," Dejan recalled at eighty-seven, slowed by a stroke. "He was a bad boy." Dejan paused. "His eye got better."

"You know, she scold me a little bit. She told me I shouldn't do that. I guess that was the reason I started playing in her church. I told her I'm going to give her a little music." The songs in the tent were hymns from the brass band repertoire for church and dirges: "Streets of the City," "Just a Little While to Stay Here," "Old Rugged Cross"—songs that Dejan's Olympia Brass Band would play for decades.

"Little Cag" the trumpeter drove Mother Catherine in a horse-drawn wagon into the Ninth Ward to buy groceries. Mother Catherine, who rarely left the compound, made her entrance by climbing a ladder outside and being helped down inside by her followers, a symbol of being heaven-sent.

Lionel Scorza, a Cagnolatti cousin, was "seven or eight" when his mother took him to the Manger with a damaged arm. "Blood poison was setting in," he told me. "My mother thought my right hand would have to be amputated; it was greenish. Mother Catherine took a live chicken and cut it in half. She put my arm in it and said the heat from the chicken's body would take out the poison. We cleaned worms off the arm the next morning. She told my mother to do the same thing. . . . The arm healed completely."

The physician-historian Jacalyn M. Duffin, who has studied miraculous cures, explains: "The application of animal meat on an inflamed surface doesn't strike me as being out of the blue. Raw meat, especially of chickens, was thought to have a healing effect in folk medicine used throughout America and in parts of Africa."

In 1928, one of Anna Cagnolatti's daughters, Juanita Maheia, gave birth to "a blue baby," writes the granddaughter, Ann. "I understand she was tiny as a mice held in one hand. The baby named Sort was not expected to survive so Sort daddy brought her to Mother Catherine at the manger.... Aunt Juanita could not go with Uncle [Elihu] Maheia to bring Sort because she was in bed sick from the birth and the thought of having to leave her newborn baby was too much for her to deal with."

Infants born with a hard blue tint typically have a blood disease, or congenital heart defect, like a perforation. For those who do not have blood disease, nonsurgical closing of the hole is possible, according to Duffin: "About a third of infants with the heart defect heal on their own. The case is impressive but not beyond explanation." Sort Maheia Young lived at the Manger into mid-adolescence; she died in 2017 at age eighty-nine.

. . . .

THE MANGER AFTER CATHERINE

In 1929 Mother Catherine built Temple of the Innocent Blood, underscoring her mission to shelter babies. In early August 1930, however, she was ailing, and said, "My time is up." She wanted to return to Kentucky. People were upset, the more so when she designated Frank Lastie to continue her work—with his vagabond past! She gave Eliza Johnson, "Mother Rita," control of the finances. Forty-three, heavy, and subject to fainting spells, Catherine, who had rarely left the Manger, wanted two virgins to travel with her, Ruth Johnson and Pearl Cie. Frank Lastie drove them to the train station. It is doubtful that Ruth or Pearl had been on a train before. Eliza Johnson told Ruth to make sure that Mother Catherine slept upright in bed.

Her heart gave out August 11, 1930, at the hotel in Lexington, Kentucky. Ruth called home. "Take the money belt," her mother said, "and put it around your waist." Eliza (Mother Rita) arranged with the Gertrude Geddes Funeral Home director in New Orleans to handle the body.

When the train arrived with the coffin, hundreds of people pressed through the gates. Mother Catherine had said upon leaving that her death would see high waters and she would have to be carried over the fence into the Manger. Mother Rita had steps built on each side of the fence. The city refused the Manger's plan to bury her in a sanctuary on the grounds, beneath the large statue of Mother Catherine, because it was not a cemetery. Mother Rita arranged for burial at St. Vincent de Paul Cemetery in the Upper Ninth. The wake ran four days and was heavily covered in the press. Guards put confiscated weapons on a table. "In 'Mother's' little chapel are hundreds of crutches tossed off by those who say they are healed by hearing her," the *Times-Picayune* reported. "Many are whites who went frankly and unashamedly to listen and tell of their cures."

Musicians came to the tent. "The wild thumping of jazz rhythms mated with the somber beat of the religious tunes ... people moaning, praying, crying, low whispering, subdued boasting," reported Harnett Kane. "White followers look on in excitement. The blacks watch the whites curiously." The following night, under "a shrouded yellow moon," wrote Hodding Carter, another journalist, "she lay beneath flickering candles, while more than 3,000 white and black, the faithful and the curious ... came in automobile, and afoot, treading the almost inaccessible flats behind the Industrial canal. Guiding them were white robed saints and sisters, brothers and coworkers, of both races, whispering their awe and sorrow."

The day of the funeral it rained so hard that Frank Lastie watched thousands of mourners slosh behind the musicians playing sacred songs, tromping up the St. Claude bridge when "the sun broke through and people started fallin' out on the bridge! People had babies in their arms and they knew it was prophecy"—her prediction that sun would shine through rain. "That was a powerful, powerful woman."

But not powerful enough to deliver peace in her wake. Several people challenged the unorthodox will; the court eventually ruled in favor of Mother Catherine's stated wish. Eliza Johnson, Mother Rita, gained control over the site and diminished resources. The 1930 Census found Eliza and fourteen others, including Sort "Mayhew," age two, at the street address. Absent Ruth or Ernie, the figure is surely skewed. Cag was playing with the clarinetist George Lewis, splitting time between the Manger and the family house in Tremé. The Manger band played as Mother Rita weathered the Great Depression. She cared for several children, including Sort, whom Ruth helped raise. But the funding flow ran slack. Hurston's profile appeared in a 1934 anthology to limited distribution and little attention. ("Mother Catherine" was published in a 1980 posthumous collection, *The Sanctified Church*.) Cag earned a trumpeter's chair in Herbert Leary's swing band in 1932. In 1936 he married Ruth Johnson. Cag and Ruth visited Eliza at the Manger, helping as they could.

In 1940, with "tears leaking from her soft eyes," Mother Rita told an LWP interviewer: "It's been a drastic road." She said that certain people she had boarded and fed "burned down some of the manger and tried to get the white folks to take what's left hyar." She avoided details. Soon thereafter she sold the land and buildings, which were torn down as the neighborhood filled out like a country town. She died in 1942.

Mother Catherine Seals (or Seal) (1887–1930). In 1922 she
founded The Manger, a compound in the Lower Ninth Ward for
homeless women, children, and pregnant girls. She is credited with
miraculous cures. Mother Catherine drew large crowds to tent
services with a large band; she also played trombone. Several jazz
musicians got their start in her tent, notably Harold "Duke" Dejan,
an alto saxophonist who led the Olympia Brass Band for many years,
and trumpeter Ernie Cagnolatti, who played with Paul Barbarin and
other bands. (Photo from the author's collection)

A scene of Mother Catherine's tent, 1920s. On another print of this photograph, the balladeer Danny Barker wrote, "Ernie Cagnolatti played the Angel Gabriel." Mother Catherine gave children the names of saints and roles in religious skits. Ernie blew his trumpet in an angel's outfit. (Photo from the author's collection)

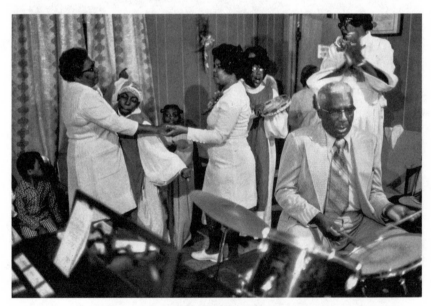

Deacon Frank Lastie, pastor of Guiding Star Spiritual Church in the Lower Ninth Ward, playing drums in the church, 1978. Lastie was baptized by Mother Catherine Seals. Three of his sons—Melvin, David, and Walter—were respected musicians who got their start playing in his church. Two of Frank and Alice Lastie's grandsons— Herlin Riley and Joseph Lastie—are third-generation drummers active in New Orleans today. (From the author's collection; gift by the photographer, the late Michael P. Smith)

Funeral for Paul Barbarin, 1969. One of the largest brass-band funerals in the civil rights era, the pageantry for this influential early drummer and composer of "Bourbon Street Parade" and "The Second Line" drew musicians from the major marching bands. (Photograph by Michael P. Smith, © the Historic New Orleans Collection, Acc. no. 2007.0103.2.3.346)

Funeral for George Lewis, 1969. A clarinetist, Lewis was a major figure of the New Orleans Revival in the late 1940s; he made a celebrated tour of Japan several years before his death. The wake was at Blandin Funeral Home, which today functions as Backstreet Cultural Museum, devoted to jazz funerals, Mardi Gras Indians, and Social Aid and Pleasure Clubs. (Photograph by Michael P. Smith, © the Historic New Orleans Collection. Acc. no. 2007.0103.2.161)

Sister Gertrude Morgan and her art dealer, Larry Borenstein, early 1970s. (Photographer unknown; from the author's collection; gift of Kelly Edmiston)

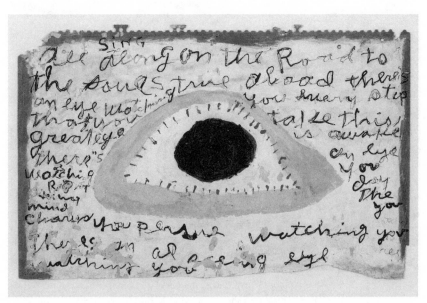

Sister Gertrude Morgan's *The All-Seeing Eye*. (Photograph by Owen Murphy, collection of Ben Jaffe; used with permission)

Willie and Percy Humphrey—grandsons of the pioneering jazz professor James Brown Humphrey—at Preservation Hall, 1993. (Photograph by Donn Young; used with permission)

JoAnn Clevenger, 1988. The proprietor of Upperline Restaurant, she was a neighbor and friend of Larry Borenstein in the French Quarter during the 1960s, when he worked with Sister Gertrude Morgan. (Photograph by Judy Cooper; used with permission)

Preservation Hall Jazz Band, 1986. Left to right: Cie Frazier, Frank Demond, Willie Humphrey, Allan Jaffe, Sing Miller, Percy Humphrey, and Narvin Kimball. (Photograph by Lee Friedlander; used with permission of Ben Jaffe and Preservation Hall)

The Bamboula, Congo Square. Slaves held large Sunday dances from the early colonial years until shortly before the Civil War at a public park, Congo Square. This picture by the artist E. W. Kimble imagined how the dances appeared based on the research of George Washington Cable, accompanying his February 1886 article in *Century Magazine*, "The Dance at Place Congo." (Collection of the author)

Second liner jumping at Emile Victor Clay funeral, February 10, 1996. The second line—performers of spontaneous choreographies during brass-band parades—extend the Congo Square tradition of street dancing. The men jumping are grand marshals ahead of the Pin Stripe Brass Band. Mr. Clay, seventy-three, was a chef and member of Young Men Olympia, Knights of Peter Claver, and the Elks Hall. The Mass was held at Holy Ghost Catholic Church. (Photograph by Michael P. Smith, © the Historic New Orleans Collection, Acc. no. 2007.0103.4.570)

Danny Barker (*right*) and Wellman Braud, ca. 1964. Braud, a bass
player from New Orleans, recorded with Danny and Blue Lu Barker
in New York and Los Angeles. He died in 1965. When Mr. Barker
lay dying in 1994, he told his wife that Braud had visited him that
day. (Photograph by the late Jack Buckley, author's collection;
gift of Sylvia Barker)

View of 1982 jazz funeral, second liners jumping on a car hood.
Danny Barker felt that burial parades were getting too wild and
told his wife, Blue Lu, that he didn't want a jazz funeral. His band
members and friends persuaded her otherwise. The 1994 funeral
parade for Mr. Barker was among the most beautiful in recent
memory. (Photograph by Michael P. Smith, © the Historic New
Orleans Collection, Acc. no. 2007.0103.4.461)

Danny and Blue Lu Barker, 1983, after fifty-three years of marriage.
(Photograph by Michael P. Smith, © the Historic New Orleans
Collection, Acc. no. 2007.0103.2.346)

A street in the Lower Ninth Ward after the epic flooding and wind damage from Hurricane Katrina in 2005. (© David G. SPIELMAN-05; used with permission)

Flood-battered house after federally run
levees broke in 2005, following Hurricane
Katrina. (Photograph by Julie Dermansky;
used with permission)

"Keep out every thing is gone." Sign on
door after Katrina, directed at looters.
(Photograph by Julie Dermansky, 2005;
used with permission)

Michael White, leader of Original Liberty Jazz Band, playing in a jazz funeral at Tulane University to memorialize the 400th anniversary of Shakespeare's death, 2016. (Freeze-frame from video; courtesy of the author)

Funeral for Black Indian leader Larry Bannock, Big Chief, Golden Starhunters, 2014. (Photograph by the author)

Zulu Social Aid and Pleasure Club, parading on Mardi Gras, 2005.
(Photograph courtesy of Kim Welsh; used with permission)

Jerome Smith, founder
of Tambourine and
Fan Club, with Big
Chief Victor Harris,
Spirit of the Fi Yi Yi,
Masked Indian, 2018.
(Photograph by Jeffrey
David Ehrenreich;
used with permission)

Mystic Krewe of Satiricon, Gay Carnival Ball, 2010. Emulating Rex, Comus, and other society balls, gay krewes held events at auditoriums with invited crowds, which began undercutting police harassment of LGBT people. (Photograph by Cheryl Gerber; used with permission)

Krewe of Rex Ball, February 28, 2017. (Photograph by Kathy Anderson; used with permission)

Mayor Mitch Landrieu, rebuilder of New Orleans after Katrina, at memorial event ten years after the storm. (Photograph by Julie Dermansky; used with permission)

Removal of Robert E. Lee statue on St. Charles Avenue, initiated by Mayor Mitch Landrieu and the majority of the City Council, after court battle with preservationists, opposition groups, and threats by white terrorist organizations against contractors, May 19, 2017. (Photograph by Julie Dermansky; used with permission)

George Landry, "Big Chief Jolley" of the Wild Tchoupitoulas, in Dot's Bar on Tchoupitoulas Street, Carnival Day, 1979—the year the New Orleans Police Department went out on strike and major parades were canceled. Landry was lead singer on major songs of the influential *The Wild Tchoupitoulas* LP of 1976 with his nephews Art, Charles, Aaron, and Cyril Neville. (From the author's collection; gift of photographer, the late Syndey Byrd)

12

....

Sister Gertrude Morgan

RUNNING FOR THE CITY

In 1957, the state built a four-lane vertical lift bridge on North Claiborne Avenue over Industrial Canal that streamlined access to the city for people in the deep Lower Nine. That year, two evangelists moved into a house several blocks from the old Manger site, and Sister Gertrude Morgan received a revelation that she was a Bride of Christ.

> He has taken me out of the black robe and crowned
> me out in white.
> We are now in revelation, he married me, I'm his
> wife.

Sister Gertrude's proximity to buried ruins of the Temple of the Innocent Blood was ironic coincidence. Gertrude Morgan was not a healer; but for some eighteen years she, too, had harbored cast-off children as a missionary on the city side of Industrial Canal. She never met Mother Catherine. Anchored in evangelical Christianity, Sister Gertrude gave Bible lessons to neighborhood kids in the house at 2538 Alabo Street that she shared with Mother Margaret Parker. But her identity as a heavenly bride and the impact of divine messages so consumed her that she began crayon drawings, scenes of her early life, which soon unloosed a torrent of paintings on varied surfaces, paintings that burst with colors and figurative renderings of earthbound folk and angels, white-robed and white-winged, swirling across the sky; churches with choirs in gowns swaying like windswept wheat stalks beneath a city in the clouds—the New Jerusalem as promised in Book of Revelation. As the scriptural account of angels and demons battling for salvation, the Book of Revelation further inspired the pencil-written passages on many of Sister Gertrude's paintings, which convey visual chapters of her spiritual odyssey.

Gertrude Morgan was a mystic, a soul in direct communication with God. In that, she resembled St. Catherine of Siena and William Blake, poetic minds charged by visions of intimacy with the Lord. No other figure of New Orleans history approaches her in this regard.

"Sister Gertrude Morgan was a self-appointed missionary and preacher, an artist, a musician, a poet, and a writer possessed of profound religious faith," writes William A. Fagaly, a New Orleans Museum of Art curator for many years and an authority on her work. Sister Gertrude's paintings, which today hang in museums and command substantial gallery prices, follow her life in settings of worship and celestial vistas as a Bride of Christ. Pictures like "Jesus Is My Airplane" are leavened by trenchant observations on evil, as when she gave a backhand to Spiritual churches in writing: "This town is running on the bases of Lucifer's tricks and luck, look out Black hawk New Jerusalem is on its way. . . . Just as well hush up your dirty Big mouth fuss. This is the lord's wife speaking to you Christ is talking to you through me. You just well take heed and make up your mind and say, lord, let it be."

As her thought field bloomed with images of the heavenly city, Sister Gertrude made regular trips into the sinful city to preach and sing on Royal Street. There, she found herself swept into currents of jazz in a changing city that carried through her most prolific years.

Born on April 7, 1900, Gertrude Williams was the seventh child of Frances and Edward Williams, a farming family in LaFayette, Alabama. The family moved several times. In 1920 Gertrude was living with her mother and three siblings in Columbus, Georgia, working as a domestic. "Gertrude apparently did not receive schooling beyond the third grade," writes Fagaly in *Tools of Her Ministry*, the catalog for a 2004 museum retrospective. "It is unclear why her education ended at such a young age ... but it's possible she had a learning disability or behavioral problems; she stated later that she 'was a peculiar little person in childhood days.' If her formal education was so abbreviated, as she reports, it is not known how she ultimately learned to read and write with such facility."

A collection of her writings, mostly on notebook paper, which surfaced after Fagaly's groundbreaking research, suggests that her ability to write improved in her sixties as she copied out long passages of scripture. Among her earlier writings, a stream-of-consciousness prose piece pinpoints how she encountered a spiritual presence, as a working fourteen-year-old, apparently without great exposure to church: "In going to my work on morning I was hearing girls talking about they got Religion. The lord put it in my mind to ask him lord teach me how to pray and what to pray for. For Jesus sakes so many sweet words came into my heart until I found my way after three days of being in pray an angel begin to sing to me lord I no I've Ben changed.... God put it into my mind to tell some of the history of my life that someone may make up their mind to come out of darkness into this marvellous light."

Many years later she painted scenes of Rose Hill Memorial Baptist Church in Columbus, Georgia, which she attended as a young woman. The pictures she made in New Orleans of those early years, in acrylic and pencil and ink, evoke a certain harmony as in a pastoral village, a starting point for her journey of the spirit. In 1928 she married Will Morgan in Columbus; she enjoyed "goin' to the picture show and I liked to dance." She did a quaint picture of their house but no image of Will. In 1934 she had a revelation.

> The strong powerful words he said was so touching to me
> I'll make thee a signet for I have chosen thee
>
> Go ye into yonders world and sing with a loud voice
> For you are a chosen vessel to call men, women, girls
> And boys.

That experience would be a heady rush for anyone; a woman so galvanized might well be challenging for any husband. She wrote nothing on why or when she and Will parted ways.

After a brief return to Alabama, where she worked as a domestic, a revelation came on February 26, 1939, telling her to keep on the holy path she had staked out in service of the Lord. And so she literally set out on the road. For an itinerant African American evangelist wending her way through the Gulf South during the Great Depression, where better to bear witness than the Babylonian city of New Orleans? She later called it "the headquarters of sin," a view harbored by upstate politicians and people in Pentecostal woodlands that hatched the televangelist Jimmy Swaggart, an anti–New Orleans mentality still strong in rural Louisiana and likely to remain so. The city more resembles tropical ports like Havana or Veracruz than Shreveport or Baton Rouge.

Sister Gertrude Morgan arrived in a time of tumultuous urban change, four years after Senator Huey P. Long's 1935 assassination in the towering Art Deco state capitol he had built in Baton Rouge. Federal agents were hunting down custodians of the Long machine. "When I took the oath of office, I didn't take any vow of poverty," Governor Dick Leche asserted in 1939. People believed him. Leche followed a parade of officials and bottom-feeders into federal prison. Huey's younger brother, Lieutenant Governor Earl K. Long, succeeded Leche, declaring, "I am determined to remove from the seat of authority every man who in any degree worships Mammon rather than God." It is a struggle in which the most charitable historians would consider Mammon to have the upper hand yet today

Huey Long's hostility to President Franklin D. Roosevelt and his plan to challenge FDR in the 1936 election did not deter Robert Maestri's ambitions. Born in 1889, a son of Italian immigrants, Bob Maestri saw his father make money in Storyville real estate. Despite a third-grade education, Bob prospered with the furniture store he inherited and invested heavily in real estate. Maestri thought nothing of a $50,000 "loan" to Long's 1927 guber-natorial campaign, knowing it would never be repaid. Long won. Appointed commissioner of conservation, Maestri allowed oil companies to exceed production quotas in exchange for funds to fuel the Long machine. Long waged war with New Orleans ward leaders, the Old Regulars, for failing to support him early and with Mayor T. Semmes Walmsley for backing a failed attempt to impeach him.

Though he slashed support for the city, Long in the late 1920s backed the Orleans Levee Board's plan to develop the area fronting Lake Pont-chartrain, including Milneburg, a working-class village of 1,600 people, heavy with fishermen, that had boomed with jazz in the early 1900s and now faced extinction. The city in 1910 built a seawall 500 feet into the lake at West End—the opposite edge of the lakefront from Milneburg, to the southeast. Restaurants mushroomed at West End; development plans for Milneburg gained momentum. In 1920 residents watched the demolition of the Washington Hotel, "a world renowned relic." A year later, the police closed seven "negro dance halls," citing disturbances. Milneburg had low-scale bordellos in certain fishing camps, a natural target for newspapers supporting progress.

In 1922 the Levee Board proposed a resettlement of all Milneburg residents in order to build a beach. The *Times-Picayune* predicted "a glorified reincarnation." It took several years to clear the people out. "Dogs bay mournfully at the moon," one Milneburger wrote to the newspaper in 1922. "There is a noticeable absence of life and gaiety. Milneburg is doomed." Indeed, the Levee Board prevailed in building a five-mile seawall extension with lake bed sentiment scooped out to create acreage for residential plots with a park along the lake drive—future homes with a view. By 1928, the Levee Board had sunk $41 million into a project that included a lakeside beach spread over the area after the fishing camps were bulldozed. The Levee Board president later went to prison for income tax evasion, along with several other Long cronies, after Huey's death. Not so Bob Maestri.

By the early 1930s, civic leaders were promoting New Orleans as a tourist destination while the city lurched toward bankruptcy. After Huey's death, Governor Leche and Lieutenant Governor Earl Long pressured Walmsley to resign. Maestri qualified for mayor in a special election. Unopposed, he won without a vote cast. Mayor Maestri mended fences with FDR. In a lunch at Antoine's Restaurant, over oysters Rockefeller, he asked the president, "How ya like dem ersters?" The rough-hewn Maestri, whose furniture store sold beds to bordellos, put New Orleans in line for 1937 U.S. Housing Act funds to build six housing projects.

Two housing projects, named Lafitte and Iberville, were built in the area of Tremé closest to Canal Street, the onset of major demolitions in downriver neighborhoods where the culture of artisans and French-speaking black Creoles once thrived. Thirty years after the closure of the Storyville prostitution zone, imposed by the city, the city demolished the mansions and ramshackle shotguns in order to build the Iberville project, one of two initially reserved for whites. The Lafitte project, across the grassy, oak-lined median of North Claiborne Avenue, housed blacks initially. By the 1960s, all of the projects housed poor blacks.

As lakeward growth accelerated, the Sewerage and Water Board extended pipelines into areas designated for white residents in Lakeview; projected resort islands in Lake Pontchartrain never materialized. New Orleans embraced the American myth of endless space with thousands of acres drained, trees cut, and bush flattened to graft streets and create neighborhoods. Developers' publicity erased any concern for a stable grid. Without the interior cypress wetlands, the city began, very slowly, to sink. "By the 1930s, Lakeview's drained land had subsided, causing street pavements to break apart," writes John Magill.

Mayor Maestri personally paid to put a wooden floor in a black Gentilly church, among other acts of personal philanthropy; he worked the federal spigot to build a new Charity Hospital, an Art Deco giant on Tulane Avenue.

He shrugged at French Quarter prostitution, the spread of slot machines, and the exposé of a bookmaking operation in a precinct station. Although crime and police corruption continued to run rampant, as Anthony J. Stanonis writes:

> Beautification programs abounded. Workmen, many of them from the WPA [Works Progress Administration], planted live oaks, azaleas, and flower plants on the medians of almost every major thoroughfare within city limits. Under Maestri, more than seventy-six thousand families and businesses signed a pledge to gather garbage from the streets, while a modernized Department of Public Works efficiently collected the refuse. On Maestri's watch, the city added 150 trash receptacles to the business district and improved conditions at the garbage dumps, notorious for emitting foul odors that wafted into the French Quarter and the central business district.

In the mid-1940s, Tennessee Williams lived at 630 St. Peter Street, where he wrote *A Streetcar Named Desire*. The city with its elegant patina, grand foodways, Carnival season, and raffish charms was ever the melting pot, which featured in the ads that the Convention and Tourist Bureau placed in national magazines to attract tourists. In 1946, Maestri faced DeLesseps ("Chep") Story Morrison, a young attorney with an old pedigree. He had won a seat in the legislature before the war and while an Army colonel in Germany was reelected in absentia thanks to his wife's campaigning for him. After the war, Maestri had grown distracted and the city shabbier when Chep Morrison, with movie-star looks, announced for mayor, promising reform. He had a brigade of Uptown ladies with brooms symbolizing clean-up needs, *Times-Picayune* editorial support, and black ministers seeking better prospects for African Americans. In a scene worthy of a Tennessee Williams play, the thirty-three-year-old glamour candidate told a secret meeting of pimps, hookers, and taxi drivers that he would not upset their sub rosa economy. Morrison won; he made the cover of *Time* as a modern Southerner. The economics of segregation hit blacks hard, pushing them deeper into poverty.

· · · · · · · · · ·

FINDING A HOME

In 1940 Sister Gertrude was living with two other evangelists at 816½ South Rampart Street amid taverns and fast life outlets. The residence had "no fewer than seventeen children under seventeen, two boarders and three women to run the 'household,'" the scholar Elaine Y. Yau writes in a probing account of Morgan's career. Sister Gertrude was listed as an assistant, along with Cora Williams, to Margaret Parker, the head of the household. The women were classified as "missionaries" caring for orphans. How Morgan joined the other Sanctified women we do not know. They moved the orphanage from Rampart to the Irish Channel, and moved again before the 1942 purchase of a large house at 533 Flake Avenue in Gentilly Woods, surrounded by small churches near Elysian Fields in the Seventh Ward. Sister Morgan helped with the down payment. "What is most striking amid the formal legal language is their economic independence as women," continues Yau. "As one notary commented upon the situation, the funds used for the purchase 'were acquired by them through their own business efforts.'"

New Orleans was like a foreign country compared to the rural towns of Morgan's past. In the 1940s, Elder Utah Smith had a warehouse church, the Two-Winged Temple in the Sky, which held 1,200 people near the Calliope Street housing project in Central City. Wearing the feathered wings of a seraphim, Elder Utah Smith played the electric guitar as he sang, pranced, and preached. He too was a survivor. Abandoned by his mother, raised by a grandmother in bleak poverty near Shreveport, Smith hurled himself into popularity through performances of rebirth. The biographer Lynn Abbott cites an early advertisement for a Shreveport revival: "The main feature of the program—Rev. Utah Smith will dramatize a Bible demonstration—the Resurrection of Lazarus. He will raise a real man out of the casket."

For his signature song, "I Got Two Wings," Smith in his wings of a seraphim would attach himself to cable wires and swing out over the stage, flying back and forth, playing the guitar and singing, his energy radiating to the worshippers in a spectacle beyond anything they had ever seen in sacred space. Smith drew attention in the *New York Times*, and eventually performed at the Museum of Modern Art.

Elder Utah Smith's singing sermons in New Orleans began airing on WJBW radio in 1944 and moved to another station with revival meetings through 1953—a soundtrack to Sister Gertrude and her two cohorts, raising children in the two-story house they had purchased in Gentilly Woods. They collected donations by visiting "Holiness" congregations, or Church of God in Christ. Radio broadcasts influenced evangelists to go outside in the spirit of Psalm 98: "Make a joyful noise unto the Lord."

In Morgan's painting of the Flake Avenue home church, a man plays guitar next to an altar, as congregants sit in robes with Sister Gertrude at the drums—she was making music before she began to paint. Another picture,

"The Flake Avenue Orphanage Band," has three black-gowned women next to a drum set, an upright lady who resembled Sister Gertrude, tilting with a tambourine, and dressed-up young women arrayed behind the sanctified ladies. "God married me himself around 1942," she would write. "When I learned I had become his wife I was so happy back in those days. Being young in the cause. O I didn't no what to do. But as the days weeks months and years rolled by I began to see greater light, and more of God's mystery see. What great love Jehova had for little me."

Her writings do not say whether she confided in Margaret Parker or Cora Williams about the 1942 revelation. Did she announce it at services or keep it secret until the years when she began to write? The many scriptural passages she wrote by hand starting in the late 1950s suggest that her literacy came from immersion in scripture. It was in 1957, after Cora Williams's death, that Sister Morgan and Mother Parker found the house on Alabo Street in the Lower Nine, the same year she had the revelation of herself as bride to both God the Father and Jesus the Son.

> The Lord of Hosts made himself known to me in my work
> through and through
> When he crowned me out he let me know I was the wife
> of my Redeemer, too

This period ignited her artistic output. She replaced the black dress of child-fostering missionary years with a bridal white that also looked like a nurse's garb. In the late 1950s, she began singing on French Quarter corners, playing the guitar and tambourine, and began selling her paintings, for even missionaries must pay bills. One day her work caught the eye of a portly art dealer, a man with thick horn-rimmed glasses who wore rumpled T-shirts and chain-smoked unfiltered cigarettes. Larry Borenstein was an unlikely sort of redeemer.

· · · · · · · · · ·

THE ODDEST COUPLE

Folk art was barely at the margins of high culture when Borenstein, moved by her naive lyricism, offered to exhibit Morgan's work at his Associated Artists Gallery at 726 St. Peter Street. They were the oddest couple in an enclave of artists, rebels, and a gay culture spreading its wings despite rough cops and Mayor Morrison's 1958 crackdown, with arrests at places known for gay patrons.

The French Quarter was not a milieu accustomed to a spouse of the Almighty; but it welcomed all comers, and Gertrude Morgan, on the cusp of sixty, was an adventuress. After being poor all her life, she had her paintings selling in an art gallery. Picture her as she walks along Royal, Chartres, and the streets near Jackson Square, taking in the myriad of artistic styles displayed in other windows of galleries that abounded in the old city core. Her journey from Alabama and Georgia had taken her into a realm she had never imagined. Noel Rockmore, a seasoned painter who exhibited with Borenstein, drank hard, and chased women, painted a portrait of her. He also did a drawing of her face. Her writings did not dwell on Rockmore or the bohemian ruckus in this new world of the city.

Borenstein had no use for religion, least of all Christianity. But in his breadth of life experience he realized that Gertrude Morgan was pure, and she had a sacred essence that made him protective, hoping to help her. Borenstein made money at nearly everything he tried. "The sound of a cash register is like a Jewish xylophone," he joked to a friend.

Born in 1919 in Milwaukee, Lorenz Borenstein came from a family of Russian Jews, his father a merchant. Larry left home at fourteen to work in a sideshow at the Chicago World's Fair but returned to finish high school in Marquette in 1938. Along the way, he sold magazine subscriptions and cleared $15,000 in nine months, huge money in the Depression. He attended Marquette University but left before graduation, working for a time as a reporter. He landed a job in Florida with a tourism promotion enterprise. Passing through New Orleans in 1941, he liked the rainbow of peoples and Old World ambience, and he decided to stay.

The city's small Jewish community gave great support to the museum, symphony, and major causes, despite the anti-Semitic exclusions by Comus and several other elite Carnival krewes with debutantes as queens and maidens of the balls. In a 1968 piece for the *New Yorker*, Calvin Trillin noted that wealthy New Orleans Jews took vacations during Mardi Gras, while homosexuals poured into town.

"For gay men in the South especially, New Orleans was a mecca, a sacred city, mentioned in hushed tones and awe, even among those Southern Baptists who despised its blatant hedonism," writes Howard Philips Smith in *Unveiling the Muse.* "Gay bars in the French Quarter were allowed to prosper as long as they made their payoffs to the police and the mob. . . . On Shrove Tuesday, however, the most flamboyant and creative costumes could be seen parading around the narrow streets."

Borenstein made friends with Miss Dixie (Yvonne Fasnacht), a lesbian and bulwark of the gay community who provided a hub at Dixie's Bar of

Music across Bourbon Street from his spacious second-story apartment. He made money trading rare stamps, running a bookstore, and speculating in foreign currencies. With so many struggling painters around him, Borenstein became an art dealer. He also became a realtor and said that he bought his first building in 1957 for $32,000, all borrowed; he slowly became one of the largest property owners in the Vieux Carré.

"Larry hung out at Bourbon House at the corner of St. Peter," says JoAnn Clevenger, the grande dame of the Upperline Restaurant, filled with the paintings she began collecting in her salad years as his neighbor.

"Tennessee Williams was a regular at Bourbon House; so was Lee Friedlander when he visited, and local artists like Noel Rockmore," Clevenger says. "People involved in gambling went there—they weren't really Mafia, they wouldn't put a price on your head, they were just running numbers and calling in bets on the telephone. The place had entrances on Bourbon and St. Peter. The bar had two sides, one gay, one straight. The cashier served both sides. There wasn't any regulation, people hung where they hung. Tennessee Williams liked to visit the straight side, listen to the juke box, and have a Brandy Alexander. He was quiet. People were reverent, they wouldn't go up and introduce themselves. His cousin introduced us; her name was Stella, like the wife in *Streetcar*."

"Most of the antique dealers I knew were gay," continues Clevenger, warming to her topic. "The My-O-My Club out by the lake had female impersonators. A lot of them lived in the Quarter. Larry lived diagonally from Bourbon House, a big place with a wrap-around balcony. He gave Mardi Gras parties and wore a black cape and black hat."

Borenstein also specialized in pre-Colombian art at his St. Peter Street gallery, Associated Artists. He got thrown in jail in Mexico three times for excavating artifacts. "In the U.S. government's zeal to stop marijuana coming across the border, they funded checkpoints for the Mexican government and it became no longer possible to slip the guard a few pesos when he was looking through your car," he later told the writer Tom Bethell. "In 1969, it cost me a great deal of money to get out. They confiscated my Buick station wagon and its cargo, plus I had to pay a large cash bribe to get out."

Borenstein also had a softer, enlightened side. He invited jazzmen to the gallery for jam sessions when race-mixing was illegal. In 1957 police hauled several musicians before a judge who called the trumpeter "Kid" Thomas Valentine a "yard boy," told him not to get "uppity," warned a visiting white trumpeter not to "mix your cream with our coffee," and then dismissed charges. Borenstein thought the music would increase traffic to the gallery. With police bribes at gay bars a fact of business in the Quarter, Borenstein probably paid cops to hold back.

The 700 block of St. Peter and surrounding streets formed a counterculture ground zero. Born in 1941, JoAnn Clevenger (née Goodwin), was raised a Southern Baptist in upstate Rapides Parish; she moved to New Orleans in high school, with daily visits to Charity Hospital as her mother slowly died of cancer. In 1960, at nineteen, she married Max Clevenger, thirty-one, a technician at LSU Medical School. Max was close with Dick Allen, who lived minutes away, a Tulane graduate doing oral history interviews of jazzmen with Bill Russell under a Ford Foundation grant for Tulane's embryonic William Ransom Hogan Jazz Archive. Clevenger recalls this period:

We lived above Dorothy Rieger's Restaurant on Chartres Street. She had a grand piano. Singer Frankie Ford and music people would stay up till all hours singing opera and show business songs. Here I am nineteen years old, I've practically been living at Charity Hospital, my mother just died, I'm pregnant and all this exotic stuff is going on downstairs. Dottie Rieger was a role model for me because she had this restaurant, we each had red hair and hers was piled up just like mine is now. From our apartment balcony I watched the ladies going to the La Petit Salon in hats and white gloves; then the ladies of the night, the streetwalkers; and on Sunday morning, the people going to church at the Cathedral and you would see nuns at the Morning Call having coffee. The nuns had such mystery for me. Caroline Durieux the artist captured their habits silhouetted against buildings of the French Quarter so beautifully. Growing up, my perception of New Orleans was that the people there were not very nice, did whatever they wanted and the priests forgave them. The Bourbon Street bus carried students at the convent school. Seeing those girls in their uniforms, and those green eyes and amazing variety of skin colors—it was very exotic to me, because growing up in central Louisiana, the schools were all segregated, you didn't come across black people hardly at all.

The school, St. Mary's Academy, run by Sisters of the Holy Family, an African American order cofounded by St. Henriette Delille, was damaged in 1965 during Hurricane Betsy and moved to another location.

Bill Russell sat at Borenstein's jam sessions, a balding, mild-mannered man whose shop across the street sold jazz records; he stacked his vast research on tall shelves in a nearby apartment with barely room for a bachelor's bed. Born in 1905 in Ohio, educated at Columbia and the University of Chicago, Russell the violinist composed avant-garde percussive music before he discovered jazz, and then he could never get enough. The author of three chapters in the influential 1939 anthology *Jazzmen*, Russell was a catalyst in the New Orleans Revival of the 1940s; he guided the comeback of trumpeter Bunk Johnson, a star of Armstrong's youth, recording the old man with George Lewis, whose quavering clarinet solos melded sorrow and sweetness in equal measure.

The New Orleans Revival was equally a product of New York, Chicago, San Francisco, London, and Paris, where jazz aficionados, writers, and producers, keen to the music of established artists, wanted more of the root sound. As Armstrong, Sidney Bechet, Red Allen, and others long gone from the Crescent City found quickened interest in the early music of the parades, churches, and fleshpots where they developed their chops, a fountain of possibilities opened for "the mens," as they called themselves, seasoned jazz musicians who had never left.

"Time after time, we saw men who had been laid low by diabetes, strokes, emphysema, alcohol, and just plain old age climb from their sick beds, like Lazarus, and live to play again," wrote the clarinetist Tom Sancton in a riveting memoir, *Song for My Fathers*. Sancton, who was taught as a teenager by George Lewis, went off to Harvard, to Oxford on a Rhodes scholarship and then to a career as a journalist based in Paris. After Hurricane Katrina, he returned to New Orleans to teach and look after his ailing parents. He plunged into collaborations with jazz pianist and bandleader Lars Edregan, a Swedish transplant who had lived in New Orleans for many years. Sancton's lyricism on the title cut of *City of a Million Dreams* (2012) pays homage to the composer, clarinetist Raymond Burke (1904–86), a son of the Irish Channel and stalwart of New Orleans Style.

Rhythm-and-blues was the commercial sound of the day. Fats Domino, who sang with a honey-sweet baritone over a rolling boogie piano, built a palatial house in the Lower Nine, riding a wave of records that got white teenagers dancing before Elvis. For jazzmen who stayed after the diaspora, the Depression was severe and the postwar years a grind. With limited venues, most musicians had to take day jobs.

Sister Gertrude had been selling pictures a short block from Mammon's lap on Bourbon Street when Borenstein took her as a client; the sales gave her the uninterrupted stretches to work that every artist needs. The condemnations of evil or Lucifer lace the handwritten lines of her pictures, with nothing on strip clubs or the fallen world on Bourbon Street. She was adjusting to daily encounters with white people, some of them strange, most of them nice. She saw the world through a scriptural prism, God's battle with fallen angels.

Lower Bourbon Street's neon strip had a few venues that featured bandmaster Oscar "Papa" Celestin, Dixieland stars Pete Fountain and Al Hirt, and the stately sunflower of Galatoire's Restaurant. But most of lower Bourbon had a tawdry tenor of fading vaudeville and was synonymous with strip clubs, joints like Stormy's, Silver Frolics, Gunga Den, and the Sho-Bar, where Governor Earl K. Long in 1959 fell for the ultrabuxom Blaze Starr. Uncle Earl, as he was known, squired the twenty-three-year-old Blaze around before his last hurrah, a 1960 congressional race in central Louisiana. He sent her off to Baltimore for the campaign, out of sight, out of mind, in an era before saturated media. Long won with a strong Pentecostal vote and died nine days later.

Some strippers danced to live music played by black musicians behind a curtain, unable to see the women, giving no scandal to white men ogling the female bodies. Evelyn West was touted as "Biggest and Best, the Girl with the $50,000 Treasure Chest Insured by Lloyd's of London." Bebop saxophonist and bandleader Al Belletto recalled a New Year's Eve "with a dead guy in the dressing room.... they weren't going to notify the police until all that good business had come in and gone."

....

JAZZ IN THE CLASH OF POLITICS

In 1960, Borenstein let a California jazz enthusiast, Ken Mills, use the patio behind the gallery at 726 St. Peter Street for recordings that included Ernie Cagnolatti on trumpet. In March 1961, Mills and a gung-ho jazz maven named Barbara Reid, who lived with her husband Bill Edmiston and their infant daughter, Kelly, in a flat above the gallery, formed the Society for the Preservation of Traditional Jazz with Bill Russell. As the music salon developed legs, Allan and Sandra (Sandy) Jaffe, a young couple from Philadelphia, moved to New Orleans, following the music's magnetic pull. Enthralled by a parade that featured Percy Humphrey on trumpet and Willie Humphrey on clarinet—Allan had the Humphreys' records!—the Jaffes followed the crowd to an art gallery on St. Peter to hear more music.

Born in 1935, Allan Jaffe grew up in Pottsville, Pennsylvania, and attended Valley Forge Academy, playing tuba on a music scholarship. His grandfather had played French horn in the Russian Imperial Army; his father played mandolin. In 1957 he graduated from Wharton, the University of Pennsylvania's elite business school. Allan and Sandy were elated to be in the city where jazz began. At the gallery jam session they met Larry Borenstein, an avuncular Jewish soulmate eager to help them put down roots.

As the friendship grew, Borenstein shared leads on Quarter real estate. Allan Jaffe had financial smarts balanced by a joy for music, and a growing affection for musicians like the trumpeter Punch Miller, the Humphreys, trombonist Jim Robinson, the supreme George Lewis, and other players he got to know from the jam sessions.

Meanwhile, Borenstein's life took a dramatic turn. Divorced since the mid-1950s, Larry fell in love with Pat Sultzer, a willowy, dark-haired beauty of eighteen, reeling from her parents' divorce. She was a part-time student at the recently opened Louisiana State University in New Orleans, and a waitress in Quarter bars, when she was raped and discovered she was pregnant. She had no way to identify the father. With a rescuer's tenderness, Larry proposed marriage; he wanted to raise the baby with Pat, regardless of paternity. Pat feared that Larry, though soothing in the moment, would be unable to love a child not his own. She entered a home for unwed mothers, gave birth to a girl, and, after nurturing the baby for six weeks, allowed a childless couple to adopt the infant.

Borenstein's complex personality was at a crossroads of midlife. He had become the art manager for a sixty-year-old black woman who considered herself a bride of Jesus Christ, while opening his heart to a woman young enough to be his daughter. Larry had his own vulnerability, a hunger to be loved. Pat responded with blazing reciprocity.

Larry Borenstein entrusted Reid and Mills to supervise the upstart jam sessions, which were attracting growing crowds, and left on a buying trip to Mexico. He was gone so long people wondered why. Several friends later speculated that he had been put in jail for digging up antiquities. When at last he returned, Borenstein decided to move his gallery next door and let the music hall operate at 726 St. Peter.

In the summer of 1961, Pat traveled to Eureka, California, to visit her mother, who had remarried. Nineteen now, she sent word to Larry that she was carrying his child. "I am glad you are pregnant and I'm looking forward with as much enthusiasm as you are," he wrote on May 28, 1961. He drove out to Eureka with Bruce Brice, a young African American who was learning to paint with a day job making frames for Borenstein's gallery. The car broke down in Baton Rouge; they had to sleep in separate hotels because of segregation laws. Once the car was repaired, they headed west. Brice, who went on to a successful career as a folk artist focused on funerals, parades, and New Orleans neighborhoods, stayed behind in Encino, Cali-

Sister Gertrude Morgan

fornia, painting the house of Larry's sister and brother-in-law. Larry and Pat headed on to San Francisco and married in a Buddhist temple.

After the honeymoon, back in New Orleans, Borenstein fired Reid and Mills, who had worked tirelessly to launch the Slow Drag Hangout. His brusque move left Reid feeling bitter; but Larry couldn't see two idealists running a business, and if the music didn't pay for itself, he'd have to swallow the losses before pulling the plug. He was confident in Allan with his Wharton degree. Renamed Preservation Hall, the venue reopened in the fall of 1961 with rustic benches, no beverage sales, no cover charge (donations welcome), and classic jazz for people of all ages.

Preservation Hall began just as the city was jolted by national coverage of crowds screaming at four black girls, escorted by federal marshals into two Ninth Ward schools, emptied of white children.

Governor Jimmie Davis, the country-western singer famous for the hit "You Are My Sunshine," resorted to unconstitutional devices in trying to thwart the city's public school desegregation. Davis was a cipher for Leander Perez, the overlord of St. Bernard and Plaquemines parishes downriver. A firebrand White Citizens Council leader, Perez is a creature of history worthy of Dante's *Inferno*, a titanic bigot who swindled a fortune from mineral-rich public lands under his control, systemic theft at that time unknown. (After his death, Perez's heirs settled by returning $10 million and 60,000 acres to the public.) When Governor Davis failed at "interposition," the state usurping school board powers to blunt a federal court order, Perez railed at a conspiracy of "Zionist Jews" and whipped up a crowd at Municipal Auditorium: "Don't wait until the burr-heads are forced into your schools. Do something about it now!" A white mob outside City Hall made more national news, bellowing, "Two, four, six, eight, we don't want to integrate!" Chep Morrison sat mum in the mayor's office as his national ambitions sank. Parents at two public schools Uptown had voted to accept black students; the Orleans Parish School Board threw "the entire burden of accepting a hugely unpopular social change on badly educated members of the white working class," writes Adam Fairclough.

Allan Jaffe's strategy to draw crowds at Preservation Hall was to build on word-of-mouth, and good press. The nightly performances became a center of gravity for Jim Robinson, the Humphreys, Papa John Joseph, Narvan Kimball, Billie and DeDe Pierce, Sweet Emma Barrett, Louis Cottrell, Chester Jones, George Lewis, and an occasional Ernie Cagnolatti, among others who enjoyed resurgent careers.

In late 1961, an NBC News report by David Brinkley showed Jaffe playing tuba with the band and a parade of blacks and whites together. Perez's White Citizens Council pressured the city to deny Jaffe a parading permit. Friends with the older musicians, Jaffe felt a deep moral revulsion at segregation. And with his Ivy League business school degree, he was a capitalist to his marrow. He knew segregation was bad for business at Preservation Hall.

Borenstein leased Preservation Hall to the Jaffes, their friendship secure. Eventually, he sold the property to them. As Freedom Riders rode buses through the South and endured beatings in the cause of civil rights, Jaffe rode his motor scooter to find musicians for gigs and help others with medical needs, as the club scratched along. The crowds kept coming. He helped musicians with small loans, building an esprit de corps while the city faced blowback from the very culture it needed to market New Orleans as a uniquely American place. How many jazzmen could they put in jail to resist the laws to which Leander Perez bowed?

In 1964, Congress passed the Civil Rights Act and Preservation Hall featured its first officially integrated band. Al Belletto, by then the entertainment manager at the Playboy Club, was hiring Ellis Marsalis and other black musicians to perform in bands with white musicians. Mixed bands for white tourists were not like street demonstrations for civil rights. The new mayor, Victor Hugo Schiro, abhorred confrontations. The culture forced compromises on the city. A similar breakthrough happened with gays, albeit more slowly. The Krewe of Petronious invited guests in formal attire to a lavish tableau in a rented auditorium, as mainstream Carnival krewes had done for years, thwarting the NOPD's itch for the bust-and-arrest. Complaints of police violence by gays and African Americans continued for decades; but as the drag queen beauty pageant became a fixture of Mardi Gras on Bourbon Street and gay Carnival krewes held by-invitation balls, the police attacks on closeted men in the 1960s dropped sharply by the 1980s. So, too, did the bar bribes.

Bill Russell was a nightly fixture at the Hall; he sold records, swept up, anything to keep the flame aglow. He had no telephone; people left messages for him at Preservation Hall. The place attracted attorney Lolis Elie, writer Tom Dent, and other blacks who became friends with the Borensteins, Jaffes, Clevengers, and other whites.

The photographer Diane Arbus spent time among the musicians and jazz followers in the Quarter in those years. Lee Friedlander visited often to photograph jazz players. He became friends with Borenstein and Russell. "New Orleans was a magical place," recalled Friedlander in a 1998 interview. "Bill Russell had this incredible instinct for where bands were playing, and he had a very big stride. We'd get on a bus and go into an area, and Russell would say, 'I think it's that way.' And we'd end up at a funeral or a march. Bands were used for almost any occasion. I thought I'd found a little piece of heaven."

Friedlander photographed Sister Gertrude and became an early collector of her work. He found her presence deeply moving. "God told her in a dream that she should give up her guitar and illustrate the Bible," he reflected. "She just did what God told her. He didn't tell her to stop singing."

She was a good client for a Bible salesman named Marcus Pergament; using some of the money she generated from her paintings, she bought Bibles and gave them away to all kinds of people. If there was a passage in the Bible she did not understand, she called Pergament for advice. He sold her the books; he should know the answer.

· · · · · · · · · ·

THE MYSTIC MOVING HIGHER

Sister Gertrude navigated the 1960s with an explosion of paintings obsessed by the battle between good and evil and the phenomenal beauty of heaven, the New Jerusalem. She underscored these themes with penciled lines of scripture, so that some of the pieces resembled scrolls, depicting herself in church, as a celebrant, pilgrim, witness, or just as spouse to the Almighty.

This the great master
and his darling wife.
they are using this wife
for this great Kingdom to
Brighten up their life.
They wanted some Body to work
through and its time for
them to Be well honored
and humored and well glorified too
I want to tell you darling
dada the world
is mad and it
seem like
they are mad with
I and you. But I'm gone
stand straight up not part the
way cause I no you are
able to carry me through.

Sister Gertrude Morgan

In the poem, "they" are her two husbands, two parts of the Trinity who have commissioned her to preach. In that sense, God the Father and God the Son are using "this wife" to serve their purposes ("their lives") and proselytize their people, the orphans in Gentilly now grown, black folk in the Lower Nine, the hookers, artists, tourists, and sinners along Bourbon and Royal, where she had been stationed with a guitar and jangling tambourine before the sales of her work brokered by Borenstein. Her two husbands and she, the darling wife, had a job to brighten the lives of people who needed inspiration to believe in everlasting happiness—her stated mission.

For her, the Lord was Master of creation; the poem speaks to God the Father, "dada." She did a painting of Jesus with mustache in a tuxedo as groom: a comic flair she did not lack. "I want to tell you darling / dada the world / is mad" is a metaphorical nod to the crazed zeitgeist and roiling anger of the 1960s. She had felt the pinch of condescending looks from some white tourists in her street preaching; she had sat in the back of buses, she knew why African Americans were protesting. Contrasting that to the floor show of Bourbon and other Quarter streets, she wrote, in a short piece called "armageddon," "never was national and Racial feeling stronger upon earth than it is now." The leitmotif of hope in many of her images of the 1960s and 1970s is interracial harmony, biracial choirs, angel flocks of white and black. Various of her works are marked by the refrain, "The gift of God is eternal life."

Musicians in Preservation Hall carried the melodies of church song from parades of the early 1900s—"The Saints," "Streets of the City," "By and By," among others; the culture of arrival and becoming from the dawn of jazz was reaching a new threshold. As New Orleans Style drew tourists, the official city needed the culture to cleanse its racist image.

After years of playing guitar and tambourine, Gertrude Morgan was not about to watch a new freedom train pass by. On August 19, 1961, a Sunday morning, Borenstein sat in his art gallery next door to the hall with a recording engineer, the ethereal clarinetist George Lewis, the trumpeter "Kid" Thomas Valentine—and Sister Gertrude. She was determined to record; the song "Let's Make a Record" in her gravelly alto is marred by inexperience—she was not a jazz vocalist; for all of Lewis and Valentine's effort to embroider a melody, you can almost feel them wincing. The disastrous recording, lodged in the Hogan Jazz Archive, is a time capsule showing how far Sister Gertrude had to go if her music would ever work on wax.

Jaffe the hefty tuba player joined the Preservation Hall Jazz band for tours he organized, and recordings, putting the business in the black. As one band traveled, another played the Hall, with vinyl records for sale at the breaks. Borenstein, meanwhile, arranged for Sister Gertrude to give a Sunday morning service, when the Hall was closed, for invited friends—Bill Russell, Dick Allen, the LSU folklorist Harry Oster, who drove down from Baton Rouge, Dianne Carney of Ballet Hysell, among others, thirty or forty guests each time.

"Some things are hard to put into words, they're so beautiful and spiritual," reflects Sandy Jaffe, across the bridge of time. "Sister Gertrude always wore a white bonnet and white dress; she was very sure of herself. Sometimes she did a beautiful drawing for the sermon, but wouldn't leave it for Larry. I think he understood her and she him, very well. When they spoke it evolved into a deep conversation that came around to him wanting that piece to sell. They had a discussion like two CEOs at Davos about his not having an extra painting, could she please paint another small one? She wouldn't unless she was motivated."

"My mom used to talk about Sister Gertrude as wanting to spread the gospel," recalls Sacha Borenstein Clay, born in 1963, the middle child of Larry and Pat's three. Pat's father was Jewish, her mother Baptist. "My mom believed that Sister Gertrude was the real deal, a prophet."

When Hurricane Betsy inundated the Lower Nine in 1965, Sister Gertrude was living in a home at 5444 North Dorgenois Street, which sustained heavy damage. Borenstein and Jaffe bought the house, oversaw repairs, and provided Sister Gertrude a home, rent-free. She called it the Everlasting Gospel Mission and began holding services in the front room. Old enough to be their mother, Sister Gertrude had effectively been adopted by two middle-aged Jewish boys who saw to her needs; their family members and friends formed a loose support network as the house became her space for living, painting, and worship. She could be abrupt in ending the services, telling guests, like a guardian housewife, "Time to go. Jesus needs his pills."

Borenstein arranged for her to sell works at the first New Orleans Jazz Festival and Louisiana Heritage Fair, in 1970. The program cover reproduced two of her self-portraits. That same year, he shepherded her work into three major exhibitions: *Twentieth-Century Folk Art*, at the American Folk Art Museum in New York; and the nationally traveling exhibitions *Dimensions of Black*, by the La Jolla Museum of Art, and *Symbols and Images: Contemporary Primitive Artists*, by the American Federation of Arts. In the early 1970s, Sister Gertrude also had a booth at the New Orleans Jazz and Heritage Festival, which further increased her sales and visibility. At a New Orleans Museum of Art exhibition in 1973, she sang and played guitar for the opening, which included three other folk artists.

As she did paintings of various sizes, decorated hand fans and other objects, she pressed Borenstein for another shot at recording—she wanted musical permanence, too. Since her disastrous 1961 recording attempt, Borenstein had reason to resist; however, he had seen the confidence as her tambourine rhythms melded with the singing and preaching at Jazz Fest exhibitions. She agreed to record alone; the engineer set up at Borenstein's gallery, which by 1971 was on Royal Street. By this time she was signing some of her work as "Prophetess Morgan, the lambs wife the lord of host wife to," suggesting that she felt herself a seer, a prescient evangelist with a sense of things to come.

Let's Make a Record has fourteen cuts. Her rough voice rolls in warm undulations of scripture-citing to the fluttering tambourine, until she slows the tempo of the hand percussion into a mild current, like a background chorus, to her preaching. The third cut, "I Got the New World in My View," draws from the Book of Revelation, in visions not of apocalyptical battle but of the singer as pilgrim entreating her listeners to join the road to New Jerusalem. With the tambourine thrumming, her voice drives a charging up tempo, with a lasso-like melody.

> I got a new world in my view
> And my journey I pursue ...
> Yes I'm running
> running for the city,
> I got the new world
> in my view.

In another song, she situates the Revelation author, John, on the island of Patmos and throws off an aside, "let not your heart be troubled, dear ones." She sings of "a New Jerusalem coming down, certainly a person is a city." But the most remarkable of the fourteen songs is "Power." Sister Gertrude sings "power ... power," in a chant to the throttling tambourine, reaching a state of near-ecstasy, crying,

> Yes send power!
> Power, Lord, power!
> I want my power!
> I want my power!

The drive of the hypnotic repetitions carry her into a fugue state as she beseeches heavenly power for light over darkness. "Power" stands alone in the vast canon of New Orleans gospel music; not even Elder Utah Smith with his seraphim wings and electric guitar touches the raw intensity of Sister Gertrude's spiritual witness.

. . . .

WHAT THE CHILDREN SAW

Allan and Sandy Jaffe lived near Preservation Hall in a two-story Creole cottage, raising two sons. Russ earned a law degree before becoming a specialist in speech pathology. Ben, an Oberlin graduate, plays tuba, double bass, and has been director of Preservation Hall and leader of the band for nearly two decades. When the boys were growing up, the double parlor had tubas, saxophones, valve oil, spit stains on the floor (tuba players work up lots of saliva), a piano covered with mouthpieces and a wall lined with Noel Rockmore paintings of New Orleans jazz. Born in 1971, Ben Jaffe as a kid was surrounded by musicians, from an antique Willie Humphrey on clarinet to the much younger clarinetist Michael White; he watched the men on break in the patio behind the Hall—phone calls, joshing, music talk, business talk—rituals in a way of life.

"Sister Gertrude was one of those spirit figures in our life like Sweet Emma Barrett, who played piano and sang in the Hall," says Ben Jaffe. "Sister Gertrude's art work hung on our walls. We would go to her house, sometimes for Sunday school. That's how we were raised, so it felt normal. There are certain spiritual people beyond any one doctrine. She painted the New Jerusalem. I knew about Jerusalem from synagogue. The music she played and sang sounded like kid songs to me—just stories. Making the pilgrimage to her house down in the Ninth Ward was something my dad would do with his brotherhood of friends, Larry Borenstein, Alan Lomax, and Lee Friedlander, this small group who understood New Orleans. First we'd go to the A&P on Royal and St. Peter and stock up on groceries for her. She had this amazing yard, filled with four-leaf clovers, and as kids we would pick clovers. She would sing and preach, pull out a book and do a little prayer ceremony. She used her paintings for the kids, teach scripture from the painting itself."

Borenstein was brilliant at getting her work to the public, educating collectors on outsider art, folk art, primitive art, the designation for artists who were poor, uneducated, and talented. In 1974 Sister Gertrude stunned him by saying that she was finished painting. Borenstein was perplexed: her health was good. With mounting interest from museums and collectors, she was in her prime. Why stop now? Because the Lord had told her, she reported. One can picture her stoical smile at the perplexity of her agent, friend and caretaker. All those years selling her work, opening her doors, building her reputation—and she just quits?

But the arc of her life makes perfect sense: what draws from heaven must resolve itself to earth. When God says quit, you quit.

Borenstein put together a collection of her best works, contacted a wealthy collector in Chicago, and negotiated a major sale. His interest in selling her work then dwindled. The Jaffes held a major collection for many years. Sister Gertrude made one exception in 1979 for a painting at the request of a friend, but otherwise maintained her fast. She died, at eighty, on July 8, 1980. Borenstein died a year later of heart failure at sixty-two. For all of his frustration over her decision to stop, Larry Borenstein would have been deeply pleased at the reception of her work in the 1982 landmark exhibition at the Corcoran Museum of Art in Washington, D.C.—*Black Folk Art in America, 1930-1980*, an all-consuming project by his friend, and hers, Bill Fagaly, the New Orleans Museum of Art curator. After many years of research, Fagaly organized the 2004 retrospective *Tools of Her Ministry*. In the years since her works have escalated in value.

The painted world that Sister Gertrude inhabited was purely of her own making, the mystic's dedication to God, making art to glorify Him, discovering herself in the process. The autobiographical poems and writings were like her music and sermons, acts of worship to the Lord.

The mingling of art and music that gave birth to Preservation Hall echoed a layer of her personality. The hymns that "the mens" played as dirges in the funeral processions are sacred statements, the opposite face on the cultural coin of hot, sexy lyrics of blues and dance tunes. She was there, a presence if not a player, as the rebirth of the 1960s saw segregation shackles fall as music sounded from the dawn of jazz.

There is something beautiful about her holy life in that bohemian carnival. Saints are stubborn, notoriously single-minded people. They raise hard questions and refuse easy answers. By the gauge of organized religion we know perhaps too little to call Sister Gertrude a saint. But the woman who harbored homeless children for nearly two decades after her arrival from Alabama, the missionary who sang for inmates at Parish Prison in the 1940s and in her last two decades painted a river of images celebrating Jesus as her Airplane was a rare personification of virtue pure, virtue simple, a saintly figure just the same.

less again, returned to Chicago with a Panamanian pianist, Luis Russell, joining the Creole band. On Christmas Eve the Lincoln Gardens (the old Royal Gardens) burned down. King Oliver had to scramble. He was suffering from gum disease; long solos were painful. Changing the band's name to the Dixie Syncopators, he took them to New York. In 1927 he called Red Allen in New Orleans, offering him the second trumpet job, which had been Armstrong's springboard.

Allen, nineteen, was an only child with a fair complexion and curly, close-cropped hair. Taking Oliver's solos at the Savoy Ballroom was a rush, but when Oliver turned down a job at the Cotton Club, Red Allen thought he was finished and headed home. The Cotton Club launched Duke Ellington. As the big bands' swinging rhythms overran the tight New Orleans ensemble style, Barbarin and the nucleus of Oliver's band regrouped under Luis Russell for a fuller, more expansive sound. In 1929 both Ellington and Russell called Red Allen in Algiers, offering him jobs. He chose Russell and in New York enjoyed arrangements that gave his gorgeous tone ample room to roam.

Red Allen and Paul Barbarin met Danny Barker at the train station in 1930; he moved into a two-bedroom apartment on 129th Street they shared with their wives. Paul took his nephew to the Rhythm Club. As musicians shot pool and hustled gigs, King Oliver ribbed him as "Gizzard Mouf" while playing billiards with an aloof bandleader, Fletcher Henderson, and the maverick genius Jelly Roll Morton. Jelly called Danny "Home Town" from that moment on. In *A Life in Jazz*, Barker wrote as if plotting history's curve. Oliver's career was in eclipse. Morton's classic 1920s Red Hot Peppers recordings "had become famous with bands which were smaller and gave the sidemen freedom to express themselves. As time marched on Jelly and Oliver stood on the sidelines with their plans and music."

Danny sent for his bride. Paul arranged for Lorenzo Tio Jr. to be Louise Barker's chaperone on the long train ride. Tio, forty-six, a clarinetist and veteran of the Onward and society orchestras, was the scion of an illustrious family of African and Spanish ancestry; his great-grandfather Louis Hazeur had been a colored militia bandleader at the Battle of New Orleans. Tio, the premier teacher of New Orleans reed players, was moving his family to New York, another talent thinning the pool. At the depot, Louise panicked. She'd forgotten her doll! Mr. Tio sat patiently as she ran home; she held the doll tight as the train pulled out.

"Now Mr. Tio was a handsome man," said Miss Lu in a foghorn voice, after throat surgery, with a twinkle at the memory of sixty-six years past. "When we got to Biloxi, I said: 'Mr. Tio, how long we got yet?' Instead of telling me the next day, or day after, he said: 'Not long, daughter.'" She kept asking, Mr. Tio kept answering, "Not long, daughter," till their arrival two days later.

Louise liked the bustle of Harlem, day and night. A pregnant Pearlie May Allen, and Sister (as the girls called Omelia, Paul's wife) were timid about going outside. Louise happily ran errands. The ladies enjoyed themselves; the men worked late and slept late. Alone, Louise wept, missing her mother. Soon the couples found apartments of their own.

Barbarin and Red Allen were mainstays for Luis Russell. The easy-going assemblage of Crescent City exiles in their twenties and thirties was making money in the Depression and thrilled at the ride. Louis Armstrong's manager arranged for him to perform with Russell's band. The association helped Red Allen advance in the ranks of trumpeters. In a 1989 interview, Barker recalled the era:

> You get to New York and it's a whole new opening—an element of inspiration you couldn't conceive in the South, where when blacks said something, whites looked at you as if you had no foundation. You have an attitude that you're not qualified. When you get to New York you had freedom, you meet artists in the Harlem Renaissance. You see Langston Hughes, Countee Cullen, and they're talking about their aspirations. Some who were denied in Chicago, which is Midwest and conservative toward blacks, they came East, to New York. Everybody who aspired to be somebody walked that street in front of Connie's Inn, which was next to the Lafayette Theatre which had first-rate black shows.... People talked about goin' to Europe like we talk about taking the ferry to Algiers. There was night schools, sculptors, and paintings. I'm playing music and hanging around these people. Your spine sort of stiffens.

In 1936, a writer named Milton Machlin he knew in Greenwich Village was deriding Jelly Roll Morton. Danny defended him. "Write!" said Machlin. "Tell me more." He began writing in the style of tabloid columnists Walter Winchell and Ed Sullivan, a radio-cadenced voice of the city. Jelly began hiring him; he made recordings in Red Allen's rhythm section, too.

"New York is not a blues town," Barker continued in his living room that day in 1989, five years before the body began to fail, seated beneath a photograph of himself and a young Louis Armstrong. "People would sit in the audience and look at some Southern man singing hard times 'cause he lost his wife—'ohhh, I'm gonna lay my head on a lonesome railroad track'—and they don't move a muscle. 'Cause New York's attitude was, 'You can't get

Buddy Bartley, the hot air balloonist who floated above Lincoln Park in 1905. As E. L. Doctorow would use historical figures in his novel *Ragtime* (1975), Barker uses musicians as characters. In Barker's rendering, Bolden and trombonist Frankie Duson struggle for control of the band. (Duson, in fact, led the Eagle Band after Bolden's collapse.) As Bolden loses his memory to booze, Bottley follows him home; he peeks inside. Bolden sits in a chair, playing a silver cornet.

> After a while I catch on. He is mixing up the blues with the hymns. He plays the blues real sad, and the hymn sadder than the blues and the blues sadder than the hymn. *That is the first time that I had ever heard hymns and blues cooked up together.* A strange feeling comes over me; I get sort of scared because I know the Lord doesn't like that mixing the Devil's music with his music. But I still listen because the music sounds so strange and I'm sort of hypnotized. I close my eyes, and when he blows the blues I picture Lincoln Park and all them sinners and whores, shaking and belly rubbing. Then, as he blows the hymn, I picture my mother's church on Sunday, and everybody humming with the choir. [Italics added.]

Frankie Duson arrives, coaxing Bolden to play a funeral with Henry Allen's band. The musicians gather around the grave, gently playing "What a Friend We Have in Jesus," when Bolden breaks with ritual, starting "Didn't He Ramble" for second liners in the street. The band leaves the cemetery, playing "Just a Closer Walk with Thee," and Bolden, again, in a ceremonial rupture belts out the parade strut. At this point, Henry Allen leads him by the arm to the sidewalk, telling a sympathetic woman, "Madame, he's Buddy Bolden. Send for the ambulance!"

Danny Barker's vision of the birth of jazz stems from that moment when Bolden, in his house, melds the sacred and profane, a hymn fused with the burning pathos of the blues. When Bolden reaches the cemetery—symbolically witnessing his death as an artist—Allen banishes him for violating ritual, playing hot music at a sacred moment.

Barker's creation story transcended the historical consensus of the time in which Storyville, parades, and blues were considered the wellsprings of jazz; little had been written about the link to churches in 1965. Barker was years ahead of Thomas Brothers, Ted Gioia, and other revisionist historians. Barker used the oral history interview as a structure for satire, letting Dude Bottley uncork. In an oral tradition, the telling is as important as the tale. "After all," Albert Murray has written, "what the comprehensive, valid and reliable biography or history must always add up to for all its entirely proper preoccupation with specific fact, is fiction. The subject's vital statistics are such and such and his doings and accomplishments are already a matter of public record.... *But what is his story?* What, in other words, is his functional mythology, his personal frame of reference?"

Danny Barker's story, and functional mythology, was his own odyssey, from New Orleans to New York and back, a witness to the jazz century with details to exaggerate or shade as storytelling required.

In New Orleans, rousing from segregation, he became assistant curator of a jazz museum; when the job ended he worked cleaning carpets in a hotel for a stretch. Good billing at the 1970 Jazz and Heritage Festival sparked the comeback, singing and playing guitar in ensembles with Blue Lu. Her career had been erratic. "If I didn't feel like singing I wouldn't," recalled Miss Lu. "Besides, I had Sylvia to raise."

Sylvia settled in Rochester, New York, raising a large family, as the Barkers became celebrities in New Orleans.

· · · · · · · · · ·

FAREWELL TO PAUL AND UP WITH FAIRVIEW

On February 17, 1969, the night before Mardi Gras, the Onward Brass Band marched in Proteus, an old-pedigree parade. As the maskers on floats threw beads, Paul Barbarin stumbled onto the sidewalk of oak-shrouded St. Charles Avenue, sat on the steps of an apartment building, and died at seventy-one. Among his compositions, the classic "Bourbon Street Parade" is a parade beat paean to the town he deeply loved.

Let's fly down or drive down
To New Or-leans
That city has pretty
Historic scenes
I'll take you and parade you
Down Bourbon Street
There's a lot of hot spots
See all the big shots
Down on Bourbon Street.

Barbarin's funeral that February 22 began with a Mass at a Catholic church, musicians playing inside, a first in the experience of veteran television cameraman Don Perry. The parade drew artists from the Young Tuxedo, Olympia, and Onward, as well as a healthy sprinkling of white musicians. Clarinetist Pete Fountain marched with a visiting Dizzy Gillespie. The second line stretched back several blocks, weaving behind the cortege in the shadows of the new I-10 overpass, past Tremé and the Iberville housing project. A promise of racial harmony rolled with the bands and the second line that drew white students from Tulane and young aficionados who sensed that the burial of this musician was more than just a parade. As the human river rolled toward St. Louis Cemetery Number Two, Danny Barker walked with his nephew Lucien Barbarin at the edge, keeping the grief to himself, unseen in the images of photographers and cameramen following the parade.

Since returning to New Orleans he fretted that youngsters had little access to brass bands. At the behest of Rev. Andrew Darby of the Fairview Baptist Church, two blocks from the Barkers' home, he began working with teenaged trumpeters Gregg Stafford, Leroy Jones, and Greg Davis, teaching them traditional songs. As the Fairview band became popular with parading clubs, older musicians railed that they were being undercut by players not in the musicians' union. Hauled before the union board, Barker had to give his young charges bad news: "I have to stop workin' with y'all." Otherwise, he would lose his union status and many jobs. It was a sad moment, but it emboldened the young players, many of whom went on to major careers. The Dirty Dozen emerged from the Fairview ranks. By 1980 the Dozen's racing percussion and rippling horn lines, refashioning bebop and soul hits like "Night Train," forged a second-line impressionism on Columbia recordings, while generating 200 road dates yearly.

The catalyst of the young brass bands struggled in his creative life, publishing fragments of his work in the alternative press. *Bourbon Street Black*, a 1973 study of musical families published by Oxford University Press, enhanced his status; the academic prose belonged to his coauthor, sociologist Jack V. Buerkle, who organized the material with Danny's observations and interviews with jazzmen.

He had been writing for nearly fifty years when Alyn Shipton, a British jazz scholar and editor at Macmillan in London, offered the elusive contract; Shipton made several trips to New Orleans, organizing boxes of papers, including handwritten pages, drawing the episodes into a typed draft that they read aloud to each other. "We also agreed to retain his grammar," Shipton told me in a letter. "In some of the pieces he felt uneasy about this, but he didn't want his authentic voice 'altered.' Danny was a keen critic

been in the wheelchair, Danny had tended to her needs. Now, he was sleeping on the couch, a newspaper on his chest. Sylvia decided to stay.

For years the Barkers had squabbled about his papers, spread over the kitchen table, where he wrote longhand. Miss Lu persuaded him to have an extra room built on the house and guided into it the boxes, files, photographs, clippings, and books. The house was filled with plaques, photographs, more books. She set a coffee pot in the writing room. Two weeks later Danny was at the kitchen table, writing. One day he returned to find a paper-strewn floor. "You got mad at me," he muttered.

She resented her dependence on his cooking. "Eggs and weenies—his favorite dish. Vienna sausage and boiled eggs."

With Danny unable to cook, Sylvia oversaw a support system, friends and neighbors handling food and errands. Glaucoma vexed him. Still, at Christmas, he was underlining passages in Hobbes's *Leviathan*.

Just before the cancer diagnosis, he had posed for the January 1994 cover of *Offbeat* music magazine: leather jacket open at the chest, guitar held with a swagger, eyes wide, his grin a mug of punk satire. *Danny Barker Still Rockin' after All These Years*.

"Them doctors don't know," said Miss Lu. "You ain't gonna die."

But Kerry Brown knew and Danny knew that Kerry knew. In their banter on undertaking, Kerry had told him that just before people expire, a film forms on the eyes. "The film is gettin' heavy," cracked Danny. His drummer buddy managed a grin. Barker turned serious. "Make sure they don't pump me up too much or leave me lookin' like a scarecrow."

· · · · · · · · · ·

FACING THE MUSIC

As death crawled closer, he accepted the invitation of Krewe Du Vieux to ride as king of their Carnival parade, fronting a legion of brass bands. Krewe Du Vieux was the brainchild of young Jewish celebrants determined to sharpen the satire directed at politicians in a state with a spectacular history of corruption. They offered Barker a horse-drawn wagon; he opted for a car, fearing the cold night air. On January 29, 1994, Geraldine Wyckoff, the *Gambit Weekly* music writer, helped his rail-thin frame into a gold lame coat; he wore a bright tie and sequined derby hat. As the bands gathered for photographs, he told jokes, drawing smiles from a young protégé, trumpeter James Andrews. The parade halted at Palm Court where eighty-nine-year-old Doc Cheatham, a vintage swing trumpeter down from New York (their careers had overlapped in Cab Calloway's band), raised a solo in his honor. Barker waved to crowds on streets he remembered from childhood. They reached Praline Connection, a cavernous club in the warehouse district. He took the stage with the Algiers Brass Band but became dazed. Fighting tears, Wyckoff helped him down. James Andrews, waiting to go on, began crying.

When clarinetist Michael White sat with him, Barker was candid. "Look how this stuff has gotten." He revealed an emaciated leg. "You live your life, and all of a sudden you wake up one day and find it's all over."

For Sylvia Barker Brunner Jones, sixty, plump, and witty, the memories floated back to the Bronx apartment when he played with Cab Calloway. Her daddy in his easy chair: books, newspapers, cigarettes. One night the radio warned of freezing winds; he had a gig in Hoboken. Don't go, she begged. He said: "When you have work, you go. *And always be on time.*"

He was losing track of time, sleeping a lot. A lady from Rhodes funeral home visited, Miss Lu selected a bronze coffin from the photographs. She told Sylvia that Danny would outlive her.

He was coughing hard, reusing soggy tissues. "Daddy," said Sylvia, "you don't have to do that."

"I'm trying to save them."

She told him not to worry. "You have lots of napkins."

"How many?"

"At least five hundred."

"Let me see them."

She produced two unopened packs, which set him at ease.

Mardi Gras 1994 was joyless for the Barkers. Sylvia and Lu watched Danny sleep on the couch in delirium. "Only dirges," he mumbled. "No vandalism in streets." He woke up and said he did not want a jazz funeral. He wanted no damage on his account by rowdy second liners.

Miss Lu insisted he was not dying.

Gregg Stafford, the forty-year-old trumpeter of the Jazz Hounds, sat with him one afternoon. Lean, thoughtful, impeccably mannered, Stafford had a day job as a schoolteacher. A distant cousin of Red Allen's family, he shared a coded banter with his mentor, whom he called Mr. Barker. Their phone calls always began with Mr. Barker's salutation: "How's *jazzz*?" Stafford recalled a gig in New York that included Michael White and Mr. Barker's grand-nephew, trombonist Lucien Barbarin. On the limousine ride into Manhattan, he spoke of nights long ago, a corner where Malcolm X had stirred crowds. Now he was worried, whispering, "Don't tell Sylvia I can't do anything. I was doing everything before she got here. I'm not a handicapped person."

Stafford soothingly told him not to worry.

When Tom Dent, the writer, sat with him, Danny said hoarsely: "I want to thank you for everything you've done for me. You're a friend, a good friend."

Saying goodbye to people may have fed the hallucinations.

"Look at Dean," he said, as Lu sat by the bed.

Dean Andrews, a roguish lawyer who had helped District Attorney Jim Garrison in the notorious JFK murder prosecution of businessman Clay Shaw, had done legal work for Paul in exchange for music lessons. Dean had gotten gigs for Danny and Lu. "What you tryin' to do, make me scared?" Lu hissed. "You know Dean *been* dead, Danny."

"Braud was here this morning," he reported.

Wellman Braud, Creole bassist on Blue Lu's 1938 sessions. Died in L.A. in 1965. "Danny, don't talk no stuff about Braud bein' here!"

Sylvia sat by him. He said, "Who's that lady in the red dress?"

"You see a lady in a red dress?"

"Yeah."

"Where is she?" piped Sylvia.

"Right up there by the bed."

"Well, I don't know who she is."

He paused. "Who's that black-nosed man over there?"

"You see a man with a black nose?" she parried.

"Yes."

"Do you know him?"

"No."

"Well, *tell him to get outta here!*"

"Now, Sylvia, that poor fella's not botherin' anybody. Just let him stay."

She left the room. When she returned he was gazing at the wall. She said, "Tell the lady with the red dress I said hello."

He turned toward her. "What lady?"

"The lady—"

"Sylvia, are you trying to play jokes on me? Death is a serious business."

Sylvia slept by him to make sure he didn't roll off the bed. One night he asked who she was. "It's me, Daddy," she whispered.

On March 12, 1994, she told her mother: "Don't go to bed. He's gonna die."

"Your daddy ain't gonna die. I'm going to bed."

On the morning of March 13 his throat was badly parched. "I think maybe he needs some water," said Miss Lu. "Wake him."

"*Shaddup!*" he blurted. "I don't wanna hear all this yackin'."

Sylvia asked if he wanted ice cream. "Okay." He ate three spoonfuls.

"You want some applesauce?" said Miss Lu.

"You talk too much!"

Just like their spats, thought Sylvia. Miss Lu rolled the wheelchair into the living room and said to a neighbor, helping, "Take me outside so I can smoke a cigarette."

Moments later Sylvia stepped onto the porch. "Daddy's dead."

"Your daddy ain't dead."

Sylvia called a nurse; she asked the neighbor to find a mirror to put under his nostrils. Just then Michael White arrived, an inner voice having told him to go now rather than that afternoon. A thirty-nine-year-old clarinetist with Barker in the Palm Court band, White had ancestors who played early jazz, men Barker had known. Sylvia and Miss Lu stood back. In the bedroom, White knew immediately he was dead. Sylvia and her mother mulled his last words—"Shut up!"—which triggered a flashback in Michael White: the mordant Danny Barker wit, singing his version of "St. James Infirmary," the lyrics of a poor man claiming his dead girlfriend at a hospital, which Danny transformed into a man imagining his own grand funeral (like a tale of Storyville) with white horses and chorus girls. He sings, "Be quiet! Can't you see I'm trying to pass away?" He had gone out a comedian, thought White.

But laughter was impossible. The eighty or so second-generation jazzmen he had known in Preservation Hall, coming up, were gone—Louis Nelson, Teddy Riley, Chester Zardis, Sweet Emma Barrett—a name upon a name and Michael White thinking, *I've almost gotten numb to this. Death is a part of life. I'm happy to have known these people, and what they were, their music, their spirit. They gave it to me and it is a part of my spirit and my music. So I feel a part of them is still alive. But each time this happens it's like losing your father all over again.*

He sat with Miss Lu and Sylvia.

Gregg Stafford arrived, then Tom Dent and the family attorney, Lois Elie. They sat in the living room with Miss Lu to discuss the burial. Rhodes Funeral Home contacted Mayor Marc Morial, who offered Gallier Hall for the wake: the majestic Greek Revival temple, old City Hall, the city's ceremonial building. The previous wake there had been in 1989 for Ernest "Dutch" Morial, the city's first African American mayor—Marc's father. Mr. Barker would be the first musician to lie in state, where the body of Jefferson Davis had lain in state slightly more than a century ago.

"Danny did not want a jazz funeral," croaked Miss Lu. She told them he did not want wild second liners damaging property. He wanted dignity. Gregg Stafford shared his mentor's frustration about the rawness of crack funerals—kids tromping on cars, spewing beer, even wielding handguns in second lines for some victims of the drug wars. Stafford as a boy had watched benevolent society men in uniforms, ramrod straight with pomp and majesty. He told Miss Lu that he understood how she felt. "But I can control the funeral by the music we play."

Sylvia wanted her daddy sent off in the best tradition. Tom Dent, who would stay up all night writing the funeral program, concurred. "Danny Barker's funeral had to make a statement that the culture was preserved," Stafford said later, "that second liners don't control the atmosphere— musicians do."

The wake at Gallier Hall was grand.

Harold "Duke" Dejan, the eighty-five-year-old leader of Olympia Brass Band, slowed by a stroke, using a cane, walked in the grip of Milton Batiste, the balding, gray-bearded trumpeter of sixty who guided the band. Then came Wendell Brunious, a trumpeter whose brother John played trumpet at Preservation Hall; their father had done musical arrangements for Armstrong. Freddie Lonzo, who played with Gregg Stafford in the Young Tuxedo, unpacked his trombone. Three dozen musicians in black suits, white shirts, and black ties fanned out beneath chandeliers in a parlor with tall French windows and a large mirror in ornate gold trim. Michael White hovered over Trombone Shorty, the seven-year-old marching with his brother James Andrews on trumpet. A third of the musicians were white, the transplanted British jazzmen out in force. A regal spirit suffused the room as the dirges flowed in somber, rolling rhythms, laced with sweetness. Two grand marshals carrying top hats cradled at their chest sashes led the procession into the hallway where Mr. Barker lay in an open casket, flanked by a guitar and floral arrangements in the design of musical notes. The musicians turned into the room where Miss Lu sat at the head of the receiving line in her wheelchair, next to Sylvia, the grandchildren, nieces, and nephews.

There was a beauty to the body, a smooth tan hue and curled eyebrows to suggest an eternal smile. For a dead man he looked great.

Three times the musicians made the route, the melodies echoing into far reaches of the elegant rooms.

A requiem Mass the next morning, St. Patrick's Day, at St. Raymond's Church in Gentilly, drew 500 friends and three dozen musicians. The Barkers had attended Fairview Baptist Church for years; but Danny wanted to leave life as he had entered, a Catholic. A black deacon gave a formal eulogy, reading sections of a Barker profile by Michael Tisserand. Several times the deacon checked the magazine—"and, as Mike wrote"—signaling that he had never met the man whose life he was recapping, an irony Barker would have milked in a story.

In the eulogy, Sylvia recalled the father who never went past eighth grade but inspired her to read, saying, "The libraries are free. And because a person only has a small amount of education doesn't mean they can't learn beyond what the school taught. You can't afford to go to college? Find out what books they're reading and get them."

She spoke of his near-death hallucinations as jocular examples of his compassion, worrying about the lady in the red dress. She repeated his last words: "*Shaddup* you two, I don't wanna hear all this yackin'!" As the mourners roared, Sylvia beamed. "His spirit is here and he's saying, '*Shut up! Shut up! Shut up!*'" She walked off to applause.

The musicians filed out, playing "In the Sweet Bye and Bye" under warm blue skies. TV cameramen and still photographers jostled for room as the musicians formed two lines, stretching from steps of the church to the curb of Paris Avenue. Up went the trumpets and trombones in an arched gauntlet, gleaming gold, notes in high streaming swirls. Six men in tuxedos with white sashes, hats held across the chest and then singer Wanda Rouzan, in black tights, tux shirt, and formal coat, pink sash, pink tie, and a white papier-mâché dove on the shoulder, a symbol of the spirit. One of the grand marshals, an aging Alfred "Dut" Lazard, a cousin of Miss Lu's, a charter member of the Money Wasters Social Aid and Pleasure Club, had made his trip to the hospital early that morning for kidney dialysis in order to lead the second line.

Next came the pallbearers, including Tom Dent, Lolis Elie, Danny's nephews, and grandson Larry Brunner, followed by Sylvia and Miss Lu in the wheelchair. After the dirge the musicians boarded a lift bus that followed the car caravan several miles to the intersection of North Claiborne and Orleans Avenues, six blocks from St. Louis Cemetery Number Two. With the family sat the retired drummer, Louis Barbarin, ninety-one, Danny's last surviving uncle. The procession began for the final blocks, the band playing "Just a Closer Walk with Thee." Lindy Boggs, the retired congresswoman, entered the second line in a bright blue dress. A large tuba bobbed like a golden disc beneath the shadow of the I-10 overpass. People from the Iberville housing project joined the second line as it grew to 2,000 people, a fourth of them white, passing an Art Deco movie house reincarnated as a Full Gospel church, past Holly's Automotive Repairs and over train tracks that once brought men to Storyville, young bloods moving in a shuffle, a white gal holding her baby, wizened men with red eyes bobbing as the band shifted to a slow tempo "Cloudless Day." As they turned the corner toward the pale white walls of the cemetery, the band broke into a charge on Paul Barbarin's "The Second Line," people waving handkerchiefs and umbrellas like sun-splashed mushrooms. Under Gregg Stafford's hand the band led the second liners to an impromptu jam at a club just down in Tremé.

They buried him in the Barbarin crypt next to Paul.

Miss Lu would join him there after a burial parade three years later.

"You see the music's effect on people," Mr. Barker wrote. "Foot patting, finger snapping, head and body bouncing to the beat. That's a great pleasure for me and the people. So jazz will live on, because it digs down inside the body, the brain, the heart, the nerves and the muscles."

14

Dr. Michael White and the Widow's Wail

In 1995, Dr. Michael White was in the prime of life. He had a medal from the French government as a Chevalier of Arts and Letters for the poetic way he played the clarinet. His New Orleans stature and line of recordings packed his voicemail with messages from outposts like Paris and Washington, D.C. A hefty six-foot-one, with fair brown skin and close-cropped hair, he had a doctorate in Spanish and a day job as a Xavier University professor. White enjoyed an association with Wynton Marsalis, flying to New York for Jazz at Lincoln Center performances. He took his Original Liberty Jazz Band on the summer circuit of musicians playing the festivals from Scandinavia to Nice, and since 1989 they had had a standing six-day gig at the Village Vanguard in Manhattan that climaxed on New Year's Eve.

He was moving deeper into New Orleans Style, excavating the past, imagining the dawn of jazz, emulating sounds of that fertile time when rural black folk planted a blues sensibility in the city of pianos and horns, and the new music sprouted like a thousand blossoms. White's compositions were competing with the standards of Louis Armstrong, Sidney Bechet, and Jelly Roll Morton, the great ghosts whose records still sold, their songs played by traditional jazz bands stoking the flame for younger fans who danced to the old-time heat. Alone in his house, Michael White composed parts for his instrumentalists, playing certain passages on the clarinet, then penciling the sequences onto music paper. Sometimes he pictured the string of notes circling like a halo over the genius of Jelly Roll Morton, "a master at creating moods and blending harmonies," said White.

Burial rites were vital to this language. Bolts of mirth and grief charged the funeral marches that Jelly had simulated in a few songs. Like the chorus of a Greek tragedy, brass bands in the parades of mourning sang out the psyche of a people, the rituals in which sorrow gave way to catharsis, releasing social tensions in the second line, the spectacular street dancers gyrating in a life force of their own.

Playing the funerals is a *rite de passage* for New Orleans musicians, showing the older guys you had the chops to play the march to church or mortuary, giving a gentle touch to hymns like "Just a Little While to Stay Here," comforting survivors.

> Just a little while to stay here
> Just a little while to wait
> Just a little while to labor
> In the path that's always straight
> Oh, just a little more of sorrow
> In this low and sinful state
> Then we'll enter heaven's portals
> Sweeping through those pearly gates

White had sat in countless wakes with members of the Olympia and Young Tuxedo bands as the preacher or priest washed mourners in the cascades of a pulpit eulogy. When the service was done, they escorted the coffin out to the bass drum's solemn tolling, and after the pallbearers lodged the casket in the hearse, the musicians unfurled the dirges, hymns setting the tone for the march to the cemetery, trailed by the limousines and dancers in the second line, waiting to uncoil.

White's job in the dirges was to capture melancholy. The clarinet, a dark cylinder studded with silver keys and lined with a thin reed, sang the "widow's wail," a cry of lamentation and female woe. Heading to the cemetery, the men played hymns at a slow tempo, like "Just a Closer Walk with Thee," marching to the cadence set by the grand marshal in a tuxedo or morning suit with tails, holding a top hat over the sash, leading them forth, one foot in slow drag behind the other, out again and down the street.

The musicians in their uniforms of black and white formed a shimmering color field and an image of dignity as the Masonic lodge or a given Social Aid and Pleasure Club escorted their colleague to rest. Year after year the photographs, film, and video scenes of funerals had formed an image of New Orleans, a symbol of the place that fit tourism marketing hand-in-glove. Throngs of people flanked the band and the cortege on the dead march. Ten musicians, a dozen, sometimes more from several bands if the deceased were a musician, followed the grand marshal. After the coffin had been lowered and the words of the priest or pastor had faded, the musicians filed out of the cemetery or graveyard, and hit an up-tempo charge for the "cutting loose" of the soul, sparking the second liners' dancing and drawing others off the stoops and porches, celebrating the departure of someone many of them never knew.

Creole folklore carried a belief that the soul, once loosened from the body, would roam among the living, fearful of the afterlife, and so the bereaved kinfolk had to shake and dance at the funeral to keep that wandering ghost from lodging inside their bodies.

In the vibrant cross-rhythms and shuffle of shoes in the street, the second liners moved like a rushing river. The trumpets spun out the melody, White sent up streams of countermelody; the backbeat rolled to the swish of the snare and the pounding of the bass drum, the trombones and saxophones anchored harmony; and he felt the power of the second liners surging alongside the band, catching glimpses of raggedy trousers, stained undershirts, fancy threads or raincoats, a flash-by of hair packed in rollers, others coiffed, red-eyed from booze or drugs, gunshot survivors trundling in wheelchairs, kids high-prancing under windows where old folk cheered — a river of people "answering the call to a culture back past your parents and grandparents to the very beginning, back to Congo Square where the slaves danced, like the call of a spirit that says *now is the time to express this part of your being*, free from earthly troubles and worries: shout, dance, create, transform yourself into another type of being in a world that sets you free."

After a decade of economic free-fall from the oil slump, the city in its faded splendor lumbered toward century's end. White was aghast at changes threatening the funerals. Crack cocaine had come down like a plague in the late 1980s; gun battles over drug turf or macho respect-posturing left sidewalks tattooed in blood, many of the dead boys too young to vote. A new generation of bands who played their funerals raised no widow's wail because they no longer included clarinets. Younger brass bands like ReBirth, Soul Rebels, and New Birth were largely composed of players who had grown up in households poorer than White's with fewer opportunities than he had had. The younger bands competed with established groups like Doc Paulin's band to play for the Scene Boosters, Money Wasters, and Lady Buck Jumpers, among other Social Aid and Pleasure Clubs. The younger bands kept a throbbing parade beat for second liners, a sound reliant more on tubas for melodic push and hypnotic, mesmerizing lines from saxophones and trumpets, far from the intricate countermelodies that colored New Orleans Style. Sometimes they played strong melody, sometimes not. White searched for players up to the demanding compositions of Jelly Roll Morton.

The younger bands were linked to a wider cultural web. Rhythm was the piston of youth culture, driving the long dancing lines of Carnival in the samba schools of Brazil, melding percussive beds and lyrical Afropop guitar lines in Western nightclubs that exalted world music, and pulsing in the rap and hip-hop culture that galvanized young people in an ever-more connected world. The lost clarinets of younger brass bands saddened White; but he saw a greater loss. The second lines were getting rougher—wild, drug-lit people spewing beers on hearses, even shooting off guns. The tradition faced a moral erosion.

Born in 1954, Michael White grew up in a family that never attended brass band funerals. The first one that registered on him was in a TV news clip in early January 1969. "One of those famous jazz musicians," his mother murmured. He remembered the name, George Lewis, and not much else. At fourteen he knew next to nothing about jazz.

Shy and bespectacled, White was not a campus star at St. Augustine, the premier high school for black boys in New Orleans. He didn't hang with the sons of Creole doctors and lawyers. Looking back, he wryly called himself "a New Orleans half-breed." His father, Oscar White, was a mailman, Protestant, and darker than his mother, Helen Forcia, who came from a hard-working Creole family. Helen's mother owned two houses Uptown. Helen and her sister, Natalie—the aunt who gave Michael his first clarinet—had college degrees. "My parents embodied black and Creole, Uptown and Downtown, the dichotomy of early jazz," he recalled. "But jazz was not central to their lives."

Michael spent his early years in the Lower Ninth Ward. In the 1950s houses began dotting farm fields as oil industry work grew in St. Bernard Parish. The Ninth was such a quilt that class distinctions vied with those of race. Dr. Frank Minyard, the flamboyant Orleans Parish coroner who played jazz trumpet as an avocation in a political career spanning forty years, recalled his mother saying, "They don't like us poor whites, Uptown." She refused to let him swim at Audubon Park pool, Uptown.

Two doors down from the Whites' home at 1329 Lizardi Street, a lady raised ducks. Another neighbor kept chickens. Fruit and vegetable gardens abounded. Barbecue aromas wafted in the air from Sunday cookouts. The moaning guitar strings and piano licks of the rural blues found a home in clubs and honky-tonks across "the Big Nine."

In 1957, the state began digging an artery down through St. Bernard Parish: the Mississippi River Gulf Outlet. MR-GO was an alternative route for ship traffic leading to the Gulf of Mexico. With a levee built alongside the seventy-six-mile waterway, wetlands that had long served as buffers against hurricane tidal flooding began drying up.

At St. David grammar school, White's classmate Anatole Domino bragged, "My daddy got so much money he puts it in a safe!" You could drive by Fats Domino's mansion on Caffin Avenue and see the sleek cars in the driveway of the man whose records rocked with that feel-good boogie beat. Anatole had seven siblings—his sisters Antoinette, Andrea, Anola, and Adonica and his brothers Antoine III, Andre, and Antonio. White bars across the segregated city featured Fats's music on jukeboxes as did Negro taverns. In 1962, when Oscar and Helen White moved the family across town to Carrollton, on the fringes of Uptown, the city had a white majority. As the Lower Nine gagged on the poisoned polemics of Governor Jimmie Davis and Leander Perez, ethnic whites, hostile to school desegregation, began moving to suburbs. The city would become 67 percent black by 2005, when Hurricane Katrina flooding demolished much of the Lower Nine.

Michael was seven when they moved into the home of his maternal grandmother, Natalie Gauff Forcia, on Dante Street, in a mostly white Carrollton neighborhood. His uncle, a thirty-nine-year-old doctor, had died of a heart attack upstate in Alexandria; his grieving mother invited the older daughter, son-in-law, and two grandkids to live with her and ease the sorrow. The move typified the clannish Creoles: a family under the same roof saves financially in drawing closer. White: "My grandmother looked almost white. She had lived there since the 1950s. People thought that my aunt [Natalie] was her live-in maid. She was a schoolteacher." After the Whites moved in, white boys threw rocks and eggs at the house.

Oscar White was a Boy Scout master who believed in discipline, toughness, and survival. The happiness Michael felt on camping trips went numb amid the bigotry he faced on the street. He grew up with the civil rights movement a narrative on the nightly news and neighborhood hooligans harassing him. Once he ran inside and grabbed a baseball bat, only to find they had fled. Several times the police responded to his father's calls; no one was arrested, not even the big boy with a German shepherd who had gone after Michael, hissing, "Sic that nigger!" The dog bit him on the stomach. More than his bloodied skin, it was the look of hatred on the animal's face and its owner's that gave Michael nightmares.

He attended the Holy Ghost School, a good ways down in Central City— as the Uptown part of Back o' Town now was known—returning to lonely afternoons at the house in Carrollton. He erected defenses, believing, as his father held, that one day good would defeat evil. At Mass in the corner church they sat in back pews, whites in front. The Catholic archdiocese on Carrollton Avenue was a few minutes' walk from their home. The archbishop's mansion occupied a corner of the stately grounds; behind it was the chancery office. Several white people became fixtures in media coverage, protesting the Church's decision to integrate parochial schools. In 1962, an uneasy Archbishop Joseph Rummel, prodded by Auxiliary Bishop John Cody, who would succeed him, excommunicated Leander Perez and Mrs. B. J. Gaillot, a housewife who railed against race-mixing. The expulsion humiliated those in the humiliation business, signaling a Church that was slowly reversing course. Perez later made amends with the new archbishop; he was buried in the church. Mrs. Gaillot never looked back.

In 1965 Hurricane Betsy blasted the city with fierce winds that drove water over the levee along Industrial Canal, flooding the Lower Ninth. Eighty-one people died. The black historian and poet Marcus Christian lost valuable research papers. A few days later, Michael rode with his father to the house they still owned on Lizardi Street. The place of his happy childhood was a muddy mess. One of the older boys in a family living nearby, Kenneth Ferdinand, went into his grandfather's house and found the old man's body.

A voracious reader, White turned inward, going through Ian Fleming's novels and the James Bond movies, imagining himself a secret agent, cool and powerful, gorgeous women throwing themselves at him. He barely dated as he moved through St. Augustine High. He felt like a goldfish in a pool of sharks, isolated between the socially adroit Creoles and the macho guys on athletic scholarship, several of them from the St. Bernard Avenue housing project. White was a good student with budding skills on the clarinet. St. Augustine's Purple Knights fielded a 100-member band, decked out in gold-and-purple uniforms with helmets, knees pumping as they marched in Mardi Gras parades. As a kid he watched the band with racing envy; now he felt proud to march as a Purple Knight in the parades where even white folks cheered.

He took private lessons on the clarinet; he enjoyed the classes in Spanish, the sense of discovery made him feel like a spy cracking a code.

New Orleans entered an era of prosperity in the 1970s under Mayor Moon Landrieu, a New Deal liberal who ushered blacks into city government as federal funds pumped the infrastructure projects. The Jazz and Heritage Festival boosted countless careers and became the catalyst for a burgeoning club circuit. African American artists began exhibiting in top galleries; filmmakers followed Mardi Gras Indian gangs. A biracial sensibility was emerging from the ashes of segregation. The St. Aug band director, Edwin

Hampton, carried thirty clarinetists, using the section to simulate violin and keyboard parts. In 1972, White's senior year, Hampton exposed them to records of the Olympia Brass Band.

Michael followed the path of his mother and aunt to Xavier, a mile or so from the home on Dante Street, a Catholic university with a largely African American student body. Living at home, majoring in Spanish, White found that as more blacks moved into the neighborhood, the white harassment ended. Besides, he was bigger now.

He sat in on a music history course taught by Danny Barker, who spoke in rolling stories. White listened to jazz records in his room, marveling as the instrumental voices merged and parted, creating space for the solos. Modernists like John Coltrane and Miles Davis were cultural icons; White kept listening to music of the seminal idiom with its tight ensembles. He browsed in record shops, scouring the liner notes like a guilty stand-up reader in a bookstore. One spring day he was talking with guys in the music program when a tuba player suggested he call Doc Paulin, a brass band leader who gave nonunion guys spot work. He sidled up to him at the 1975 New Orleans Jazz and Heritage Festival.

Ernest "Doc" Paulin was sixty-eight, a gruff trumpeter raised upriver in St. John the Baptist Parish. Paulin got his start playing dances, picnics, and weddings in a band with his uncle. "In the country we didn't play funerals," he told me under a tree on a steamy afternoon at a parade break near the levee in the town of Hahnville. It was Mother's Day 1996. Paulin hated interviews but consented in order to promote a CD made with his sons, *The Tradition Continues*. "You'd have to hustle 'em up"—funeral jobs. "You have to play that trumpet, representing it like a preacher.... The trumpet's gonna talk that funeral talk."

Doc Paulin and his wife Betty had thirteen children. They lived in Central City; he ran the Property Owners Voters League, a get-out-the-vote organization for elections. Six of his sons played music; a daughter sang. Doc Paulin had white hair and leathery skin. Sizing up White, he growled in a country patois, "Wha' instrument you play?" *Clarinet*. "I call you for work, you gon show up on time?" *Yes, sir*. "You gon dress right?" *Yeah*. Because a job for Doc Paulin meant you'd better show in black pants, *clean* white shirt, black tie, black shoes, a black coat if it was cold, and a clean white band cap. With six of his sons becoming musicians, the possibility loomed that a new player might be bumped in favor of a Paulin son; but if you showed up, nine times out of ten, you got work. "In this organization," Paulin declaimed, "you GOT to be on time!" At his house, Doc Paulin inspected each uniform and thought nothing of throwing out a man with scuffed shoes. He lectured them about being professional: "Handle yo own bidness not like some union says"—so much self-reliance talk that White once saw snare drummer Rickey Paulin's eyes glaze over.

From his sheltered background, Michael White found it all so fascinating. His first job with Doc Paulin was a parade for the Morning Star Baptist Church across the Mississippi in the town of Marrero. He earned eleven dollars and took his girlfriend to dinner. His first funeral job was in Hahnville, twenty-eight miles upriver. As Doc Paulin's band marched on the road below the levee, playing a slow-tempo "Just a Closer Walk with Thee," the men of the Masonic lodge wore navy blue admirals' uniforms, holding swords, the women in white gowns stately as they marched, everyone utterly solemn, and White had the overpowering sensation of water, as if the Mississippi currents were pulling the band, pulling the mourners, a sensation that filled him with a primordial sense of the music as tides of the spirit. Sending out high peals from the upper register, the wind blowing off the river, White absorbed notes placed in movement, his clarinet planting sorrow in the mind of the march. Later, when they cut loose in the second line, he saw a reserve in the strutting, twirling umbrellas and white handkerchiefs, as if they were dancing in church.

The city was opening up to him as White played gigs in neighborhoods he had once avoided, shaking hands with white socialites at the occasional high-end party. But reminders of the raw past were never far away. One gig with Doc Paulin in 1975 required the band to march down St. Charles Avenue as part of a Tulane fraternity's celebration of Robert E. Lee, the frat boys wearing Rebel uniforms with a Confederate flag, the sorority girls in hoop skirts and bonnets. Full of loathing, he protested to Doc Paulin. "A job is a job," the old man growled. "You play to get paid." White marched, but he never again took a gig like that.

His Xavier advisors counseled him to apply for Ivy League scholarships to pursue a doctorate in Spanish. But like the river at that funeral, jazz was pulling at him, a spiritual current with mysteries about himself. He landed a Ford Foundation fellowship for postgraduate studies and chose Tulane University. He wanted to go deeper into New Orleans Style. The place to do that was the city where jazz began.

. . . .

DISCOVERING GEORGE LEWIS

There are turning points in the life of a young artist, no matter the medium, when the discovery of a master fires the imagination with ideas of greater

Dr. Michael White

reach and expression. White's epiphany came in the spring of 1978; he was standing in a record store, a friend recommended *Jazz at Preservation Hall: The George Lewis Band*. A vague memory of Lewis's funeral on the TV news poked him, and he bought the album. In his room, he put needle to the vinyl. Enthralled at the quavering of Lewis's clarinet, he played the record over and over, the deep lolling passages of sorrow rising into gusts of joy as Lewis ran his notes up the register. Michael had never heard an instrument ring from the soul like George Lewis on clarinet. Why couldn't he be so alive? White suddenly saw a design to life—his family, his race, what New Orleans meant to him. Lewis and his trumpeter Kid Howard were "telling my story in what they played.... I need[ed] to know the fullness of that story."

In Lewis's signature song, "Burgundy Street Blues," the reed-thin clarinetist fashions a wondrous female persona in the vibrato, like a woman crying, then rising in a swoon at her lover's tender touch. Lewis was packing the sorrow White felt in playing funeral dirges, eliding to sensuous arpeggios suggesting an erotic release. He spent hours playing along with the record, trying to emulate the power and beauty that Lewis had recorded fifteen years earlier, when Michael was a kid with no idea who the great musician was.

George Lewis mined a subconscious story of his race. Born in 1900 in New Orleans, he was a child when his parents parted. His father remained close; he was raised by his mother, Alice Zeno, in a small brick house on Tremé Street, sharing a courtyard with a cousin, two uncles, his maternal grandmother, and his great-grandmother Zaier. Born in about 1800 in Senegal, Zaier was a child kidnapped and sold into slavery. She spent most of her life in New Orleans, first as a house slave, then as a servant after the Civil War for the descendants of the same family. A woman of profound Christianity, Zaier delivered babies as a midwife; she was content to witness the birth of her great-grandson. Alice Zeno lost two infants at birth. Zaier named him George. He was six when his African grandmother died at age 106.

George Lewis joined the Young Veterans Benevolent Association, wearing a bowler hat and knee pants to march in their parades. Alice Zeno had a neighbor, a widow who lived in a water cistern, a large wooden cone without ventilation, only one room for a bed, table, and stove. Alice scraped together funds to buy her a benevolent society policy, ensuring her funeral would be paid. A delegation from the group paid a visit to the cistern, invited the old lady to lunch, and helped her find a decent place to live. When she died, Alice found herself the beneficiary of funds that the burial costs had not consumed.

The biographer Ann Fairbairn saw Lewis's style as forged "through the open window of the churches, at the picnics and in the churches during the funeral services, and it moved him as no other type of music ever had … remember[ing] the transcendent lyricism of a woman's voice." Working his E-flat clarinet, Lewis in his early twenties joined the Eureka Brass Band, which would become the city's preeminent midcentury marching unit. Lewis began "playing for funerals about 1923," he said. "I liked it better than playing dance music; I could hear that clarinet singing all the time." His own high quavering caused a woman at one funeral to break into the band, snatch the clarinet from his mouth, and cry, "Make him stop, for the love of Jesus! He's breakin' my heart."

As White pored through articles and biographies about George Lewis, he played the music, seeking his own voice on the B-flat clarinet, the instrument on which Lewis made most of his recordings.

Unlike the Creole clarinetists from family traditions of the Seventh Ward, Lewis drew his inspiration from the chant-like rhythms of small churches and the bent pitches of blues and country. George Lewis was the supreme talent of early jazzmen who did not follow the diaspora of musicians like Armstrong and Jelly to Chicago and New York. He was a catalyst in the New Orleans Revival of the 1940s, when William Russell began producing records in the Crescent City. Bill Russell fostered a reunion of Lewis and the trumpeter Bunk Johnson, who had played together in the 1920s. At a 1931 gig in the Cajun town of Rayne, as the band was setting up, a guy with a knife stormed the stage and stabbed the second trumpeter, Evan Thomas, convinced that he was having sex with his wife. Thomas's blood spewed over Lewis's shirt. The trumpeter bled to death as musicians scattered. The killer trashed their instruments. Bunk Johnson retreated to his home in New Iberia, abandoning music for years. Lewis made it back home. Russell, who discovered Bunk years later in New Iberia, rehabilitated him for the first of many recordings on his American Music label, in 1945, that one done in George Lewis's backyard.

Lewis worked for years as a stevedore on the river dock, unloading heavy cargo. After the 1961 founding of Preservation Hall, he spent his last seven years as a full-time musician. His concert tours in Europe, and a famous trip to Japan with his band, drew huge press coverage, establishing him as a major musician. "His slim body had the energy of a coiled snake," wrote Tom Sancton. "His clarinet seemed to fill the room with soul and spirit, something deep, dark, and eternal."

After a long immersion in Lewis's recordings, and reading heavily about early jazz, White began digging into his own history.

His grandmother had a shotgun-double house on South Liberty Street where Michael's mother grew up, near the Tulane campus. White moved into one side of the double as he advanced in his doctoral studies. Liberty ran like a plumb line through black Uptown in a rough parallel with elegant St. Charles Avenue seven blocks away. The Humphrey brothers, Percy and Willie, lived nearby. His mother told him about concerts the grandsons of James Brown Humphrey played in the 1930s at a playground near the house as part of the Works Progress Administration, stopping to talk to her on the way back. He began to see the old men in the neighborhood. Percy the trumpeter began hiring White on jobs when Willie the clarinetist was unavailable.

From his front porch White could see a small cemetery where an ancestral cousin on his mother's side, Willie "Kaiser" Joseph, a clarinetist, was buried. When he found Kaiser's 1927 recordings with the Jazzola Eight in a used-record bin, White began researching the name on the grave.

Born in 1892 to a family of five boys and seven girls, Kaiser Joseph was like many of the seminal jazzmen who moved to the city from outlying rural areas, in his case St. James Parish. "Everybody played a little something," one of the Joseph sisters told White in an interview. "We all played different instruments." Kaiser played clarinet in the Storyville bordello district before World War I but faded from the music scene and moved to California. He died in 1951. Kaiser's older brother, "Papa John" Joseph (born in 1877), lived much longer. Papa John Joseph played standup bass in several of George Lewis's recordings. Papa John also cut hair at a barbershop owned by one of his brothers on Liberty Street, farther down in Central City. The place was a hub for musicians he booked for gigs. Buddy Bolden hung at the barbershop in the early 1900s. The great Buddy Bolden, first man of jazz, had been Papa John's neighbor. White considered Bolden a figure as tragic as any out of Shakespeare, the pioneer of a new art form who broke into pieces, doomed in his prime to a quarter century of silence.

Bolden's fate shadowed White's research. White wanted to know how jazz began and the role of his ancestral line in the years of the great flowering; he wanted to remember Kaiser and Papa John with his own music carrying their spirit and give praise to Buddy Bolden each time the clarinet met his lips. It wasn't until the early 1960s that the white-haired Papa John

Joseph stopped cutting hair. Imagine the secrets the old man knew! How Michael wished to have been there! To sit in the old barber's chair on Liberty Street, sink his elbows in the timeworn leather, feel some property of the past and ask Papa John about Bolden, Kid Ory, King Oliver, and "little Louis," as they called the teenaged Armstrong. What were they like? What did Bolden's music really sound like? Papa John made the famous 1963 tour of Japan with George Lewis's band that exposed a vast new audience to the New Orleans Revival. In 1965, the eighty-eight-year-old bassist finished a solo at Preservation Hall, turned to the piano player and said, "That piece just about did me in." Then Papa John Joseph keeled over dead of a heart attack.

Michael White was eleven when Papa John died. Researching the lives of George Lewis, Kaiser and Papa John Joseph, not one of whom he had ever met, filled White with questions about the stylistic attack of the early bands, how the funerals and the second line took shape. Papa John played on several of Lewis's recordings. What did they talk about?

White's parents were not musicians, which made him curious about the mystery of a musical gene, skipping a mother, surfacing in her son. There were days when he felt the pull from the graveyard at his corner on Liberty Street like the magnetic force of the old men he got to know at Preservation Hall and in parades; he asked them about Lewis and Papa John, keen for their memory shards. *A piece of those old men is in me, a current passing from them, through me, every time I play.* One afternoon he had to pick up someone in Algiers and found himself in the McDonoghville cemetery, wandering among the tombstones till he found the grave of George Lewis. Staring at the headstone, he wondered if he had the skill and stamina to emulate the stunning beauty of Lewis's playing.

· · · · · · · · · ·

A CALL OF THE STREETS

In the early 1980s, White began playing in Preservation Hall and touring with the house band under the auspices of Allan Jaffe, the tuba player and portly, gentle shepherd in the lives of many older musicians. Playing in the drafty room with the creaky benches at 726 St. Peter Street, where George Lewis and Papa John had held court fifteen years before, deepened White's personal bond with the music.

He found a sidekick, trumpeter Gregg Stafford. As White had come up with Doc Paulin, Stafford had started a bit earlier with the Fairview Baptist Church Brass Band under the tutelage of Danny Barker. In the 1980s

Stafford became the leader of the Young Tuxedo Brass Band, a group founded in 1938 by the clarinetist John Casmir. Marching in the third generation of the Young Tuxedo, White enjoyed the human sea in Social Aid and Pleasure Clubs, many of them from poor neighborhoods, their parades a pageantry of the spirit for folk who saved to make their costumes and his job was to swing the music and make them dance.

Earning his doctorate in Spanish in 1983 was a moment of great pride for the clarinetist. Percy Humphrey gave him fifty dollars with a card of congratulations. The women of White's life—his mother, aunt, sister, and now a wife—formed his own proud ring; he regretted that his father, who had passed away two years earlier, was not there to share in the happiness. Several years later, as the music career became more consuming, White and his wife parted ways.

As White moved through his twenties and thirties, he worked with older men. "These were the last performing years of the surviving second generation jazz musicians, many of whom had been active during the 1920s with some of most important figures in early jazz," he wrote years later. "Being among them made me part of an extended family. We rode together to jobs, talked on the phone, visited, ate out, and had one-on-one practice sessions. They not only shared their music, but the essence of their lives; their secrets and true feelings."

Some had had private lessons and could read music well, while others could not read and were self-taught. They were all very individual players with their own personal styles and expression. What they shared was a similar understanding of the roles of each instrument and how a New Orleans–style ensemble should sound. . . . They came from a time when New Orleans jazz was mainly played for dancing—not stage concerts. They spent most of their lives making hot swinging music largely devoid of the concessions sometimes made for concerts and shows.

One day he ended up with "Kid" Thomas Valentine. White had his records with the Algiers Stompers. Kid Thomas was eighty-three and had driven across from Algiers for a gig in Jackson Square at union scale. As the old man took a seat, the antique banjo player Emmanuel Sayles arrived, a legend in White's eyes for his recordings with George Lewis. Sayles smiled, extending his hand. "How you doing, young man?" As the other guys set up, White realized he was by far the youngest and least experienced member of the band. This made him nervous as they began to play.

"Up to that point I had only really played brass band style clarinet: upper register fills, riffs, and extended high notes. Playing in the lower register, having featured solos, and doing songs in different tempos and tunes that were more harmonically involved—all that was new to me."

The set began, he got into the groove. Kid Thomas called "Burgundy Street Blues," the signature George Lewis song. White blinked, said nothing, nodded. After weeks of playing along to the record in his room, he was about to perform it with Emanuel Sayles, who had recorded it with Lewis. He closed his eyes, counting off 1-2-3, and released the fabled three-note figure that begins the song. A feeling of calm washed through him, his clarinet and body felt guided by some spiritual force, and after the second chorus he started climbing the octaves in search of that piercing vibrato when the splash hit his forehead, then another and another—he opened his eyes to a thunderstorm and the musicians running for cover into the Cabildo. He ran, too, and took shelter with them. He was sad. Watching the sheets of rain, he felt he had come so close! The thin, ancient fingers of Mr. Sayles enveloped his hand: "You made the sky cry. That was beautiful, young man. I haven't played that since George Lewis."

He began billing himself as "Dr. Michael White," the musician with the doctorate gaining confidence as a cat who could really blow. He had occasionally wept while playing the funeral marches of friends passing on; but he maintained the discipline of ritual. Like his idol George Lewis, he wanted to capture his people's story through his music.

· · · · · · · · · ·

POLITICS AND BLOWBACK

As the long recession begun in 1985 slowly hit bottom, a spectacle of demagoguery jolted Louisiana, and the blowback rocked the moorings of Mardi Gras. In 1989, David Duke, a former Ku Klux Klan leader with a face remade by plastic surgery, ran for a vacant statehouse seat as a born-again Republican, attacking government programs benefiting blacks and stoking fears of crime. By a 224-vote margin, Duke won the special election in Metairie, the white suburb bordering New Orleans. In Louisiana's history of political charlatans, Duke was beyond category.

Speaking in the cadences of a television news anchor, he seemed as cool as the other side of the pillow, projecting an aura of the reasoned conservative who had evolved from a hardline past. Before the age of search engines and attached files, the local media did a poor job of probing his past in the short election period in early 1989. The Klan background made international headlines, drawing an army of journalists to the state over the next three years as dogged reporters opened the doors on his life as a closet Nazi. Duke had a mail-order business selling books that debunked the Holocaust as a myth. National television made him a celebrity as he parried shallow questions from talk show hosts who failed to spotlight the extensive record of his links to Neo-Nazi and Klan groups. And yet, as reporters exposed more about his past, Duke's white base held steady, a long foreshadowing of Donald Trump's die-hard evangelical support. Running as an outsider in a state jaded by corruption, Duke showed that when economies contract, so does reason and the human heart.

In 1990, despite a report that he had celebrated Hitler's birthday, Duke pulled a majority of white voters in a race for the U.S. Senate, losing heavily to the incumbent, J. Bennett Johnson. In 1991 he made the gubernatorial runoff with Edwin Edwards, the scandal-stained former governor. A bumper sticker said it all: *Vote for the Crook. It's important.* Edwards won in a landslide; Duke again won a white majority, but he was soon a spent force. He later earned a fifteen-month federal prison term, for mail fraud and filing false tax returns, after fundraising letters telling supporters he was about to lose his house, which yielded $200,000 that he tapped into for trips to casinos in Mississippi, Las Vegas, and the Bahamas.

On December 19, 1991, not two months after the gubernatorial election, with the long Duke nightmare finally done, the New Orleans City Council held a hearing in which several civic leaders—men from Rex, Momus, Proteus, and Comus, also members of elite gentlemen's clubs—found themselves in the awkward position of defending their membership practices under tough questioning by Councilwoman Dorothy Mae Taylor. A veteran civil rights activist, Taylor was pushing an ordinance to desegregate certain private clubs whose members paraded in old-line Carnival krewes. She framed it as an issue of public accommodations—the city covered costs of police for the street parades. Taylor's proposed ordinance drew hard protests from two white colleagues on the council, Jackie Clarkson and Peggy Wilson, who defended the parade groups saying they provided public spectacles that generated huge revenues for the city. Clarkson wanted the ordinance deferred "before we ruin the best things this city has."

Beau Bassich, a former Rex and a philanthropist who ran City Park on a dollar-a-year salary, faced Taylor as she asked if he was a member of any krewes. Like a good Southern gentleman, he replied, "Yes, ma'am."

"Which ones?"

After several silent seconds, he replied, "One of the things that has made Carnival work is tongue-in-cheek secrecy."

"You can't say which krewes you belong to?"

"I cannot. I have been a member for forty years of more than one."

"Have you ever recommended anyone for membership?"

"Yes."

"Have you ever recommended blacks, Jews, or Italians?"

"I don't know about Italians."

"Blacks?"

"No, ma'am."

"Do you think that generating monies through discrimination is right?" Bassich and other Rex leader, John Charbonnet, sat wordlessly.

"Can't answer that?" said Taylor, sarcastically.

Councilwoman Wilson riposted with sarcasm of her own: "I object. We have not yet established the Inquisition, but we're getting close to it."

Taylor was angry. "What's before us today is discrimination!"

Taylor was hitting on a nerve ending of history; men who had prospered through generations of an elite white society were members of krewes that paid the city fees for their parades in a Carnival season—a season that that had grown into the city's biggest industry other than the port, a near-defining essence of New Orleans, with upstart parade groups rolling for nearly a month every winter, generating huge revenues for the city's restaurants, hotels, and a range of vendors. Harry McCall, a lawyer and Comus member, insisted that the clubs had a First Amendment right to private association. After a break for backroom discussions, Bassich and Charbonnet announced that they had reached an agreement with the city. James Gill offers his account of the meeting in *Lords of Misrule*:

> They would drop their opposition to the ordinance, which the council would pass that day. But no action would be taken against the krewes for a year while a "blue ribbon committee on Carnival reconsidered the issue." The council would then vote on any changes the committee might recommend. The faces of krewemen in the audience dropped, for they felt they had been betrayed by their leaders. Meeting beforehand, several krewe members had decided that the most effective strategy would be to announce that, if the ordinance passed, all [of their] parades would be cancelled. Many in the audience were dumbstruck when Bassich and Charbonnet failed to use the threat of economic havoc to force Taylor to back down.

Comus, the oldest parade, and the Knights of Momus, which had begun in 1872 with equally scalding satire of Reconstruction-era politicians and African Americans, announced that they would no longer parade. In 1992, the Krewe of Proteus, which was founded in 1882, withdrew as a parading group. All of them continued having balls. Rex, which took pride in its motto *Pro bono publico*—For the public good—announced a more flexible membership policy.

The blue-ribbon committee proposed a compromise that stripped the ordinance of penalties, with krewe captains signing affidavits pledging that they did not discriminate. In 2000, Proteus returned, singing the non-discrimination pledge, which had no real enforcement mechanism. "The world's changing, and we're changing with the world," Proteus official Gary Brewster told the *Times-Picayune*. Within a decade of the dispute, ten new parade organizations had formed with open admission policies.

· · · · · · · · · ·

FUNERALS CHANGING

As Carnival became a greater engine of culture and commerce, the cultural tides of music and parading in funerals brought more difficult changes, ones that made White and Gregg Stafford, among other traditional jazzmen, uneasy.

"The funerals in the sixties were like ballets compared to the ones today," remarked Jules Cahn on a summer day in 1994. A wealthy businessman and avocational photographer, Cahn had been filming funerals and second lines of the Social Aid and Pleasure Clubs since the early 1960s. His lens had followed second liners in ring dance steps, the Afro hair styles bobbing like cushions, the parasols pumping as circles dissolved in gyrating shoulders and hip-rolling street folk who did some serious getting down.

When Cahn died in 1995, at seventy-eight, Dejan's Olympia Brass Band with musicians from other groups played in the parlor of a mortuary on Rampart Street. Milton Batiste, the Olympia's balding, gray-bearded lead trumpeter, sang "This Train Is Bound for Glory" in a softly rolling baritone, a Christian hymn spawned by the freedom quest of slaves, honoring the genial Jewish businessman. Cahn's family and friends from synagogue, sitting with music aficionados, rocked and swayed in place. "Jules is riding that train now," purred Batiste. "Jules saw it all, did it all."

This was the community that Michael White had come to cherish. His recordings and work with Gregg Stafford in the Young Tuxedo Brass Band gave White an anchor in the society of musicians and aficionados joined by a passion for New Orleans as a place apart. Each funeral strengthened his ties to a culture that honored the dead with music in the daily rites of living. In 1988 he formed the Original Liberty Jazz Band. Recording opportunities blossomed; by the early 1990s he had a national profile among jazz writers and cultural journalists. He still crossed paths with Doc Paulin, who was nearly ninety, still marching, and voicing a concern many musicians felt: "Funerals are changin.' Too much *wildness*."

As the crack plague ate into the 1990s, a string of Sunday second lines for parading clubs erupted in shootings. The drug culture's crooked finger hit Doc Paulin's family the night his son Rickey, thirty-seven, stepped off the bus after a gig. Some dude jumped out of a car and pumped thirteen bullets into his lower torso, legs, and left hand—a total stranger, a gang initiation rite. A father of six, working two jobs, Rickey Paulin miraculously stumbled home. His wife got him to the hospital. Surgeons removed ten bullets; three were too close to the spine to extract. Eight weeks later he walked out and, despite piercing pain, began to rebuild, resuming his work and music.

White felt numb watching TV news, a nightly show on homicide: the yellow police tape strung across another street, sobbing women, a new murder squeezed into forty-five seconds or fewer. The cycle of splintered families and drug killings became a media cliché as the cradle of jazz outpaced Detroit as the nation's leader in per capita homicides.

Nevertheless, White's career was blossoming. His dialogue with Wynton Marsalis led to consulting work on a Jazz at Lincoln Center concert and recordings of Jelly Roll Morton on the New Orleans Masters programs. He drew critical praise for his own discs, particularly *Crescent City Serenade* (1991) and *New Year's at the Village Vanguard* (1993), both on the Antilles label.

The charging section-riff approach of younger bands was as uncomplicated to White as disco or rap. Polyphony, the interweave of instrumental voices tied to a melodic line, was the pulse of the tradition that White was extending in his music and compositions. As the crack killings ate into a culture that, for him, had always been spiritual at the root, he wondered if the deep pull of second lining, a reach across the city's history, was turning against itself. Releasing anguish through dance, the second liners had forged a language of street drama by *not* being predictable. But when parades grew self-destructive, with bullets and violence, where were the spiritual roots? What were the limits?

In 1995 he took his Original Liberty Jazz Band on a first-ever concert tour of China. The tradition he carried was the function of jazz to make people dance. Traditions resist change or develop an adaptive capacity to absorb what is new without compromising the integrity that one generation passes to the next. The brass band burials with the stately procession of musicians in which White had come of age in the 1970s were still the norm, still the center. As funerals for homicide victims rocked over scarred streets that few cameras followed, the idea of the center was up for grabs, each funeral a drama of the city's lurching progress in the ebbing of a century that had opened with the birth of jazz.

Moving into the new millennium, needing more time to compose, he began cutting back on the parade work, balancing his teaching tasks at Xavier with ensemble work at clubs, events, and private parties. He was on a vibrant path with his compositions, reassembling the instrumental voices associated with the elders, improvising melodies off the deep root, when Hurricane Katrina hit on August 29, 2005. He evacuated to Houston with the women in his life, and while following Google maps realized that his house was nine feet underwater.

15

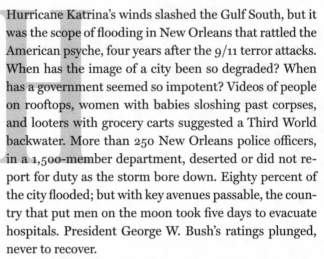

After the Flood

Hurricane Katrina's winds slashed the Gulf South, but it was the scope of flooding in New Orleans that rattled the American psyche, four years after the 9/11 terror attacks. When has the image of a city been so degraded? When has a government seemed so impotent? Videos of people on rooftops, women with babies sloshing past corpses, and looters with grocery carts suggested a Third World backwater. More than 250 New Orleans police officers, in a 1,500-member department, deserted or did not report for duty as the storm bore down. Eighty percent of the city flooded; but with key avenues passable, the country that put men on the moon took five days to evacuate hospitals. President George W. Bush's ratings plunged, never to recover.

New Basin Canal, which ran from the lake to Carrollton with a long turn toward South Rampart, had long since been filled in and paved over to create the Pontchartrain Expressway, the highway that merged with Interstate 10, linking downtown to the suburbs, heading west to Baton Rouge and Texas. More than a million people fled along that route by car before the storm hit. For many of us who crossed the Lake Pontchartrain Causeway to stay in St. Tammany Parish towns, when power went down, battery-powered radio carried news. The haggard voice of WWL-AM reporter Dave Cohen stuck as deep as a surgical implant: "New Orleans is over. Where do I live?"

Once the winds died down, Governor Kathleen Blanco sent National Guardsmen to secure the city; whole areas were underwater and most citizens unable to return. On the second day, Lieutenant Governor Mitch Landrieu drove from Baton Rouge and found Mayor C. Ray Nagin, a former Cox Cable TV executive, on the upper floor of a downtown hotel, dazed. Landrieu recounts their conversation in his recent book *In the Shadow of Statues*:

"What do you need?" I said.

He sat in a chair unable to focus. *He seems out of it*, I thought.

Standing in the Hyatt Regency room with Nagin, I knew we had work to do. The city had a bus fleet for evacuation needs. "Where are the buses?" I asked.

"We don't have the keys," he said. I had not yet seen TV footage of the city's bus fleet engulfed by the flood, or learned what went wrong in that chain of command.

Nagin rebounded to give a furious, free-associating interview on WWL-AM radio with Garland Robinette. The NOPD's communication system was down and rumors flying when Nagin, after a fleeting reference to a phone call with Bush, declared, "I been out there, man, flew these helicopters, been in the crowds, talking to people," and shifted to a rant against the Iraq war and drug addicts "walking around the city looking for a fix ... they don't have anything to take the edge off. And they've probably found guns. So what you're seeing is drug-starving, crazy addicts, drug addicts that are wreakin' havoc. And we don't have the manpower to adequately deal with that." In projecting his powerlessness, Nagin ignited unfounded fears of marauding addicts in a defenseless city.

As he regained some self-control, Nagin pinned his hopes on President George W. Bush, who gave a prime-time speech at Jackson Square promising a new city; Bush was soon distracted, however, by the Iraq War. Senator Mary Landrieu (Mitch's sister) became a major advocate for recovery, but social Darwinists who controlled Congress yawned at the moribund city.

· · · · · · · · · ·

DIMENSIONS OF THE FLOOD

Katrina's tidal wave slammed into villages and hamlets south of the city where the Laffites once roamed, shredding buildings, tossing cars and boats onto trees and roofs, barreling up the alley of denuded flora straddling the Mississippi River Gulf Outlet, and crashing through Plaquemines and St. Bernard parishes. Another surge line rolled across Lake Borgne into Lake Pontchartrain, driving a barge through the Industrial Canal protective wall, exploding water into the Lower Ninth Ward. That torrent filled or toppled hundreds of houses, wiping out the largest neighborhood. A swollen Lake Pontchartrain cracked the barriers of outfall canals along the northern perimeter, inundating areas by the lake, Seventh Ward, Gentilly, and Carrollton as never before.

The flooded area was seven times the size of Manhattan Island; tens of thousands of houses sat in oily saltwater for several weeks. The unflooded areas followed the river's curve on higher ground. In mid-October, people began returning to dry areas in the French Quarter, patches in Lakeview, high ridge streets between the river and St. Charles Avenue, and parts of Uptown off South Claiborne Avenue. Most of the city still had no electricity at Thanksgiving; most of the people were gone.

In the months that followed the flood, FEMA-funded subcontractors and understaffed city departments began clearing debris and rewiring essential buildings. Rebuilding the city would take untold billions, and years. Soon, though, tradition-bearers of the cultural memory, musicians, Mardi Gras Indians, and Social Aid and Pleasure Club members began trickling back to wrecked homes or lost apartments in the hard-hit downriver wards determined to dig out, regroup, and claim their place.

Culture prevailed as politics failed. The life force of music and memory, determined to survive, came back to the shattered city. Without a rejuvenating roots culture, the $4.9 billion tourism industry would have been crippled. "We're blues people," Wynton Marsalis said, with prescience, that first September. "We absorb pain but we come back. It's our way of life. We play dirges. We play hymns. We bury the dead above ground. We're always close to death.... This is an unbelievable tragedy. It's going to leave a certain type of scar on the psyche, but we're going to cover that scar over with so much soul and depth that we're going to astound people. We will definitely be back."

Marsalis, the Jazz at Lincoln Center director, spearheaded a PBS telethon to raise funds on September 18, flying in musicians from stranded outposts. Michael White was in Houston, where he had rented an apartment and arranged nursing care for his mother. The universities had canceled fall semesters. At least he had his paycheck from Xavier.

Former presidents George H. W. Bush and Bill Clinton formed a commission that raised $90 million by December for institutional rebuilding. Oil-rich Qatar donated $17.5 million to assist Xavier University rebuilding, as part of a $60 million package announced the following spring.

"Our first objective is to bring back the talent pool," Marsalis told the *Chicago Tribune* in January 2006. He released a consultant's report documenting the extent of second-line clubs, Mardi Gras Indians, and other groups. "We're not going to let our culture slip away."

The following month, as the White House tried to thwart congressional investigators' access to documents on its pathetic Katrina response, Marsalis announced the release of $2.8 million generated by the Higher Ground PBS concert. Checks for $100,000 each went to the Ogden Museum of Southern Art, the Zulu Social Aid and Pleasure Club, the Contemporary Arts Center, cultural organizations across the southern parishes, and nearly 200 individual grants of $15,000 to displaced artists like White. As the broken mud town waited on Washington, a jazz composer handed out money.

Despite heroic work by first responders, the Coast Guard, and volunteers in the "Cajun Navy," the city did not receive a huge financial lifeline from Baton Rouge.

Blanco threatened to block oil and gas leases, worth hundreds of millions of dollars to the federal treasury, unless the state received crucial funding. "The threat worked," writes Gary Rivlin. Donald Powell, the White House liaison to the region for Katrina recovery, and Sean Reilly, chair of the Louisiana Recovery Authority formed by Blanco, "hatched a plan that would help make drowned-out Louisiana homeowners whole again." Powell announced that Bush would seek $4.2 billion from Congress for funds to Louisiana homeowners for rebuilding costs: many adjustors refused to cover water damage from collapsed rooftops, terming it "flood damage." Thousands of homeowners who never flooded had no flood coverage. Blanco added funds from federal block grants providing an initial $7.5 billion base when the legislation passed in July 2006; the grants would take years to reach applicants under ICF, the Virginia-based company to which the governor outsourced the job. ICF paid generous bonuses to its executives and created a labyrinth of red tape for homeowners seeking relief. "The state had to add benchmarks under intense public pressure," reported David Hammer in *The Advocate*. Eventually, Road Home spent $10 million in helping 130,000 flooded homeowners. The program was also a huge bailout for the insurance industry.

Human error produced the flood—the worst civil engineering disaster in American history. A government investigation found that the U.S. Army Corps of Engineers had relied on flawed levee design and faulty maintenance of the system. State government had done its share with a mindset of environmental cynicism that for decades winked at oil companies, carving 20,000 miles of navigational canals through coastal forests to lay oil and gas pipelines and to service off-shore derricks. Long a buffer to storm surges from the Gulf, the wetlands had been reduced to green patches like shards of soggy cardboard. Since 1932, the state had lost 1,900 square miles of wetlands, an area larger than Rhode Island.

Cars with muddy windshields sat for months under the North Claiborne overpass median between Tremé and the Seventh Ward as Nagin convened a blue-ribbon Bring New Orleans Back Commission. The hearings that autumn of 2005 at a downtown hotel with architects, academics, planners, civic leaders, and consultants from the Urban Land Institute in Chicago produced a plan for a smaller urban footprint—the Lower Nine and swaths of the emptied New Orleans East would revert to marsh, a buffer to future floods; a smart city would help people relocate to medium-rise apartments built on dry ridge streets. The blueprint infuriated homeowners trying to get back to marsh-designated areas. Nagin abandoned the plan, declared the city open for all, and geared up for his 2006 reelection race.

With a 484,674 population in 2000, New Orleans was 67 percent African American. A limited tax base saw reduced support for public schools, compounded by the school board's decline into a patronage hive. Twenty-eight percent of the population was at poverty level.

For months after Katrina, people overwhelmed by the loss of their homes were stuck in motels, transitional apartments, or with kith or kin in Houston, Atlanta, Baton Rouge, and elsewhere. Anticipation raced in other quarters that recovery would rinse away the city's poverty and crime. Shortly after the hurricane, James Reiss, a major Uptown supporter of Mayor Nagin, told the *Wall Street Journal*: "Those who want to see this city rebuilt want to see it done in a completely different way: demographically, geographically, and politically. I'm not just speaking for myself here. The way we've been living is not going to happen here."

The day Reiss's comment appeared, Republican congressman Richard Baker of Baton Rouge referenced the brick housing units built in the 1940s that had become riddled with drugs, crime, and teenage births: "We finally cleaned up public housing in New Orleans. We couldn't do it, but God did."

God's closer approximation came from churches and civic groups sending truckloads of water, diapers, and hygienic items; volunteers came by the dozens to clean and gut houses for willing homeowners. Wynton Marsalis in a TV interview the night of Baker's comment, scored "the incompetence in our government in terms of how politicians try to polarize everybody.... The poetic truth is that Americans are coming together to save lives regardless of race and class."

When New Orleans most needed potent influence in Washington, the city's veteran congressman, William Jefferson, suffered a loss of $90,000 in tinfoil from the freezer of his Capitol Hill home, taken by FBI agents in August 2005, less than a month before Katrina made landfall. Politically crippled, Jefferson spent years preparing for trial. Convicted in 2009 of using his office for bribes to further business deals in Africa, Jefferson's fate was a dynastic tragedy worthy of Faulkner. Born in 1947 in the upstate plantation town of Sweet Providence, Jefferson was the sixth of ten children in a sharecropping family whose valiant matriarch stood up against bigoted local officials. At the historically black Southern University in Baton Rouge, Bill became a civil rights leader, won a scholarship to Harvard Law, built a practice in New Orleans, and in 1979 won a state senate seat. Bill and Andrea Jefferson raised five daughters. Three would graduate from Harvard and Harvard Law, two from Brown and Boston University, respectively. In 1990 he was earning $400,000 a year as a lawyer when he was elected to Congress.

"Traditionally, in Louisiana, using political office or political favors to enrich oneself and one's friends has not been swept under the rug," observed "Big Bad" Bill Dodd, a lieutenant governor in the 1950s. "For as long as I can remember, a big-time state politician who failed to get rich and make his friends and relatives rich has been considered stupid."

Eloquent, amiable, thoughtful Bill Jefferson built a political machine around his family. Older brother Mose Jefferson, a whirlwind at mobilizing voters, began buying or operating low-rent properties in Central City as Bill gained power in Baton Rouge. Another brother, Archie, lost his law license after borrowing against client accounts. In the 1980s, with half of the ten siblings in or around New Orleans, Bill formed Jefferson Interests, a company that ran stores with monthly appliance rentals to poor people. When he ran for mayor in 1986, an opponent correctly charged that the company "harassed and intimidated" housing project dwellers late on payments. Large families can be messy. Was Bill dragged into milk-the-poor schemes or was he the mastermind?

In 2004, a former Orleans Parish School Board president pleaded guilty to fraud and bribery, testifying that she took $140,000 from Mose for her support of a software math program in the schools; Mose reportedly earned $900,000 in fees from the software company before going to federal prison, where he died. His longtime companion, the former New Orleans councilwoman Renee Gill Pratt, served time too.

A sister, Betty Jefferson, rode Bill's coattails to become a city tax assessor, and in 2010 pleaded guilty to racketeering.

Ray Strother, a top Washington, D.C., political consultant, got his start in Baton Rouge. In 1982, Strother ran Jefferson's media campaign when he challenged New Orleans mayor Dutch Morial.

"Jeff still owes me $25,000 from that race," Strother told me. "I'm convinced that Jefferson was corrupted by his years in the legislature in Baton Rouge. The perception in the black community was that white politicians got rich, and blacks wanted in on that."

Legislators with insurance licenses did business with the state; others worked as (or for) vendors to state agencies. "The state" was there to milk for many politicians. Governor Edwin Edwards in the 1970s gave carte blanche to oil waste disposal operators who did business with his cronies and brothers with no state oversight. The Jeffersons' corruption, and that of other black officials after the flood, made the city seem a graveyard of the civil rights era.

New Orleans city councilman Oliver Thomas, who rescued people in the flooding, pleaded guilty in 2007 to taking $20,000 in bribes from a politically connected restaurateur, Stan "Pampy" Barre, whose fingers reached into lots of pies. A year later, Pampy pleaded guilty and said: "This city trusted me, and I stabbed her in the back in the dead of night." After serving time, Thomas went to work at Covenant House, helping to rehabilitate teenagers off the streets; he took a role in *Tremé*, the popular HBO series, portraying himself before the fall.

· · · · · · · · · ·

TREMÉ IN TIME

My wife and I returned in late October 2005 to a raised house in Carrollton, luckily dry, unlike the yard and garage. The long reach of darkness, a ghost town off the grid, stretched from crosstown Claiborne Avenue six miles to Lakeview, most of the area developed after mass drainage in the early 1900s. Along those eerie streets, with houses stained by a horizontal waterline, backstories of the city floated like hungry ghosts.

A short drive north on Carrollton Avenue got me on the up-ramp for the Pontchartrain Expressway, heading east to the exit at Tremé. Between 1980 and 1990, Tremé lost 26 percent of its population; its poverty level rose from 37 to 50 percent. The exodus of an African American middle class from traditional urban enclaves was a national phenomenon. In New Orleans, City Hall produced the decay.

In 1946, Mayor Morrison embraced a consultant's plan by Robert Moses, "the master builder" of New York who razed neighborhoods that got in his way, for an elevated riverfront bypass along the French Quarter linking Esplanade Avenue with the Pontchartrain Expressway. Moses also advised a highway overpass on North Claiborne Avenue through the Seventh Ward and Tremé as another link to the Expressway. The Eisenhower administration's Interstate Highway Program covered 90 percent of funds for new highways. Moses contended that a French Quarter riverside highway would reduce traffic congestion caused by the Pontchartrain Expressway. The plan meant demolishing some colonial-era buildings and blocking the river view around which Adrien de Pauger, the original French engineer, planned the city. By the time Morrison left to take an ambassadorship, a preservation movement had risen in angry opposition, sending documents and well-supported arguments to the Department of Transportation and congressional offices. After a series of delays, the federal government withdrew the plan.

Mayor Victor H. Schiro, a short man with a pencil-thin mustache who won reelection in 1965 before mobilization of the black vote, pushed a "Lincoln Center of the South" for development in Tremé, where the city had been quietly acquiring property. The artist's rendering envisaged a happy theme park with white faces across from Municipal Auditorium, which had been built in 1929, next to Congo Square's remaining acres. The city demolished fourteen square blocks of Tremé. An architectural history called the razed houses "a living history of the city.... Hundreds of brick-between-post Creole cottages and center-hall, side-gabled houses had been designed, built, owned and lived in by the prosperous free black community of the first half of the nineteenth century."

Down, too, went the Gypsy Tea Room, where Olympia Brass Band leader Harold Dejan met his wife, Rose, a dancer in the shows. Anthony Bennett, a musician who worked for Doc Minyard in the city morgue, recalled, "A whole piece of my childhood was torn down. Reverend Alexander's church is gone! I played my first instrument in that church, a silver clarinet. There was an Italian grocery store on Ursulines and Villere. Two Italian ladies lived next door. Where did they go? It all became a big empty space." Many Sicilians headed for the suburbs.

Another casualty of the era was the Caldonia Inn, where Armstrong got off the float to pay a call in his 1949 ride as King of Zulu. Funeral parades stopped at the Caldonia, coffins occasionally hoisted on the bar, second liners toasting the deceased. "Uncle" Lionel Batiste, a drummer with a mortuary day job, organized a funeral for Caldonia. Uncle Lionel borrowed a casket. "I was the corpse," he said of his role, supine on velvet. Pallbearers followed Dejan's Olympia playing dirges to the New Caldonia; a mannequin garbed as a weeping widow sat at the bar.

And with all that federal highway money like low-hanging fruit, the city in the mid-1960s erected an I-10 overpass link on North Claiborne Avenue that tore through Tremé and the Seventh Ward. North Claiborne had a long grassy median thick with oak trees. Commerce along the avenue hummed in bakeries, mortuaries, seafood markets, shoeshine stands, barber shops, tailors' stores, pharmacies, restaurants, and small clubs. The linear park drew courting teenagers. Creole ladies on benches did needlepoint. Bells jangled as vendors pushed wagons, singing, "I got watermellllons . . . I got bannanas."

City Hall barely publicized notices on the 1966 demolitions. One day bulldozers began gutting the oak trees in the 13.5-acre lane. Thundering pile drivers secured foundations for the elevated highway. North Claiborne was the economic backbone of black downtown, with 115 businesses in 1965. Six years later, 64 survived. "How quickly the neighborhood disintegrated," Edgar Chase III, the Dillard University business dean, told the *Times-Picayune*.

North Claiborne's oak grove had been the hub of black Carnival, drawing people from all over town for cookouts, showing off costumes, watching Zulu floats and marches of the Masked Indians of Mardi Gras. Raised in the Seventh Ward, Jerome Smith was a civil rights activist who came back from frontline years in Mississippi to found the Tambourine and Fan Club, which used cultural traditions as a teaching tool for youth. He likened the oak grove of his adolescence to "a neighborhood mall."

"The music was a constant. You had the lyrical tap dancers on the street and you had the music from the vendors, the rag man, the produce man. . . . That made a lot of magic for young people on the street."

When we met on a wintry day in 1982, Smith sat in Tambourine and Fan headquarters beneath the I-10 in a triangular park called Hunter's Field, a reference to black Indian tribes of Carnival. "We wanted something for ourselves out of that thing," said Smith, a brawny six-foot-two, eyes raised at the whizzing traffic above.

"First we had to clear the junkies off this ground. Place was filled up with dope addicts. We took care of that."

How?

"They just left."

"You have to see Tambourine and Fan in the context of history. Tambourine, which is the Mardi Gras Indians, and fan, which is the music popular-ized by Louis Armstrong—the hand fan, the artifact of the street parade."

Smith had pushed Mayor Moon Landrieu to provide the space for Hunter's Field. Landrieu was a former city councilman elected in 1969 with 95 percent of the newly enfranchised black vote. As a young state legislator, Landrieu had stood nearly alone in opposing Jim Crow laws. As Smith and other activists engaged City Hall to provide more neighborhood services, Tambourine and Fan became a grassroots force in the tradition of Congo Square. "Tambourine and Fan gave me strength," recalled Victor Harris, who grew up in the Seventh Ward, worked for many years in food services at Charity Hospital, and became a renowned Mardi Gras Indian Big Chief, as Spirit of the Fi Yi Yi: "It taught us who we were. It was a struggle, but it was never violent. We lived in a troubled world, but it was all about to build and provide and protect."

Schiro's envisioned cultural complex had tanked for lack of money, leaving Landrieu to fill the empty space, and soothe a bitter wound in Tremé.

When Louis Armstrong died in 1971, Mayor Landrieu flew to New York for the funeral in Queens. Armstrong in late life had let it be known that he would not return to his beloved hometown owing to ill-treatment of blacks. The solemn funeral had no second line. The mayor knew that the city's image owed greatly to Armstrong, yet it was saddled by a history of racism. In New Orleans, he announced a commemorative ceremony with African American leaders. A massive second line flooded the streets, throwing off a release of emotions as people overran the dais outside City Hall, forcing three of Armstrong's relatives out of their seats. "The eulogy was cancelled," reported the *Times-Picayune*.

Landrieu had the city do landscaping in the flattened area, built a per-forming arts theater, and, after negotiations with Tremé leaders, built a gymnasium and community center in a corner, outside the park wall with iron rods. Landrieu's advisory commission, chaired by state appellate judge Ernest "Dutch" Morial, recommended naming the park for Louis Arm-strong. Succeeding Landrieu as the city's first African American mayor, Dutch Morial had the theater named for Mahalia Jackson. Tensions be-tween Tremé leaders and City Hall over a master plan for the park, and over affordable housing, ran through Morial's mayoralty. Morial commissioned a bronze statue of Satchmo for the park by the esteemed Elizabeth Catlett. In 1994, Mayor Marc Morial (Dutch's son) put funds into renovation of a Tremé manor house for a museum of African American history. But with so much poverty, and reduced federal funds, City Hall had its limits. As the crack plague worsened, squatter houses sold drugs amid worsening gun violence.

Nevertheless, Tremé, with partial flooding, had the first museum to re-open after Katrina—Backstreet: A Powerhouse of Knowledge, a tiny temple to funerals, second-line clubs, and Mardi Gras Indians opposite St. Augustine Church. Backstreet was the brainchild of Sylvester Francis, once a house painter and club bouncer who started collecting radiant Indian suits and funeral memorabilia in his garage. In 1999, the Rhodes funeral home gave him dollar-a-year use of the tiny Blandin mortuary. "When word got out that I was opening, more people started calling, saying, *I got my daddy's stuff, I got my momma's stuff,*" Francis told me. Sunlight doused the yellow plumes of an Indian suit. "These things are precious to me."

He followed second lines with a video camera, showing tapes at Backstreet, which survived on twenty-dollar dues from 300 members, a five-dollar admission fee, donations, and grants. The flood drove Francis and eleven family members out of a Ninth Ward apartment into a long march on the I-10 overpass under burning sun; he got his people into the squalor of the overcrowded Convention Center. The government evacuated them by helicopter, then an airplane to Texas, with weeks in jammed motels on a FEMA cash card. "I was like Dorothy and the Wizard, bra, *just get me home.*" He reopened Backstreet in late October, using the office and kitchen for living space. "Nagin's not a culture man," he snorted. "They're trying to keep poor people from coming back. But the poor people is the culture." He lit a Kool. "They're worried about the French Quarter, the tourists.... If you don't have Indians and second liners, you ain't got a real Mardi Gras."

Francis had an unlikely echo in Bishop Charles Jenkins of the Episcopal Diocese of Louisiana, who told me later, with a graven brow, "I cannot prove the urban myth of a conspiracy to keep poor people from returning, but too much evidence points toward *someone* not wanting the poor to come home." A genteel Southerner who had opposed the ordination of a gay bishop, Jenkins fled Katrina to stay with friends in Baton Rouge. Watching the coverage of beleaguered people outside the Convention Center sent Jenkins to his knees, weeping, begging God for a message. On his return, he threw himself into fundraising for a neighborhood health clinic and worked with Jerome Smith, among others, in building several houses at affordable rates for the poor. He protested in vain the city's decision under Nagin to demolish the housing projects for a vast rebuilding of mixed-use affordable housing, the long wait for which did not help the displaced working poor. Jenkins resigned as bishop in 2009, citing post-traumatic stress.

In 2004, Xavier University had awarded Michael White the Rosa and Charles Keller Endowed Chair in the Humanities, which freed him from teaching Spanish to focus on jazz courses, research, and composing. He took the Original Liberty Jazz Band to Europe that summer, promoting *Dancing in the Sky* (Basin Street Records), with tight New Orleans Style ensemble pacing on White's compositions, notably the title cut with trumpeters Gregg Stafford, Nicholas Payton, and Mark Braud in robust harmonizing. White had reached a new level of artistic harmony when his evacuation to Houston, normally a seven-hour drive, had taken thirty. By the time he found an apartment, and got his mother into nursing care, White had relatives, friends, and band members scattered across several states. Watching New Orleans collapse on television became a waking nightmare. From an aerial map online he calculated that his home, which backed onto the London Avenue Canal floodwall, sat in water from the lake for three weeks. In early October we finally connected by cell phone. I was at my sister-in-law's home in a Dallas suburb. White was the protagonist in a documentary on jazz funerals I was producing, which had gone into a free fall. For two hours we caught up on our lives and our friends. He agreed to let me film him returning to his home.

On October 21, cameraman Philip Braun and I followed White along a once-serene Mirabeau Avenue with cast-off refrigerators and mounds of debris. He turned onto Pratt Drive; fallen trees and trash packed the sidewalk. He parked outside the ranch house, slipping on a mask protecting his mouth and nostrils as health authorities advised.

In a city crawling with journalists, I was not surprised when the *Times-Picayune* music writer Keith Spera materialized with a photographer. Spera's time was short; we agreed to give each shooter focus on Dr. White. Going to bed each night in a dry house, I felt like a voyeur as he adjusted thick gloves at the door, sighing, "I don't know if I should pray before or after." We, too, wore face masks, gazing at plumes of mold that branched up the walls. "It's like your whole life drowned and you get to look at it." His treasured painting of George Lewis had floated across the room and come down, tilted against a wall. Books driven out of his study by the water sank in mush underfoot, biographies of Oliver, Bechet, Jelly, and countless others. "This is where I kept much of my research. Four thousand books. I built these bookcases. Part of me is here and I think died in this." A Baptist hymnal from which he culled dirges, books, culture, and African American history, layers on lumps.

A framed photograph, gone black from the water, had been a rare photograph of Papa John Joseph, his bass-playing ancestor. "It was the most beautiful picture I'd seen of Papa John. Wherever you went in the room, those eyes followed you. There was wisdom, but also truth."

A closet door, warped shut by water, held forty antique clarinets. Five thousand CDs; a thousand vinyl LP and 78 rpm records; hundreds of films and documentaries; dozens of his own unrecorded compositions, rare original sheet music, photographs of countless artists and himself with Danny Barker, "Kid" Thomas Valentine, Emmanuel Sayles, Doc Paulin, President Clinton; interview transcripts and research on Papa John Joseph—layers in mud insurance wouldn't cover. Gone, too, the mouthpieces of Sidney Bechet and the Irish Channel–born Raymond Burke, an eccentric player he had befriended in his twilight years and the composer of "City of a Million Dreams," a song he so enjoyed.

When the January 2006 semester began, White had a FEMA trailer at Xavier's campus. He kept dreaming of water crashing through a wall, people drowning.

Gregg Stafford had it tough, too. A longtime public school teacher, the trumpeter lost his salary and health insurance two weeks after the storm. The Orleans Parish School Board, unable to account for $70 million in federal dollars, saw most of its students evacuated and put 7,500 employees on "disaster leave," eligible for unemployment only. In November, the Recovery School District, which the legislature created in 2003 to take over failed schools, assumed authority for 102 of the city's 126 public schools. Of the 24 remaining, 7 closed due to damage and 12 became charter schools. Five remained under auspices of the board, which took a severe funding cut. The Recovery School District fostered start-up charter schools and became a national case study in education reform.

Stafford had sixteen years as a second-grade teacher, before an approved leave of absence, when Katrina hit.

They were trying not to hire veteran teachers, but they found places for Teach for America people to live, paying the rent and a sign-up bonus. It was bad the way they treated us, as if we had never taught before. With my health insurance cut off right after the storm, I became short-winded after helping my sister work on her house, which took ten feet of water. I had to get checked for bronchitis. A friend—a doctor—instructed me to go to a state [public] hospital in Houma. I had to drive at 5 A.M. for a 7 A.M. appointment. It was almost 10 o'clock when I finally saw someone.

Gregg Stafford got a job in 2007 at a Recovery District school. "I taught for two years and they laid us off to bring in Teach for America teachers." He found work at another charter, "teaching second and third grade. Again I was laid off. I lost health insurance again. I was able to get on at Eisenhower. The assistant principal knew me. I went back as a teacher's aide, making $600 a week—a big cut from $45,000 a year. I got up every morning thinking if the storm hadn't come I'd be eligible to retire and draw pension. Thank God I had the music, or I would have lost my house and been just about homeless."

A nine-year lawsuit to compensate the fired school employees won a $1.5 billion verdict, which the Louisiana Supreme Court reversed. The U.S. Supreme Court declined the plaintiffs' appeal.

The charter school experiment, with its access to corporate and foundation resources, provided greater autonomy for principals and closer focus on children with learning challenges. The results after nine years were impressive. Before Katrina, slightly more than a third of New Orleans public school students scored at their grade level in state standardized tests. In 2014, the figure rose to 62 percent. The drop-out rate before Katrina was nearly 50 percent, and less than 20 percent went to college. The four-year graduation rate rose to 73 percent in 2014, and 59 percent of graduates entered college.

In ordinary times, Stafford's two-hour drive to the Houma hospital to be treated for his bronchial infection would have been a fifteen-minute trip to Charity Hospital on Tulane Avenue, near the Central Business District. Charity was the major treatment center for the indigent poor; its trauma center treated many of the city's gunshot victims. Soon after Katrina, doctors and nurses from Charity assisted troops under U.S. Army Lt. Gen. Russell Honoré in restoring the facility, where the basement flooded, getting it ready for service. A south Louisiana native, Honoré knew the city needed an acute care facility. Advising Governor Blanco that Charity was ready, he was taken aback when she said the state had other plans. The LSU medical system, which ran Charity with medical interns training there, had long wanted a new, state-of-the-art hospital. "We were in desperate need of this facility," then-state treasurer John Kennedy told the journalist Roberta Brandes Gratz. "The lights and a/c were on. It was clean and functional."

Kennedy asked LSU hospital CEO Don Smithburg why they shouldn't move back into Charity on a temporary basis. "If we do, we will never get a new one," said Smithburg. When the state closed Charity in 2005, it marked the end of a medical facility that in different locations had provided service to the poor since Bienville's time.

"The lengths to which the U.S. military sought to restore Charity Hospital's most vital functions cannot be overstated," writes the sociologist Brad Ott, who spent years researching the Charity saga for a master's thesis. FEMA authorized up to $1 billion for the military transportation of relief supplies and to establish medical facilities. But as Ott writes:

> A possible attempt by the Department of Defense to allocate substantial monetary resources to cover necessary repair costs of Charity Hospital was initiated—*but declined* by Louisiana state officials in September 2005. Under normal FEMA Public Assistance program guidelines, the federal agency would pay 75 percent of the project costs and a state would be responsible for 25 percent. Under special expedited rules, FEMA pledged "to reimburse state agencies and local governments for costs involving lifesaving emergency work related to Hurricane Katrina" *reimbursing 100 per cent of all eligible costs.*

Louisiana's Department of the Treasury received $352 million during the third week of September 2005, adding to $105 million already on hand for a total of $457 million in FEMA-approved disaster assistance. Louisiana's Department of Health and Hospitals (DHH) officials, however, expressed confusion over what the funds were intended to reimburse. DHH officials said that if they accepted the funds without accounting for actual expenditures, the state would be charged interest and potentially blocked from future FEMA Public Assistance funding—so DHH promptly returned to FEMA almost $340 million.

After closing the Charity Hospital, which FEMA and the Department of Defense wanted open, Louisiana officials then engaged in hard bargaining over four years with FEMA, whose initial estimate of $23 million for a full remediation of Charity escalated under negotiations with the state, to $475 million. The law allowed certain criteria, which of course the state met, to apply the funds toward a replacement building. Voilà! A down payment for the new University Medical Center begat a saga of cost overruns that reached a final price tag of $1.1 billion. As Gratz reported in *The Nation*:

> Mayor Ray Nagin's recovery czar, Ed Blakely, used $75 million in HUD funds as leverage to persuade the Department of Veterans Affairs to

move its facility to a more densely populated, thirty-acre site even farther from the downtown core. Blakely even went so far as to threaten the VA at a public meeting on August 11, 2008, with the loss of those funds should they refuse to relocate. Thus, LSU obtained ... a joint complex with some shared facilities on thirty-seven acres [which] ballooned into two stand-alone, totally separate hospitals on sixty-seven acres (twenty-seven square blocks).

The LSU grand plan encountered a minor obstacle: the Mid-City neighborhood on the projected site, and some 265 homes, many of which had been restored with federal grants under the Road Home program. The state used eminent domain to force the homeowners to sell, followed by a massive removal of houses to scattered locations.

The city had an interim public hospital while the University Medical Center was under construction; it opened in 2015. In a more encouraging development, the city moved toward neighborhood satellite clinics and walk-in care facilities to streamline health service.

· · · · · · · · · ·

THE WORST OF TIMES

Mayor Nagin wisely let Mardi Gras floats roll in 2006 to pump an economy with only a third of the population back. Tour buses rolled through the Lower Nine, showing visitors the dead houses choked in flora like some tropical Pompeii. Carnival parades along St. Charles Avenue sent a message of revival. Across town in Tremé, Sylvester Francis was jubilant: "They comin' out!" Backstreet had red beans and rice selling at five bucks a plate. "Innians from all over. Spirit of Fi-Yi-Yi, Lil Charles, Bo Dollis and Wild Magnolias marching' Uptown. Donald Harrison 'n Congo Nation in Tremé. Ain't no real Mardi Gras without Innians."

The Rockefeller Foundation provided major support for long-term neighborhood revival planning; other foundations came to the city's aid despite Nagin's ham-fisted strategies. The Jazz and Heritage Festival, a major piece of the cultural economy, came back in the spring of 2006, providing a big boost to the roots culture, downtown hotels, and restaurants throughout town.

But the racial fault lines were jagged. The city in the 1970s had 12,000 workers. Nagin took office with 6,300 after years of federal cutbacks. With revenues crippled by the flood, Nagin fired half the city workforce. In 2002, Nagin had run as the outsider, gaining 80 percent of the white vote; after news broke that he had donated $1,000 to Bush's campaign in 2000, many conservatives viewed him as a de facto Republican. He won with only 20 percent of the black vote. In 2006, Nagin campaigned as the great black hope, keeping City Hall from going back to the Man. Jesse Jackson and Al Sharpton helped rally displaced African American voters for him. On the Martin Luther King Jr. birthday holiday, Nagin announced that God had told him the city would always be "chocolate." As pundits and talk show hosts scoffed, blacks crammed in FEMA trailers or temporary lodging got the message.

Lieutenant Governor Mitch Landrieu (the fifth of Moon and Verna Landrieu's nine children) entered the mayor's race with a strong African American base. Having never faced so polarized an electorate, he held back from a full attack on Nagin. "Race trumps everything at a certain point," Landrieu later wrote. With strong black support, Nagin won.

As Michael White waded through Road Home red tape, seeking options for his blighted home and commuting to see his mother in Houston, his band members flew in from different places for the jobs he landed at Carnegie Hall, Lincoln Center, the Apollo Theater, and the Smithsonian. "Prayer, playing music, and the kindness shown toward the Gulf Coast storm victims by individuals around the world have kept me going," he wrote in 2007. "I am told that there is a deeper passion in my playing.... I have often considered the philosophy of the jazz funeral—of sadly grieving the loss of life and joyously celebrating the beginning of its glorious resurrection. My old life has ended, but a new one has begun."

His life took a good turn with a month-long residency at A Studio in the Woods, an artists' retreat in a bottomland hardwood forest at the far edge of Orleans Parish. Without the daily interruptions, he practiced in the mornings and composed through the afternoons, sometimes into the night. In 2008 he released *Blue Crescent*, one of his finest recordings.

The "old life" in New Orleans came back with a vengeance in the shooting deaths of Dinerral Shavers, a school bandleader and Hot 8 Brass Band snare drummer, on December 28, 2006, and Helen Hill, a young Harvard-trained filmmaker, on January 4, 2007. Musicians led a march to City Hall with speakers blasting Nagin. He promised to make changes but drifted into passivity, touting a "market-driven recovery," which many people took as a dog whistle for keeping the poor from returning. With hundreds of miles of streets gouged and rutted from the flood, there wouldn't be much of a market without major government intervention. As the Road Home grants reached their applicants at an achingly slow pace, Governor Blanco, who had outsourced the program to the Virginia company ICF, read the poll numbers and chose not to run for reelection.

As people slowly got back into houses, the medical district Blakely had helped orchestrate with the LSU system promised to pump money into the city, regardless of how much red ink the state would swallow for its overreach in construction costs. But the great need for the city's infrastructure repair lagged ... and lagged. Nagin never cultivated allies in Washington and Baton Rouge to secure the stream of federal dollars. A Commerce Department official who suggested available projects to the mayor was flummoxed when Nagin waved them off, saying the city wasn't yet able to write those kinds of grants! Ineligible for a third consecutive term, Nagin left a broken mud town when his second term ended in 2010. By then FBI agents were on to him. Four years later he was sentenced to ten years in a federal penitentiary for tax evasion, wire fraud, and bribery.

Mitch Landrieu won the 2010 mayor's race with 65 percent in the primary, becoming the first white mayor since his father, who hugged him at the victory party. The next night, fireworks lit the sky as the New Orleans Saints won their first Super Bowl, beating the Indianapolis Colts 31–17 in Miami. The city, at long last, seemed on the rebound.

Facing a $97 million deficit, ravaged streets, and miles of leaking pipes, Landrieu made surgical cuts for short-term budget stability. Having a sister in the U.S. Senate was a huge advantage; so was his rapport with President Barack Obama. Obama approved his request for city officials to meet monthly with regional FEMA directors in order to access available funding streams. As Landrieu targeted other Washington agencies for support, the city had some 750 meetings over eight years. "The Obama administration furthered this effort by making important bureaucratic changes to free up federal money," a 2015 report by the Federal Reserve Bank of Atlanta noted. The city's new relationship with the White House had led to federal block grants for schools ($247.5 million), the local criminal justice system ($130 million), housing vouchers ($85 million), and medical services in underserved areas ($47 million). Where federal funds fell short, nonprofits, foundations, and community organizations stepped in.

Today, New Orleans is seeing the results of this reconstruction. On the one hand, the city is now one of the hottest places in the country for new businesses. The influx of major chains and companies expanding into New Orleans has created 14,000 jobs and brought $7 billion in capital investment to the city over the past five years. Its exuberant growth and diversification can be found almost everywhere, from the new 1,500-acre biomedical district to the revived neighborhood corridors with their trendy bars; from the added streetcar line to the budding New Orleans film industry. The city has become a hub for tech start-ups and young urban professionals.

On the other hand, the cost of living is increasing. Moreover, affordable housing, mostly destroyed by Katrina's powerful storm surge, has not been entirely rebuilt. New Orleans has only twenty-five affordable housing units for every 100 people living in extreme poverty. This subsidized housing—in which mortgage costs usually do not exceed 30 percent of annual household income—is a vital part of the social infrastructure in New Orleans.

In 2014, the city received $2.4 billion for the largest street and water system repair in its history. As traffic slowed on thoroughfares because of street rebuilding, grass on the St. Charles and South Claiborne Avenue medians seemed manicured, and cleaner, without the litter. In 2013, New Orleans still had 100,000 fewer people, but it also had 500 more restaurants than on August 29, 2005.

Rebuilding under Landrieu played out on many fronts. Blighted houses, a major problem after the flood, particularly in the downriver wards, dropped from 43,755 in 2010 to below 29,000 five years later. The city went from 16,000 burned-out streetlights in 2010 to 889 in 2015.

And yet, as of 2015, according to the Data Center of New Orleans, for all of the federal largesse, support by major foundations, and generosity of the church groups and many volunteers, the city faced major shortfalls in restoring the urban land mass a decade after the failure of the federally managed levees. The majority of the $120.5 billion in federal spending ($75 billion) was allocated for emergency services, not rebuilding. Philanthropy of $6.5 billion and $30 billion in coverage of insurance claims left a deep impasse that hit hardest on the working poor. Nevertheless, the levee system that had been so compromised before Katrina had a $14 billion upgrade under the Army Corps of Engineers.

The University Medical Center proudly opened in 2015; the hospital's operating costs exceeded $500 million a year. The state was wallowing in a billion-dollar deficit after a scheme by former governor Bobby Jindal to privatize the public hospital system, which required government grants and subsidies, while building the new hospital. Health-care expenditures had become a Trojan horse for legislators in Baton Rouge who had marched loyally behind Jindal as he slashed education to stanch the fiscal bleeding. New Orleans was reaping the benefits of the state's overreach; downtown office buildings were converting to condos and apartments as doctors, nurses, and researchers walked to work in the biomedical district.

After the Flood

Landrieu won reelection in 2014 with 64 percent of the vote; the accelerating recovery augured well for his future. "Mitch Landrieu is the best stand-up politician in Louisiana," said Jim Engster, an interviewer of studied neutrality for Louisiana Radio News. "He won statewide as lieutenant governor because of his speeches."

Landrieu had a moral barometer that was rare for a Louisiana politician. The gun killings that kept New Orleans high in per capita urban homicide rates gnawed at Landrieu for years. He visited prisons and the local jail, arranging encounter sessions for young inmates with cops, judges, and prosecutors, trying to steer men slated for parole into counseling to build coping skills. "I don't understand why it's okay in America—a country that's supposed to be the greatest country in the world, a place with more wealth than anywhere else—for us to leave so many of our citizens basically dead," he told Jeffrey Goldberg of the *Atlantic* in 2015. "We have basically given up on our African-American boys. I'd be a cold son of a bitch if I ignored it, if I just focused on the other side of town, or focused just on tourism."

Shortly after Landrieu's reelection, Wynton Marsalis was in town for a concert; Landrieu persuaded him to meet at a downtown Starbucks; he wanted Wynton involved in Tricentennial event planning for 2018. Landrieu was fifty-three, fourteen months older than Marsalis. They came from two of the city's fabled dynasties. Ellis Marsalis the jazz pianist, professor, and recording artist had four sons in the music industry—Branford, Wynton, Delfeayo, and Jason—each a confident, forceful personality. Of the nine Landrieu children, Mary had served three terms in the U.S. Senate and Madeline was an elected Orleans Parish judge before becoming dean of the Loyola University College of Law. Mitch was long friendly with Wynton but held him in a certain awe for the prolific recordings, the Pulitzer Prize for music, and his national stature as director of Jazz at Lincoln Center. Over coffee, Landrieu outlined his Tricentennial planning, asking Wynton to participate and offer ideas. Marsalis said yes, and, as Landrieu would recall, surprised him by asking that he take down the Robert E. Lee statue.

"You lost me on that," said Landrieu.

"I don't like the fact that Lee Circle is named Lee Circle."

"Why is that?"

"Let me help you see it through my eyes. Who is he? What does he represent? And in that most prominent space in the city of New Orleans, does that space reflect who we were, who we want to be, or who we are?" Marsalis was on a roll. "Louis Armstrong left and never came back. You ever think about what Robert E. Lee means to someone black?"

"Black and white people watch Carnival parades there."

Marsalis wasn't buying. Black people had left New Orleans because they didn't feel welcome, he insisted. Landrieu replied that the city was now 60 percent African American and his policies fostered a welcoming city. Marsalis hammered back on the symbolic weight of other Confederate monuments. Landrieu averred that it would be a big political fight. "But it's the right thing to do," said Marsalis.

Landrieu wondered if the squeeze was worth the juice for his career ambitions. His African American base would support the dismantling of Confederate icons; some liberals too. But among traditionalists proud of the architectural fabric and the floral beauty of St. Charles Avenue over which Lee towered, Landrieu stood to lose popularity and would surely damage his statewide chances with whites who might otherwise support him as the man who rebuilt New Orleans after the great flood. His father advised him not to take down statues.

A lawyer trained in arbitration, Landrieu directed his staff and the city attorney to research city archives on four monuments—Lee, Jefferson Davis on Canal Street in Mid-City, the raised statue of Gen. P. G. T. Beauregard on horseback at the entrance to City Park, and the White League obelisk the City Council in 1993 had declared a public nuisance and stuck behind a downtown aquarium. The research showed that city government starting in the 1890s had erected the monuments without a referendum vote. What the city put up, the city could take down.

Landrieu was laying the legal groundwork in 2015, when a white supremacist shot to death nine worshippers in the Emanuel African Methodist Episcopal Church in downtown Charleston. Founded in 1816, Emanuel AME is "the oldest African Methodist Episcopal church in the southern United States." South Carolina governor Nikki Haley called for the Confederate flag atop the statehouse to come down. At that point Landrieu announced that the four New Orleans monuments should come down. The idea was a political firecracker; but in gathering support from six of the seven city council members, the mayor had an air-tight legal case.

The most intriguing of the four was Beauregard. As a postwar politician, the Civil War general had been active in an effort to defeat Radical Republicans by voicing support for African American political rights. He was not a liberal but a pragmatist who thought the city should embrace racial reconciliation. He was dead when the Lost Cause partisans elevated his bronze figure in uniform, on horseback, using the image of his war years to mute any sense of personal or political evolution.

The fervor of Lost Cause mythology that arose after the Civil War and fashioned a story line of southern redemption became fuel for the white violence against the civil rights movement of the 1950s and 1960s. The outrage felt at white churches and country clubs, at Chamber of Commerce meetings, and among good old boys in the duck blinds was over the very questioning of white innocence. A century after the Civil War, a way of life was simply what it was: white people superior and black people expected to be submissive. The success of the Lost Cause mythology, or cult, as Landrieu called it, registered precisely in the unblinking pride many whites had for monuments whose actual purpose—as symbols of white might—had faded into a nebulous history, symbols of a war long forgotten, ancestors who stood for what they believed. That was then, this is now.

In *Race and Reunion*, historian David W. Blight draws a bead on how the Lost Cause spread, on "the movement's effort to write and control the *history* of the war and its aftermath; its use of *white supremacy* as both means and ends.... Frequently disclaiming partisanship, and eager to establish what they so frequently called 'the truth of history,' diehard Lost Cause advocates, many of them high-ranking officers and political leaders of the Confederacy, forged one of the most highly orchestrated grassroots partisan histories ever conceived."

That partisanship all but rode into New Orleans on a horse as the debate intensified over the meaning of the four Confederate monuments that Landrieu and the council majority proposed to dismantle. The spectacle of people arguing over the legitimacy of historic symbols stood out in ironic relief from the tolerance achieved by Carnival and Jazz Fest as rites of public harmony.

"The victim of the Lost Cause legend has been *history*, for which the legend has been substituted in the national memory," wrote the late historian Alan T. Nolan. "The Lost Cause was expressly a rationalization, a cover-up."

As the city council held public hearings, registering opposition from preservationists and people who opposed the city's position for political reasons, the Lost Cause seemed a cover-up of continuing strength, concealing the ethos of white supremacy, and subjugation of blacks, behind their erection in the first place. The argument over aesthetics, the statues as artistry of the city's past, evaded the issue of why they were put there—to memorialize a power structure that had long stripped African Americans of the right to vote and enforced an economic system that had for nearly a century denied blacks a path of upward mobility in a genuine democracy. As preservation groups filed suit to block dismantlement of the icons, the City of New Orleans had vaulted to the truthful side of history. The long delay over appeals saw the haunting power of sanitized history as white supremacists staged protests, and terrorists torched the $200,000 Lamborghini owned by a contractor who had agreed to remove the monuments, and quickly withdrew. Upper-crust conservatives who would never set fire to a car had acquired a sleazy set of political bedfellows.

The violence tried to subvert what legal appeals could not halt. In the spring of 2017, the U.S. Fifth Circuit Court of Appeals—which had become one of the nation's most conservative federal appellate courts—ruled that the city indeed had the authority to make the decision. At two in the morning on April 24, two flatbed trucks with cardboard taped over the company's name removed the Liberty Place monument to a warehouse after it was taken down by workers wearing masks and bullet-proof vests. A clutch of protesters jeered behind a police barricade. In order to protect truck drivers and crane operators and keep protesters clear of the work site, the city hired a Texas-based security firm to find a crane outside the metro area. The city spent $1 million for what should have cost $200,000, but there was no violence. The Robert E. Lee statue came down on May 17, 2017.

Earlier that day, Landrieu spoke at Gallier Hall.

These monuments purposefully celebrate a fictional, sanitized Confederacy; ignoring the death, ignoring the enslavement, and the terror that it actually stood for.... Consider these four monuments from the perspective of an African American mother or father trying to explain to their fifth grade daughter who Robert E. Lee is and why he stands atop of our beautiful city. Can you do it? Can you look into that young girl's eyes and convince her that Robert E. Lee is there to encourage her? Do you think she will feel inspired and hopeful by that story?

The speech streamed across the Internet, generating favorable coverage for Landrieu in the national media, with some pundits suggesting he run for president. On the Uptown street where Mitch and Cheryl Landrieu lived with their family, neighbors stopped speaking to them. But after weeks of obscene calls to City Hall and the couple's home, the worst of it seemed over.

In the quirky patterns of New Orleans society, a certain mantra began— *Mitch took down Robert E. Lee so he could run for president*—a view that would be laughable if put to a basic test. How many politicians intentionally alienate a large portion of white voters to pursue a plan that he could have just as easily avoided? Had Landrieu told Marsalis, "I can't get the support to take down the icons," what would Wynton have done? What power did the jazz genius have to rally public opinion? Landrieu had the power and could have just as easily left office as the Great Rebuilder with strong popularity and begrudging respect from white conservatives who realized that a remade city was good for business. Whatever his calculation about the potential for one speech to boost his image, in national politics a speech can put you on the map and one severe verbal blunder slide you off just as fast. Drawing on a moral calculus in his decision, Landrieu embodied Hemingway's notion of "grace under pressure."

· · · · · · · · · ·

INDIANS FOR THE NATION

As the recovery rolled on, memory dramas that held a mirror to the society resumed their pageantry. Elite families in carefully worded press announcements of Carnival balls described their tableaux, listing parents, grandparents, and sometimes great-grandparents of the debutante queens and princesses. Black Creole society had an established ball tradition of its own. An important, if symbolic, gesture of interracial harmony came in 2010, when the Zulu king, arriving at the downtown river dock by barge on Lundi Gras, the day before Fat Tuesday, greeted Rex, the Carnival king, in what became a televised show of mutual respect. Each year since then, the two kings have met in a media event with the mayor, spreading good wishes for Mardi Gras.

Michael White settled with the Road Home bureaucracy, taking a heavy loss in the equity of his Gentilly home, but with enough to buy a house in a high-ground neighborhood near the lake. He became more prolific in his recordings, playing as a guest artist on an Eric Clapton album, and released his own *Adventures in New Orleans Jazz*, part 1, inspired in part by African diaspora rhythms.

Congo Square traditions rocked to another narrative rhythm.

The May 10, 2014, funeral for Larry Bannock, Big Chief of the Golden Starhunters, included a cortege fit for a pharaoh. Fifteen black Indians from different tribes in their many-feathered costumes, shimmering in the noon sun, waited outside City of Love Church, two blocks behind the huge Costco complex built over a Carrollton Avenue shopping mall destroyed in the flood.

Bannock, sixty-five, was lionized in the urban warrior culture of working-class African Americans who sew the gorgeous costumes, parading on

Carnival day, the night of St. Joseph's Day, for selected events through late spring, and for special events like the Jazz and Heritage Festival. As family and loved ones followed the preacher behind the casket, men from the Wild Tchoupitoulas, Mohawk Hunters, Yellow Pocahontas, and White Cloud Hunters swayed in their billowing costumes, thrumming tambourines, singing as the pallbearers hoisted the casket into an antique, horse-drawn hearse provided by the Charbonnet-Labat-Glapion Funeral Home. An Indian in an orange costume swaggered up behind the hearse, his costume catching the shafts of sunlight like a burning bush.

We are In-diannns
Inn-diannns
Indians of the nation
The whole wide creation
Oh how I love to hear
Them call
My Indian Red

Kidney dialysis for diabetes and congestive heart failure had forced Bannock to stop parading, but as an Indian costume artist and bard of the tradition, he held sway in Gert Town, a poor enclave on the far side of Carrollton Avenue where he was raised by an aunt and stepmother. A burly man who didn't mince words, Larry Bannock had a persona that to some could be forbidding. "No man will ever love me the way you did," his adopted daughter, Cymonde Ford, thirty-three, said in a church eulogy. "I realized after bringing a few guys around, you would give them a really hard time and showed every last one of them your gun collection. I thought maybe I should give you a little more time to accept my dating." A welder by trade, he worked on a crew in the 1970s that helped finish the Louisiana Superdome. But it was the intricate, beaded designs he sewed into the breastplates and back patches for his feathered outfits that brought Bannock renown as a folk artist. He got his start in 1971 when he met Gerald Moore, a 400-pound bartender at Metairie Country Club. Moore was a member of the Golden Star tribe in Gert Town; he and an Indian called Gilly Boy coaxed Larry into sewing.

In his mid-forties, Bannock saw his costumes exhibited at the Smithsonian Institution and St. Louis Museum of Art, among other prominent venues. He elaborated on the wellsprings of the tradition in a 1989 interview: "It's a proud culture and it symbolizes to me the paying respects of the black and the red man." He sat in the living room of his shotgun house in

Gert Town, the winter light suffusing feathers, thread, needles, and ribbon. He rubbed the yellow ostrich plumes for his headdress like silk between the fingers. "When the blacks were slaves, the Indians were the first people to accept us."

The Choctaw and other Indians had indeed lived on the outskirts of Place Congo, traded with Africans at the Sunday market, and played a ballgame called *raquette*. The relationship of Native Americans and African Americans is more complex than a story of allied resistance fighters; but the power of myth carries in storytelling that distills certain core truths. The two defeated peoples of colonial Louisiana rose to radiance in the Black Indian parades. Carnival provides a revolving stage for performance myths, as the baroque lineages of faux-royalty in Comus, Rex, and other old-pedigree Mardi Gras societies attest. Myths of nobility and rebellion share a ritual stage in Carnival.

Discussing the Spy Boy, who scouts ahead for Big Chief to warn of rival tribes nearing the turf of a given gang, Bannock broke into song:

I'm the Spy Boy that walked through the graveyard
Kicking over tombstones
I'm the Spy Boy jumped
the St. Louis Cemetery fence
Barked at thunder
Roared at lightning
Made death wonder!

When you meet me that morning
You better step aside.
A lot of men didn't,
A lot of men died.

City of Love Church faced two-lane Palmetto Avenue and a long canal that only floods in the monsoon downpours. A cobalt sky greeted the mourners filing out of the church, about 150 of whom melded with the crowd of onlookers waiting to follow the funeral, riveted at the sight of Indians. The crowd numbered about 450 as the mortuary attendants secured the casket inside the glass-paneled buggy and carefully fastened an enormous shroud of yellow plumes and feathers atop the hearse for Larry Bannock's final ride.

"Bigggg Chieffff!" cried one of the Indians. "Myyy big chief!" boomed another. A man in a yellow T-shirt walked behind the hearse, his back bearing the logo *Ain't No Star Like a Shining Star.*

A group of young brass band musicians, wearing shorts and jeans and T-shirts, carried the "Indian Red" melody into an up-tempo march behind the booming bounce of the bass drummer. The cracked street that bore the scarification lines of the 2005 flood made it difficult for people in the second line to dance, so they jostled along in stutter steps to avoid falling face forward. The hearse driver in his black suit, white shirt, and black tie shook the reins, coaxing the white horses ahead. They pulled the elegant wagon at a slow pace for a block and then made a U-turn beneath the Palmetto Street overpass. The pounding drums, rubato horns, and shaking tambourines boomed and echoed off the steel girders as the horses emerged in the sunlight. A policeman stopped traffic on Palmetto for the cortege and second line to pass, and as the street became less cracked, people broke out dancing.

Three-story apartment buildings built since Katrina lined the right side of the avenue. The music drew people in clusters onto balconies, porches, and corners, black folk waving to friends, people twirling white handkerchiefs to signal a soul released from earthly ties. "Go head on, Larry," called a lady from a balcony.

"Big Chief don't never bow down!" yelled a man.

An Indian in an orange outfit swaggered up behind the hearse in a blaze of light. Behind him came a woman in a suit of bright turquoise feathers and plumes with red fringe, meandering along in no special hurry as people absorbed the flurry of bluish-green and her two little girls, dressed in identical turquoise outfits, marched with stoic resolve. A man in a wheelchair, perhaps a gunshot survivor, pushed hard, keeping up with an Indian from the Mohawk Hunters who carried a saber and wore a blue vest like a Union jacket from the Civil War. His shoulders bore the logo *Buffalo Hunters*, and the feather-fringed apron displayed a black soldier in military blue with a chest of ribbons on horseback, rescuing an Indian woman clutching a baby with an African face.

A man pulled an ice chest on wheels, selling water for a dollar a bottle. Policemen on motorcycles halted traffic at the major intersection of Carrollton and Washington Avenues. Several motorists opened their doors and stood by their cars, taking pictures as the Indians and second liners moved slowly across Carrollton. Another man in a wheelchair crossed Carrollton. A man walking slowly, with a cane, followed him. The most spectacular Indian appeared to be a woman, wearing a suit of royal blue feathers and plumes, the face covered like an African mask with a mere horizontal slit for the eyes, the back of the costume a beaded image of an African women in a tiara of cowry shells, a long green dress and rising bubbles of many colors at the edge to convey a sense of the female figure in movement.

Palmetto becomes Washington Avenue after it crosses Carrollton and approaches the campus of Xavier University. One block south lies Gert Town. The crowd trailed the hearse into the neighborhood where Bannock lived his life. Cracked, creased, and pockmarked streets again made dancing harder. Sun beat down as the procession halted behind the parking lot for Pep Boys, a repair garage. The buggy hearse stopped. The funeral home staff moved the coffin into a motorized hearse.

People touched the yellow feather shroud, singing "Indian Red" until the transfer of the coffin to the vehicle was done. Then the hearse and vehicles with family drove off. As people dispersed, a man and woman walked toward the Costco.

"Larry was a man," said he.

"Larry loved that lul girl," said she.

"Larry stood his ground."

"That's right. And Larry knew how to sew."

. . . .

CODA

As New Orleans begins its fourth century, the grim epidemic of gun violence has supplanted that of yellow fever. Poverty has deepened its roots over generations of neglect and racial politics. The city that Moon Landrieu once touted for its unique biracial housing patterns has become more gentrified and segregated since the flood of 2005; yet it is still a city where people of different colors and cultures have daily interactions as they have done for generations. The resilience of a society composed of people whose roots lie across the world has been a rudder through the storms and violent upheavals throughout three centuries. The city that nearly drowned on global television in 2005 in the short span of thirteen years has unveiled a new persona, as a cultural mecca and a city of the young. The 2016 population of 391,195 remained less than the 484,000 who lived in the city when Hurricane Katrina hit; but New Orleans has become a magnet to dreamers drawn to a flourishing digital economy, an $800-million-dollar film industry, a resurgent music scene, art galleries, festive folkways, and neighborhoods with the character that comes from an authentic culture.

New Orleans in its long tension between culture and law, order and lawlessness, has fashioned a kaleidoscopic personality, seducing writers as diverse as Benjamin Latrobe, George Washington Cable, Grace King, Lafcadio Hearn, Kate Chopin, Tennessee Williams, Walker Percy, John Kennedy Toole, Anne Rice, Valerie Martin, Ellen Gilchrist, Brenda Marie Osbey, James Lee Burke, John Gregory Brown, Danny Barker, and Louis Armstrong, among others, with the promise of imagination lived large. The village on the Mississippi River oxbow that began as an outpost of the French Empire has become the American city with the deepest African identity. New Orleans rocks along through the pageantries and memory rituals of its varied people, a map of the world in miniature, a blue city floating against the odds of sea rise and climate convulsions, blue forever in its long sweet song.

ACKNOWLEDGMENTS

William Ferris, the eminent scholar, folklorist, and documentarian of the American South, has been a peerless guide over the long haul in which this work found its final form. I thank him for his support, influence, and friendship.

My thanks in equal measure to the historian Lawrence N. Powell, Tulane University emeritus professor and author of *The Accidental City: Improvising New Orleans*, for his close reading of my chapters and for offering criticism, advice, and citations.

Mark J. Davis, an attorney and literary critic in Santa Fe, and a friend since our undergraduate years at Georgetown, read the work as I wrote it with instructive comments at every turn. I owe him more than I can say.

I am likewise indebted to historian Howard Hunter, the dean of academics at Metairie Park Country Day School and an authority on New Orleans in the Civil War and the Lost Cause movement, for providing citations and constructive comments. I also wish to thank Professor Richard Campanella of Tulane for his prolific work on New Orleans geography and history, and for reading several chapters and sharing citations for others.

The National Endowment for the Humanities, Alicia Patterson Foundation, and John Simon Guggenheim Foundation provided research fellowships during the early and middle phases of this work, which helped me greatly. I owe a special thanks to Sheila Biddle, who embraced the early research as a grant officer at the Ford Foundation and provided support for a video oral history project on jazz funerals that I directed for the William Ransom Hogan Jazz Archive at Tulane University in 1997–98. The interviews and funeral footage deepened my journey into the city's cultural history and provided a baseline of material for a documentary film connected to this book.

My research on this book evolved over a course of more than twenty years before the final stretch of writing. I was taken away from this pursuit for long periods by other projects, primarily on the crisis in the Catholic Church. Time and again, I came back to New Orleans from research, production work, or assignments in distant places to attend the wake and brass band funerals for musicians and culture-carriers. The catastrophic impact of the Hurricane Katrina flooding threw me into a free fall, like so many others, and as I wrote about the city's recovery, I realized the approach of the book had to change. I am deeply indebted to Dr. Michael White, clarinetist and Xavier University jazz scholar, and trumpeter Gregg Stafford, leader of the Young Tuxedo Brass Band, for their patience with my endless questions. A special note of thanks to Bruce Sunpie Barnes and Deacon John Moore. To the many tradition-bearers of my native city, thank you for renewing my faith in the spiritual imagination and giving me the viewfinder on the city's cultural vistas.

Among New Orleanians who are no longer here and exerted a profound influence on me I must single out Tom Dent, a poet, author, and friend; the photographers Michael P. Smith and Syndey Byrd; Danny and Blue Lu Barker; Milton Batiste of Dejan's Olympia Brass Band; Big Chief Donald Harrison Sr. of Guardians of the Flame; and cameraman Don Perry for sharing his knowledge of funerals with music.

I received early research support from the Louisiana Endowment for the Humanities and for several years contributed to its magazine *Louisiana Cultural Vistas*. I am grateful to Michael Sartisky, the former LEH president; former editor David Johnson; cultural historian John Kemp, a former LEH official; and Brian Boyles, the current editor. I am likewise grateful to Tulane University for a Monroe Fellowship from the New Orleans Center for the Gulf South that facilitated my research on the French colonial era.

My abundant thanks to Bruce Boyd Raeburn, who recently retired after many years as director of the Hogan Jazz Archive at Tulane. Bruce shared his reservoir of knowledge on countless occasions and read the middle chapters of this book. His presence will be missed by many of us. My gratitude extends to his colleagues at the archive, Lynn Abbott, an industrious historian of African American music, and Alaina Hebert, who has helped me on many occasions. I also wish to thank Dr. William E. Bertrand of Tulane at the Payson Center for his support of the early stages of the film work.

In the late nineties, I was fortunate to work as a consultant to The Historic New Orleans Collection after the acquisition of the William J. Russell jazz archive. Jon Kukla, the director, allowed me to immerse myself in Russell's substantial collection of interviews, articles, photographs, and other materials. Much later, after Jon's move to Virginia and the publication of *A Wilderness So Immense*, his notable book on the Louisiana Purchase, he kindly read portions of my work-in-progress. I thank the late Mary Louise Christovich, the longtime board chair of the THNOC, for her support during my consultancy and for the information she shared near the end of her long, productive life on the early cultivation patterns of the city after her publication of *Garden Legacy* with Roulhac Toledano. THNOC director Priscilla Lawrence; her husband, John Lawrence; and staffers at the Williams Research Center, particularly Mary Lou Eichorn, Mark Cave, Pamela Arcenaux, and Rebecca Smith, each of whom assisted me in various ways, for which thanks to all.

The late Dr. Samuel A. Floyd Jr., author of *The Power of Black Music* and founder of the Center for Black Music Research at Columbia College, Chicago, was a longtime friend and colleague with whom I worked on several projects; Sam's spirit pervades these pages.

Gwendolyn Midlo Hall, a pioneering scholar of slavery and the author of *Africans in Colonial Louisiana*, a landmark work, kindly read my early chapters, for which many thanks. Special thanks to James Wilson of UL Press.

Charles B. Davis, an art dealer and authority on African mask and dance rituals, has helped me over many years in understanding the spiritual dimensions of sub-Saharan cultures and read several chapter drafts. I am grateful for his help and the friendship shared with his wife, Kent.

William A. Fagaly, a longtime curator at the New Orleans Museum of Art, introduced me to Sister Gertrude Morgan's work and enlisted me for a catalog essay in the 2004 traveling exhibition he organized, *Tools of Her Ministry*. Bill's milestone biographical essay in the catalog was a bedrock source in my chapter about Sister Gertrude's life. His reading of the draft was an enormous help, for which my lasting thanks. I am likewise grateful to the scholar Elaine Y. Yau, an authority on Gertrude Morgan, for her close reading and sharing information. Author and musician Tom Sancton, who got his start on jazz clarinet during the rise of Preservation Hall, gave a perceptive reading of the chapter, for which I thank him.

I am also indebted to Sacha Borenstein Clay for providing information on her parents, particularly the early history of her father, Larry Borenstein. JoAnn Clevenger's interview and conversations on those years were of great help as well.

Warmest thanks to Ann Cagnolatti for providing a copy of her family history and information on her parents' and grandmother's involvement with Mother Catherine and the Manger in the Lower Ninth Ward.

The following scholars read various chapters, providing insights and critiques that helped me along the way. To all of you, my thanks.

Professor Daniel H. Usner Jr. of Vanderbilt University, an esteemed authority on the history of Native Americans in the Gulf South; Professor William C. Davis of Virginia Tech, the author of *The Pirates Laffite* and a forthcoming history of the Battle of New Orleans; James F. Barnett Jr., author of *The Natchez Indians: A History to 1735*; Ned Sublette, author of *The World That Made New Orleans*, an indispensable work; Professor Bryan Wagner of the University of California, Berkeley, an authority on New Orleans culture and literature; Professor Emily Suzanne Clark of Gonzaga University, author of *A Luminous Brotherhood*, kindly shared French translations of the Cercle Harmonique séances; Professor Fatima Shaik of St. Peter's University generously provided information on Pierre Casanave from her forthcoming book on Economy Hall; Patricia Brady, a colonial scholar and authority on Benjamin Latrobe, gave an informed opinion on the death of Latrobe's son. Tom Smith, the author of *The Crescent City Lynchings*, was unfailingly helpful with insights and in his reading of chapter 10. Dr. Jacalyn M. Duffin, a physician and historian who has written on the Vatican's canonization procedures, offered rare insights on the oral histories of Mother Catherine Seals. For assistance on the same chapter, I am grateful to Professor D. Ryan Gray, an anthropologist at University of New Orleans, for sharing his research on the area that was once The Manger. Dr. Ibrahima Seck, academic director of the Whitney Plantation, provided helpful insights on my treatment of slavery. Russell Desmond of Acadian Books was extremely helpful in providing translations from the French and guidance on the trail of my colonial research.

As an investigative journalist, I have been fortunate to work with a number of editors who gave me the space for probing politics, yielding material that after further research became part of this narrative. Three editors at *Gambit Weekly*—Michael Tisserand, Allen Johnson, and Clancy DuBos—have been fine colleagues; they knew when to cut and also gave me length on cultural pieces. I am particularly indebted to Clancy for a close reading of the final chapter, and Allen for eleventh-hour help in tracking down source citations.

Errol Laborde, the editor of *New Orleans Magazine*, has published my music column for better than twenty years now, for which my thanks.

Bob Hall was the editor of *Southern Exposure* many years ago when I wrote about Governor Edwin Edward's cynical environmental policies. Albert LaFarge was the deputy editor of *DoubleTake*, a wonderful magazine too short-lived, when I did a profile of Danny Barker.

Malcolm Jones of *The Daily Beast* has been an ideal editor for my on-going pieces about culture and politics and always a pleasure to work with, as was John Avlon, the former editor in chief. I carry a lasting appreciation to Tom Roberts and Dennis Coday, the editors at *National Catholic Reporter*, who welcomed my articles about New Orleans (and other topics) over many years. Warm thanks, as well, to Carl Cannon and Melinda Henneberger, the editors at *Politics Daily*, which in its grand if abbreviated run gave space for many of my pieces. I appreciate, too, the outlet at Global-Post that Charles Sennott provided for reports on New Orleans in the long aftermath of Hurricane Katrina.

Tim Watson of Ariel Montage has been my friend and editor on film projects for many years and a great help in assisting with illustrations and photographs on this book, for which the warmest of thanks.

For various favors, I am grateful to the late Christina Vella; the late Leon René; Sylvia Barker; Professor J. H. Kwabena Nketia of the University of Ghana in Legon; Garry Wills; Carol Gelderman; Karl Koenig; Adam Rothman and John Tutino of the Georgetown University history department; authors Ben Sandmel, Rick Coleman, Michael Tisserand, Lolis Elie, Gregory Orfalea, Keith Spera, John Pope, Susan Larson, Rodger and Moira Kamenetz, Mark Hertsgaard, and the late Deb "Big Red" Cotton; Rosemary James; Jacques Morial; Dr. Stephen Hales and the School of Design; Arthur Hardy; Henri Schindler; photographers Kathy Anderson, David Spielman, Donn Young, Julie Dermansky, Kim Welsh, Judy Cooper, and Cheryl Gerber and videographers Philip Braun, Harris Done, and Jake Springfield; Frank Maselli and Sal Serio of the American Italian Cultural Center; Adam and Sharon Nossiter; Gerard Wimberly; Stephen Hanselman; Cherice Harrison-Nelson of the Mardi Gras Indian Council; Herreast Harrison; Mark F. Fernandez and Justin A. Nystrom of the Loyola New Orleans history department; Professor Carla Kaplan of Northeastern University; Hodding Carter; Marcie Cohen Ferris; James Carville; Walter Isaacson; Carolyn Goldsby Kolb; Phoebe Ferguson; Roxie Wright; Leon Miller, the head of the Louisiana Research Collection at the Tulane University Howard-Tilton Memorial Library; Gregory Osborne, archivist in the Louisiana Division of the New Orleans Public Library; Daniel Samuels; Lisa Clark; Ned Hémard; Rob and Missy Couhig; Sheridan Philipp; Jim Brown; Michael and Emily Arata; Mary Lou Dauray and Alan Davis; Fred and Lynn Lyon; Stephen Smith of Herman Leonard Photography LLC; Ray Strother; Katie Kleinsasser; Joseph Logsdon and Arnold R. Hirsch, scholars well remembered; Deputy Clerk Siva M. Blake; and Dale N. Atkins, clerk of Civil District Court for the Parish of Orleans.

After a long history of attacking elected officials and certain religious authorities in print, I was delighted when Mayor Mitch Landrieu called one morning in September of 2017 to ask if I had interest in providing editorial assistance for his book, just then under way, *In the Shadow of Statues*. Having already interviewed him about the issues he faced over the Confederate monuments, and after a great deal of my own reading on the Lost Cause mythology by then, I found it a rare pleasure to assist on his book and get to know Deputy Mayor Ryan Berni. Warm thanks to them both.

I am deeply grateful to John Boutté for allowing the use of his lyrics from "The Tremé Song" in this book.

A very special expression of appreciation to my literary agent, John Taylor "Ike" Williams, and his assistant, Hope Denekamp, of the Kneerim & Williams Agency LLC, for their assistance on many fronts. I am also deeply grateful to Mark Simpson-Vos, the University of North Carolina Press editorial director, for a most rewarding dialogue as this work took shape, and to his colleagues Jessica Newman, Jay Mazzocchi, Alex Martin, Gina Mahalek, and Joanna Ruth Marsland.

Finally, to the personal infrastructure that every writer needs, I am ever grateful to my wife, Melanie McKay, who in her final year before retirement as vice-provost for academic affairs at Loyola University New Orleans managed, despite the working hours, to read these chapters with a sharp editorial eye, providing assistance on the endnotes and patience with a man who has no dissertation, much less one on Nabokov. My inspiring daughter Simonette Berry, who works as an artist in the film industry with her husband, David Whatley; and my stepson, Keith Wood, his wife, Nicole, and their children, Colin, Grace, and Julia, are all a source of joy. And to the memory of my parents, Mary Frances and Jason Sr., and my late daughter, Ariel, for the light each of them has given to my life.

NOTES

Prologue

1. **"Symbols should reflect who we really are"**: quoted in Robert McClendon, "New Orleans Mayor Mitch Landrieu Calls for Removal of Lee Circle Statue," *Times-Picayune*, June 24, 2015, http://www.nola.com/politics/index.ssf/2015/06/lee_circle_statue_robert_e_lee.html.

1. **Elton John sent carnations**: Keith Spera, "Stars Send Off Allen Toussaint with His Own Songs," *New Orleans Advocate*, November 24, 2015, http://www.theadvocate.com/new_orleans/news/article_fc7403d3-68db-565e-afbe-88f84cbad36c.html.

1. **"The tunes you gave us"**: quoted in Jason Berry, "Can Soul Icon Allen Toussaint Topple Robert E. Lee in New Orleans?," *The Daily Beast*, November 26, 2015, http://www.thedailybeast.com/can-soul-icon-allen-toussaint-topple-robert-e-lee-in-new-orleans.

3. **"The end of a perfect death"**: quoted in Marshall W. Stearns, *The Story of Jazz* (Oxford: Oxford University Press, 1958), 57.

3. **"Because it's so quiet"**: Jason Berry, "Allen Toussaint: On the Spiritual Side," *OffBeat Magazine*, May 1, 1996, http://www.offbeat.com/articles/allen-toussaint-on-the-spiritual-side/.

3. **In response, Glen David Andrews**: Berry, *The Daily Beast*, "Can Soul Icon Allen Toussaint Topple Robert E. Lee?"

3. **"an attempt to 'hide' history"** and **"The statue never bothered anybody"**: quoted in ibid.

4. **"Lee had the least"**: Campbell Robertson, "From Lofty Perch, New Orleans Monument to Confederacy Comes Down," *New York Times*, May 20, 2017, http://www.nytimes.com/2017/05/19/us/confederate-monument-new-orleans-lee.html.

4. **"Zulu caricatured Rex"**: Reid Mitchell, *All on a Mardi Gras Day: Episodes in the History of New Orleans Carnival* (Cambridge, Mass.: Harvard University Press, 1995), 151.

5. **"putting on masks at Mardi Gras"**: Walker Percy, *Lancelot* (New York: Farrar, Straus and Giroux, 1977), 4.

Chapter 1. Bienville

6. **"They are all nude"**: Jean François Bertet de la Clue, *A Voyage to Dauphin Island in 1720: The Journal of Bertet de la Clue*, trans. and ed. Francis Escoffier and Jay Higginbotham (Mobile: Museum of the City of Mobile, 1974), 63–64.

6. **"acts of bravery"**: Arnaud Balvay, "Tattooing and Its Role in French–Native American Relations in the Eighteenth Century," *French Colonial History* 9 (2008): 1–14.

7. **On that oxbow**: Richard Campanella, *Bienville's Dilemma: A Historical Geography of New Orleans* (Lafayette: University of Louisiana at Lafayette Press, 2008), 20.

7. **the king lay dying**: Duc de Saint-Simon, *The Memoirs of Louis XIV, His Court and the Regency, Complete*, Project Gutenberg EBook no. 3875, September 29, 2006, chap. 72, 3–4.

7. **a bold plan by John Law**: Janet

Gleeson, *Millionaire: The Philanderer, Gambler, and Duelist Who Invented Modern Finance* (New York: Simon and Schuster, 1999), 168–72.

7. **Where to situate the port?**: Lawrence N. Powell, *The Accidental City: Improvising New Orleans* (Cambridge, Mass.: Harvard University Press, 2012), 46. Campanella, *Bienville's Dilemma*, 21, 110.

7. **two corporate officials *above him***: Grace King, *Jean Baptiste Le Moyne, Sieur de Bienville* (New York: Dodd, Mead, 1893), 229.

8. **"We are working on New Orleans"**: Baron Marc de Villiers, "A History of the Foundation of New Orleans (1717–1922)," trans. Warrington Dawson, *Louisiana Historical Quarterly* 3, no. 2 (April 1920): 179.

8. **"Crayfish abound"**: quoted in ibid.

8. **"Of the seven thousand"**: Daniel H. Usner Jr., *Indians, Settlers, and Slaves in a Frontier Exchange Economy: The Lower Mississippi Valley before 1783* (Chapel Hill: University of North Carolina Press, 1992), 35.

8. **"I told them"**: André Pénicaut, *Fleur de Lys and Calumet: Being the Pénicaut Narrative of French Adventure in Louisiana*, trans. and ed. Richebourg Gaillard McWilliams (Baton Rouge: Louisiana State University Press, 1935), 218–19.

8. **"The Chitimachas stepped out"**: Shane Lief, "Singing, Shaking, and Parading at the Birth of New Orleans," *Jazz Archivist* 28 (2015): 15.

8. **"I purchased from"**: Le Page Du Pratz, *History of Louisiana* (1924; New Orleans: Pelican, 1947), 19.

9. **"the bad man"** and **"Formerly the sun was red"**: quoted in John R. Swanton, *Indian Tribes of the Lower Mississippi Valley and Adjacent Coast of Mexico* (1911; Mineola, N.Y.: Dover, 1998), 340–41.

9. **"fresh meat that is consumed"**: Dunbar Rowland and Albert Godfrey Sanders, eds. and trans., *Mississippi Provincial Archives, 1704–1743, French Dominion*, vol. 3 (Jackson: Press of the Mississippi Department of Archives and History, 1932), 535.

9. **"Chance and Bienville's cunning"**: Powell, *The Accidental City*, 51.

10. **"infinite embarrassment"**: Philomena Hauck, *Bienville: Father of Louisiana* (Lafayette: Center for Louisiana Studies, 2006), 71.

10. **"murders, debauchery"**: Gwendolyn Midlo Hall, *Africans in Creole Louisiana: The Development of Afro-Creole Culture in the Eighteenth Century* (Baton Rouge: Louisiana State University Press: 1997), 5–6.

10. **newlyweds had their shackles removed**: Gleeson, *Millionaire*, 176.

10. **the Crown halted the forced emigration**: James D. Hardy Jr., "The Transportation of Convicts to Colonial Louisiana," in *The French Experience in Louisiana*, ed. Glenn R. Conrad, vol. 1 of *The Louisiana Purchase Bicentennial Series in Louisiana History* (Lafayette: Center for Louisiana Studies, University of Southwestern Louisiana, 1995), 119.

10. **Bienville's cultivation of Pauger**: Powell, *The Accidental City*, 55–57.

10. **"necessities of urban life"**: quoted in Mary Louise Mossy Christovich and Roulhac Bunkley Toledano, *Garden Legacy* (New Orleans: The Historic New Orleans Collection, 2017), 45.

11. **"the last thing the Biloxi faction wanted to see"**: Powell, *The Accidental City*, 57.

11. **Bienville genealogy**: Nellis M. Crouse,

Lemoyne d'Iberville: Soldier of New France (Baton Rouge: Louisiana State University Press, 2001), 6–7.

11. **Biographical sketch of Charles Le Moyne**: King, *Jean Baptiste Le Moyne, Sieur de Bienville*, 3. The surname is alternately spelled Lemoyne and Le Moyne by the respective biographers of Pierre and Jean-Baptiste. Since the Bienville biographers—Grace King and Philomena Hauck—use Le Moyne, so have I.

12. **a commanding presence to Count Pontchartrain**: see Sara E. Chapman, *Private Ambition and Political Alliances: The Phélypeaux de Pontchartrain Family and Louis XIV's Government, 1650–1715* (Rochester, N.Y.: University of Rochester Press, 2004).

12. **In 1682, on mudflats**: Mathé Allain, *"Not Worth a Straw": French Colonial Policy and the Early Years of Louisiana* (Lafayette: Center for Louisiana Studies, University of Southwest Louisiana, 1988), 40, 42. On LaSalle, see Jon Kukla, *A Wilderness So Immense: The Louisiana Purchase and the Destiny of America* (New York: Knopf, 2003), 30–31; and Charles L. Dufour, *Ten Flags in the Wind: The Story of Louisiana* (New York: Harper & Row, 1967), 9–10.

12. **"We looked with admiration"**: Pénicaut, *Fleur de Lys and Calumet*, 14.

12. **"It is almost certain"**: Campanella, *Bienville's Dilemma*, 106.

13. **"attracts many buzzards"**: *Iberville's Gulf Journals*, trans. and ed. Richebourg Gaillard McWilliams (Tuscaloosa: University of Alabama Press, 1981), 68–69.

13. **explorers' memories of candlelit solemnities**: Philippe Ariès, *The Hour of Our Death* (New York: Random House, 1982), 167.

13. **"He who goes unburied"**: ibid., 31.

13. **"Fifteen of the prettiest"**: *Iberville's Gulf Journals*, 68.

13. **"They offered the women"**: quoted in Robert S. Weddle, *The French Thorn: Rival Explorers in the Spanish Sea, 1682–1762* (College Station: Texas A&M University Press, 1991), 145.

14. **Tonti was a legendary explorer**: Marcel Giraud, *A History of French Louisiana*, vol. 1, *The Reign of Louis XIV, 1698–1715* (Baton Rouge: Louisiana State University Press, 1974), 6.

14. **Henri de Tonti**: Francis Parkman, *LaSalle and the Discovery of the Great West: France and England in North America, Part Third* (Boston: Little, Brown, 1908), 128–29; Jay Higginbotham, *Old Mobile: Fort Louis de la Louisiane, 1702–1711* (Mobile: Museum of the City of Mobile: 1977), 54–55.

14. **the Bayogoula camp**: *The French Thorn*, 148.

14. **Bienville bargained**: King, *Jean Baptiste Le Moyne, Sieur de Bienville*, 64.

14. **Some 3,500 Indians**: Usner, *Indians, Settlers, and Slaves*, 17.

14. **Pontchartrain and Iberville**: Allain, *"Not Worth a Straw,"* 53.

14. **Invading the island of Nevis**: Giraud, *A History of French Louisiana*, 119.

15. **Love-starved men**: Carl Brasseaux, "The Moral Climate of French Colonial Louisiana, 1699–1763," *Louisiana History* 27 (1986): 27–41.

15. **Death and burial of Tonti**: Higginbotham, *Old Mobile*, 196.

15. **Bienville and LaVente**: Charles Edward O'Neill, *Church and State in*

French Colonial Louisiana: Policy and Politics to 1732 (New Haven, Conn.: Yale University Press, 1966), 54–58, 246–50.

15. "All the Indians of these countries": 15wland and Sanders, *Mississippi Provincial Archives*, 38.

15. patching together a Choctaw-Chickasaw alliance: James F. Barnett Jr., *The Natchez Indians: A History to 1735* (Jackson: University Press of Mississippi, 2007), 83.

15. In 1712 Pontchartrain negotiated: John G. Clark, *New Orleans, 1712–1812: An Economic History* (Baton Rouge: Louisiana State University Press, 1970), 14–15.

16. On Cadillac: "LAUMET, dit de Lamothe Cadillac, ANTOINE," *Dictionary of Canadian Biography Online, 1701–1740*, vol. 11.

16. "I have enthralled him": quoted in Allain, *"Not Worth a Straw,"* 61.

16. "to determine how much money": James F. Barnett Jr., "The Yamasee War, the Bearded Chief, and the Founding of Fort Rosalie," *Journal of Mississippi History* 74, no. 1 (2013): 1–24.

16. "I have been here for thirteen years": quoted in Rowland and Sanders, *Mississippi Provincial Archives*, 168.

16. "His Majesty will be regardful": quoted in ibid., 167–68.

16. "He is the most artificial": quoted in King, *Jean Baptiste Le Moyne, Sieur de Bienville*, 200.

16. "I had the misfortune": quoted in ibid.

17. The Natchez: Pénicaut, *Fleur de Lys and Calumet*, 91. Archaeological digs in the 1980s found deposits of bones at the mound where the temple once stood. Barnett, *The Natchez Indians*, 47.

17. was strangled: Pénicaut, *Fleur de Lys and Calumet*, 94.

17. Some Natchez area chieftains traded captives: Barnett, "The Yamasee War," 14.

17. "unfortunate newborns strangled": Pénicaut, *Fleur de Lys and Calumet*, 87–88.

18. "him in a mud hole": ibid., 176.

18. Bienville and capture of the Natchez: Pénicaut, *Fleur de Lys and Calumet*, 177. The more extensive report on which I rely is a translation of Richebourg's account, quoted at length in Swanton, *Indian Tribes of the Lower Mississippi Valley*, 199.

20. "This is a country": quoted in Shannon Lee Dawdy, *Building the Devil's Empire: French Colonial New Orleans* (Chicago: University of Chicago Press, 2008), 30–31.

20. "smugglers, loose women": ibid., 30.

20. In view of the fragmented Natchez districts: Barnett, *The Natchez Indians*, 88–89.

20. "screed of complaints": Hauck, *Bienville*, 96.

21. He met with Great Sun and Tattooed Serpent: George Milne, *Natchez Country: Indians, Colonists, and the Landscapes of Race in French Louisiana* (Athens: University of Georgia Press, 2015), 113–15.

21. In March 1725, Bienville left: Powell, *The Accidental City*, 80–81.

21. "because the clergy competed": Thomas N. Ingersoll, *Mammon and Manon in Early New Orleans: The First Slave Society in the Deep South, 1718–1819* (Knoxville: University of Tennessee Press, 1999), 109.

21. "open enemy of the church": quoted in O'Neill, *Church and State in French Colonial Louisiana*, 161–65.

22. Bienville's "Memoir of Louisiana": Rowland and Sanders, *Mississippi Provincial Archives*, 499–539.

22. **"kiss of death"**: Hauck, *Bienville*, 104–5.

22. **"The great copper vats"**: quoted in Richard N. Ellis and Charlie R. Steen, "An Indian Delegation in France, 1725," *Journal of Illinois State Historical Society* 67, no. 4 (September 1974), 385–405. A translation of the entire *Mercure* report begins on page 389.

22. **"I regard myself"**: quoted in ibid., 386.

22. **"an impressive peace offering"**: Emily Clark, *Masterless Mistresses: The New Orleans Ursulines and the Development of a New World Society, 1727–1834* (Chapel Hill: University of North Carolina Press, 2007), 46.

23. **took up residence in Bienville's two-story townhome**: King, *Jean Baptiste Le Moyne, Sieur de Bienville*. **"the most beautiful house"**: in Emily Clark, ed., *Voices from an Early American Convent: Marie Madeleine Hachard and the New Orleans Ursulines, 1727–1760* (Baton Rouge: Louisiana State University Press, 2007), 78.

23. **In 1728, the King's Council annulled**: Powell, *The Accidental City*, 84.

23. **"acts of injustice"**: Daniel H. Usner Jr., *American Indians in the Lower Mississippi Valley: Social and Economic Histories* (Lincoln: University of Nebraska Press, 1998), 26.

23. **The Natchez forged ties**: Gwendolyn Midlo Hall, *Africans in Colonial Louisiana: The Development of Afro-Creole Culture in the Eighteenth Century* (Baton Rouge: Louisiana State University Press, 1992), 100.

23. **Alerted by seven of his men**: Barnett, *The Natchez Indians*, 104.

23. **"some of these people completely naked"**: Marc-Antoine Caillout, *A Company Man: The Remarkable French-Atlantic Voyage of a Clerk for the Company of the Indies*, ed. Erin M.

Greenwald, trans. Teri F. Chalmers (New Orleans: The Historic New Orleans Collection, 2013), 124.

24. **Fifteen blacks were among the troops**: Roland C. McConnell, *Negro Troops of Antebellum Louisiana: A History of the Battalion of Free Men of Color* (Baton Rouge: Louisiana State University Press, 1968), 7.

24. **Chief Chicagou in St. Louis church**: Lief, "Singing, Shaking, and Parading," 18.

24. **"more delight and pleasure in chanting"**: ibid., 19.

25. **"Indians never begin any exercise"**: Caillout, *A Company Man*, 122.

25. **"labors, the anxieties, and the mental strain"**: in Rowland and Sanders, *Mississippi Provincial Archives*, 738.

25. **"We went out in order"**: in Clark, *Voices from an Early American Convent*, 125–26.

Chapter 2. St. Maló in the Memory Rings

27. **The evolution of the land**: Freddi Williams Evans, *Congo Square: African Roots in New Orleans* (Lafayette: University of Louisiana Press, 2011), 18; Richard Campanella, *Bienville's Dilemma: A Historical Geography of New Orleans* (Lafayette: University of Louisiana at Lafayette Press, 2008), 20.

27. **brickyard on Bayou Road**: Roulhac Toledano and Mary Louise Christovich, *Faubourg Tremé and Bayou Road*, vol. 6 of *New Orleans Architecture* (Gretna, La.: Pelican, 1980), 4.

27. **The 1724 Code Noir**: Judith Kelleher Schaefer, *Slavery, the Civil Law, and the Supreme Court of Louisiana* (Baton Rouge: Louisiana State University Press, 1994), 1.

28. **in 1757, two Sephardic Jews**: Bertram

Wallace Korn, *The Early Jews of New Orleans* (Waltham, Mass.: American Jewish Historical Society, 1969), 15.

28. **"a humanitarian document"**: Robert Harris, *The Diligent: A Voyage through the Worlds of the Slave Trade* (New York: Basic Books, 2003), 26. Other dimensions of the code: Thomas Ingersoll, *Mammon and Manon in Early New Orleans: The First Slave Society in the Deep South, 1718–1819* (Knoxville: University of Tennessee Press, 1999), 135–41; Lawrence N. Powell, *The Accidental City: Improvising New Orleans* (Cambridge, Mass.: Harvard University Press, 2012), 73.

28. **"work their own garden plots"**: Jerah Johnson, "New Orleans's Congo Square: An Urban Setting for Early Afro-American Cultural Formation," *Louisiana History: The Journal of the Louisiana Historical Association* 32, no. 2 (Spring 1991): 120.

28. **the land had been a primordial site**: Fred B. Kniffen, Hiram F. Gregory, and George A. Stokes, *The Historic Indian Tribes of Louisiana: From 1542 to the Present* (Baton Rouge: Louisiana State University Press, 1987), 260.

28. **"The circle is linked"**: Sterling Stuckey, *Slave Culture: Nationalist Theory and the Foundations of Black America* (New York: Oxford University Press, 1987), 11–12.

28. **Artists in West Africa carved**: Robert Farris Thompson, *African Art in Motion: Icon and Art* (Berkeley: University of California Press, 1974).

28. **We have eyewitness descriptions**: On Pinkster dances in Albany, see Herbert G. Gutman, *The Black Family in Slavery and Freedom, 1750–1925* (New York: Vintage, 1976), 333–34. On slave dancing in the South, see Katrina

Hazzard-Gordon, *Jookin': The Rise of Social Dance Formations in African-American Culture* (Philadelphia: Temple University Press, 1990); Dena J. Epstein, *Sinful Tunes and Spirituals: Black Folks Music to the Civil War* (Champagne: University of Illinois Press, 1977); and Lynne Fauley Emery, *Black Dance from 1619 to Today*, 2nd rev. ed. (Hightstown, N.J.: Princeton Book, 1988).

29. **Rice seeds came**: Gwendolyn Midlo Hall, *Africans in Colonial Louisiana: The Development of Afro-Creole Culture in the Eighteenth Century* (Baton Rouge: Louisiana State University Press, 1992), 49.

29. **"Nothing is to be more dreaded"**: *The History of Louisiana: Translated from the French of M. Le Page Du Pratz*, ed. Joseph G. Tregle Jr. (Baton Rouge: Louisiana State University Press, 1975), 387.

29. **"With over two thousand"**: Evans, *Congo Square*, 18.

29. **"that the negroes have wives"**: Le Page Du Pratz, *The History of Louisiana*, 386.

29. **"The life of a slave was marked"**: Ibrahima Seck, *Bouki Fait Gombo: A History of the Slave Community of Habitation Haydel (Whitney Plantation), Louisiana, 1750–1860* (New Orleans: University of New Orleans Press, 2014), 105.

30. **"fringes, ribbons, little bells"**: David C. Estes, "Traditional Dances and Processions of Blacks in New Orleans as Witnessed by Antebellum Travellers," *Louisiana Folklore Miscellany* 6 (1990): 2.

30. **a priest at St. Louis Church filed**: Emilie Gagnet Leumas, "St. Peter Street Cemetery," Office of Archives and Records, Archdiocese of New Orleans, n.d. See also Roger Baudier,

The Catholic Church in Louisiana (New Orleans: Approval by Archbishop Joseph Rummel, 1939), 130–31.

30. **Alabama, Virginia, and New York had laws**: David R. Roediger, "And Die in Dixie: Funerals, Death and Heaven in the Slave Community," *Massachusetts Review* 22 (Spring 1981): 166.

30. **Many of the blacks sent to New World plantation regimes**: Albert J. Rabouteau, *Slave Religion: The "Invisible Institution" of the Antebellum South* (1978; New York: Oxford University Press, 2011), 22.

30. **The Yoruba of present-day Nigeria**: Wole Soyinka, *Myth, Literature and the African World* (Cambridge: Cambridge University Press, 1976), 1979.

30. **Dropping bits of food**: Robert Farris Thompson, "An Aesthetic of the Cool II," *Aesthetic of the Cool: Afro-Atlantic Art and Music* (New York: Periscope, 2011), 22.

30. **Two-thirds of the 5,951**: Hall, *Africans in Colonial Louisiana*, 48.

31. **"The Bambara belief in"**: ibid., 50.

31. **"the fertility of their crops"**: Charles B. Davis, *The Animal Motif in Bamana Art* (New Orleans: Davis Gallery, 1981), 4.

31. **In *Gouan*, a secret society**: See Pascal James Imperato, *Buffoons, Queens, and Wooden Horsemen: The Dyo and Gouan Societies of the Bambara of Mali* (New York: Kima House, 1983).

31. **"to the unseen world of the dead"**: J. H. Kwabena Nketia, "Traditional Funerals and Social Change," Symposium on Funerals, Institute of African Studies, University of Ghana, Legon, July 12, 1972, monograph photocopy, gift of Professor Nketia to the author.

31. **Senegalese warlord of Wolof royalty**: Seck, *Bouki Fait Gombo*, 41.

32. **"Dancing the slaves"**: Hazzard-Gordon, *Jookin'*, 9.

32. **in 1721 on a ship with some 294 *captifs***: Hall, *Africans in Colonial Louisiana*, 60.

32. **"This job"**: Ingersoll, *Mammon and Manon in Early New Orleans*, 71.

32. **"Let us punish"**: quoted in Shannon Lee Dawdy, *Building the Devil's Empire: French Colonial New Orleans* (Chicago: University of Chicago Press, 2008), 190.

32. **"His personal freedom"**: ibid., 191.

33. **"head rotting in some farmer's field"**: Brenda Marie Osbey, "The Head of Luís Congo Speaks," in *All Saints: New and Selected Poems* (Baton Rouge: Louisiana State University Press, 1997), 103.

33. **"When very young slaves"**: Jennifer M. Spear, *Race, Sex and Social Order in Early New Orleans* (Baltimore: Johns Hopkins University Press, 2009), 86.

34. **"senior delinquents"**: Ned Sublette, *The World That Made New Orleans: From Spanish Silver to Congo Square* (Chicago: Lawrence Hill, 2008), 78.

34. **Police criticized slave owners**: Carl A. Brasseaux, "The Administration of Slave Regulations in French Louisiana, 1724–1766," *Louisiana History* 21, no. 2 (Spring 1980): 146.

34. **"little Versailles" and "grandeur and elegance"**: Grace King, *New Orleans: The Place and the People* (New York: MacMillan, 1895), 79.

34. **tons of sugar with 100,000 slaves**: Simon Henochsberg: "Public Debt and Slavery: the Case of Haiti (1760–1915)," Paris School of Economics, December 2016, 7.

35. **Louis XV offered New Orleans**: Jon Kukla, *A Wilderness So Immense: The Louisiana Purchase and the Destiny of America* (New York: Knopf, 2003), 32–33.

35. **In contrast, the Jesuits had**: John W. O'Malley, S.J., *The Jesuits: A History from Ignatius to the Present* (Lanham, Md.: Rowman & Littlefield, 2014), 77; Vivienne Morell, "'The Mission' and Historical Jesuit Missions in Paraguay in the 1750s," Wordpress.com, August 19, 2004; Christine Vogel, "The Suppression of the Society of Jesus, 1758–1773," *EGO: European History Online*, March 3, 2010, http://ieg -ego.eu/en/threads/european-media /european-media-events/christine -vogel-suppression-of-the-society-of -jesus-1758-1773; Rev. Cornelius Buckley, S.J., "When Jesuits Ignore Papal Decrees," *Crisis Magazine*, September 6, 2016.

35. **"stuffed [them] into"**: O'Malley, *The Jesuits*, 78.

36. **In Haiti, the Jesuits educated 25,000 slaves**: George Breathett, *The Catholic Church in Haiti, 1704–1785* (Salisbury, N.C.: Documentary Publications, 1983), 14–15; Anne Greene, *The Catholic Church in Haiti: Political and Social Change* (East Lansing: Michigan State University Press, 1993), 77.

36. **The papacy was conflicted**: Joel S. Panzer, *The Popes and Slavery* (New York: Alba House, 1996), 79–81.

36. **The Ursulines in New Orleans promoted tight family groupings**: Emily Clark, *Masterless Mistresses: The New Orleans Ursulines and the Development of a New World Society, 1723–1834* (Chapel Hill: University of North Carolina Press, 2007), 176–77.

36. **"to increase the value"** and **"The Church ornaments"**: Baudier, *The Catholic Church in Louisiana*, 163–64.

36. **Bienville, white-haired at eighty-four**: Powell, *The Accidental City*, 160–61.

36. **Ulloa, a fifty-year-old distinguished**

scientist and diplomat: Sublette, *The World That Made New Orleans*, 90.

36. **O'Reilly had the rebel leaders arrested**: Powell, *The Accidental City*, 157–59.

37. *coartación*: Schaefer, *Slavery, the Civil Law, and the Supreme Court of Louisiana*, 2.

37. **"The effect this had"**: Sublette, *The World That Made New Orleans*, 98–99.

37. **"With so many strangers"**: quoted in ibid., 102.

37. **strong, healthy, free, and clever**: Hall, *Africans in Colonial Louisiana*, 226–27. See also Gilbert C. Din, "'Cimarrones' and the San Malo Band in Spanish Louisiana," *Louisiana History: The Journal of the Louisiana Historical Association* 21 (Summer 1980): 237–62.

38. **"The runaways left in families"**: Hall, *Africans in Colonial Louisiana*, 233–34.

38. **Stealing supplies from plantations** and **allies**: Gwendolyn Hall, "The Formation of Afro-Creole Culture," in *Creole New Orleans: Race and Americanization*, ed. Arnold R. Hirsch and Joseph Logsdon (Baton Rouge: Louisiana State University Press, 1992), 58–87.

38. My account of St. Maló relies on Hall, *Africans in Colonial Louisiana*; Hall, "The Formation of Afro-Creole Culture," in Hirsch and Logsdon, *Creole New Orleans*; Gilbert C. Din, *Francisco Bouligny: A Bourbon Soldier in Spanish Louisiana* (Baton Rouge: Louisiana State University Press, 1993); and Ingersoll, *Mammon and Manon in Early New Orleans*.

39. **"confessed his crimes"**: Gilbert C. Din and John E. Harkins, *The New Orleans Cabildo: Colonial Louisiana's First City Government, 1769–1803* (Baton Rouge: Louisiana State University Press, 1996), 166.

40. *shouted his protest*: Baudier, *The Catholic Church in Louisiana*, 202–3. Baudier spells the bishop's name with two *l*'s—Cirillo. More recent accounts use one *l*. For the sake of consistency, I have used the latter spelling.

40. "happy with the imprisonment": quoted in Din, *Francisco Bouligny*, 97.

41. "Negroes who at the vespers hour": quoted in Evans, *Congo Square*, 103.

41. "to remember" or "to remind": Sublette, *The World That Made New Orleans*, 180–81, 110.

41. *Bamboula* and other dances spread: Lynne Fauley Emery, *Black Dance from 1619 to Today*, 2nd rev. ed. (Hightstown, N.J.: Princeton Book, 1988), 9, 18, 24–27.

41. Ordered to forego plumes: Sublette, *The World That Made New Orleans*, 126. See also *In Search of Julien Hudson: Free Artist of Color in Pre–Civil War New Orleans*, with essays by William Keyse Rudolph and Patricia Brady (New Orleans: The Historic New Orleans Collection, 2010).

41. For Fon people from Dahomey, **vodun**: Melville J. Herskovits, *Life in a Haitian Valley* (Garden City, N.Y.: Doubleday, 1971), 23.

42. "Africa reblended": Robert Farris Thompson, *Flash of the Spirit: African & Afro-American Art & Philosophy* (New York: Vintage, 1984), 164.

42. Historical context of vodun: Donald J. Cosentino, ed., *Sacred Arts of Haitian Vodou* (Los Angeles: UCLA Fowler Museum of History, 1995). Among the essays in this collection, see in particular Susan Preston Blier, "Vodun: West African Roots of Vodou," 62–63.

42. "Voodoo was the medium of conspiracy": C. L. R. James, *The Black Jacobins: Toussaint L'Ouverture and the San Domingo Revolution*, 2nd rev. ed. (New York: Vintage, 1963), 86.

43. "The steel blue of the western horizon": *Inventing New Orleans: Writings of Lafcadio Hearn*, ed. S. Frederick Starr (Jackson: University Press of Mississippi, 2001), 90.

43. "Dirge of St. Malo": George Washington Cable, *Creoles and Cajuns: Stories of Old Louisiana*, ed. Arlin Turner (New York: Doubleday Anchor, 1959), 418–19.

44. "St. Marron, a folk saint": Carolyn Morrow Long, *A New Orleans Voudo Priestess: The Legend and Reality of Marie Laveau* (Gainesville: University Press of Florida, 2006), 109. See also Maya Deren, *Divine Horsemen: The Living Gods of Haiti* (New York: Vanguard, 1961), 58–66.

44. "stories about St. Malo well known": interview with Bruce Sunpie Barnes, New Orleans, March 17, 2017. Song lyrics quoted with permission. See also Jason Berry, "Pro Linebacker Resurrects the Legend of a Runaway Slave," *The Daily Beast*, April 2, 2017.

Chapter 3. The Great Fire and Procession for Carlos III

46. A network of ditches: Richard Campanella, *Bourbon Street: A History* (Baton Rouge: Louisiana State University Press, 2014), 17.

46. as an archaeological excavation discovered: *tDAR: The Digital Archeological Record*, "Douglas W. Owsley," 2017, https://core.tdar.org /browse/creators/12144/douglas-w -owsley; *tDAR*, "Charles E. Orser, Jr.," 2017, https://core.tdar.org/browse /creators/53723/charles-e-orser-jr; *tDAR*, "Robert Montgomery," 2017, https://core.tdar.org/browse/creators /64867/robert-montgomery; *tDAR*, "Claudia C. Holland," 2017, https://

core.tdar.org/browse/creators/62790
/claudia-c-holland; *An Archaeological
and Physical Anthropological Study
of the First Cemetery in New Orleans*
(Baton Rouge: Louisiana State
University, 1985).

46. **eight private schools**: Caroline Maude
Burson, *The Stewardship of Don
Esteban Miró, 1782-1792* (New Orleans:
American Printing, 1949), 264.

47. **People tended orange and lemon
trees**: Mary Louise Mossy Christovich
and Roulhac Bunkley Toledano, *Garden
Legacy* (New Orleans: Historic New
Orleans Collection, 2017), 52.

47. **The night sky emboldened rats**:
Christina Vella, *Intimate Enemies:
The Two Worlds of the Baroness de
Pontalba* (Baton Rouge: Louisiana State
University Press, 1997), 8–9.

47. **"The puddles, hoofs, feet"**:
Campanella, *Bourbon Street*, 23.

47. **"Carlos III hunted"**: Jon Kukla,
*A Wilderness So Immense: The
Louisiana Purchase and the Destiny of
America* (New York: Alfred A. Knopf,
2003), 24–25.

47. **A catechism for Indians**: David J.
Weber, *Bárbaros: Spaniards and Their
Savages in the Age of the Enlightenment*
(New Haven, Conn.: Yale University
Press, 2005), 111–12.

48. **The elegant thoroughfare begun
in 1835**: Ned Hémard, "Charles and
His Avenue," *New Orleans Nostalgia:
Remembering New Orleans History,
Culture and Traditions* (New Orleans:
New Orleans Bar Association, 2012).
For a less precise interpretation, see
John Chase, *Frenchmen, Desire, Good
Children ... and Other Streets of New
Orleans* (Gretna, La.: Pelican, 2007),
72.

48. **The superintendent of the king's mint**:
Kukla, *A Wilderness So Immense*, 38.

48. **Pollack with Unzaga**: Ned Sublette,
*The World That Made New Orleans:
From Spanish Silver to Congo Square*
(Chicago: Lawrence Hill, 2008), 98.

48. **A seasoned soldier**: John Walton
Caughey, *Bernardo de Gálvez in
Louisiana, 1776-1783* (Berkeley:
University of California Press, 1934),
66–67.

48. **charmed a young widow**: ibid., 84.

48. **despite a prohibition barring top
Spanish officials**: Gilbert C. Din,
"Bernardo de Galvez: A Reexamination
of His Governorship," in *The Spanish
Presence in Louisiana, 1763-1803*, ed.
Gilbert C. Din, vol. 3 of *The Louisiana
Purchase Bicentennial Series in
Louisiana History* (Lafayette: Center
for Louisiana Studies, University of
Southwestern Louisiana, 1996), 78.

49. **"La Compagnie des Mulâtres"**:
Kimberly S. Hanger, *Bounded Lives,
Bounded Places: Free Black Society
in Colonial New Orleans, 1769-1803*
(Durham, N.C.: Duke University Press,
1997), 118.

49. **To boost Louisiana's population**:
Diana C. Monteleone, "Isleños,"
University of Louisiana at Lafayette:
Center for Louisiana Studies, cls
.louisiana.edu/programming-special
-projects/louisiana-101/peoples ...
/isleños. Accessed June 15, 2017.

49. **Gálvez learned from an intercepted
letter**: Eric Beerman, "Victory on the
Mississippi, 1779," in Din, *The Spanish
Presence in Louisiana*, 19.

49. **"Although I am disposed"**: quoted
in Caughey, *Bernardo de Gálvez in
Louisiana*, 152–53.

49. **On August 27**: Beerman, "Victory on
the Mississippi," 295. Hanger, *Bounded
Lives*, 119. See also Thomas Fleming,
"Bernardo de Gálvez: The Forgotten
Revolutionary Conquistador Who Saved

Louisiana," *American Heritage* 33, no. 3 (April–May 1982): 3–5, http://www.americanheritage.com/content/bernardo-de-g%CS%A1lvez.

50. **Gálvez honored ten black militia leaders**: Hanger, *Bounded Lives*, 120.

50. **"The grand tradition began"**: Sublette, *The World That Made New Orleans*, 101.

50. **Mulatto soldiers, called *pardos*, wore the round hat**: Kimberly S. Hanger, "Free Black Militia of Spanish Louisiana," in Din, *The Spanish Presence in Louisiana*, 395.

50. **extending a European tradition**: Henry George Farmer, *The Rise & Development of Military Music* (London: Wm. Reeves, 1912), reissue by CPSIA, www.ICCGtesting.com; Raoul F. Camus, *Military Music of the American Revolution* (Westerville, Ohio: Integrity, 1975).

50. **marching soldiers as a guardian force**: Sublette, *The World That Made New Orleans*, 101.

50. **"in reading and writing"**: Hanger, "Free Black Militia of Spanish Louisiana," 395.

50. **nearly two-thirds of them owned at least one slave**: Mary Gehman, *The Free People of Color of New Orleans: An Introduction* (New Orleans: Margaret Media, 1994), 32; Hanger, *Bounded Lives*, 18.

50. **after the November harvest, when the planters moved**: Gilbert C. Din and John E. Harkins, *The New Orleans Cabildo: Colonial Louisiana's First City Government, 1769–1803* (Baton Rouge: Louisiana State University Press, 1996), 18.

51. **The Cabildo . . . functioned**: Gilbert C. Din, "The Offices and Functions of the New Orleans *Cabildo*," in Din, *The Spanish Presence in Louisiana*, 143–45.

51. **In 1779, the Cabildo opened a public market**: Robert A. Sauder, "The Origin and Spread of the Public Market System in New Orleans," *Louisiana History: The Journal of the Louisiana Historical Association* 22, no. 3 (Summer 1981): 282.

51. **"were the disciples of rival ministries"**: Vella, *Intimate Enemies*, 46.

52. **"His Majesty honors"**: Samuel Wilson Jr., "Almonaster: Philanthropist and Builder of New Orleans," in *The Spanish in the Mississippi Valley, 1762–1804*, ed. John Francis McDermott (Urbana: University of Illinois Press, 1974), 185.

52. **"Hundreds of documents"**: Vella, *Intimate Enemies*, 42.

52. **"the founding of a free hospital"**: quoted in Stella O'Connor, "The Charity Hospital of Louisiana at New Orleans: An Administrative and Financial History, 1736–1941," *Louisiana Historical Quarterly* 31, no. 1 (January 1948): 9. The qualifier "(until 2005)" refers to the State of Louisiana's closure of Charity Hospital, New Orleans, treated in the final chapter of this book.

52. **"It is clear from the Spanish laws"**: quoted in ibid., 18.

53. **the regidores protested**: Vella, *Intimate Enemies*, 47.

53. **In 1785 when the hospital opened**: ibid., 49.

53. **smaller facility for lepers**: Wilson, "Almonaster," 187; Vella, *Intimate Enemies*, 49.

53. **the ecclesiastical court in Cartagena**: Richard E. Greenleaf, "The Inquisition in Spanish Louisiana, 1762–1800," in Din, *The Spanish Presence in Louisiana*, 545, first published in *New Mexico Historical Review* 50 (1975): 45–72.

53. **Despite routine communications**

with **Sedella**: microfilm edition of the *Records of the Diocese of Louisiana and the Floridas, 1576–1803*, ed. Thomas T. McAvoy and Lawrence J. Bradley, 12 reels (Notre Dame, Ind.: 1967) (hereafter *DLF*), IV-4-c, A.D.S., August 29, 1787; Hamilleton (Hamilton) Therese (Opelousas, Louisiana) to Estevan Miro (gov. of Louisiana), New Orleans, IV-4-c, A.D.S., 9 pp., 8 vols. (French).

54. **"I kiss the hand of Your Lordship"**: Letters of Antonio de Sedella, Cura of San Luis Cathedral, New Orleans, Work Projects Administration of Louisiana, trans. 1940, project sponsored by Louisiana State University, Louisiana Collection, Howard Tilton Memorial Library, Tulane University, bundle 602, letter 2, May 25, 1785.

54. **On March 20, 1787**: Vella, *Intimate Enemies*, 52.

54. **"a constant and more or less furtive traffic"**: ibid.

54. **in any of the city's seventy-five taverns**: Jack D. L. Holmes, "Spanish Regulation of Taverns and the Liquor Trade in the Mississippi Valley," in McDermott, *The Spanish in the Mississippi Valley*, 181 (see appendix 4).

54. **Spain helped French-speaking farmers**: Carl A. Brasseaux, *The Founding of New Acadia: The Beginnings of Acadian Life in Louisiana, 1765–1803* (Baton Rouge: Louisiana State University Press, 1987), 124.

54. **Miró gave a welcoming speech**: Charles Gayarré, *History of Louisiana: The Spanish Domination*, vol. 3, 4th ed. (New Orleans: Pelican, 1965), 191–92.

54. **a ball where Creole ladies in fine dresses**: Grace King, *New Orleans: The Place and the People* (New York: Macmillan, 1895), 140.

54. **Núñez lit upward of fifty votive candles**: Lauro A. de Rojas, "The Great Fire of 1788 in New Orleans," *Louisiana Historical Quarterly* 3, no. 3 (July 1937): 579. The article draws on several sources, including official reports by Miró as well as newspaper accounts in Mexico and England discovered by scholars long after the fire.

55. **Sedella reported to a Cuban bishop**: *Microfilm Edition (DLF)*, March 28, 1788, Sedella, Father Antonio de (vicar and ecclesiastical judge of Louisiana), New Orleans to (Santiago Joseph de Hechavarria y Ellguenzua), bp. of (Santiago de) Cuba, Havana, IV-4-c, A.L.S., 2 pp., 8 vols. (Spanish).

55. **claim contrary to other eyewitness accounts**: "The Great Fire of 1788" includes supplementary notes added by the editor of the quarterly, with the text from a letter to the *London Chronicle*, dated March 26, 1788, but published in the issue of August 19–21 that year, stating, "There was neither fire engines, buckets, hooks or ladders, so that every effort was in vain" (585).

55. **In less than five hours**: de Rojas, "The Great Fire of 1788," 582.

55. **"With dawn the scene appeared"**: Kukla, *A Wilderness So Immense*, 36.

55. **"Soon Madrid was pouring silver"**: Lawrence N. Powell, *The Accidental City: Improvising New Orleans* (Cambridge, Mass.: Harvard University Press, 2012), 200.

56. **Faubourg Sainte-Marie**: Richard Campanella, *Geographies of New Orleans: Urban Fabrics before the Storm* (Lafayette: Center for Louisiana Studies, 2006), 8.

56. **Another street, San Carlos**: "Thomas Jefferson's Statement of Facts in the Batture Case, [ca. March 23, 1811]," *Founders Online*, National Archives,

last modified June 29, 2017, http://
founders.archives.gov/documents
/Jefferson/03-03-02-0370. Original
source: *The Papers of Thomas Jefferson,*
Retirement Series 3 (August 12, 1810,
to June 17, 1811), ed. J. Jefferson Looney
(Princeton, N.J.: Princeton University
Press, 2006), 489–99.

56. **a well-trained corps of blacksmiths**:
Marcus Christian, *Negro Ironworkers
of Louisiana, 1718–1900* (Gretna, La.:
Pelican, 1972), 16–21.

56. **"most regular, well-governed city"**:
Rojas, "The Great Fire of 1788," 584.

56. **"epidemic which has raged"**:
Microfilm Edition (DLF), October
25, 1788, Estevan Miro (governor
of Louisiana) to Father Antonio de
Sedella, auxiliary vicar (New Orleans,
Louisiana), IV-4-c A.L.S., 7 pp., 8 vols.
(Spanish).

56. **Digging began on the new St. Louis
Cemetery**: Florence M. Jumonville,
*Nameless Graves: Indigent Cemeteries
of New Orleans* (New Orleans: Save Our
Cemeteries, 2016), 2.

56. **"Because of isolation and ignorance"**:
Gilbert C. Din and John E. Harkins,
"Spanish New Orleans," in *The
Louisiana Purchase Bicentennial Series
in Louisiana History,* vol. 14, *New
Orleans and Urban Louisiana,* part
A, *Settlement to 1860,* ed. Samuel C.
Shepherd Jr. (Lafayette: Center for
Louisiana Studies, University of
Louisiana at Lafayette, 2005), 202. The
essay also appears as the first chapter
in Din and Harkins, *The New Orleans
Cabildo: Colonial Louisiana's First City
Government, 1769–1803* (Baton Rouge:
Louisiana State University Press, 1966).

57. **"the two mace-bearers"** and other
quotations from the account by the
Cabildo secretary, Pedro Pedesclaux:
"Ceremonies for Funeral Rites for

Carlos III," Records and Deliberations
of the New Orleans Cabildo, Louisiana
State Museum, April 4 and 24, 1789.

59. **"What is clear from diocesan
records"**: Greenleaf, "The Inquisition
in Spanish Louisiana," 545.

59. **"grave disturbances"**: Rev. Michael J.
Curley, *Church and State in the Spanish
Floridas, 1783–1822* (Washington, D.C.:
Catholic University of America Press,
1940), 121. Curley has the most detailed
account of the conflict between Sedella
and Cirilo.

60. **"furnish me immediately"**: The
Letters of Antonio de Sedella, Tulane
University, bundle 102, letter 52 (Sedella
to Miró), April 28, 1790. See also
Greenleaf, "The Inquisition in Spanish
Louisiana," 546.

60. **"Your Lordship will please advise"**:
Sedella letters, Tulane University,
bundle 102, letter 53.

Chapter 4. City of Migrants

61. **"blood flowed and cries of joy"**: Simon
Schama, *Citizens: A Chronicle of the
French Revolution* (New York: Vintage,
1990), 670.

61. **People fleeing the French island**:
Alfred N. Hunt, *Haiti's Influence on
Antebellum America: Slumbering
Volcano in the Caribbean* (Baton Rouge:
Louisiana State University Press, 1988),
48.

61. **Saint-Domingue's estimated 452,000
slaves**: ibid., 9.

61. *Slaves'* **life expectancy**: Madison
Smartt Bell, *Toussaint Louverture:
A Biography* (New York: Pantheon,
2007), 16. Several variations on the
spelling of the name exist. "Louverture"
is the most common, and I have used it
throughout.

61. **The 27,548 free blacks**: Philippe

Girard, *Toussaint Louverture: A Revolutionary Life* (New York: Basic Books, 2016), 56.

62. **"The quarrel between"**: C. L. R. James, *The Black Jacobins: Toussaint L'Ouverture and the San Domingo Revolution*, 2nd rev. ed. (New York: Vintage, 1963), 75.

62. **"Louisiana was the most desirable"**: Hunt, *Haiti's Influence on Antebellum America*, 45–46.

62. **The 1791 New Orleans census**: ibid., 46.

62. **Carondelet was greeted**: Christina Vella, *Intimate Enemies: The Two Worlds of the Baroness Pontalba* (Baton Rouge: Louisiana State University Press, 1997), 54.

62. **"The public Buildings are capacious"**: John Pope, *A Tour through the Southern and Western Territories of the United States of North-America*, facsimile reproduction of the 1792 edition, with an introduction and indexes by Barton Starr (Gainesville: University Press of Florida, 1979), 37.

62. **General background on Carondelet**: Thomas M. Fiehrer, "The Baron de Carondelet as Agent of Bourbon Reform: A Study of Spanish Colonial Administration in the Years of the French Revolution" (PhD diss., Tulane University, 1977); Thomas D. Watson, "Francisco Luis Héctor, Barón de Carondelet," in *Know Louisiana: The Digital Encyclopedia of Louisiana History and Culture*, ed. David Johnson (New Orleans: Louisiana Endowment for the Humanities), August 4, 2011, http://www.knowlouisiana.org/entry /francisco-luis-hector-baron-de -carondelet. A number of biographies spell Carondelet's name in Spanish; I have opted for the French version, given his place of birth.

62. **With a brother in the priesthood**: Fiehrer, "The Baron de Carondelet as Agent of Bourbon Reform," 376–78.

62. **As a governor in Guatemala**: Jack D. L. Holmes, *Honor and Fidelity: The Louisiana Infantry Regiment and the Louisiana Militia Companies, 1766–1821* (Birmingham: Louisiana Collection Series of Books and Documents on Colonial Louisiana, 1955), 45.

62. **New Orleans now had a theater**: John R. Kemp, *New Orleans: An Illustrated History* (Woodland Hills, Calif.: Windsor, 1981), 46.

62. **Hang the aristocrats**: Caryn Cossé Bell, *Revolution, Romanticism, and the Afro-Creole Protest Tradition in Louisiana, 1718–1868* (Baton Rouge: Louisiana State University Press, 1997), 25.

62. **"cochon de lait"**: Jon Kukla, *A Wilderness So Immense: The Louisiana Purchase and the Destiny of America* (New York: Knopf, 2003), 150.

63. **"Hot headed, all imagination"** and **biographical information on Genêt**: ibid., 161.

63. ***The Freemen of France***: quoted in Ernest R. Liljegren, "Jacobinism in Spanish Louisiana, 1792–1797," *Louisiana Historical Quarterly* 22 (January–October 1939): 53.

63. **"Now is the time"**: ibid., 54–55.

64. **On June 23, 1793**: Paul F. LaChance, "The Foreign French," in *Creole New Orleans: Race and Americanization*, ed. Arnold R. Hirsch and Joseph Logsdon (Baton Rouge: Louisiana State University Press, 1992), 103.

64. **Short, stout, and fastidious**: Fiehrer, *The Baron de Carondelet*, 259.

64. **"Taverns, gambling-dens and bawdy-houses"**: Herbert Asbury, *The French Quarter* (New York: Garden City Publishing, 1938), 60–61.

64. **To reduce crime**: Fiehrer, *The Baron de Carondelet*, 371.

64. **"colonel and adjutant major"**: Holmes, *Honor and Fidelity*, 50.

65. **Patrician women took swims**: Lawrence N. Powell, *The Accidental City: Improvising New Orleans* (Cambridge, Mass.: Harvard University Press, 2012), 206.

65. **Spanish building codes and design**: Malcolm Heard, *French Quarter Manual: An Architectural Guide to New Orleans' Vieux Carré* (New Orleans: Tulane School of Architecture, 1997), 21.

66. **"The *French* and *Spanish* Subjects"**: Pope, *A Tour through the Southern and Western Territories*, 38.

66. **Miró groused to a captain-general**: Alfred E. Lemmon, "Music and Art in Spanish Colonial Louisiana," in *The Spanish Presence, 1763–1803*, ed. Gilbert C. Din, vol. 3 of *The Louisiana Purchase Bicentennial Series* (Lafayette: Center for Louisiana Studies, University of Southwestern Louisiana, 1996), 435.

66. **According to one study, at least half of the 214**: ibid., 435.

67. **"the concubine of the friars"**: Bell, *Revolution, Romanticism*, 14.

67. **Sedella in his Spanish exile**: Rev. Michael J. Curley, *Church and State in the Spanish Floridas, 1783–1822* (Washington, D.C.: Catholic University of America Press, 1940), 128.

68. **"You have exceeded your powers"**: ibid., 129.

68. **"probably the stormiest of any priest"**: Roger Baudier, *The Catholic Church in Louisiana* (New Orleans: Approval by Archbishop Joseph Rummel, 1939), 209.

68. **he ordered a two-year prison sentence**: Bell, *Revolution, Romanticism*, 26–27.

68. **"To preserve emancipation"**: Laurent Dubois, *Avengers of the New World: The Story of the Revolution in Haiti* (Cambridge, Mass.: Belknap Press of Harvard University Press, 2004), 4.

69. **"undercover plots"**: Bell, *Revolution, Romanticism*, 28.

69. **"were well informed about the war between France and Spain"**: Gwendolyn Midlo Hall, *Africans in Colonial Louisiana: The Development of Afro-Creole Culture in the Eighteenth Century* (Baton Rouge: Louisiana State University Press, 1992), 349.

70. **Portuguese ministers converted**: Susan Cooksey, Robin Poynor, and Hein Vanhee, introduction to *Kongo across the Waters*, ed. Susan Cooksey, Robin Poynor, and Hein Vanhee (Gainesville: University Press of Florida, 2013), 1.

70. **"Beyond heraldry, swords appeared"**: Cécile Fromont, "By the Sword and the Cross: Power and Faith in the Arts of Christian Kongo," in Cooksey, Poyner, and Vanhee, *Kongo across the Waters*, 29.

70. **"the crosses of the brotherhoods, the clergy and dignitaries"**: Jeroen Dewulf, introduction to *From the Kingdom of Kongo to Congo Square: Kongo Dances and the Origins of the Mardi Gras Indians* (Lafayette: University of Louisiana at Lafayette Press, 2017), xviii.

70. **About 40 percent of African victims**: ibid., xv.

70. **"the election ritual of a Kongo king in the diaspora"**: Dewulf, *From the Kingdom of Kongo to Congo Square*, 126.

70. **"meet on the green"**: quoted in Ned Sublette, *The World That Made New Orleans: From Spanish Silver to Congo Square* (Chicago: Lawrence Hill, 2008), 3.

71. **The Mardi Gras Indians, parading**: Jason Berry, Jonathan Foose, and Tad Jones, *Up From the Cradle of Jazz: New Orleans Music since World War II* (Lafayette: University of Louisiana at Lafayette Press, 2009), 235.

71. **"The Kongo dance should, in fact"**: Dewulf, *From the Kingdom of Kongo to Congo Square*, 126.

71. **In 1800, free black militia members**: ibid., 4.

71. **"They dance in the country"**: Henry Kmen, *Music in New Orleans: The Formative Years, 1792–1841* (Baton Rouge: Louisiana State University Press, 1966), 4.

71. **The city's first known burial society**: Claude F. Jacobs, "Benevolent Societies of New Orleans Blacks during the Late Nineteenth and Early Twentieth Centuries," *Louisiana History: Journal of the Louisiana Historical Association* 29, no. 1 (Winter 1988): 22.

71. **"between the levée and the front row of houses"**: Francis Baily, *Journal of a Tour in Unsettled Parts of North America, in 1796 & 1797*, ed. Jack L. Holmes (Carbondale: Southern Illinois University, 1967), 165.

71. **"The inhabitants of this place"**: ibid., 168.

72. **"fore part of the day"**: ibid., 174–75.

72. **"vast numbers of negro slaves"**: Dena J. Epstein, *Sinful Tunes and Spirituals: Black Folk Music to the Civil War* (Champagne: University of Illinois Press, 1977), 84.

72. **"planted with green boughs"**: Baily, *Journal of a Tour*, 175.

73. **"The Presbytère was not completed until 1813"**: Vella, *Intimate Enemies*, 100.

74. **"There is on the globe one single spot"**: quoted in Kukla, *A Wilderness So Immense*, 216.

74. **"Rid us of these gilded negroes"**: quoted in Dubois, *Avengers of the New World*, 255.

74. **Louverture negotiated his French military rank**: ibid., 275.

74. **"General, we have not come here"**: quoted in James, *The Black Jacobins*, 334.

75. **"It is not only New Orleans"**: quoted in Thomas Ruys Smith, *Southern Queen: New Orleans and the Nineteenth Century* (New York: Continuum, 2011), 18.

75. **a land mass of 909,130 square miles**: Kukla, *A Wilderness So Immense*, 415n4.

75. **By then, 24,000 of the 34,000 troops**: James, *The Black Jacobins*, 355.

76. **"More than 50,000 European soldiers"**: Powell, *The Accidental City*, 319.

76. **"One of the elder women"**: Grace King, *New Orleans: The Place and the People* (New York: Macmillan, 1896), 158.

76. **"Slaves bearing lanterns"**: ibid., 159.

76. **"souls of filth"**: C. C. Robin, *Voyage to Louisiana, 1803–1805*, abridged trans. Stuart O. Landry (1965; Gretna, La.: Pelican, 2000), 62. The translator's note attributes the letter quoting Madame Laussat to *"Daniel Clark, that advance agent of the American government,"* with the following citation: *"Territorial Papers of the United States, Volume IX*, 'The Territory of Orleans, 1812–1812,' p. 201–121 [*sic*]."* Clark's quotation also appears in Joseph T. Hatfield, *William Claiborne: Jeffersonian Centurion in the American Southwest*, USL History Series (Lafayette: University of Southwestern Louisiana, 1976), 113.

76. **Casa-Calvo . . . with a cordial front**: Hatfield, *William Claiborne*, 113. See also Kukla, *A Wilderness So Immense*, 317.

77. **a vibrant presence at the Café de**

Réfugiés: Nathalie Dessens, *From Saint-Domingue to New Orleans: Migration and Influences* (Gainesville: University Press of Florida, 2007), 78.

77. **"France has ceded Louisiana"**: quoted in Robin, *Voyage to Louisiana*, 63.

77. **"Claiborne and Wilkinson knew"**: Kukla, *A Wilderness So Immense*, 323.

77. **"lugubriousness of silence"**: Robin, *Voyage to Louisiana*, 66.

77. **his wife and young daughter**: Jared William Bradley, ed., *Interim Appointment: William C. C. Claiborne Letter Book, 1804–1805* (Baton Rouge: Louisiana State University Press, 2002), 25n3.

Chapter 5. Claiborne

78. **Claude Tremé carved out tracts**: Roulhac Toledano and Mary Louise Christovich, *Faubourg Tremé and the Bayou Road*, vol. 6 of *New Orleans Architecture* (Gretna, La.: Pelican, 1980), 13.

78. **shotgun houses, an import from Haiti**: John Michael Vlach, *By the Work of Their Hands: Studies in Afro-American Folklife* (Charlottesville: University Press of Virginia, 1991), 195.

78. **"twenty different dancing groups"**: quoted in Dena J. Epstein, *Sinful Tunes and Spirituals: Black Folk Music to the Civil War* (Champagne: University of Illinois Press, 1977), 93.

79. **"Hangin' in the Tremé"**: "Tremé Song," lyrics by John Boutté, from the CD *Jambalaya* (2003), used with permission.

79. **Established as a hat-maker** and **"some dogs barked"**: quoted in Toledano and Christovich, *Faubourg Tremé and the Bayou Road*, 13–14.

80. **"to five years imprisonment"**: quoted in ibid., 14.

80. **"a pure white person by birth"**: quoted in ibid., 13.

80. **"Enumeration of thirty-seven persons who bought lots"**: ibid., 15.

80. **"Our lodgings at the gates"**: Pierre-Clément de Laussat, *Memoirs of My Life*, ed. Robert D. Bush, trans., with an introduction, Sister Agnes-Josephine Pastwa (Baton Rouge: Louisiana State University Press, 1978), 32.

80. **"The country is so infested with snakes"**: quoted in ibid., 51.

80. **"We cursed hundreds of times"**: quoted in ibid., 49.

81. **"much anxiety"**: quoted in Joseph I. Stoltz III, "The Preservation of Good Order: William C. C. Claiborne and the Creation of the Orleans Territorial Militia, 1803–1805," *Louisiana History: The Journal of the Louisiana Historical Association* 54, no. 4 (Fall 2013): 431–32.

81. **"Horrible Scenes of Bloodshed"**: quoted in Jon Kukla, *A Wilderness So Immense: The Louisiana Purchase and the Destiny of America* (New York: Knopf, 2003), 165.

81. **"The militia of colour shall be confirmed"**: quoted in ibid., 168.

81. **Governor Casa-Calvo in 1802 had put the black militia**: Roland C. McConnell, "Louisiana's Black Military History, 1729–1865," *Louisiana's Black Heritage*, ed. Roland C. Macdonald, John R. Kemp, and Edward F. Haas (New Orleans: Louisiana State Museum, 1979), 37–38.

81. **"heavy, squat [and] good natured"**: Laussat, *Memoirs*, 73.

81. **secretly renounced citizenship**: Kukla, *A Wilderness So Immense*, 127.

81. **Casa-Calvo . . . settled with him for $12,000**: Gilbert C. Din, *An Extraordinary Atlantic Life: Sebastián Nicolás Calvo de la Puerta y O'Farrill,*

Marqués de Casa-Calvo (Lafayette: University of Louisiana at Lafayette Press, 2016), 234.

82. **Claiborne biographical material**: Hatfield, *William Claiborne*, 3–21; Glen Jeansonne and David Luhrssen, "William C. C. Claiborne," in *Know Louisiana: The Digital Encyclopedia of Louisiana History and Culture*, ed. David Johnson (New Orleans: Louisiana Endowment for the Humanities), May 7, 2013, http://www.knowlouisiana.org/entry/william-charles-cole-claiborne; John D. Winters, "William C. C. Claiborne: Profile of a Democrat," *Louisiana History: The Journal of the Louisiana Historical Association* 10, no. 3 (Summer 1969): 189–209.

82. **"The Jacksons needed a home"**: Jon Meacham, *American Lion: Andrew Jackson in the White House* (New York: Random House, 2008), 9.

82. **"systematically destroying the household"**: H. W. Brands, *Andrew Jackson: His Life and Times* (New York: Anchor, 2006), 26.

82. **"their American captors couldn't afford to keep"**: ibid., 29.

83. **"His face was long and narrow"**: quoted in ibid., 40.

83. **"an enigma that at present"**: quoted in George Dargo, *Jefferson's Louisiana: Politics and the Clash of Legal Traditions* (Cambridge, Mass.: Harvard University Press, 1975), 29.

83. **"a mere stranger here"**: quoted in Lawrence N. Powell, *The Accidental City: Improvising New Orleans* (Cambridge, Mass.: Harvard University Press, 2012), 321.

83. **Eliza stayed in Nashville**: Hatfield, *William Claiborne*, 207.

83. **"as many Spaniards as Americans and Frenchmen"**: Laussat, *Memoirs*, 80.

84. **"Coffee was served"**: ibid., 81.

84. **city of about 8,000 people**: Roland C. McConnell, *Negro Troops of Antebellum Louisiana: A History of the Battalion of Free Men of Color* (Baton Rouge: Louisiana State University Press, 1968), 34.

84. **"If the women have a drop of French blood"**: quoted in Ann Ostendorf, *Sounds American: National Identity and the Music Cultures of the Lower Mississippi River Valley, 1800–1860* (Athens: University of Georgia Press, 2011), 73.

84. **"We have been Spanish for thirty years"**: quoted in Henry A. Kmen, *Music in New Orleans: The Formative Years, 1792–1841* (Baton Rouge: Louisiana State University Press, 1966), 29.

85. **"There you have a picture"**: quoted in Laussat, *Memoirs*, 93.

85. **"Insofar as slaveholding planters"**: Samuel Kinser, *Carnival American Style: Mardi Gras at New Orleans and Mobile* (Chicago: University of Chicago Press, 1990), 30.

85. **"the blame of these misfortunes"**: quoted in Ostendorf, *Sounds American*, 77.

85. **"Noel Carriere, a skilled tanner"**: Emily Clark, *The Strange History of the American Quadroon: Free Women of Color in the Revolutionary Atlantic World* (Chapel Hill: University of North Carolina Press, 2013), 74.

85. **"somehow managed to acquire"**: ibid., 76.

85. **"Carriere officially witnessed"**: ibid., 79.

85. **"the period's foremost black agitator"** and **"almost single-handedly"**: Kimberly S. Hanger, "Conflicting Loyalties: The French Revolution and Free People of Color

in Spanish New Orleans," *Louisiana History: The Journal of the Louisiana Historical Association* 34, no. 1 (Winter 1993): 12.

86. **"They have conceded men their rights"**: quoted in ibid., 26.

86. **"tirades against the Spanish"**: quoted in ibid., 13.

87. **"fidelity and zeal"**: quoted in McConnell, "Louisiana's Black Military History," 39.

87. **advice of Secretary of War Henry Dearborn**: Stoltz, "The Preservation of Good Order," 440.

87. **"to prevent the emergence of an internal slave trade"**: Adam Rothman, *Slave Country: American Expansion and Origins of the Deep South* (Cambridge, Mass.: Harvard University Press, 2005), 31.

87. **In a city where smuggling had long fed a black market economy**: John G. Clark, *New Orleans, 1712-1812: An Economic History* (Baton Rouge: Louisiana State University Press, 1970), 232; Shannon Lee Dawdy, *Building the Devil's Empire: French Colonial New Orleans* (Chicago: University of Chicago Press, 2008), 121.

87. **with a garden so large it gave the Spanish family**: Jane Lucas de Grummond, *Renato Beluche: Smuggler, Privateer, and Patriot, 1780-1860* (Baton Rouge: Louisiana State University Press, 1999), 37.

87. **"The female of the species needs"**: Benjamin H. Trask, *Fearful Ravages: Yellow Fever in New Orleans, 1796-1905* (Lafayette: Center for Louisiana Studies, University of Louisiana at Lafayette, 2005), 6.

87. **"With the importation of millions"**: ibid., 6–7.

88. **"The climate and spells of excessive heat"**: Laussat, *Memoirs*, 42.

88. **"sponged their burning faces"**: Winters, "William C. C. Claiborne," 202.

88. **Eliza and Cornelia died within hours of each other**: Jared William Bradley, ed., *Interim Appointment: W. C. C. Claiborne Letter Book, 1804-1805* (Baton Rouge: Louisiana State University Press, 2002), 70n2.

88. **"bent her willing steps"**: quoted in Hatfield, *William Claiborne*, 156–57.

88. **Bishop Peñalver left**: Roger Baudier, *The Catholic Church in Louisiana* (New Orleans: Approval by Archbishop Joseph Rummel, 1939), 245.

88. **Casa-Calvo, who arranged funds**: Din, *An Extraordinary Atlantic Life*, 231.

89. **The Irish vicar retorted**: Bradley, *Interim Appointment*, 488; Baudier, *The Catholic Church in Louisiana*, 255.

89. **The Vatican had given authority**: Peter Guilday, *The Life and Times of John Carroll, Archbishop of Baltimore (1735-1815)* (Westminster, Md.: Newman, 1954), 704.

89. **"On March 14, 1805," and "We want Père Antoine"**: Baudier, *The Catholic Church in Louisiana*, 256.

89. **Mayor James Pitot asked**: ibid., 256–57.

89. **Casa-Calvo, in transferring**: Stanley Faye, ed., "The Schism of 1805 in New Orleans," *Louisiana Historical Quarterly* 22 (January–October 1939):100; Caryn Cossé Bell, *Revolution, Romanticism, and the Afro-Creole Protest Tradition in Louisiana, 1716-1868* (Baton Rouge: Louisiana State University Press, 1997), 69.

89. **"artful Spanish friar" and "The attempt has completely miscarried"**: quoted in Guilday, *The Life and Times of John Carroll*, 707. Letter to Madison quoted at length. Carroll's title was bishop during the events recounted in this chapter, not yet archbishop.

90. **"The case is entirely ecclesiastical"** and **"The accounts here agree"**: quoted in Guilday, *The Life and Times of John Carroll*, 708–9.

90. **"as dangerous to politics as religion"**: Baudier, *The Catholic Church in Louisiana*, 258.

90. **Bishop Carroll dispatched**: Guilday, *The Life and Times of John Carroll*, 708.

90. **"for the keys to the said church"**: New Orleans Notarial Archives, courtesy of Dale N. Atkins, Clerk of Civil District Court, Parish of Orleans, March 26, 1805, B. Van Pradelles, notary, June 15, 1807, Complaint of Rev. John Olivier, p. 96.

90. **"low Spaniards, free Mullatos"** and **a move that cut across lines**: Thomas N. Ingersoll, *Mammon and Manon in Early New Orleans: The First Slave Society in the Deep South, 1718–1819* (Knoxville: University of Tennessee Press, 1999), 262.

91. **"Keep a watchful eye"**: quoted in Dargo, *Jefferson's Louisiana*, 54. Peter J. Kastor, *The Nation's Crucible: The Louisiana Purchase and the Creation of America* (New Haven, Conn.: Yale University Press, 2004), 137–38; Powell, *The Accidental City*, 340–41.

91. **affaire d'honneur**: Hatfield, *William Claiborne*, 161.

91. **"apologize for my imprudence"**: quoted in Kastor, *The Nation's Crucible*, 74.

91. **In 1808, she gave birth**: Stanley Clisby Arthur, ed., *Old Families of Louisiana* (New Orleans: Harmanson, 1931), 147.

91. **Data on migrations from Cuba**: Bell, *Revolution, Romanticism*, 37.

92. **"He repairs instruments"**: *Louisiana Courier*, June 21, 1809.

92. **"In what sense and by what right"**: Rebecca J. Scott, "Paper Thin: Freedom

and Re-enslavement in the Diaspora of the Haitian Revolution," *Law and History Review* 4, no. 4 (November 2011): 1062.

92. **"Governor Claiborne was caught"**: ibid., 1072.

92. **"possess, sell and dispose"**: ibid., 1074.

92. **"the 3,000 people sold as slaves"**: Edward E. Baptist, *The Half Has Never Been Told: Slavery and the Making of American Capitalism* (New York: Basic Books, 2014), 16.

93. **"50 Dollars Reward"**: *Louisiana Courier*, July 30, 1810.

93. **branded his initials**: ad for Pierre La Puce, *Louisiana Courier*, August 2, 1811. See also Albert Thrasher, *On to New Orleans! Louisiana's Heroic 1811 Slave Revolt* (New Orleans: Cypress, 1996), 172–73.

93. **The police force, founded in 1805**: See Dennis C. Rousey, *Policing the Southern City: New Orleans, 1805–1889* (Baton Rouge: Louisiana State University Press, 1996), 11–33.

93. **"As to the custom"**: Epstein, *Sinful Tunes and Spirituals*, 93; my emphasis.

94. **"A Negro WENCH"**: *Louisiana Courier*, December 11, 1807. See also Thrasher, *On To New Orleans!*, 157.

94. **"a negro boy named CIPIO"**: *Louisiana Courier*, "Runaway," March 21, 1810. Thrasher, *On to New Orleans!*, 164.

94. **"my maroon Mulatress"**: *Le Moniteur*, "20 or 40 Piasters Reward," April 13, 1808. Thrasher, *On to New Orleans!*, 160.

95. **"a barber"**: *Courier*, "50 Dollars Reward," August 2, 1811. Thrasher, *On to New Orleans!*, 172.

95. **where many wealthy families now had French names**: Thrasher, *On to New Orleans!*, 70.

95. **"extensive network"**: ibid., 58.

95. **"We only know"**: Baptist, *The Half Has Never Been Told*, 58.

95. **slipped on Andry's military uniforms**: Daniel Rasmussen, *American Uprising: The Untold Story of America's Largest Slave Revolt* (New York: Harper, 2011), 100.

95. **The slave army faced**: Baptist, *The Half Has Never Been Told*, 62–63.

96. **"Local authorities orchestrated"**: Rothman, *Slave Country*, 114.

96. **the territorial legislature awarded planters $300**: ibid., 116.

96. **Advocates for statehood**: Baptist, *The Half Has Never Been Told*, 63–64.

96. **a Spanish Creole who eight years earlier**: de Grummond, *Renato Beluche*, 35–37.

96. **"Claiborne's third marriage"**: Kastor, *The Nation's Crucible*, 223.

Chapter 6. Pirates, Black Soldiers, and the War under Jackson

97. **Napoléon's defeat in Haiti**: Edward F. Baptist, *The Half Has Never Been Told: Slavery and the Making of American Capitalism* (New York: Basic Books, 2014), 65.

97. **The subsequent embargo choked the port economy**: John G. Clark, *New Orleans, 1718–1812: An Economic History* (Baton Rouge: Louisiana State University Press, 1970), 326.

97. **flying the flag of Cartagena**: William C. Davis, *The Pirates Laffite: The Treacherous World of the Corsairs of the Gulf* (New York: Harcourt, 2005), 68.

97. **"He stopped at Cap Français"**: ibid., 2. See also William Davis, "Jean and Pierre Laffite," in *Know Louisiana: The Digital Encyclopedia of Louisiana History and Culture*, ed. David Johnson (New Orleans: Louisiana Endowment for the Humanities, 2010–), September 4, 2013, http://www.knowlouisiana.org/entry /jean-and-pierre-laffite.

98. **"robust, powerfully built"**: Davis, *The Pirates Laffite*, 51.

98. **"side whiskers down his chin"**: ibid., 52.

98. **goods plundered at sea**: ibid., 60.

98. **The Barataria pirates had shot**: ibid., 136.

99. **"hot temper, prickly sense of honor"**: Daniel Feller, "Andrew Jackson: Life before the Presidency," Miller Center, https://millercenter.org/president /jackson/life-before-the-presidency.

99. **Claiborne met resistance**: Tom Kanon, *Tennesseans at War, 1812–1815: Andrew Jackson, the Creek War, and the Battle of New Orleans* (Tuscaloosa: University of Alabama Press, 2014), 136–37.

99. **It must have been difficult for Claiborne**: Michael J. Edwards, "A 'Melancholy Experience': William C. C. Claiborne and the Louisiana Militia, 1811–1815" (MA thesis, University of New Orleans, 2011), 17.

99. **"make every sacrifice"**: quoted in Jon Meacham, *American Lion: Andrew Jackson in the White House* (New York: Random House, 2008), 29.

99. **"heterogeneous mass"**: quoted in Edwards, "A 'Melancholy Experience,'" 20.

100. **a $500 reward to "any person delivering"**: quoted in Robert V. Remini, *The Battle of New Orleans: Andrew Jackson and America's First Military Victory* (New York: Penguin, 1999), 33.

100. **offering $5,000 "to any person"**: quoted in ibid., 33.

100. **a leading New Orleans merchant complained**: Davis, *The Pirates Laffite*, 109.

100. **men who nicknamed him "Old Hickory"**: Meacham, *Andrew Jackson*, 29.

100. **"You conducted it in a savage, unequal"**: quoted in H. W. Brands, *Andrew Jackson: His Life and Times* (New York: Anchor, 2006), 189.

100. **Benton and Jackson both fired**: ibid., 190.

100. **war-for-survival speeches**: ibid., 166–69.

101. **"Half of the 100-man garrison"**: Gregory A. Waselkov, "Fort Mims Battle and Massacre," *Encyclopedia of Alabama Online*, January 11, 2017.

101. **"Brave Tennesseans!"**: Brands, *Andrew Jackson*, 196.

101. **Coffee's forces annihilated the Creeks**: Kanon, *Tennesseans at War*, 75–76; Herbert J. "Jim" Lewis, "Battle of Talluschatchee," *Encyclopedia of Alabama Online*.

101. **"We now shot them like dogs"**: quoted in Steve Inskeep, *Jacksonland: President Andrew Jackson, Cherokee Chief John Ross, and a Great American Land Grab* (New York: Penguin, 2015), 40.

101. **"elegant style"**: quoted in Brands, 198.

102. **"Jackson and the baby"**: Inskeep, *Jacksonland*, 41.

102. **"were nearly a spent force"**: ibid., 43.

102. **surrendered 23 million acres**: Remini, *Battle of New Orleans*, 14–15.

102. **"Thirty-four of the thirty-five Creek leaders"**: Adam Rothman, *Slave Country: American Expansion and the Origins of the Deep South* (Cambridge, Mass.: Harvard University Press, 2005), 138.

102. **redcoats set fire**: Joel Achenbach, "D.C.'s Darkest Day, a War That No One Remembers," *Washington Post*, August 23, 2014.

103. **Clerks at the Department of State**: Anthony S. Pitch, "The Burning of Washington," n.d. White House Historical Association, https://whitehousehistoryorg./the-burning-of-washington. Jessie Kratz, "Rescue of the Papers of State During the Burning of Washington," The White House Historical Association. *White House History* Number 35, Summer 2014.

103. **"commanded, counseled, & advised"**: quoted in Davis, *Pirates Laffite*, 164.

103. **"You may be a useful assistant"**: quoted in ibid., 166.

104. **"With a population differing"**: quoted in Caryn Cossé Bell, *Revolution, Romanticism, and the Afro-Creole Protest Tradition in Louisiana, 1768–1868* (Baton Rouge: Louisiana State University Press, 1997), 51.

104. **"They must be for us or against us"**: quoted in ibid., 52.

104. **"perfectly sincere insubordination"**: *The New Orleans of George Washington Cable: The 1887 Census Office Report*, ed. Lawrence N. Powell (Baton Rouge: Louisiana State University Press, 2008), 126.

104. **Claiborne stressed to Jackson**: Robert C. Vogel, "Jean Laffite, the Baratarians, and the Battle of New Orleans: A Reappraisal," *Louisiana History: The Journal of the Louisiana Historical Association* 41, no. 3 (Summer 2000): 261–76.

104. **"Your intelligent minds"**: quoted in Bell, *Revolution, Romanticism and the Afro-Creole Protest Tradition*, 53.

104. **"wretches" and "hellish banditti"**: quoted in Remini, *Battle of New Orleans*, 38.

104. **Claiborne, shifting to**: Brands, *Andrew Jackson*, 256.

104. **The next morning, at Grand Isle**: Davis, *Pirates Laffite*, 191.

105. **"medicinal herbs and flowers"**: ibid., 192.

105. **"letters of several New Orleans merchants"**: quoted in ibid., 200–201.

105. **Born in 1764, schooled as a boy**: Mark J. Fernandez, *From Chaos to Continuity: The Evolution of Louisiana's Judicial System, 1712–1862* (Baton Rouge: Louisiana State University Press, 2001), 74.

106. **"hospitable, honest, and polite"**: quoted in Christian Garcia, "Edward Livingston," in Johnson, *Know Louisiana*, September 13, 2013, http://www.knowlouisiana.org/entry/edward-livingston.

106. **he wrote President Madison**: Vogel, "Jean Laffite, the Baratarians, and the Battle of New Orleans," 263.

106. **Jackson was then marching to Pensacola**: Kanon, *Tennesseans at War*, 128–32.

107. **to greet the public, he was forty-seven**: Remini, *Battle of New Orleans*, 42.

107. **"drive enemies into the sea"**: ibid., 45.

107. **"Good citizens"**: ibid., 45.

107. **Planters agreed to let slaves**: Rothman, *Slave Country*, 149.

107. **Savary raised a second battalion**: Gene Allen Smith, *The Slaves' Gamble: Choosing Sides in the War of 1812* (New York: Palgrave MacMillan, 2013), 162–63.

107. **Lieutenant Colonel Nicolls, meanwhile, was moving**: ibid., 155–59.

107. **people were on edge**: Remini, *Battle of New Orleans*, 47.

107. **Marigny and another member met with Dominic Hall**: Remini, *Battle of New Orleans*, 47; Davis, *Pirates Laffite*, 209.

108. **The Laffite brothers met with General Jackson**: Davis, *Pirates Laffite*, 210.

109. **Planters sent slaves**: Rothman, *Slave Country*, 149.

109. **Among them, Henry Latrobe, twenty-one**: Smith, *The Slaves' Gamble*, 166; Carolyn Goldsby Kolb, "At the Confluence of Science and Power: Water Struggles of New Orleans in the Nineteenth Century" (PhD diss., University of New Orleans, 2006), 67.

109. **"The citizens were preparing for battle"**: Arsène Lacarrière Latour, *Historical Memoir of the War in West Florida and Louisiana in 1814–1815, with an Atlas* (Philadelphia: John Conrad, 1816), 73.

109. **Upcountry soldiers tended to urinate**: Jerry Brock, "Jordan Noble: Drummer, Soldier, Statesman," *Louisiana Cultural Vistas*, Winter 2015, www.knowlouisiana.org.

109. **"then sold Judith and Jordan"**: ibid.

110. **"At eight o'clock, when the fog"**: Marcus Christian, *Negro Soldiers in the Battle of New Orleans* (Originally published by the Battle of New Orleans 150th Anniversary Committee of New Orleans, 1965; rprt. Washington, D.C.: Eastern National, 2004), 32.

110. **which included his son Joseph**: Rothman, *Slave Country*, 153.

110. **"En Main! En Main!"**: quoted in Smith, *The Slaves' Gamble*, 166.

110. **Pierre Laffite served as a guide**: Davis, *Pirates Laffite*, 213.

110. **"Jackson's troops' self-confidence"**: Roland C. McConnell, *Negro Troops of Antebellum Louisiana: A History of the Battalion of Free Men of Color* (Baton Rouge: Louisiana State University Press, 1968), 78.

111. **Pakenham carried a secret proclamation**: Brands, *Andrew Jackson*, 272.

111. **Pakenham and his officers**: Remini, *Battle of New Orleans*, 128.

111. **excruciating work, carving canals**: Smith, *The Slaves Gamble*, 168.

111. **British boats began**: Remini, *Battle of New Orleans*, 75.

112. **"Reverend Sir," said Jackson**: Robert V. Remini, *The Life of Andrew Jackson* (New York: Penguin, 1988), 106. The book is a condensation of the author's three-volume biography originally published between 1944 and 1984.

112. **Hall acted on jurisprudence back to normal**: ibid., 109–10.

113. **John Noble died three years later**: Brock, "Jordan Noble."

113. **"Ultimately, Jackson never fulfilled his promises"**: Smith, *The Slaves Gamble*, 173.

113. **"did provide several thousand musket flints"**: Davis, "Jean and Pierre Laffite."

113. **Spanish warships were stalking him**: ibid.

113. **Jean Laffite got into a firefight**: Davis, *The Pirates Laffite*, 462–63.

Chapter 7. The Builder and the Priest

115. **"A sound more strange"**: Benjamin Henry Latrobe, *Impressions Respecting New Orleans: Diary & Sketches, 1818–1820*, ed. Samuel Wilson Jr. (New York: Columbia University Press, 1931), 18.

115. **"a stark naked Indian girl"**: ibid., 21.

115. **"all hues of brown"**: ibid., 22.

116. **"a contemptible wretch"**: Talbot Hamlin, *Benjamin Henry Latrobe* (New York: Oxford University Press, 1955), 477.

116. **"Do you know who I am, sir?"** and **"Yes, I do"**: ibid., 477.

116. **"wild duck, oysters, poultry"**: Latrobe, *Impressions Respecting New Orleans*, 22.

116. **In 1795, his wife, Lydia**: Hamlin, *Benjamin Henry Latrobe*, 32.

116–17. **"his charm, his musical knowledge"**: ibid., 68–69.

117. **A trip to Philadelphia**: ibid., 130–32.

117. **a witty, elegant patrician** and **"from the first hour"**: ibid., 145.

117. **Latrobe used steam pumps to power water**: Gary A. Donaldson, "Bringing Water to the Crescent City: Benjamin Latrobe and the New Orleans Waterworks System," *Louisiana History: The Journal of the Louisiana Historical Association* 28, no. 4 (Autumn 1987): 381–96.

117. **Governor Claiborne met Latrobe**: Hamlin, *Benjamin Henry Latrobe*, 349.

117. **"your feelings and affection"**: Latrobe, *Impressions Respecting New Orleans*, 83n19.

117. **a precursor of the funerary architecture of neoclassical design**: Peter B. Dedeck, *The Cemeteries of New Orleans: A Cultural History* (Baton Rouge: Louisiana State University Press, 2017), 18–19.

118. **"below the age of 24 or 25"**: Latrobe, *Impressions Respecting New Orleans*, 33.

118. **"all the beautiful girls"**: ibid., 35.

118. **"famous also as a seamstress"**: ibid., 53.

118. **"till she bled"**: ibid., 54.

118. **"Madam Lanusse is another"**: ibid.

119. **"What is more remarkable"**: C. C. Robin, *A Voyage to Louisiana*, abridged trans. Stuart O. Landry Jr. (Gretna, La.: Pelican, 2000), 239.

119. **"pale, languid & mild"**: Latrobe, *Impressions Respecting New Orleans*, 54.

119. **"savage pleasure [as] those soft eyes"**: ibid., 53.

119. **In 1816 a traveling "Congo Circus"**: Freddi Williams Evans, *Congo*

Square: African Roots in New Orleans (Lafayette: University of Louisiana at Lafayette Press, 2011), 142.

119. **"5 or 600 persons . . . *blacks*"**: Latrobe, *Impressions Respecting New Orleans*, 49.

119. **"They held each a coarse handkerchief"**: ibid., 49–50.

120. **"The drummer sitting astride his drum"**: Evans, *Congo Square*, 70.

120. **"Though he does not use the word"**: Ned Sublette, *The World That Made New Orleans: From Spanish Silver to Congo Square* (Chicago: Lawrence Hill, 2008), 276.

120. **"the parade of funerals"**: Latrobe, *Impressions Respecting New Orleans*, 60.

121. **"like a heap of sticks"**: ibid., 137–38.

121. **A shift began to the Spanish custom**: Decker, *The Cemeteries of New Orleans*, 33.

121. **so close that he was paying**: Edward C. Carter II, John C. Van Horne, and Lee W. Formwalt, eds., *The Journals of Benjamin Henry Latrobe, 1799–1820, from Philadelphia to New Orleans*, vol. 3 (New Haven, Conn.: Yale University Press, 1980), xivn1.

121. **"my friend"**: Latrobe, *Impressions Respecting New Orleans*, 43.

122. **"In the truest sense he epitomized"**: Joseph G. Tregle Jr., *Louisiana in the Age of Jackson: A Clash of Cultures and Personalities* (Baton Rouge: Louisiana State University Press, 1999), 47.

122. **"We have a Spanish priest here"**: Herbert Asbury, *The French Quarter: An Informal History of the New Orleans Underworld* (New York: Garden City Publishing, 1938), 58.

122. **Père Antoine had become a spy for Spain**: William C. Davis, *The Pirates Laffite: The Treacherous World of the Corsairs of the Gulf* (New York: Harvest, 2006), 297–305.

123. **The Vatican tried again in 1815**: For an analysis of the canon law issues surrounding Père Antoine's conflicts, see Charles Edward O'Neill, "'A Quarter Marked by Sundry Peculiarities': New Orleans, Lay Trustees and Père Antoine," *Catholic Historical Review* 76, no. 2 (April 1990): 235–77.

123. **he reported to Rome rumors of the housekeeper**: Caryn Cossé Bell, *Revolution, Romanticism, and the Afro-Creole Protest Tradition in Louisiana, 1718–1868* (Baton Rouge: Louisiana State University Press, 1997), 71.

123. **"A mob formed"**: Roger Baudier, *The Catholic Church in Louisiana* (New Orleans: Approval by Archbishop Joseph Rummel, 1939), 263.

123. **"From all that I can learn"**: quoted in Liliane Crété, *Daily Life in Louisiana, 1815–1830* (Baton Rouge: Louisiana State University Press, 1981), 148.

123. **"New Orleans is the most tolerant place"**: ibid., 149.

123. **"I wrote to Father Anthony begging"**: Latrobe, *Impressions Respecting New Orleans*, 166.

123. **He imported engine parts**: Carolyn Goldsby Kolb, "At the Confluence of Science and Power: Water Struggles of New Orleans in the Nineteenth Century" (PhD diss., University of New Orleans, 2006), 64.

123. **"vile hole"**: quoted in Hamlin, *Benjamin Henry Latrobe*, 525.

124. **"I cannot express to you"**: Carter, Van Horne, and Formwalt, *The Journals of Benjamin Henry Latrobe, 1799–1820*, vol. 3, xivn1.

124. **"After his death"**: Kolb, "At the Confluence of Science and Power," 68.

124. **"much less efficient than"**: ibid., 69.

124. **invited General Lafayette to visit America**: Patricia Brady, "Gilbert du Motier, Marquis de Lafayette," in *Know Louisiana: The Digital Encyclopedia of Louisiana History and Culture*, ed. David Johnson (New Orleans: Louisiana Endowment for the Humanities, 2010–), February 14, 2011. http://www.knowlouisiana.org/entry/guilbert-du-motier-marquis-de-lafayette.

125. **city officials had allocated $15,000**: Crété, *Daily Life in Louisiana*, 229.

125. **"Wealthy citizens lent"**: Brady, "Gilbert du Motier, Marquis de Lafayette."

125. **The Place d'Armes, lit up**: Patricia Brady, "Carnival of Liberty: Lafayette in Louisiana," *Louisiana History: The Journal of the Louisiana Historical Association* 41, no. 1 (Winter 2000): 35.

125. **"Oh my son"**: quoted in Crété, *Daily Life in Louisiana*, 233.

125. **"His exemplary piety"**: Mortuary notice, *American Mercury*, reprint of *New Orleans Bee*, February 24, 1829.

126. **Judge Edward Livingston adjourned his courtroom**: Bell, *Revolution, Romanticism, and the Afro-Creole Protest Tradition*, 74.

Chapter 8. The Burial Master

143. **A colored Creole born**: Linda Epstein, "Pierre André Destrac Cazenave: Judah Touro's 'Pet' or a Man of Means?" *Louisiana History* 53, no. 1 (Winter 2012): 9. Epstein's important article with biographical data on the Casanave family corrects a long-standing misperception by historians who thought that Pierre Casanave was a secretary and heir to the Jewish philanthropist Judah P. Touro. Pierre A. D. Cazenave, who was white and close to Touro, became conflated with the free black man with a similar surname. The late Robert C. Reinders's important research on the undertaker Casanave unknowingly used financial information on the wealth amassed by Pierre A. D. Cazenave in the 1850s, from a Dun Bradstreet financial analysis of his assets at the time. The confusion was complicated by other scholars because of the variation in the spellings of their names. Epstein's article is a benchmark for establishing reliable biographical data on both men.

143. *New Orleans Argus*: April 13, 1825. "Removal. Pierre Casanaze, cabinet maker, informs the public …"

143. **By 1830, the city with a population of 46,082**: Virginia R. Domínguez, *White by Definition: Social Classification in Creole Louisiana* (New Brunswick, N.J.: Rutgers University Press, 1997), 116–17.

144. **Between 1833 and 1839, Rose gave birth to four sons**: Archdiocese of New Orleans, database on sacramental registries, courtesy of Emilie Gagnet Leumas, archivist.

144. **"the graceful lines of decorative balcony railings"**: Mary Gehman, *The Free People of Color of New Orleans: An Introduction* (New Orleans: Margaret Media, 1994), 55.

144. **"incredible laxity of morals"**: George Wilson Pierson, *Tocqueville in America* (Baltimore: Johns Hopkins University Press, 1996), 629.

144. **"dressed or masked balls composed of men and women of color"**: Caryn Cossé Bell, *Revolution, Romanticism, and the Afro-Creole Protest Tradition in Louisiana, 1718–1868* (Baton Rouge: Louisiana State University Press, 1997), 78.

144. **"most often the mix-blooded heirs won in court"**: Joan M. Martin,

"*Plaçage* and the Louisiana *Gens de Couleur Libre*: How Race and Sex Defined the Lifestyles of Freewomen of Color*," in *Creole: The History and Legacy of Louisiana's Free People of Color*, ed. Sybil Kein (Baton Rouge: Louisiana State University Press, 2000), 68.

144. **"fancy girls"**: Walter Johnson, *Soul by Soul: Life inside the Antebellum Slave Market* (Cambridge, Mass.: Harvard University Press, 1999), 114.

144. **"entertained his dinner guests"**: ibid., 114.

144. **"a total exceeding the value of black-owned property"**: Loren Schweninger, *Black Property Owners in the South, 1790–1915* (Urbana: University of Illinois Press, 1999), 71.

144. **Casanave had branched out**: An 1844 *City Directory* identifies "Peter Casanave" as a "fine cabinet-maker and undertaker."

145. **La Sociedad Española de Beneficencia Mutua**: "The Spanish Mutual Benevolent Society," *New Orleans Bee*, July 13, 1857.

145. **In January 1836, fifteen free black men**: Fatima Shaik, "The Economy Society and Community Support for Jazz," *Jazz Archivist: A Newsletter of the William Ransom Hogan Jazz Archive* 18 (2004): 2.

145. **In 1836 the legislature carved out**: Henry Rightor, ed., *Standard History of New Orleans* (1900; Forgotten Books, 2012, www.forgottenbooks.com), 96–98.

145. **"Thus, by 1829"**: Henry A. Kmen, *Music in New Orleans: The Formative Years, 1791–1841* (Baton Rouge: Louisiana State University Press, 1966), 39.

146. **"Coinciding with the building"**: Laura D. Kelley, *The Irish in New Orleans* (Lafayette: University of Louisiana at Lafayette Press, 2014), 34.

146. **People dumped refuse in the river**: Robert C. Reinders, *End of an Era: New Orleans, 1850–1860* (New Orleans: Pelican, 1964), 93.

146. **three municipal cemeteries boosted pay**: John Duffy, "Pestilence in New Orleans," in *The Past as Prelude: New Orleans, 1718–1968*, ed. Hodding Carter (New Orleans: Tulane University and Pelican, 1968), 95.

146–47. **cotton receipts** and **"the main reason that"**: Scott P. Marler, *The Merchants' Capital: New Orleans and the Political Economy of the Nineteenth-Century South* (New York: Cambridge University Press, 2013), 37.

147. **"The staple subjects were Latin, Greek"**: Rev. Tom Clancy, S.J., "The Last 150 Years," Jesuits' New Orleans Province. http://norprov.jesuitscholar.com/identity/150years.htm.

147. **In 1904 the Jesuits purchased land**: "Our History," Loyola University of New Orleans. http://www.loyno.edu/2012/history.

147. **and in 1926, changing the name**: "History, College of the Immaculate Conception," Jesuit High School of New Orleans. www.jesuitnola.org/about/history/.

148. **"a family might use a single room to raise"**: Reinders, *End of An Era*, 95.

148. **"As the procession passed along"**: Mike Scott, "When Jackson Square Became Jackson Square," NOLA.com/ *The Times-Picayune*, December 6, 2017. http://www.nola.cm/300/2017/jackson _square_history_new_orleans_2062017 .html.

148. **the council moved to impeach**: Duffy, "Pestilence in New Orleans," 108.

148. **"an obsolete idea in New Orleans"**: quoted in Reinders, *End of an Era*, 96.

148. **"no prevalent diseases"**: quoted in ibid., 96.

148. **"When thousands of people"**: Duffy, "Pestilence in New Orleans," 108.

148. **"Some physicians believed"**: Benjamin H. Trask, *Fearful Ravages: Yellow Fever in New Orleans, 1796–1905* (Lafayette: Center for Louisiana Studies, University of Louisiana at Lafayette Press, 2005), 53.

148. **In July of that deadly 1853**: Shaik, "The Economy Society and Community Support," 2.

149. **"even the workhouse"**: Reinders, *End of an Era*, 96.

149. **"at the rate of 7,950 deaths"**: "The Yellow Fever in New Orleans: Fearful Mortality," *New York Times*, August 29, 1853.

149. **"the full horror and virulence"**: quoted in Reinders, *End of an Era*, 91.

149. **"the odors of rotting corpses"**: quoted in ibid., 100.

149. **"In times of an epidemic"**: "Music at Funerals," *Daily Picayune*, August 21, 1853.

150. **"The high point of the funeral"**: Reinders, *End of an Era*, 106.

150. **"flat broke and without a piano"**: S. Frederick Starr, *Bamboula! The Life and Times of Louis Moreau Gottschalk* (New York: Oxford University Press, 1995), 206.

150. **"His sisters sang them"**: ibid., 42.

151. **"Give me your hand"**: quoted in Peter Collins, "Louis Moreau Gottschalk," in *Know Louisiana: The Digital Encyclopedia of Louisiana History and Culture*, ed. David Johnson (New Orleans: Louisiana Endowment for the Humanities, 2010–), April 3, 2013. http://www.knowlouisiana.org/entry /louis-moreau-gottschalk.

151. **"felt ashamed of myself"**: quoted in Starr, *Bamboula!*, 207.

151. **Once aloft**: ibid., 209.

151. **"Embalming the Dead"**: "Embalming

the Dead: P. Casanave, Undertaker," *New Orleans Daily Creole*, July 2, 1856.

152. **The "Dr. [Thomas S.] Holmes" he referenced**: E. B. White and Ivan Sandrof, "The First Embalmer," *New Yorker*, November 7, 1942.

152. **Casanave was president of**: Fatima Shaik, personal communication.

152. **"large two-story building"**: Shaik, "The Economy Society," 4.

152. **Casanave made a major move**: "424–426 Bourbon Street Pegneguy's Stables (Site)," Vieux Carré Survey, n.d., Historic New Orleans Collection.

152. **"The lead was carried off"**: "A Heavy Load," *Daily Picayune*, December 6, 1959.

153. **In the 1850s policemen spied**: Bell, *Revolution, Romanticism, and the Afro-Creole Protest Tradition*, 85–86.

153. **"for political and social quality"**: Shaik, "The Economy Society," 5.

153. **"In our own city a new inventor"**: "Embalming," *New Orleans Crescent*, April 22, 1856.

153. **would see Thomas Holmes of Washington**: Drew Gilpin Faust, *This Republic of Suffering: Death and the American Civil War* (New York: Knopf, 2008), 94.

153. **"the extinction of slavery"**: quoted in Bruce Levine, *The Fall of the House of Dixie: The Civil War and the Social Revolution That Transformed the South* (New York: Random House, 2014), 37.

154. **"It is impossible to learn"**: Roger W. Shrugg, *Origins of Class Struggle in Louisiana: A Social History of White Farmers and Laborers during Slavery and After, 1840–1875* (Baton Rouge: Louisiana State University Press, 1966), 163.

154. **Beauregard came from a long Creole line**: T. Harry Williams, *P. G. T. Beauregard: Napoleon in Gray* (Baton

Rouge: Louisiana State University Press, 1955), 4–6.

154. **making the triumphal 1848 march**: ibid., 31–32.

155. **an estimated 49,000 white men of military age**: G. Howard Hunter, "The Politics of Discontent: New Orleans Unionist Regiments, 1862–1864" (MA thesis, Tulane University, 1995), 49.

155. **Jordan Noble, the drummer boy**: Stephen J. Ochs, *A Black Patriot and a White Priest: André Cailloux and Claude Paschal Maistre in Civil War New Orleans* (Baton Rouge: Louisiana State University Press, 1995), 65.

155. **"foundations are laid"**: quoted in James W. Loewen and Edward H. Sebesta, eds., *The Confederate and Neo-Confederate Reader: The "Great Truth" about the "Lost Cause"* (Jackson: University Press of Mississippi, 2010), 12.

155. **"set it apart"**: Eric Foner, *A Short History of Reconstruction, 1863–1877*, updated ed. (New York: Harper Perennial, 1990), 21.

155. **"The highest cash price"**: "Second-Hand Furniture Bought," *Times-Picayune*, September 20, 1861. The undersigned is "S. F. Casanave."

155. **"Cailloux was one of 156 Afro-Creole cigar makers"**: Ochs, *A Black Patriot and a White Priest*, 49.

156. **Rey's father-in-law had been a founder**: Melissa Daggett, *Spiritualism in Nineteenth-Century New Orleans: The Life and Times of Henry Louis Rey* (Jackson: University Press of Mississippi, 2017), 42.

156. **the soldiers had to purchase uniforms**: ibid., 72.

156. **"free white males capable of bearing arms"**: James G. Hollandsworth Jr., *The Louisiana Native Guards: The Black Military Experience during the Civil War* (Baton Rouge: Louisiana State University Press, 1995), 8.

156. **"The new major general arrived in early October"**: Shelby Foote, *The Civil War: A Narrative—From Fort Sumter to Perryville*, vol. 1 (New York: Random House, 1958), 361.

156. **After recruiting, training, and arming 30,000 volunteers**: Chester G. Hearn, *The Capture of New Orleans 1862* (Baton Rouge: Louisiana State University Press, 1995), 3–5.

156. **vessels bearing General Benjamin Butler**: James M. McPherson, *Battle Cry of Freedom: The Civil War* (New York: Oxford University Press, 1988), 412.

156. **foreigners forced into duty at bayonet point**: Howard G. Hunter, "Fall of New Orleans and Federal Occupation," in Johnson, *Know Louisiana*, July 27, 2011. http://www.knowlouisiana.org/entry/fall-of-new-orleans-and-federal-occupation.

156. **The mayor told the black soldiers**: Hollandsworth, *The Louisiana Native Guards*, 9–10.

157. **His father, Barthélemy Rey**: Bell, *Romanticism, Revolution, and the Afro-Creole Protest Tradition*, 215.

157. **When Barthélemy died in 1845**: ibid., 215–16.

157. **You are not tired**: Emily Suzanne Clark, *A Luminous Brotherhood: Afro-Creole Spiritualism in Nineteenth-Century New Orleans* (Chapel Hill: University of North Carolina Press, 2016), 31.

157. **"In Rey's early years"**: ibid., 86.

157. **Pierre Casanave was one of five men**: Daggett, *Spiritualism in Nineteenth-Century New Orleans*, 44.

158. **General Lovell sent twelve gunboats**: McPherson, *Battle Cry of Freedom*, 419–20.

158. **As a prewar Massachusetts lawyer**: Gerald M. Capers, *Occupied City: New Orleans under the Federals, 1862–1865* (Lexington: University of Kentucky Press, 1965), 56–57.

158. **"setting up a welfare state"**: Hunter, "Fall of New Orleans."

158. **"contempt for any officer or soldier"**: Chester C. Hearn, *When the Devil Came Down to Dixie: Ben Butler in New Orleans* (Baton Rouge: Louisiana State University Press, 1997), 103.

158. **shuttered a Catholic paper**: ibid., 100.

158–59. **"A very intelligent looking set of men"**: Benj. F. Butler, *Butler's Book: A Review of His Legal, Political, and Military Career* (Boston: A. M. Thayer, 1892), 492.

159. **"In parade, you will see a thousand white bayonets"**: quoted in Hollandsworth, *Louisiana Native Guards*, 29.

159. **Polished in manners, bilingual**: Ochs, *A Black Patriot and a White Priest*, 80.

159. **"the drudgery of garrison duty"**: Daggett, *Spiritualism in Nineteenth-Century New Orleans*, 59.

159. **"syphilitic rheumatism"**: ibid., 59.

160. **"calculation that the stench"**: Ochs, *A Black Patriot and a White Priest*, 148.

160. **"one of the bravest soldiers"**: quoted in ibid., 156.

160. **"I have left your world"**: Bell, *Romanticism, Revolution, and the Afro-Creole Protest Tradition*, 241.

160. **"Those noble dead"**: quoted in Ochs, *A Black Patriot and a White Priest*, 154.

160. **Odin championed the white South**: ibid., 107.

160. **White musicians of the Forty-Second Massachusetts**: ibid., 4.

161. **several weeks later, a full page inside *Harper's Weekly***: "Funeral of the Late Captain Cailloux, First Louisiana Volunteers (Colored): Sketched by a Native Guard," *Harper's Weekly Magazine*, August 29, 1863.

161. **On April 21, 1865, a mass meeting**: Evans, *Congo Square*, 158.

162. **The police shot, clubbed, and slaughtered**: James G. Hollandsworth Jr., *An Absolute Massacre: The New Orleans Race Riot of July 30, 1866* (Baton Rouge: Louisiana State University Press, 2001).

162. **Anthony Dostie was shot, stabbed**: James Gill, *Lords of Misrule: Mardi Gras and the Politics of Race in New Orleans* (Jackson: University Press of Mississippi, 1997), 78.

162. **The massacre triggered a congressional investigation**: Justin A. Nystrom, *New Orleans after the Civil War: Race, Politics, and a New Birth of Freedom* (Baltimore: Johns Hopkins University Press, 2010), 67.

162. **"God is to be your judge"**: Clark, *A Luminous Brotherhood*, 59.

162. **Two sons took over the mortuary business**: "G. & St F. Casanave, Undertakers, Etc.," announcement, *Times-Democrat*, February 21, 1867.

162. **Oscar J. Dunn was a leading light**: Charles Vincent, "Oscar Dunn," in Johnson, *Know Louisiana*, August 1, 2013. http://www.knowlouisiana.org/entry/oscar-dunn-2.

163. **"blind ambition and social aplomb"**: Nystrom, *New Orleans after the Civil War*, 47.

163. **new laws allowed him to appoint state officials**: Ted Tunnell, "Henry Clay Warmoth," in Johnson, *Know Louisiana*, January 25, 2011. http://www.knowlouisiana.org/entry/henry-clay-warmoth.

163. **"and he seemed to speak directly"**: Clark, *A Luminous Brotherhood*, 65.

163. **"For the sake of harmony"**: ibid., 65.

163. **"power to secure victory"**: ibid., 66.

163. **Politics descended into madness**: Justin A. Nystrom, "Reconstruction," in Johnson, *Know Louisiana*, October 30, 2015. http://www.knowlouisiana.org /entry/reconstruction.

163. **"so shot through with fraud"**: quoted in Nystrom, *New Orleans after the Civil War*, 131.

164. **"Each Link was attended"**: Henri Schindler, *Mardi Gras New Orleans* (Paris: Flammarion, 1997), 50–52.

164. **"The racism that informed the satire"**: James Gill, *Lords of Misrule: Mardi Gras and the Politics of Race in New Orleans* (Jackson: University Press of Mississippi, 1997), 103.

164. **"served as a defining moment"**: Justin A. Nystrom, "The Battle of Liberty Place," in Johnson, *Know Louisiana*, January 3, 2011, http://www .knowlouisiana.org/entry/the-battle-of -liberty-place.

165. **"I have to reconcile with many Beings here"**: Translation courtesy of Emily Suzanne Clark, René Grandjean Collection, Louisiana and Special Collections Department, Earl K. Long Library, University of New Orleans; Register 85–55; May 28, 1874, message signed P. Casanave.

Chapter 9. The Time of Jazz

166. **"playing the melody with a beat"**: Bill Russell, *New Orleans Style*, comp. and ed. Barry Martyn and Mike Hazeldine (New Orleans: Jazzology, 1994), 8.

166. **Rural churches released a memory stream**: Samuel A. Floyd Jr., *The Power of Black Music* (New York: Oxford University Press, 1995), 39; Burton W. Peretti, *The Creation of Jazz; Music, Race, and Culture in Urban America* (Urbana: University of Illinois Press, 1994), 12.

166. **many of the 40,000 black folk**: Thomas Brothers, "Who's on First, What's Second, Where Did They Come From? The Social and Musical Textures of Early Jazz," in *Early Twentieth-Century Brass Band Idioms*, ed. Howard T. Weiner (Lanham, Md.: Scarecrow, 2009), 17.

166. **The flowing spirituality in small New Orleans churches**: Thomas Brothers, *Louis Armstrong's New Orleans* (New York: Norton, 2006), 34–36.

166. **"My sister played mandolin"**: quoted in Russell, *New Orleans Style*, 98. For an overview of musical families, see Jason Berry, Jonathan Foose, and Tad Jones, *Up from the Cradle of Jazz: New Orleans Music since World War II* (Lafayette: University of Louisiana at Lafayette Press, 2009), chap. 1, "Musical Families: The Founding Tradition," 1–14.

167. **John Robichaux, a drummer and violinist**: Al Rose and Edmond Souchon, *New Orleans Jazz: A Family Album* (Baton Rouge: Louisiana State University Press, 1967), 107–8. See also Tom Hook, *The New John Robichaux Orchestra* at www.TomHook.com.

167. **"rode a smoke-filled balloon"**: John McCusker, *Creole Trombone: Kid Ory and the Early Years of Jazz* (Jackson: University Press of Mississippi, 2012), 66.

167. **"one fine-lookin' brownskin man"**: quoted in Nat Shapiro and Nat Hentoff, *Hear Me Talkin' to Ya: The Story of Jazz as Told by the Men Who Made It* (New York: Dover, 1966), 36–37.

167. **"Buddy Bolden is the first man who played blues for dancing"**: Papa John Joseph, oral history interview, November 26, 1958, Hogan Jazz

Archive, Tulane University, 18, 21. Also quoted in McCusker, *Creole Trombone*, 54. For biography of Joseph, see Michael G. White, "Papa John Joseph: The Man and His Music," *Second Line* (Fall 1980): 4–5.

167. **With an intuitive grasp**: Donald M. Marquis, *In Search of Buddy Bolden: First Man of Jazz* (Baton Rouge: Louisiana State University Press, 1978), 107–8.

168. **formative years at 2390 First Street**: ibid., 22–25.

168. **"Destitute and excluded"**: Richard Campanella, *Bienville's Dilemma: A Historical Geography of New Orleans* (Lafayette: Center for Louisiana Studies, University of Louisiana at Lafayette, 2008), 181.

168. **"There is no way of concealing filth"**: *New Orleans Daily Picayune*, January 3, 1891.

168. **Black infant mortality was 45 percent**: Ted Gioia, *The History of Jazz*, 2nd ed. (New York: Oxford University Press, 2011), 28.

168. **Bolden's sister died**: ibid., 32–33.

168. **In response to the misery**: Carolyn Goldsby Kolb, "At the Confluence of Science and Power: Water Struggles of New Orleans in the Nineteenth Century" (Ph.D. diss., University of New Orleans, 2006), 238.

168. **that allowed growth**: Richard Campanella, *Geographies of New Orleans: Urban Fabrics before the Storm* (Lafayette: Center for Louisiana Studies, University of Louisiana at Lafayette, 2006), 151.

168. **"Imagine the bright summer sunshine"**: In Clint Bolton, "All Gone Now," *New Orleans Magazine*, May 1971, 33–34. Bolton, in a preface, called the article an excerpt from a work-in-progress on Barbarin's life. Barbarin

was deceased two years by then; Bolton died before finishing the project. The only known part of the work is the article.

169. **"Milenburg Joys"**: Howard Reich and William Grimes, *Jelly's Blues: The Life, Music and Redemption of Jelly Roll Morton* (New York: DaCapo, 2003), 86.

169. **The shotgun house on First Street**: Marquis, *In Search of Buddy Bolden*, 22–25.

169. **"from the 'Holy Roller' Baptist Church"**: quoted in Russell, *New Orleans Style*, 175.

170. **"moan in his cornet"**: quoted in Brothers, *Louis Armstrong's New Orleans*, 43.

170. **"The ministers, sometimes unordained"**: Marquis, *In Search of Buddy Bolden*, 31.

170. **"Traditionally, the highest praise"**: Albert Murray, *Stomping the Blues* (New York: McGraw-Hill, 1976), 27.

170. **"On Sunday mornings"**: Marquis, *In Search of Buddy Bolden*, 67.

170. **"sung in towns up and down the Mississippi"**: ibid., 109–10.

170. **Jelly Roll Morton recorded "Buddy Bolden Blues"**: ibid., 110.

171. **"The police put you in jail"**: quoted in Gioia, *The History of Jazz*, 34.

171. **"Bolden's ragged and raucous music"**: ibid., 34.

171. **As brass bands spread**: William J. Schafer with assistance from Richard B. Allen, *Brass Bands and New Orleans Jazz* (Baton Rouge: Louisiana State University Press, 1977), 8.

171. **flourished in towns near New Orleans**: The most detailed research on brass bands in rural southern Louisiana is by Karl Koenig. His voluminous writings are arranged as e-books readable at no charge and posted at

www.Basinstreet.com. See Koenig, *Music in the Parishes Surrounded New Orleans: Plaquemines*, hereafter referred to as *Plaquemines*.

172. **"a performance of memory"**: Joseph Roach, *Cities of the Dead: Circum-Atlantic Performance* (New York: Columbia University Press, 1996), 34. In the growing literature on the second line, see particularly Michael P. Smith, *A Joyful Noise: A Celebration of New Orleans Music*, introduction and interviews by Alan Governar (Dallas: Taylor Publishing, 1990); Sybil Kein, "The Celebration of Life in New Orleans Jazz Funerals," in *Feasts and Celebrations in North American Ethnic Communities*, ed. Ramón A. Gutiérrez and Geneviève Fabre (Albuquerque: University of New Mexico Press, 1995), 101–10; Jacqui Malone, *Steppin' on the Blues: The Visible Rhythms of African American Dance* (Urbana: University of Illinois Press, 1996), 140; Bruce Sunpie Barnes and Rachel Bruenlin, *Talk That Music Talk: Passing on Brass Band Music in New Orleans the Traditional Way* (Center for the Book at the University of New Orleans, 2014); and Eric Waters, photography, and Karen Celestan, narrative, *Freedom's Dance: Social, Aid and Pleasure Clubs in New Orleans* (Baton Rouge: Louisiana State University Press, 2018).

172. **an anthem, "When the Saints Go Marching In"**: Bruce Boyd Raeburn, "Jazz Notes: The Anthem of New Orleans," *Louisiana Cultural Vistas*, Summer 2005, 85.

172. **"Oh, when the drums begin to bang"**: Kallie Berens, "When the Saints Go Marching In: Origins of the Gospel Song," www.mysendoff.com, accessed December 22, 2017.

172. **"Slavery contradicts God"**: James H.

Cone, *The Spirituals and the Blues: An Interpretation* (Maryknoll, N.Y.: Orbis, 1997), 65.

172. **"Wading in the Water"**: John Lovell Jr., *Black Song: The Forge and the Flame—The Story of How the Afro-American Spiritual Was Hammered Out* (New York: Paragon, 1972), 196.

173. **"Reverend Satchmo"**: The 1938 recording is third cut on *Louis Armstrong: Gospel, 1931–41*, F&A 001.

173. **Born to fifteen-year-old May Ann Albert**: Armstrong gave his birthday in writings and interviews as July 4, 1900, a date that James Lincoln Collier questioned, given the absence of a birth certificate, in *Louis Armstrong: An American Genius* (New York: Oxford University Press, 1983). Gary Giddins, in researching the text for *Satchmo: The Genius of Louis Armstrong* (New York: Dolphin/Doubleday, 1988), commissioned New Orleans author and researcher Tad Jones, who found a baptismal certificate at Sacred Heart of Jesus church in New Orleans with the August 4, 1901, date. See Giddins, *Satchmo*, 48.

173. **"In that one block between Gravier and Perdido"**: Louis Armstrong, *Satchmo: My Life in New Orleans* (New York: DaCapo, 1986), 8.

173. **"It all came from the Old 'Sanctified' Churches"**: *Louis Armstrong in His Own Words: Selected Writings*, ed. Thomas Brothers (New York: Oxford University Press, 1999), 170.

173. **trusty typewriter**: The DaCapo reissue of *Satchmo* includes an introduction in which Dan Morgenstern writes: "We know that Armstrong already owned a typewriter and knew how to use one when he arrived in Chicago [in 1922]," ix. Armstrong wrote the memoir himself.

173. **"May Ann made a choice"**: Brothers, *Armstrong's New Orleans*, 38.

173. **"When I was in church"**: Armstrong, *Satchmo*, 24.

174. **"cooling board"**: Olympia Brass Band leader Harold Dejan, in conversation with the author, 1997.

174. **"In New Orleans, we would often wonder where a dead person was located"**: quoted in Alan Lomax, *Mister Jelly Roll: The Fortunes of Jelly Roll Morton, New Orleans Creole and "Inventor of Jazz"* (Berkeley: University of California Press, 1958), 15.

174. **"A fiddler is *not a violinist*"**: ibid., 86.

175. **"a titan of early jazz"**: Souchon and Rose, *New Orleans Jazz: A Family Album*, 98.

175. **James Brown Humphrey**: Richard H. Knowles, *Fallen Heroes: A History of New Orleans Brass Bands* (New Orleans: Jazzology, 1996), 72–80; Karl Koenig, "The Plantation Belt Brass Bands and Musicians, Part I: Professor James Brown Humphrey," *Second Line* (Fall 1981): 28–29. See also Koenig, *Plaquemines*.

175. **"Jim Humphrey would bring a new piece"**: quoted in Koenig, *Plaquemines*, 19.

175. **"These rhythms were characteristic"**: ibid., 4.

176. **"One of the surest signs"**: quoted in ibid., 11.

176. **"Grandfather made his money"**: quoted in ibid., 18.

176. **A wealthy man**: Ted Tunnell, "Henry Clay Warmoth," in *Know Louisiana: The Digital Encyclopedia of Louisiana History and Culture*, ed. David Johnson (New Orleans: Louisiana Endowment for the Humanities, 2010–), January 25, 2011. http://www.knowlouisiana.org/entry/henry-clay-warmoth;

Henry Clay Warmoth, *War, Politics, and Reconstruction: Stormy Days in Louisiana*, new introduction by John C. Rodrigue (Columbia: University of South Carolina Press, 2006), 260. See also Karl Koenig, "Magnolia Plantation: History and Music," *Second Line* 34 (Spring 1982): 35.

176. **Warmoth's five-day incarceration in 1874**: John Wilds, *Afternoon Story: A Century of the New Orleans States-Item* (Baton Rouge: Louisiana State University Press, 1976), 108–9.

176. **"march all around the quarters"**: quoted in Koenig, *Plaquemines*, 34.

176. **"generally showed a tender love"**: Warmoth, *War, Politics, and Reconstruction*, 267.

176. **"We must encourage"**: ibid., 269.

177. **Between 1882 and 1903**: William Ivy Hair, *Bourbonism and Agrarian Protest: Louisiana Politics, 1877–1900* (Baton Rouge: Louisiana State University Press, 1969), 186.

177. **"More often than not"**: ibid., 188–89.

177. **"dark blue helmet hats, ribbed with burnished brass"**: Charles B. Hersch, *Subversive Sounds: Race and the Birth of Jazz in New Orleans* (Chicago: University of Chicago Press, 2007), 135.

177. **"The high point"**: Lawrence N. Powell, "Reinventing Tradition: Liberty Place, Historical Memory, and Silk-Stocking Vigilantism in New Orleans Politics," *Slavery and Abolition* 20, no. 1 (1999): 127–49.

178. **"While northern publications"**: Howard Hunter, "Late to the Dance; New Orleans and the Emergence of a Confederate City," *Louisiana History* 56, no. 3 (Summer 2016): 297–322.

178. **"universal justice and equity"**: George W. Cable, "The Freedman's Case in Equity," in *The Negro Question:*

A Selection of Writings on Civil Rights in the South, ed. Arlin Turner (Garden City, N.Y.: Doubleday, 1958), 53.

178. **"I have seen the two races"**: ibid., 72–73.

178. **"Social relations must not impose"**: ibid.; Cable, "The Silent South," 86–87.

179. **flowers shaped as guns and swords**: Charles Reagan Wilson, *Judgment and Grace in Dixie: Southern Faiths from Faulkner to Elvis* (Athens: University of Georgia Press, 1995), 42.

179. **"judges, justices, tax collectors"**: Charles McCain, "A President's New Orleans Funeral," *New Orleans Magazine*, February 1981. See also www.CharlesMcCain.com.

179. **"The Lost Cause had its icons"**: Wilson, *Judgment and Grace in Dixie*, 20. See also Gary W. Gallagher and Alan T. Nolan, eds., *The Myth of the Lost Cause and Civil War History* (Bloomington: Indiana University Press, 2000); Gaines M. Foster, *Ghosts of the Confederacy: Defeat, the Lost Cause, and the Emergence of the New South* (New York: Oxford University Press, 1987); James W. Loewen, *Lies across America: What Our Historic Sites Get Wrong* (New York: Touchstone, 1999); and James W. Loewen and Edward H. Sebesta, eds., *The Confederate and Neo-Confederate Reader: The "Great Truth" about the "Lost Cause"* (Jackson: University Press of Mississippi, 2010).

179. **"a civil religion"**: Wilson, *Judgment and Grace in Dixie*, 21.

179. **"Can a cause be lost?"**: quoted in William Ivy Hair, *The Kingfish and His Realm: The Life and Times of Huey Long* (Baton Rouge: Louisiana State University Press, 1991), 3.

180. **loosening the military spine of parades**: Schafer, *Brass Bands and New*

Orleans Jazz, 37–40; Gioia, *The History of Jazz*, 31.

180. **"considerable opposition"**: *New Orleans Daily States*, November 30, 1890; my emphasis.

180. **probably the bellicose editor, Henry James Hearsey**: Wilds, *Afternoon Story*, 41–49.

181. **"benevolent societies to abolish the custom"**: "Reform in Funerals," *New Orleans Daily States*, December 2, 1890.

181. **"young white hoodlums" for "a small-sized riot"**: quoted in Schaefer, *Brass Bands*, 27–28.

181. **"Anybody can be a Second Liner"**: Armstrong, *Louis Armstrong, in His Own Words*, 27.

182. **"Erato to Carondelet"**: quoted in Freddi Williams Evans and Zada Johnson, "Freedom Dances across the Diaspora: The Cultural Connections of New Orleans Second Line, Cuban Conga, and Haitian Rara," 35. Eric Waters, photographs, and Karen Celestan, narrative, *Freedom's Dance: Social Aid and Pleasure Clubs in New Orleans* (Baton Rouge: Louisiana State University Press, 2018).

182. **led the Reliance**: Rose and Souchon, *New Orleans Jazz: A Family Album*, 198.

182. **"ended at about the same time"**: Jack Stewart, "Funerals with Music" (New Orleans: Save Our Cemeteries, 2004).

182. **"It is strictly forbidden"**: quoted in ibid.

183. **Holy Ghost parish . . . sponsored a brass band**: Jason Berry, "Leader of the Band," *Mature Times* (New Orleans) 8, no. 1 (March 1996): 10.

Chapter 10. Sicilians in the Meld

184. **arrival of 69,937 Italians**: A. V. Margavio and Jerome J. Salomone, *Bread and Respect: The Italians of Louisiana* (Gretna, La.: Pelican, 2002), 37.

184. **New Orleans by 1900 had 21,000 Italians**: Bruce Boyd Raeburn, "Sons of David and Sons of Sicily: Constellations beyond the Canon in Early New Orleans Jazz," *Jazz Perspectives* 3, no. 2 (2009): 123–52.

184. **Within nine years, the number of Italians doubled**: Margavio and Salomone, *Bread and Respect*, 37.

184. **at least a dozen pasta factories**: Donna Shrum, "When the French Quarter Was Italian," *Country Roads*, November 22, 2016.

184. **flamboyant singer-bandleader**: Garry Boulard, *Louis Prima* (Urbana: University of Illinois, 2002), 4.

184. **"The smells of the food and sounds of the music"**: Anna Harwell Celenza, *Jazz Italian Style: From Its Origins in New Orleans to Fascist Italy and Sinatra* (Cambridge: Cambridge University Press, 2017), 11.

184. **St. Mary Parish, on Decatur Street**: Joseph Macelli and Dominic Candeloro, *Images of America: Italians in New Orleans* (Charleston, S.C.: Arcadia, 2004), 61.

184. **On St. Joseph's Day**: ibid., 59.

185. **The Ring turned the police into a patronage hive**: Tom Smith, *The Crescent City Lynchings: The Murder of Chief Hennessy, the New Orleans "Mafia" Trials, and the Parish Prison Mob* (Guilford, Conn.: Lyons, 2007), 28.

185. **with heavy-handed tactics toward African Americans**: Dennis C. Rousey, *Policing the Southern City: New Orleans, 1805–1889* (Baton Rouge: Louisiana State University Press, 1996), 167.

185. **City governance crawled along**: Joy J. Jackson, *New Orleans in the Gilded Age: Politics and Urban Progress, 1880–1896* (Lafayette: Louisiana Historical Association: Center for Louisiana Studies, University of Southwestern Louisiana, 1997), 38.

185. **"in some cases"**: Alecia P. Long, *The Great Southern Babylon: Sex, Race, and Respectability in New Orleans, 1865–1920* (Baton Rouge: Louisiana State University Press, 2004), 74.

185. **helping elect Joseph A. Shakspeare**: Jackson, *New Orleans in the Gilded Age*, 36–37.

185. **"Brothel and casino operators"**: Justin A. Nystrom, "Sicilian Lynchings in New Orleans," in *Know Louisiana: The Digital Encyclopedia of Louisiana History and Culture*, ed. David Johnson (New Orleans: Louisiana Endowment for the Humanities, 2010–), June 24, 2013. See also Nystrom, *New Orleans after the Civil War: Race, Politics, and a New Birth of Freedom* (Baltimore: Johns Hopkins University Press, 2012), 220–22; and Humbert S. Nelli, *The Business of Crime: Italians and Syndicate Crime in the United States* (New York: Oxford University Press, 1976), 47–66.

185. **Hennessy befriended the three Provenzano brothers**: Herbert Asbury, *The French Quarter: An Informal History of the New Orleans Underworld* (New York: Garden City Publishing, 1938), 409.

185. **"It ill becomes the head of the police force"**: James Gill, *Lords of Misrule: Mardi Gras and the Politics of Race in New Orleans* (Jackson: University Press of Mississippi, 1997), 145.

186. **"reputedly left a trail of bodies"**: Smith, *The Crescent City Lynchings*, 45.

186. **padroni . . . "found jobs for immigrants"**: Margavio and Salomone, *Bread and Respect*, 71.

186. **the African American idiom forged of blues and church song**: Raeburn, "Sons of David and Sons of Sicily."

186. **ballots to control**: Jackson, *New Orleans in the Gilded Age*, 31.

187. **seen the faces of shooters**: Smith, *The Crescent City Lynchings*, 70.

187. **"Who gave it to you, Dave?"**: Numerous sources recount Boylan's exchange with Hennessy. I have relied on Smith, *The Crescent City Lynchings*; and Richard Gambino, *Vendetta* (New York: Doubleday, 1977), 4.

187. **"Florid-faced and goateed"**: William Ivy Hair, *The Kingfish and His Realm: The Life and Times of Huey Long* (Baton Rouge: Louisiana State University Press, 1991), 24.

187. **"These are all Dave's enemies"**: quoted in Smith, *The Crescent City Lynchings*, 81.

188. **"despicable assassins" and "total annihilation"**: quoted in Gary Krist, *Empire of Sin: A Story of Sex, Jazz, Murder, and the Battle for Modern New Orleans* (New York: Crown, 2014), 37–38.

188. **"the Italian vendetta cases"**: quoted in Gill, *Lords of Misrule*, 149.

188. **"The vendetta"**: quoted in John Wilds, *Afternoon Story: A Century of the New Orleans States-Item* (Baton Rouge: Louisiana State University Press, 1976), 95.

188. **"The evidence presented"**: Gill, *Lords of Misrule*, 150.

188. **"Rise in your might"**: quoted in ibid., 151.

189. **"Talk is idle!"**: quoted in Smith, *The Crescent City Lynchings*, 218–19.

189. **"The law has proven a farce"**: quoted in Lawrence N. Powell, "Reinventing

Tradition: Liberty Place, Historical Memory, and Silk-Stocking Vigilantism in New Orleans Politics," *Slavery and Abolition* 20, no. 1 (1999): 127–49.

189. **"the grand choir"**: ibid., 233.

190. **"had no relation to the war"**: quoted in Howard Hunter, "Late to the Dance; New Orleans and the Emergence of a Confederate City," *Louisiana History* 56, no. 3 (Summer 2016): 297–322.

190. **Società Italiana del Tiro al Bersaglio**: Raeburn, "Sons of David and Sons of Sicily," 136.

190. **"much older than the segregation laws"**: ibid., 126.

190. **Many of these Italian-American**: ibid., 138.

191. **"fluent in French and English"**: Keith Weldon Medley, *We as Freemen: Plessy v. Ferguson* (Gretna, La.: Pelican, 2003), 125.

191. **The Comité recruited Albion W. Tourgée**: In my synthesis of *Plessy v. Ferguson*, I have relied on Medley, *We as Freemen*; and Liva Baker, *The Second Battle of New Orleans: The Hundred-Year Struggle to Integrate the Schools* (New York: HarperCollins, 1996), particularly chapter 2, "The Stubborn Creoles," 12–42. For citations from Tourgée and Harlan, 39 of Baker, *The Second Battle of New Orleans*.

191. **"Our defeat sanctioned the odious principle"**: Rodolphe Desdunes, *Our People and Our History: Fifty Creole Portraits*, ed. and trans. Sister Dorothea Olga McCants, Daughter of the Cross (Baton Rouge: Louisiana State University Press, 2001), 144.

192. **"This quaint and sunny old city"**: *The 1897 Picayune's Guide to the City of New Orleans* (New Orleans: Picayune, 1897), 1. The newspaper published several subsequent editions of the guide in the early 1900s.

192. **Prostitution was rampant in many late nineteenth-century American cities**: Emily Epstein Landau, *Spectacular Wickedness: Sex, Race, and Memory in Storyville, New Orleans* (Baton Rouge: Louisiana State University Press, 2013), 1–2; Karen Abbott, *Sin and the Second City: Madams, Ministers, Playboys, and the Battle for America's Soul* (New York: Random House, 2008); Thomas Ruys Smith, *Southern Babylon: New Orleans in the Nineteenth Century* (New York: Continuum, 2011), 165–66.

192. **Lumber merchant George L'Hote**: Long, *The Great Southern Babylon*, 104–20.

192. **"one of the few places in turn-of-the-century New Orleans"**: ibid., 198.

192. **"that depict the fussy, over-decorated domestic interiors"**: Pamela D. Arcenaux, *Guidebooks to Sin: The Blue Books of Storyville, New Orleans* (New Orleans: The Historic New Orleans Collection, 2017), 42–43.

193. **"You think, it is pretty low"**: quoted in Sally Asher, "Last Days of Storyville," *New Orleans Magazine*, October 2017.

193. **"Storyville served a fantasy"**: Landau, *Spectacular Wickedness*, 118.

193. **"the most handsome"**: Arcenaux, *Guidebooks to Sin*, 84.

193. **Mahogany Hall, four stories**: Al Rose, *Storyville, New Orleans: Being an Authentic Account of the Notorious Red-Light District* (Tuscaloosa: University of Alabama Press, 1978), 80.

193. **"The girls would come down"**: quoted in Nat Shapiro and Nat Hentoff, *Hear Me Talkin' to Ya: The Story of Jazz as Told by the Men Who Made It* (New York: Dover, 1966), 11.

193. **"One thing that always puzzled me"**: Frank J. Gillis and John W. Miner, eds., *Oh, Didn't He Ramble: The Life Story of Lee Collins as Told to Mary Collins*, forewords by Danny Barker and Art Hodes, afterword by Max Jones (Urbana: University of Illinois Press, 1989), 64.

193. **Ferdinand LaMothe was about seventeen**: Jelly Roll Morton's birth year, alternately given as 1885 and 1890, would mean he was twelve when he began playing the District, the point at which he later claimed to have invented jazz. A seventeen-year-old getting into that life makes more sense. Otherwise, I have relied on Howard Reich and William Gaines, *Jelly's Blues: The Life, Music and Redemption of Jelly Roll Morton* (New York: DaCapo, 2003); and Alan Lomax, *Mister Jelly Roll: The Fortunes of New Orleans Creole Jelly Roll Morton and "Inventor of Jazz"* (Berkeley: University of California Press, 1950).

194. **Playing "Hot Time in the Old Town"**: Reich and Gaines, *Jelly's Blues*, 20.

194. **"Champagne flowed like water"**: Jelly Roll Morton, letter, 1938, William Russell Collection, The Historic New Orleans Collection.

194. **"I'd just stand there"**: quoted in Shapiro and Hentoff, *Hear Me Talkin' to Ya*, 43.

194. **"Most of the funerals I used to play"**: Ory interview, in Bill Russell, *New Orleans Style*, comp. and ed. Barry Martyn and Mike Hazeldine (New Orleans: Jazzology, 1994), 179.

194. **Spawned as a British drinking ditty**: Frank J. Gillis, "The Metamorphosis of a Derbyshire Ballad into a New World Jazz Tune," in *Discourse in Ethnomusicology: Essays in Honor of George List* (Bloomington: Indiana University, Ethnomusicology Publications Group, Archives of Traditional Music, 1978), manuscript

copy at Hogan Jazz Archive, Tulane University.

195. **"The only evidence that Charles was a desperate man"**: Ida B. Wells-Barnett, *Mob Rule in New Orleans: Robert Charles and His Fight to Death, the Story of His Life, Burning Human Beings Alive, Other Lynching Statistics*, Project Gutenberg, online reprint of the pamphlet published in 1900, www.Gutenberg.net. The definitive account is William Ivy Hair, *Carnival of Fury: Robert Charles and the 1900 Race Riot of New Orleans* (Baton Rouge: Louisiana State University Press, 1976).

196. **"Hundreds of policemen were about"**: quoted in Wells-Barnett, *Mob Rule*.

196. **"A mob of some two thousand whites formed"**: Krist, *Empire of Sin*, 96.

196. **"The fact that colored men and women had been made the victims"**: Wells-Barnett, *Mob Rule*.

197. **"In the frenzy of the moment"**: ibid.

197. **"They had a song out"**: Jelly Roll Morton and Alan Lomax, "Library of Congress Narrative" (1938), transcribed by Michael Hall, Roger Richard, and Mike Meddings, www.doctorjazz.co.uk/locspeech1.html. See also Lomax, *Mister Jelly Roll*, 69–70.

198. **he thought his mother-in-law was lurking**: Donald M. Marquis, *In Search of Buddy Bolden: First Man of Jazz* (Baton Rouge: Louisiana State University Press, 1978), 113.

198. **"CAUSE OF INSANITY"**: quoted in ibid., 121.

198. **"Paranoid delusions"**: quoted in ibid., 129.

198. **"He continues to get along nicely"**: quoted in ibid., 130.

199. **"None of the white bands"**: Johnny Wiggs, in Russell, *New Orleans Style*, 164.

200. **"Nothing so rhythmically free"**: Reich and Grimes, *Jelly's Blues*, 36.

200. **"If it wasn't for the nice Jewish"**: Louis Armstrong, "Louis Armstrong + the Jewish Family in New Orleans, La., the Year of 1907," in *Louis Armstrong in His Own Words: Selected Writings*, ed. Thomas Brothers (New York: Oxford University Press, 1999), 9.

200. **"a hardheaded idealist who believed"**: Terry Teachout, *Pops: A Life of Louis Armstrong* (New York: Houghton Mifflin Harcourt, 2009), 34–35.

200. **Armstrong had at least two substantial stays**: Will Buckingham, "Louis Armstrong in the Waifs' Home," *Jazz Archivist* 24 (2011): 7.

200. **"We used to go fishing behind the home"**: Author's interview with Deacon Frank Lastie, February 25, 1976, Louis Armstrong Oral History Project, Hogan Jazz Archive, Tulane University. See also Jason Berry, Jonathan Foose, and Tad Jones, *Up from the Cradle of Jazz: New Orleans Music since World War II* (Lafayette: University of Louisiana Lafayette Press, 2009), 44.

201. **"the madams bought their bedding"**: Christine Wiltz, *The Last Madam: A Life in the New Orleans Underworld* (New York: Faber and Faber, 2000), 51.

201. **"Louis was with me"**: Ory interview, in Bill Russell, *New Orleans Style*, 179.

201. **The African American pioneers back home listened**: Bruce Boyd Raeburn, "Jazz and the Italian Connection," *Jazz Archivist* 6, no. 1 (May 1991): 4.

202. **"Musicians are like gypsies"**: quoted in H. O. Braun, *The Original Dixieland Jazz Band* (Baton Rouge: Louisiana State University Press, 1969), 5.

203. **"Jass and Jassism"**: *Times-Picayune*, June 20, 1918.

Chapter 11. Mother Catherine and
the Lower Ninth Ward

205. **red-and-white terrazzo marble**:
Anthony J. Stanonis, *Creating the Big
Easy: New Orleans and the Emergence
of Modern Tourism, 1918-1945* (Athens:
University of Georgia Press, 2006), 73;
*The WPA Guide to New Orleans: The
Federal Writers' Project Guide to 1930s
New Orleans* (New York: Pantheon,
1983), 286.

205. **At Spanish Fort**: Samuel Charters,
*A Trumpet around the Corner: The
Story of New Orleans Jazz* (Jackson:
University Press of Mississippi, 2008),
240.

205. **Ships unloaded cargo**: Louis
Vyhnanek, *Unorganized Crime: New
Orleans in the 1920s* (Lafayette: Center
for Louisiana Studies, University of
Southwestern Louisiana, 1998), 54.

205. **white artists and literati barely
interacted with blacks**: John Shelton
Reed, *Dixie Bohemia: A French Quarter
Circle in the 1920s* (Baton Rouge:
Louisiana State University Press, 2012),
59-60.

206. **The engineer Albert Baldwin
Wood**: Nicole Romagossa, "Albert
Baldwin Wood, the Screw Pump, and
the Modernization of New Orleans"
(MA thesis, University of New Orleans,
2010), http://scholarworks.uno.edu
/td/1245.

206. **"Within the city limits"**: quoted in
Joy Jackson, *New Orleans in the Gilded
Age: Politics and Urban Progress,
1880-1896* (Lafayette: Center for
Louisiana Studies of the University of
Southwestern Louisiana, 1997), 4. See
also Juliette Landphair, "The Forgotten
People of New Orleans: Community,
Vulnerability, and the Lower Ninth

Ward," *Journal of American History* 94
(December 2007): 837-45.

206. **The sisters "worshiped, taught
girls"**: Richard Campanella, *Cityscapes
of New Orleans* (Baton Rouge:
Louisiana State University Press, 2017),
126.

206. **The Dock Board subsequently dug a
link**: ibid., 126.

206. **Several large houses rose**: Clarence
John Laughlin, *Clarence John Laughlin:
The Personal Eye* (New York: Aperture,
1974), 109. A companion house in the
"Steamboat Gothic" style is a block away
from the one Laughlin photographed.

206. *Mother Seal is a holy spirit*: Zora
Neale Hurston, *The Sanctified Church*
(Berkeley, Calif.: Turtle Island, 1983),
23.

207. **"the spyglass of anthropology"**:
Robert E. Hemenway, *Zora Neale
Hurston: A Literary Biography*,
foreword by Alice Walker (Urbana:
University of Illinois Press, 1978), 115.

207. **Village folkways seeded her
imagination**: Deborah G. Plant, *Zora
Neale Hurston: A Biography of the
Spirit* (Westport, Conn.: Praeger, 2007),
18-19.

207. **"jump at de sun"**: Hemenway, *Zora
Neale Hurston*, 18.

207. **"That hour began my wanderings"**:
Zora Neale Hurston, *Dust Tracks on a
Road* (New York: Arno, 1969), 177.

207. **"the archetypal Good Mother"**:
Valerie Boyd, *Wrapped in Rainbows:
The Life of Zora Neale Hurston*
(London: Virago, 2004), 65.

207. **"savage smelting of outrage"**: ibid.,
66.

207. **deducted a decade**: Hemenway, *Zora
Neale Hurston*, 17-19; Plant, *Zora Neale
Hurston*, 32-33.

207. **"a place of barbaric splendor"**: Zora

Neale Hurston, "Mother Catherine," in *Negro: An Anthology*, ed. Nancy Cunard (New York: Frederick Ungar, 1970), 23. The same piece is included in the posthumous collection, *The Sanctified Church*.

208. **"Catherine of Russia"**: ibid., 24; my emphasis.

208. **"We are happy living together"**: Mother Catherine's will, a two-page autobiographical document dictated to typist E. M. Barnett, is filed in Civil District Court of Orleans Parish, File no. 188001, dated October 11, 1929. A typed copy appears in the Robert Tallant Papers, Louisiana Research Division, New Orleans Public Library, Main Branch. The death certificate is in the same collection.

208. **"Mother Catherine's religion is matriarchal"**: Hurston, "Mother Catherine," 28.

209. **"God tells me to tell you"**: ibid., 26.

209. **Catherine's cosmology**: See Jessie L. Weston, *From Ritual to Romance* (Mineola, N.Y.: Dover, 1997); Robert Graves, *The White Goddess: A Historical Grammar of Poetic Myth* (New York: Farrar Straus and Giroux, 1966); and Sir James George Frazer, *The Golden Bough: A Study in Magic and Religion* (New York: Macmillan, 1894). Many editions of *The Golden Bough* have been published since, including a Gutenberg e-book, which is available for free download.

209. **The Manger was a unique outgrowth**: Claude F. Jacobs and Andrew J. Kaslow, *The Spiritual Churches of New Orleans: Origins, Beliefs, and Rituals of an African-American Religion* (Knoxville: University of Tennessee Press, 1991), 38.

210. **Nineteenth-century Spiritualism**: Ann Braude, *Radical Spirits: Spiritualism and Women's Rights in Nineteenth-Century America* (Boston: Beacon, 1989), 56. On background to the New Orleans branch, see Hans A. Baer, *The Black Spiritual Church Movement: A Religious Response to Racism* (Knoxville: University of Tennessee Press, 1984).

210. **Leafy Anderson, a charismatic woman**: Jason Berry, *The Spirit of Black Hawk: A Mystery of Africans and Indians* (Jackson: University Press of Mississippi, 1995), 57–61.

210. **A 1926 notice**: Unsigned, *Louisiana Weekly*, December 11, 1926.

210. **"Mother Anderson's followers"**: Zora Neale Hurston, "Hoodoo in America," *Journal of American Folklore* 44 (October–December 1931): 321.

211. **"Chris Kelly played"**: Danny Barker, *A Life in Jazz*, ed. Alyn Shipton with introduction by Gwen Thompkins (New Orleans: Historic New Orleans Collection, 2016), 66.

211. **More details come**: The most detailed listing of news articles on Mother Catherine from the Louisiana Writers' Program Collection is in Catherine B. Dillon, "The Manger of True Light" (revised copy), February 11, 1941. The twenty-nine-page unpublished biographical essay, under the rubric "Folklore, Fanatic Cults, Mother Catherine," is in the Federal Writers' Project Collection, Watson Memorial Library, Northwestern State University of Louisiana, Nachitoches. Another extensive collection of FWP materials is in the New Orleans Public Library, main branch, Robert Tallant and Lyle Saxon Collections. Saxon directed the Louisiana Writers' Program

as part of the FWP with various field researchers and writers. Dillon's essay is striking because Saxon and Tallant ignored most of her research in their major work, coauthored with Edward Dreyer, *Gumbo Ya Ya: Louisiana Folk Tales* (New York: Houghton Mifflin, 1945), with several reissues since. The brief chapter titled "The Temple of the Innocent Blood" is largely based on another field reporter's visit to the religious compound, which was in an advanced state of decay a decade after Mother Catherine's death. The tone of the chapter is derisive if not patently racist and has little on Mother Catherine, a pity considering the abundant information the authors had available.

211. **(Hurston supervised the Negro unit . . .)**: Carla Kaplan, ed., *Zora Neale Hurston: A Life in Letters* (New York: Doubleday, 2002), 181–82.

211. **After press reports of his reputed healing powers**: The story of Brother Isaiah drew extensive scrutiny in the *Times-Picayune* and other local papers, which led to national attention. See in particular Doris Kent, "Scientists Observe 'Miracle Man' Work before Huge Throngs," *Times-Picayune*, March 14, 1920; Unsigned, "Mrs. Barrow, Nearly Blind, Asserts 'Healer' Cured Her," *Times-Picayune*, March 27, 1920; Unsigned, "Crisis Is Reached at 'Healer's' Camp,'" *Times-Picayune*, April 11, 1920; Unsigned, "'Brother Isaiah' John Cudney: Faith Healer Hides Himself from Afflicted," July 25, 1924, *San Francisco Chronicle*; and Unsigned, "Cult Is Awaiting 'Resurrection' of 'Prophet' in West," *Times-Picayune*, July 25, 1934.

211. **"He told me he was not healing colored folks"**: quoted in Marguerite

Young, "Mother Catherine's Manger," *Item-Tribune*, December 25, 1927.

211. **"We were all supposed"**: quoted in Michael P. Smith, photographs and journal, *Spirit World: Pattern in the Expressive Folk Culture of African-American New Orleans* (1984; reprint Gretna, La.: Pelican, 1992), 46.

212. **In 1922, she paid $1,100**: "Negro Woman Healer Plans Retreat for Life," *New Orleans Item*, March 24, 1922.

212. **"African devil dance"** and **"automobiles wending their way"**: quoted in Wm. Hunter, "'Mother Catherine' and Her Followers," *New Orleans Item Magazine*, November 23, 1924.

212. **"I never saw any miraculous cures"**: Hazel Breaux, interview with Mrs. Fuccich, 814 Dauphine Street (New Orleans), in *Mother Catherine*, Robert Tallant Collection, New Orleans Public Library, 1. The first name of interviewee and date are not provided, as in several other field reports of the Louisiana Writers' Program; however, Mother Catherine was deceased when the interview took place.

212. **"My grandmother gave her five hundred dollars"**: interview with Gloria Rosselli, February 8, 1996. Jason Berry, "Mother Catherine Seals: A Healer in the City," *Historic New Orleans Collection Quarterly* 17, no. 1 (Winter 1999): 8.

212. **"That was exactly what the kid needed"**: Telephone interview with Jacalyn M. Duffin, January 11, 2018, with email correspondence.

213. **Several people told the LWP writers**: Miscellaneous LWP reports, Robert Tallant Collection.

213. **"Ernie Cagnolatti played the Angel Gabriel"**: Photograph of the Manger with Danny Barker inscription, William

Russell Collection, The Historic New Orleans Collection.

213. **"The 'black' Cagnolattis"** and Cagnolatti genealogy: Bruce Boyd Raeburn, "Italian Americans in New Orleans Jazz: Bel Canto Meets the Funk," *Italian American Review* 4, no. 2 (Summer 2014): 92–93.

214. **Ernie, nine, lived briefly:** Ernie Cagnolatti, interview with William Russell, Ralph Collins, and Harold Dejan, April 5, 1961, Hogan Jazz Archive, Tulane University.

214. **"My grandmother needed help"**: Ann Cagnolatti, family memoir, "All about Us," 2. The undated manuscript begins on page 2; she provided a copy to me and shared information in interviews and phone calls between 2012 and 2018.

214. **Eliza Johnson:** Biographical information from "All about Us" and a five-page addendum by Ann Cagnolatti on her mother. Another granddaughter, Yolanda Johnson of Los Angeles, spoke to me by telephone on January 15, 2018.

214. **"There is sin in this house!"**: Ann Cagnolatti interview.

214. **Jenkins died in 1927:** "Mother Catherine's Succession Opened," *The Times-Picayune*, January 14, 1931. George Jenkins's death, January 16, 1927, in East Louisiana State Hospital, the town of Jackson, is referenced in coverage of the probate.

214. **"The oldest one"**: Mother Catherine's will.

215. **"Grandpa was told"**: Cagnolatti, "All about Us," 4.

215. **Frank Lastie:** Author's interview with Frank Lastie, February 25, 1976; Jason Berry and Jonathan Foose, interview with Frank Lastie and Lewis Rock, March 11, 1982.

216. **"The people she healed"**: Jason

Berry, Jonathan Foose, and Tad Jones, *Up from the Cradle of Jazz: New Orleans Music since World War II* (Lafayette: University of Louisiana Lafayette Press, 2009), 45.

216. **"They couldn't set the eye straight"**: quoted in Jason Berry, "Leader of the Band," *Mature Times* (New Orleans) 8, no. 1, March 1996: 11.

216. **"Blood poison was setting in"**: interview with Lionel Scorza, November 20, 1998.

216. **"The application of animal meat"**: Telephone interview with Jacalyn M. Duffin, January 11, 2018, with email correspondence.

216. **"a blue baby"**: Cagnolatti, "All about Us," 3.

217. **Sort Maheia Young lived at the Manger:** The 1930 census lists Sort "Mayhew" among the fifteen residents at the 2420 Charbonnet address of the Manger. D. Ryan Gray, "Effacing the 'Imagined Slum': Space, Subjectivity and Sociality in the Margins of New Orleans" (PhD diss., University of Chicago, 2012), 79.

217. **"My time is up"**: quoted in Berry, Foose, and Jones, *Up from the Cradle of Jazz*, 45.

217. **"Take the money belt"**: quoted in Cagnolatti, "All about Us," 5.

217. **When the train arrived with the coffin:** "Mother Catherine's Body Reaches City," *Times-Picayune*, August 14, 1930.

217. **"In 'Mother's' little chapel"**: "Mother Catherine, Servent [*sic*] of 'De Lawd Jehovy,' Dies in Kentucky," *Times-Picayune*, August 12, 1930.

218. **"The wild thumping"**: Harnett Kane, "Mother Catherine Will Rise from Her Grave, Negroes Say," *New Orleans Morning Tribune*, August 15, 1930.

218. **"under a shrouded yellow moon"**:

Hodding Carter, "Thousands Gather to Pay Tribute as Mother Catherine Returns Home," *New Orleans Morning Tribune*, August 14, 1930.

218. **"the sun broke through"**: quoted in Berry, Foose, and Jones, *Up from the Cradle of Jazz*, 47.

218. **The 1930 Census**: Gray, "Effacing the 'Imagined Slum,'" 24.

218. **Hurston's profile**: Hurston, "Mother Catherine," 39.

218. **Cag earned a trumpeter's chair**: Larry Borenstein and Bill Russell, *Preservation Hall Portraits*, paintings by Noel Rockmore (Baton Rouge: Louisiana State University Press, 1968), "CAGNOLATTI, ERNIE – trumpet."

218. **"tears leaking"** and **"It's been a drastic road"**: Robert McKinney, "Mother Catherine's Manger," LWP field reports, Robert Tallant Collection, July 10, 1940.

Chapter 12. Sister Gertrude Morgan

235. **"He has taken me out of the black robe"**: Sister Gertrude Morgan, "A Poem of My Calling" (1962), in William A. Fagaly, *Tools of Her Ministry: The Art of Sister Gertrude Morgan* (New York: American Folk Art Museum, Rizzoli, 2004), 34.

236. **"Sister Gertrude Morgan was a self-appointed"**: Fagaly, *Tools of Her Ministry*, 3.

236. **"This town is running on bases"**: Sister Gertrude Morgan, "Composed by the Lord's Wife. New Jerusalem," n.d., manuscript collection of Sacha Borenstein Clay.

236. **"Gertrude apparently did not receive schooling beyond the third grade"**: Fagaly, *Tools of Her Ministry*, 4.

237. **"In going to my work one morning"**: Sister Gertrude Morgan, "some history

of my life!," n.d., Collection of Sacha Borenstein Clay.

237. **"goin' to the picture show"**: quoted in Fagaly, *Tools of Her Ministry*, 5.

237. **"The strong powerful words"**: Morgan, "A Poem of My Calling," 51.

237. **"headquarters of sin"**: ibid., 7.

238. **Federal agents were hunting down custodians of the Long machine**: Harnett Kane, *Louisiana Hayride: The American Rehearsal for Dictatorship, 1928–1940* (Gretna, La.: Pelican, 1971).

238. **"When I took the oath of office"**: quoted in Cyril E. Vetter, *Fonville Winans' Louisiana: Politics, People and Places* (Baton Rouge: Louisiana State University Press, 1995), 10.

239. **"I am determined to remove"**: Michael L. Kurtz and Morgan D. Peoples, *Earl K. Long: The Saga of Uncle Earl and Louisiana Politics* (Baton Rouge: Louisiana State University Press, 1990), 100.

239. **Maestri thought nothing of $50,000 "loan"**: T. Harry Williams, *Huey Long: A Biography* (New York: Knopf, 1970), 253–54.

239. **Appointed commissioner of conservation**: Glen Jeansonne and David Luhrssen, "Robert Maestri," in *Know Louisiana: The Digital Encyclopedia of Louisiana History and Culture*, ed. David Johnson (New Orleans: Louisiana Endowment for the Humanities, 2010–), August 21, 2013, http://knowlouisiana.org/entry/robert -maestri.

239. **The city in 1910 built a seawall**: Robert J. Cangelosi Jr., "West End," *New Orleans Preservation in Print*, September 1984.

239. **"a world renowned relic"** and **"seven negro dance halls"**: Betty A. Smallwood, "Milneburg, New Orleans: An Anthropological History of a

Troubled Neighborhood" (MS thesis, University of New Orleans, 2011), 34.

239. **"Dogs bay mournfully"**: quoted in ibid., 36. Craig E. Colten, *An Unnatural Metropolis: Wresting New Orleans from Nature* (Baton Rouge: Louisiana State University Press, 2005), 144.

239. **By 1928, the Levee Board had sunk $41 million**: Smallwood, "Milneburg, New Orleans," 38.

239. **The Levee Board president later went to prison**: Kane, *Louisiana Hayride*, 166.

239. **the city lurched toward bankruptcy**: Anthony J. Stanonis, *Creating the Big Easy: New Orleans and the Emergence of Modern Tourism, 1918–1945* (Athens: University of Georgia Press, 2006), 88–90.

239. **"How ya like dem ersters?"**: quoted in Edward F. Haas, *DeLesseps S. Morrison and the Image of Reform: New Orleans Politics, 1946–1961* (Baton Rouge: Louisiana State University Press, 1974), 13.

239. **put New Orleans in line for**: Jeansonne and Luhrssen, "Robert Maestri."

239. **"By the 1930s, Lakeview's drained land had subsided"**: John Magill, "A Conspiracy of Complicity," *Louisiana Cultural Vistas*, Fall 2006.

239. **Maestri personally paid to put a wooden floor**: Haas, *DeLesseps S. Morrison*, 18.

240. **"beautification programs abounded"**: Stanonis, *Creating the Big Easy*, 93–94.

240. **was reelected in absentia thanks to his wife**: Haas, *DeLesseps S. Morrison*, 32.

240. **In a scene worthy of a Tennessee Williams play**: ibid., 38.

240. **The economics of segregation hit blacks hard**: Kent B. Germany, *New Orleans after the Promise: Poverty, Citizenship, and the Search for the Great Society* (Athens: University of Georgia Press, 2007), 24.

240–41. **"no fewer than seventeen children"**: Elaine Y. Yau, "Acts of Conversion: Sister Gertrude Morgan and the Sensation of Black Folk Art, 1960–1982" (PhD diss., University of California, Berkeley, 2015), 38.

241. **"What is most striking"**: ibid., 40–41.

241. **"The main feature"**: quoted in Lynn Abbott, *I Got Two Wings: Incidents and Anecdotes of the Two-Winged Preacher and Electric Guitar Evangelist Elder Utah Smith* (Brooklyn: Case Quarter, 2008), 58.

241. **wings of a seraphim**: Jason Berry, "Elder Utah Smith," *New Orleans Magazine*, November 2010.

241. **a soundtrack to Sister Gertrude and her two cohorts**: Yau, "Acts of Conversion," 76–78.

241. **she was making music before she began to paint**: ibid., 39.

242. **"God married me himself around 1942"**: Sister Gertrude Morgan, "Poem by Jehova's Wife," n.d., Collection of Sacha Borenstein Clay.

242. **"The Lord of Hosts"**: Morgan, "A Poem of My Calling," 34.

242. **a man with thick horn-rimmed glasses**: Tom Bethell, "Profile: Larry Borenstein," *Vieux Carré Courier*, February 9–15, 1973.

242. **Mayor Morrison's 1958 crackdown**: Howard Philips Smith, *Unveiling the Muse: The Lost History of Gay Carnival* (Jackson: University Press of Mississippi, 2018), 5–6.

243. **Noel Rockmore, a seasoned painter**: For a compendium of Rockmore's life and work, see Shirley Marvin, Rich Marvin, and Tee Marvin, *Noel Rockmore & Shirley Marvin: Our Journey to the*

Discovery of Rockmore (New Orleans: Golden Era of the French Quarter, 2013). I have also relied on interviews with William Fagaly and JoAnn Clevenger.

243. **"The sound of a cash register"**: In conversation with photographer Judy Cooper, 2018.

243. **Born in 1919 in Milwaukee**: Bethell, "Profile: Larry Borenstein."

243. **despite the anti-Semitic exclusions**: James Gill, *Lords of Misrule: Mardi Gras and the Politics of Race in New Orleans* (Jackson: University Press of Mississippi, 1997), 7.

243. **Calvin Trillin noted**: Calvin Trillin, "U.S. Journal: New Orleans Mardi Gras," *New Yorker*, March 9, 1968.

243. **"For gay men in the South"**: Smith, *Unveiling the Muse*, xiii–xiv.

244. **he bought his first building in 1957**: Bethell, "Profile: Larry Borenstein."

244. **"Larry hung out at Bourbon House"**: interview with JoAnn Clevenger, January 29, 2018.

244. **He got thrown in jail three times**: Bethell, "Profile: Larry Borenstein."

244. **"In the U.S. government's zeal"**: ibid.

244. **a judge who called the trumpeter "Kid" Thomas Valentine "a yard boy"**: Tom Sancton, *Song for My Fathers: A New Orleans Story in Black and White* (New York: Other, 2006), 107.

245. **"We lived above Dorothy Rieger's Restaurant"**: interview with JoAnn Clevenger, January 29, 2018.

245. **Bill Russell sat at Borenstein's jam sessions**: For biographical information, and Russell's role in the New Orleans Revival, see Bruce Boyd Raeburn, "The Musical Worlds of William Russell," *Southern Quarterly* 36 (Winter 1998): 11–18; and Jason Berry, "William Russell and His Collection," *Southern Quarterly* 36 (Winter 1998): 81–93.

246. **"Time after time"**: Sancton, *Song for My Fathers*, 96.

247. **Long in 1959 fell for the ultrabuxom Blaze Starr**: Kurtz and Peoples, *Earl K. Long*, 215.

247. **Some strippers danced to live music**: Elizabeth Manley, "Cream with Our Coffee: Preservation Hall, Organized Labor, and New Orleans's Musical Color Line, 1957–1969," in Thomas J. Adams and Steve Striffler, *Working in the Big Easy: The History and Politics of Labor in New Orleans* (Lafayette: University of Louisiana at Lafayette Press, 2014), 140.

247. **Evelyn West**: Angus Lind, "A Shot of Bourbon Street, the Way It Was," *Times-Picayune*, August 2, 1998.

247. **"with a dead guy in the dressing room"**: in Peggy Scott Laborde, producer, *The French Quarter That Was* (New Orleans: WYES TV, 1999). See also David Cuthbert, "Deja Vu Carre …," *Times-Picayune TV Focus*, November 7, 1999.

247. **Borenstein let a California jazz enthusiast**: William Carter, *Preservation Hall: Music from the Heart* (New York: W. W. Norton, 1991), 140–44.

247. **Allan had the Humphreys' records!**: interview with Sandra Jaffe, January 25, 2018.

247. **Allan Jaffe grew up**: Tom Sancton, "The Venerable, Musical History of Preservation Hall in New Orleans," *Vanity Fair*, January 2012, https://www.vanityfair.com/culture/2012/01/preservation-hall-201201.

248. **Larry fell in love with Pat**: interview with Sacha Borenstein Clay, January 31, 2018.

248. **"I am glad you are pregnant"**: letter, May 28, 1961, quoted from the collection of Sacha Borenstein Clay.

249. **Borenstein fired Reid and Mills**: Carter, *Preservation Hall*, 144–58.

249. **Davis was a cipher**: Adam Fairclough, *Race & Democracy: The Civil Rights Struggle in Louisiana, 1915–1972* (Athens: University of Georgia Press, 1995), 242. On Perez, see Glen Jeansonne, *Leander Perez: Boss of the Delta* (Baton Rouge: Louisiana State University Press, 1977). For an inspired character portrait of Perez, see Robert Sherrill, *Gothic Politics in the Deep South* (New York: Ballantine, 1969).

249. **"Don't wait until these burr-heads"**: quoted in Fairclough, *Race & Democracy*, 244.

249. **"the entire burden of accepting"**: ibid., 250–51.

249. **an NBC News report**: Manley, "Cream with Our Coffee," 157.

250. **Al Belletto, by then the entertainment manager**: Jason Berry, Jonathan Foose, and Tad Jones, *Up from the Cradle of Jazz: New Orleans Music since World War II* (Lafayette: University of Louisiana at Lafayette Press, 2009), 157.

250. **The Krewe of Petronious invited guests**: Smith, *Unveiling the Muse*, 25–26.

250. **"New Orleans was a magical place"**: quoted in Jason Berry, "American Photographer: Lee Friedlander Comes to Town with a New Book and an Old Painting by Sister Gertrude Morgan," *Gambit Weekly*, November 10, 1998. See also Berry, "New Orleans in the Years of Sister Gertrude Morgan," in Fagaly, *Tools of Her Ministry*, 77–83.

251. **"This is the great master"**: Sister Gertrude Morgan, *Jesus Christ the Lamb of God and His Little Bride*, an artwork in the collection of Gordon W. Bailey, citation courtesy of Elaine Y. Yau.

252. **"never was national and Racial feeling stronger"**: Sister Gertrude Morgan, "armageddon," n.d., collection of Sacha Borenstein Clay.

253. **"Some things are hard to put into words"**: interview with Sandra Jaffe.

253. **"My mom used to talk about Sister Gertrude"**: interview with Sacha Borenstein Clay.

254. **"I got a new world in my view"**: Sister Gertrude Morgan, *Let's Make a Record*, reissue 1971 vinyl, remastered for compact disc by Benjamin Jaffe and Parker Dinkins (Preservation Hall Recordings, 2004), www.Preservationhall.com.

255. **"Sister Gertrude was one of those spirit figures"**: interview with Ben Jaffe, January 24, 2018.

Chapter 13. The Last Days of Danny Barker

257. **"Death affects people all kinda ways"**: quoted in Jason Berry, "Jazz Funerals: Second-Line through Time," *Times-Picayune, Lagniappe*, October 29, 1988.

257. **"Well, when you come up with families and religious training"**: quoted in Jason Berry, "The Elder Statesman of Jazz, Danny Barker," *Atlanta Journal/Atlanta Constitution*, January 2, 1994.

257. **He called his smile "a weapon"**: Michael Tisserand, "The Enduring Contribution of Danny Barker," *Louisiana Cultural Vistas* 4, no. 2 (Summer 1993): 8–15.

258. **bequeathed a mummy by the mortician Pierre Casanave II**: Rodolphe Lucien Desdunes, *Our People and Our History: Fifty Creole Portraits*, translated and edited by Sister Dorothea Olga McCants, Daughter of the Cross (Baton Rouge: Louisiana

State University Press, 2001), 80. In Sister McCants's translation of the original 1911 edition, Desdunes refers to Pierre Cazenave—with a "z" instead of "s"—as "the leading undertaker and embalmer in New Orleans during the mid-1880s." The author does not make a distinction between the father, Pierre, who died in 1866, and the son Pierre II, who carried on the family business.

258. **"The doctor, the undertaker"**: Danny Barker, *A Life in Jazz* (New York: Oxford University Press, 1986), 50.

258. **Spun off from benevolent societies**: Harry Joseph Walker, "Negro Benevolent Societies in New Orleans: A Study of Their Structure, Foundation and Membership" (PhD diss., Fisk University, 1937); Mary Louise Christovich, ed., *New Orleans Architecture*, vol. 3, *The Cemeteries* (Gretna, La.: Pelican, 1974), 19–20; William J. Schafer with Richard B. Allen, *Brass Bands and New Orleans Jazz* (Baton Rouge: Louisiana State University Press, 1977), 66, 79–80.

258. **"silk and satin-ribboned streamers"**: Barker, *A Life in Jazz*, 50.

258. **Isidore was hit in the side**: Richard Knowles, *Fallen Heroes: A History of New Orleans Brass Bands* (New Orleans: Jazzology, 1996), 47. Knowles mistakenly writes that Barbarin was shot at a "white" Mardi Gras ball. In a January 7, 1959, oral history interview for Tulane University's Hogan Jazz Archive, Barbarin said he was shot "when a white fellow came there."

258. **Red Allen as a boy**: John Chilton, *Ride Red Ride: The Life of Henry "Red" Allen* (London: Continuum, 200), 12.

258. **"The snare was taken off"**: quoted in Whitney Balliett, *American Musicians: 56 Portraits in Jazz* (New York: Oxford University Press, 1986), 42.

259. **"so quick to get emotionally upset"**: Barker, *A Life in Jazz*, 7.

259. **"All they do in the Barbarin home is talk about music"**: interview with Danny Barker, May 12, 1981, Hogan Jazz Archive, Tulane University. See also Jason Berry, Jonathan Foose, and Tad Jones, *Up from the Cradle of Jazz: New Orleans Music since World War II* (Lafayette: University of Louisiana at Lafayette Press, 2009), 12.

259. **Her father, August**: Mona MacMurray and Sue Hall, "Blue Lu Barker (and a Bit about Danny Too)," *Second Line*, Fall 1984, 27.

259. **the girl had to watch from the porch**: Geraldine Wyckoff, "Blue Lu Barker Remembers," *Offbeat*, October 1996.

259. **One of Danny's Barbarin aunts introduced Louise to him**: interview with Blue Lu Barker, April 3, 1997.

259. **he thought she looked at least sixteen**: Barker, *A Life in Jazz*, 110.

260. **He was earning twenty-five dollars a week**: Danny Barker, interview with William Russell, December 21, 1985, The Historic New Orleans Collection.

260. **Paul Barbarin spent his early years on Barracks Street**: Paul Barbarin, oral history interview with Richard B. Allen and William Russell, March 27, 1957, Hogan Jazz Archive, Tulane University.

261. **He was suffering from gum disease**: Balliett, *American Musicians*, 11.

261. **In 1929 both Ellington and Russell called Red Allen**: ibid., 36.

261. **"had become famous with bands"**: Barker, *A Life in Jazz*, 118.

261. **his great-grandfather Louis Hazeur**: Gene Allen Smith, *The Slaves' Gamble: Choosing Sides in the War of 1812* (New York: Palgrave Macmillan, 2013), 206. Jerry Brock, "Jordan Noble: Drummer,

Soldier, Statesman," *Louisiana Cultural Vistas*, Winter 2005, www .knowlouisiana.org.

261. **She'd forgotten her doll!**: Elizabeth Mullener, "This Lady Still Sings the Blues," *Times-Picayune*, March 3, 1991.

261. **"Now Mr. Tio was a handsome man"**: interview with Blue Lu Barker, April 5, 1997.

262. **"You get to New York"**: interview with Danny Barker, April 14, 1989.

262. **"Write!"**: ibid.

262. **"New York is not a blues town"**: ibid.

263. **"could not dance to that kind of rhythm"**: Barker-Russell interview, The Historic New Orleans Collection.

263. **"that knew nothing of press agents"**: ibid.

263. **"He had a culture acquired from New Orleans"**: interview with Danny Barker, April 14, 1989.

263. **"to pray for deliverance"**: Howard Reich and William Gaines, *Jelly's Blues: The Life, Music and Redemption of Jelly Roll Morton* (New York: Da Capo, 2003), 220.

263. **"He died in my arms"**: quoted in Alan Lomax, *Mister Jelly Roll: The Fortunes of Jelly Roll Morton, New Orleans Creole and "Inventor of Jazz"* (Berkeley: University of California Press, 1959), 261.

263. **"I sat up all night with Nat Hentoff"**: interview with Danny Barker, April 14, 1989.

264. **"That's about right"**: telephone interview with Nat Hentoff, March 26, 1997.

264. **"one of the best rhythm-section guitarists"**: Nat Hentoff, *Listen to the Stories: Nat Hentoff on Jazz and Country Music* (New York: Harper Collins, 1995), 197.

264. **She asked the drummer**: interview with Blue Lu Barker, April 3, 1997.

265. **Calloway was personally earning $200,000**: Cab Calloway and Bryant Rollins, *Of Minnie the Moocher and Me* (New York: Thomas H. Crowell, 1976), 184.

265. **"Women flocked around the band like bees"**: Danny Barker, *Buddy Bolden and the Last Days of Storyville*, ed. Alyn Shipton (New York: Cassell, 1998), 64.

265. **"houses where a musician, performer"**: ibid., 124.

266. **"flim-flam town"**: Blue Lu Barker interview.

266. **In 1959, Danny Barker published his first article**: Danny Barker, "Jelly Roll Morton in New York," *Jazz Review*, May 1959. Much of the material appears in the chapter on Morton in Barker's memoir, *A Life in Jazz*.

266. **"I'd rather be a lamp post in New York"**: interview with Placide Adams, May 23, 1996.

266. **his 7,500-word piece**: Danny Barker, "Memory of King Bolden," *Evergreen Review* 9 (March 1965): 67–74; reprinted and revised as "A Life in Jazz," in Barker, *Buddy Bolden and the Last Days of Storyville*.

266. **"After a while"**: ibid., 38; my emphasis.

266. **Henry Allen leads him by the arm**: ibid., 46.

267. **"After all"**: Albert Murray, *The Blue Devils of Nada: A Contemporary American Approach to Aesthetic Statement* (New York: Pantheon, 1996), 27.

268. **"If I didn't feel like singing I wouldn't"**: interview with Blue Lu Barker, April 5, 1997.

268. **Barbarin's funeral that February 22**: interview with Don Perry, February 3, 1990. Footage of funeral: Don Perry, producer, *A Collection of New Orleans*

Jazz Films, VHS, 1987. David Cuthbert, "Barbarin Funeral Draws Throngs of Admirers," *Times-Picayune*, February 23, 1969; Barbara Pyle, "More than a Funeral, Barbarin Rites Reveal New Orleans Culture," *Tulane Hullabaloo*, April 18, 1969. Articles and footage are at the Hogan Jazz Archive, Tulane University.

269. **At the behest of Rev. Andrew Darby**: Jason Berry, "New Orleans Brass Band Revival," *Reckon: The Magazine of Southern Culture* 1, nos. 1 and 2 (1995): 28–39.

269. **"I have to stop workin' with y'all"**: quoted in ibid.

269. **"We also agreed"**: Personal correspondence with Alyn Shipton.

270. **"a remarkable contribution"**: *Jazztimes* blurb on back cover of *A Life in Jazz*, Oxford University Press paperback ed., 1988 (hardcover ed.: Oxford University Press, 1986).

270. **"What is wrong with you, crying?"**: interview with Kerry Brown, August 8, 1995.

270. **"When the Wolves had a parade"**: ibid.

270. **"You got to keep up your front"**: interview with Blue Lu Barker, April 3, 1997.

270. **"When I die"**: ibid.

270. **"Lot of jazz funerals ended up here"**: Rob Florence, in conversation with the author, 1994.

270. **"Well," he said**: interview with Tom Dent, March 12, 1995.

270. **"Doctor don't know nothin'"**: Blue Lu Barker interview, April 3, 1997.

271. **"You got mad at me"**: ibid.

272. **"Eggs and weenies"**: ibid.

272. **"Them doctors don't know"**: ibid.

272. **"The film is gettin' heavy"**: interview with Kerry Brown, August 8, 1995.

273. **Fighting tears, Wyckloff helped him down**: Geraldine Wyckloff, in conversation, 1994.

273. **"Look how this stuff has gotten"**: interview with Michael White, May 7, 1994.

273. **"When you have work, you go"**: interview with Sylvia Barker, April 5, 1995.

273. **"Daddy," said Sylvia**: ibid.

273. **"How's *jazz*?"**: interview with Gregg Stafford, April 21, 1994.

273. **"Don't tell Sylvia I can't do anything"**: ibid.

274. **"I want to thank you"**: interview with Tom Dent.

274. **"Look at Dean"**: interview with Blue Lu Barker, April 5, 1997.

274. **"Who's that lady in the red dress?"**: Sylvia Barker interview.

274. **"Shaddup!" he blurted**: Sylvia Barker interview, and from her eulogy at Danny Barker's funeral.

275. **"Be quiet! Can't you see I'm trying to pass away?"**: Michael White interview.

276. **"Danny Barker's funeral had to make a statement"**: Gregg Stafford interview.

278. **"You see the music's effect on people"**: Barker, *A Life in Jazz*, 199. *A Life in Jazz* had gone out of print by 2016, when the Historic New Orleans Collection, as part of its Louisiana Musicians Biography Series, published a handsome new edition with photographs, illustrations, and previously unpublished material provided by Alyn Shipton, the editor of the original edition, and a new introduction by Gwen Thompkins. My chapter by then was done, utilizing page numbers from the 1988 softcover edition; the new edition is eminently worthy of its author.

Chapter 14. Dr. Michael White
and the Widow's Wail

279. **White enjoyed an association with Wynton Marsalis**: John Swenson, *New Atlantis: Musicians Battle for the Survival of New Orleans* (New York: Oxford University Press, 2011), 211.

279. **"a master at creating moods"**: interview with Michael White, May 8, 1994.

281. **Creole folklore carried a belief**: Vernel Bagneris, *The New Orleans Jazz Funeral: Rejoice When You Die*, photographs by Leo Touchet, introduction by Ellis L. Marsalis Jr. (Baton Rouge: Louisiana State University Press, 1998).

281. **"answering the call to a culture"**: video interview with Michael White, September 9, 1997.

281. **changes threatening the funerals**: Brenda Marie Osbey, "One More Last Dance: Ritual and the Jazz Funeral," *Georgia Review* 50, no. 1 (1996): 97–107; Matt Sakakeeny, *Roll with It: Brass Bands in the Streets of New Orleans*, artwork by Willie Birch (Durham, N.C.: Duke University Press, 2013), 144–48.

281. **Rhythm was the piston of youth culture**: Jason Berry, "New Orleans Brass Band Revival," *Reckon: The Magazine of Southern Culture* (University of Mississippi) 1, nos. 1 and 2 (1995): 28–39.

282. **"One of those famous jazz musicians"**: interview with Michael White, December 7, 2005.

282. **"a New Orleans half-breed"**: ibid.

282. **"They don't like us poor whites"**: quoted in Dan Baum, *Nine Lives: Death and Life in New Orleans* (New York: Spiegel and Grau, 2009), 26.

282. **Mississippi River Gulf Outlet**: Gary Rivlin, *Katrina: After the Flood* (New York: Simon and Schuster, 2015), 118–19.

283. **"My daddy got so much money"**: White interview, December 7, 2005.

283. **"My grandmother looked almost white"**: ibid.

283. **an uneasy Archbishop Joseph Rummel**: Adam Fairclough, *Race & Democracy: The Civil Rights Struggle in Louisiana, 1915–1972* (Athens: University of Georgia Press, 1995), 258.

284. **Mrs. Gaillot never looked back**: Bruce Nolan, "Daring to Discipline," *Times-Picayune*, July 18, 2004.

285. **Ernest "Doc" Paulin was sixty-eight**: Michael G. White, "Dr. Michael White: The Doc Paulin Years," *Jazz Archivist* 23 (2010): 2–20. See also essay brochure by Alden Ashforth, "Doc Paulin's Marching Band: Recording Doc Paulin," Folkways Records Album no. FS2856, 1982.

285. **"In the country we didn't play funerals"**: quoted in Jason Berry, "Doc Paulin's Long Goodbye," *Gambit Weekly*, December 4, 2007.

285. **"Wha' instrument you play?"** White interview, September 9, 1997.

287. **"telling my story in what they played"**: White interview, December 7, 2005.

287. **Born in 1900 in New Orleans**: Tom Bethell, *George Lewis: A Jazzman from New Orleans* (Berkeley: University of California Press, 1977).

288. **"through the open window"**: Ann Fairbairn, *Call Him George: A Biography of George Lewis: The Man, the Faith and His Music* (New York: Crown, 1969), 54.

288. **"playing for funerals about 1923"**: quoted in ibid., 13.

288. **"His slim body had the energy of a coiled snake"**: Tom Sancton, *Song for My Fathers: A New Orleans Story*

in Black and White (New York: Other, 2006), 53.

289. **"Everybody played a little something"**: Michael White, "Papa John Joseph," *Second Line*, vol. 32 (Fall 1980): 4.

290. **"That piece just about did me in"**: ibid., 8.

291. **"These were the last performing years"**: Michael G. White, "Dr. Michael White: My Years among the Elders, 1990–1995," *Jazz Archivist* 29 (2016): 16.

291. **"Some had private lessons"**: ibid., 19.

291. **"How are you doing, young man?"**: ibid., 18.

291. **"Up to that point"**: ibid.

292. **"You made the sky cry"**: ibid.

292. **By a 224-vote margin**: Jason Berry, "A Master Racist Jumps Parties to Land in the Louisiana Legislature," *Los Angeles Times*, February 26, 1989. See also Lawrence N. Powell, "Slouching toward Baton Rouge: The 1989 Legislative Election of David Duke," in *The Emergence of David Duke and the Politics of Race*, ed. Douglas A. Rose (Chapel Hill: University of North Carolina Press, 1992), 12.

292. **the local media did a poor job**: Clancy DuBos, "Eyes on the Prize," *Gambit*, December 17, 1991. Jeanne W. Amend, "The *Picayune* Catches Up with David Duke," *Columbia Journalism Review* (January/February 1992): 1.

293. **"National television made him a celebrity"**: Jason Berry, "Louisiana Hateride," *The Nation*, December 9, 1991. Jason Berry, "David Duke: Triumph of the Image," *Television Quarterly*, January 1992.

293. **he had celebrated Hitler's birthday**: Tyler Bridges, the reporter assigned by the *Times-Picayune* to cover Duke, broke the story in 1990.

See Tyler Bridges, *The Rise of David Duke* (Jackson: University Press of Mississippi), 120.

293. **He later received a fifteen-month federal prison term**: David M. Halbfinger, "National Briefing, South: Louisiana: Prison Term for David Duke," *New York Times*, March 13, 2003.

293. **"before we ruin the best thing"**: quoted in James Gill, *Lords of Misrule: Mardi Gras and the Politics of Race in New Orleans* (Jackson: University Press of Mississippi, 1997), 22.

293. **"Yes ma'am"**: ibid., 22–23.

294. **They would drop**: ibid., 26.

295. **"The world's changing"**: Bruce Nolan, "Bitter Mardi Gras Debate of Race, Class Evolves 20 Years Later into a Diverse Celebration, *The Times-Picayune*, February 12, 2012.

295. **"The funerals in the sixties"**: Jules Cahn, in conversation at Congo Square, White Buffalo Day, August 20, 1994.

295. **"Jules is riding that train"**: Jason Berry, "Ancestors in the Infield," *New Orleans Magazine*, May 2013.

295. **"Funerals are changin'"**: Michael White, in conversation, 1998.

295. **Rickey, thirty-seven, stepped off the bus**: Sheila Stroup, "13 Bullets Shatter Plans but Not Family's Spirit," *The Times-Picayune*, June 15, 1997.

Chapter 15. After the Flood

298. **More than 250 New Orleans police officers . . . deserted**: Bootie Costrove-Mather, "60 New Orleans Police Fired," Associated Press, December 9, 2005.

298. **Eighty percent of the city flooded**: "New Orleans in Peril," *New York Times*, August 31, 2005.

299. **"What do you need?"**: Mitch

Landrieu, *In the Shadow of Statues* (New York: Viking, 2018), 102.

299. **"I been out there, man"**: transcript of Ray Nagin–Garland Robinette WWL Radio interview, September 1, 2005. David Rutledge, ed., *Do You Know What It Means to Miss New Orleans* (Seattle: Chin Music, 2006), 35.

300. **The flooded area was seven times**: Jim Amoss, "Awaiting a Commitment," *Los Angeles Times, Opinion*, August 27, 2007.

300. **the $4.9 billion tourist industry**: Sarah Whitten, "New Orleans' Tourism Booms 10 Years after Hurricane Katrina," CNBC.com, August 28, 2015, https.//www.cnbc.com/2015/08/28 /new-orleans-tourism-booms-10-years -after-hurricane-katrina.html.

300. **"We're blues people"**: Wynton Marsalis, interview with Tavis Smiley, PBS, September 8, 2006, www.pbs .org./tavissmiley/archive.

300. **Former presidents George H. W. Bush and Bill Clinton**: Phil Hirschorn, "Katrina Relief Fund to Distribute $90 Million," CNN, December 7, 2005.

300. **Oil-rich Qatar donated**: Stephanie Strom, "Qatar Grants Millions in Aid to New Orleans," *New York Times*, May 2, 2006.

300. **"Our first objective"**: quoted in Howard Reich, "Katrina Decimated New Orleans' Cultural Life, Report Concludes," *Chicago Tribune*, January 26, 2006.

300. **He released a consultants' report**: *Report of the Bring New Orleans Back Commission*, Cesar R. Burgos, chairman, Wynton Marsalis, cochairman, January 10, 2006.

301. **Despite heroic work**: Douglas Brinkley, *The Great Deluge: Hurricane Katrina, New Orleans, and the*

Mississippi Gulf Coast (New York: William Morrow, 2006), 372–81.

301. **"The threat worked"**: Gary Rivlin, *Katrina: After the Flood* (New York: Simon and Schuster, 2015), 222.

301. **"The state had to add"**: David Hammer, "Examining post-Katrina Road Home program: 'It's more than the money. It's the hoops we had to jump through to do it,'" *Baton Rouge Advocate*, August 23, 2015. *The Advocate* has a New Orleans edition and news partnership with WWL-TV, where Hammer is a reporter. http://www .theadvocate.com/baton_rouge/news /article_f9763ca5-42ba-5a62-9935 -c5f7ca94a7c4.html

301. **A government investigation**: John Schwartz, "Army Corps Admits Flaws in New Orleans Levees," *New York Times*, June 1, 2006.

301. **State government had done its share**: Jason Berry, "Memory of the Flood," *Gambit Weekly*, August 22, 2006.

302. **"Those who want to see this city rebuilt"**: quoted in Christopher Cooper, "Old-Line Families Plot the Future," *Wall Street Journal*, September 8, 2005.

302. **"We finally cleaned up"**: quoted in Richard Harwood, "Washington Wire," *Wall Street Journal*, September 9, 2005.

302. **"the incompetence in our government"**: Wynton Marsalis, interview with Tavis Smiley, PBS, September 8, 2006, www.pbs.org ./tavissmiley/archive.

303. **suffered a loss of $90,000**: Jason Berry, "The Rise and Fall of Bill Jefferson," *Gambit Weekly*, December 11, 2007.

303. **"Traditionally, in Louisiana"**: William J. "Bill" Dodd, *Peapatch Politics: The Earl Long Era in*

Louisiana Politics (Baton Rouge, La.: Claitor's, 1991), 5.

303. **"harassed and intimidated"**: quoted in Berry, "The Rise and Fall of Bill Jefferson."

303. **testifying that she took $140,000**: Cindy Chang, "Ellenese Brooks-Simms Gets Sentence Reduced as Reward for Helping Prosecutors," *Times-Picayune*, March 11, 2010.

304. **"Jeff still owes me $25,000"**: quoted in Berry, "The Rise and Fall of Bill Jefferson."

304. **Governor Edwin Edwards in the 1970s**: Jason Berry, "The Spoiling of Vermilion Parish," *Gambit*, April 10, 1982. (The alternative weekly in 2009 changed its name to *Gambit Weekly*.) Berry, "The Poisoning of Louisiana," *Southern Exposure*, May 1984.

304. **guilty in 2007 to taking $20,000**: Frank Donze, "Summary of the Government's Case against Oliver Thomas," *Times-Picayune*, August 13, 2007. Adam Nossiter, "New Blow to New Orleans in Council Member's Plea," *New York Times*, October 4, 2007.

304. **"This city trusted me"**: quoted in Gordon Russell, "Stan 'Pampy' Barre Gets 5 Years in Prison," *The Times-Picayune*, July 9, 2008, http://www .nola.com/news/index.ssf/2008/07/do _not_publish_pampy_blog.html.

304. **Between 1980 and 1990**: Daniel Robert Samuels, "Remembering North Claiborne: Community and Place in Downtown New Orleans" (MA thesis, University of New Orleans, 2000), 94.

305. **a consultant's plan by Robert Moses**: Richard O. Baumbach Jr. and William E. Borah, *The Second Battle of New Orleans: A History of the Vieux Carré Riverfront Expressway Controversy* (Tuscaloosa: University of Alabama Press, 1981), 30–32. Robert A. Caro, *The Power Broker: Robert Moses and the Fall of New York* (New York: Vintage, 1975), chronicles the neighborhood destructions in New York.

305. **"a living history of the city"**: Roulhac Toledano and Mary Louise Christovich, *Faubourg Tremé and the Bayou Road*, vol. 6 of *New Orleans Architecture* (Gretna, La.: Pelican, 1980), 66.

305. **"a whole piece of my childhood"**: interview with Anthony Bennett, November 20, 2002.

306. **"I was the corpse"**: in conversation, Uncle Lionel Batiste.

306. **erected an I-10 overpass link**: Michael E. Crutcher Jr., *Tremé: Race and Place in a New Orleans Neighborhood* (Athens: University of Georgia Press, 2010), 50–65.

306. **"How quickly the neighborhood disintegrated"**: quoted in Ronette King, "Shifting Landscape," *Times-Picayune*, March 26, 2001.

306. **"a neighborhood mall"**: Samuels, "Remembering North Claiborne," transcript of Samuels's interview with Jerome Smith, June 12, 2000.

306. **"We wanted something for ourselves"**: quoted in Jason Berry, "Carnival Claiborne Comeback," *Gambit*, February 13, 1982.

307. **"Tambourine and Fan gave me strength"**: *Fire in the Hole: The Spirit Work of Fi Yi Yi & the Mandingo Warriors. A Collaborate Ethnography with the Committee Members of Fi Yi Yi*, ed. Rachel Bruenlin, photographs Jeffrey Ehrenreich (University of New Orleans Neighborhood Story Project, 2018), 11.

307. **The solemn funeral had no second line**: Joseph Lelyveld, "Louis

Armstrong's Simple Funeral Shuns Sadness and Display of Bands," *New York Times*, July 10, 1971.

307. **"The eulogy was cancelled"**: Bruce Nolan, "Thousands Attend Memorial Services Given for Satchmo," *Times-Picayune*, July 12, 1971.

307. **Tensions between Tremé leaders and City Hall**: Jason Berry, "The Upgrading of New Orleans: Neighborhoods as Real Estate," *The Nation*, September 23, 1978.

307. **and reduced federal funds**: Kent B. Germany, *New Orleans after the Promise: Poverty, Citizenship, and the Search for the Great Society* (Athens: University of Georgia Press, 2007), 50–53.

308. **"When word got out"**: quoted in Jason Berry, "Tremé's Cultural Heartbeat," *Gambit Weekly*, March 7, 2006.

308. **"I was like Dorothy and the Wizard, bra."** In conversation, Sylvester Francis.

308. **"Nagin's not a culture man"**: quoted in Berry, "Tremé's Cultural Heartbeat."

308. **"I cannot prove the urban myth"**: quoted in Jason Berry, "Memory of the Flood," 307. Jason Berry, Jonathan Foose, and Tad Jones, *Up from the Cradle of Jazz: New Orleans Music since World War II* (Lafayette: University of Louisiana at Lafayette Press, 2009).

309. **"I don't know if I should pray before or after"**: Video-taped sequence with Michael White, October 21, 2005.

310. **"It was the most beautiful picture I'd seen of Papa John"**: quoted in Keith Spera, "Facing Music: Michael White Returns Home," *Times-Picayune*, October 22, 2005.

310. **The Recovery School District**: For the historical background, I have relied on *Eddy Oliver, Oscarlene*

Nixon and Mildred Goodwin versus Orleans Parish School Board, Supreme Court of Louisiana, no. 2014-C-0329, consolidated with no. 2014-C-0330, October 31, 2014.

310. **"They were trying not to hire veteran teachers"**: quoted in Jason Berry, "It Was New Orleans' Musicians—Not Its Politicians—Who Saved the City Post-Katrina," *The Daily Beast*, August 23, 2015, www .thedailybeast.com/it-was-new-orleans -musiciansnot-its-politicianswho-saved -the-city-post-katrina.

311. **"I taught for two years"**: ibid.

311. **Before Katrina, slightly more than a third of New Orleans public school students**: David Osborne, "How New Orleans Made Charter Schools Work," *Washington Monthly*, June 2015, https://washingtonmonthly.com/ ... 2015/how-new-orleans-made-charter -schools-work.

311. **he was taken aback**: Alex Glustrom's documentary *Big Charity*, with interviews from Honoré, medical personnel, and various officials, is a probing account of the hospital's closure; www.BigCharityFilm.org. The most thorough work on this topic is Kenneth Brad Ott, "The Closure of New Orleans' Charity Hospital: A Case of Disaster Capitalism," M.A. thesis, sociology, University of New Orleans (2012), *University of New Orleans Theses and Dissertations*, 1472, http:// scholarworks.uno.edu/td/1472.

311. **"We were in desperate need"**: quoted in Roberta Grandes Gratz, "Why Was New Orleans's Charity Hospital Allowed to Die?," *The Nation*, April 27, 2011.

312. **"If we do, we will never get a new one"**: quoted in ibid.

312. **"The lengths to which the U.S.**

military": Ott, "The Closure of New
Orleans' Charity Hospital," 81.

312. a **final price tag of $1.1 billion**: Abby
Goodnough, "New Orleans Hospital Is
Replaced, with Hope of Preserving Its
Mission," *New York Times*, August 1,
2015.

312. **Mayor Ray Nagin's recovery czar**:
Gratz, "Why Was New Orleans's Charity
Hospital Allowed to Die?"

313. **"They comin' out!"**: quoted in Berry,
Foose, and Jones, *Up from the Cradle of
Jazz*, 310.

314. **"chocolate city"**: Manuel Roig-
Franzia, "New Orleans Mayor
Apologizes for Remarks about God's
Wrath," *Washington Post*, January 18,
2006.

314. **"Race trumps everything"**: Landrieu,
In the Shadow of Statues, 121.

314. **"Prayer, playing music, and
the kindness"**: Michael G. White,
"Reflections of an Authentic Jazz Life in
Pre-Katrina New Orleans," *Journal of
American History* 94 (December 2007):
833.

314. **Musicians led a march**: Jason Berry,
"Hot 8 Fights for the Big Easy," *Los
Angeles Times*, January 21, 2007.

314. **"market-driven recovery"**: quoted
in Adam Nossiter, "New Orleans Mayor
Pleads for Patience in Meeting Goals,"
New York Times, September 13, 2006.

315. **A Commerce Department official**: To
the author, on background, 2009.

315. **Four years later he was sentenced**:
David Zucchino, "C. Ray Nagin, Former
New Orleans Mayor, Sentenced to 10
Years in Prison," *Los Angeles Times*,
July 9, 2014.

315. **The city had some 750 meetings**:
Landrieu, *In the Shadow of Statues*,
133–34.

315. **"The Obama administration
furthered this effort"**: Priyanka

Juneja, "Economics of Disaster: New
Orleans and Katrina," Federal Reserve
Bank of Atlanta, Publications, Fall 2015.
https://www.frbatlanta.org/economy
-matters/.../new-orleans-10-years-after
-katrina.

316. **Blighted houses**: Tyler Bridges, "See
How New Orleans Pre–Mitch Landrieu
Compares to 2017 Version of the City,"
New Orleans Advocate, July 8, 2017.

316. **The majority of the $120.5 billion in
federal spending**: Allison Plyer, "Facts
for Features: Katrina Impact," August
26, 2016. The Data Center. https://www
.datacenterresearch.org/data-resources
/katrina/facts-for-impact/

316. **the hospital's operating costs
exceeded $500 million**: Goodnough,
"New Orleans Hospital Is Replaced."

317. **"Mitch Landrieu is the best stand-up
politician in Louisiana"**: Jim Engster,
in conversation, 2017.

317. **"I don't understand why it's okay in
America"**: quoted in Jeffrey Goldberg,
"A Matter of Black Lives," *Atlantic*,
September 2015.

317. **"You lost me on that"**: Landrieu, *In
the Shadow of Statues*, 163.

318. **Landrieu wondered if the squeeze
was worth the juice**: Jason Berry, "New
Orleans' Confederate Monuments Are
Coming Down under Mayor Landrieu,"
National Catholic Reporter, July 3, 2017.

318. **Emanuel AME is the oldest**: http://
www.emanuelamchurch.org/pages
/staff.

318. **As a postwar politician, the Civil
War general had been active**: T. Harry
Williams, *P. G. T. Beauregard: Napoleon
in Gray* (Baton Rouge: Louisiana State
University Press, 1995), 268–269.

319. **"the movement's effort to write
and control the history"**: David W.
Blight, *Race and Reunion: The Civil
War in American Memory* (Cambridge,

Mass.: The Belknap Press of Harvard University, 2001), 259. Italics in the original text.

319. **"The victim of the Lost Cause legend has been *history*"**: Alan T. Nolan, "The Anatomy of the Myth," in *The Myth of the Lost Cause and Civil War History*, ed. Gary W. Gallagher and Alan T. Nolan (Bloomington: Indiana University Press, 2000), 14.

320. **torched the $200,000 Lamborghini**: Danielle Kinchen, "$200,000 Lamborghini Found Burned in Baton Rouge Raises Questions about Possible Link to New Orleans Confederate Monuments Debate," *Baton Rouge Advocate*, January 20, 2016.

320. **the U.S. Fifth Circuit Court of Appeals ruled**: On January 26, 2016, Judge Carl J. Barbier of the United States District Court, Eastern District of Louisiana, denied the plaintiffs' motion in *Louisiana Monumental Task Committee Inc. et al. versus Anthony R. Foxx et al.*, Civil Action no. 15-6905. The U.S. Fifth Circuit Court of Appeals upheld Barbier's ruling on March 6, 2017, no. 16-30107. In upholding the authority of the City of New Orleans to make the decision, the Fifth Circuit observed, "We do not pass judgment on the wisdom of this local legislature's policy determination, nor do we suggest how states and their respective political subdivisions should or should not memorialize, preserve, and acknowledge their distinct histories. Wise or unwise, the ultimate determination made here, by all accounts, followed a robust democratic process."

320. **The city spent $1 million**: Landrieu, *In the Shadow of Statues*, 195.

320. **"These monuments purposefully"**: ibid., 219–22.

321. **symbolic gesture of interracial harmony**: Errol Laborde, *Mardi Gras: Chronicles of the New Orleans Mardi Gras* (Gretna, La.: Pelican, 2013).

322. **"No man will ever love me"**: quoted in Jason Berry, "Mardi Gras Indian Chief Larry Bannock's Last Ride," *The Daily Beast*, May 16, 2014.

322. **"It's a proud culture"**: quoted in Jason Berry, "Cross Cultural Tradition Starts a New Chapter," *Times-Picayune*, March 19, 1989.

323. **"I'm the Spy Boy that walked through the graveyard"**: quoted in ibid.

325. **"Larry was a man"**: quoted in Berry, "Mardi Gras Indian Chief."

INDEX

Page numbers appearing in *italics* refer to photographs.

blues, 167–71, 174, 179–80, 186, 193–94, 199, 210–11, 262–63, 267, 279, 282, 288. *See also* jazz

Boas, Franz, 207

Boggs, Lindy, 277

Boisbriant, Pierre Dugué, Sieur de, 21

Bolden, Charles Joseph (Buddy), 167–71, 174, 195, 198–99, 202, 214, 289–90; Barker's memoir on, 266–67; influences on, 175–77

Bonaparte, Napoléon, 69, 73–76, 81, 89, 91–92, 97, 102, 115, 125

Borenstein, Larry, *222*, 223, 242–45, 247–48, 255–56

Borenstein, Pat Sultzer, 248

Boston Club, 164, 177

Boukman (plantation headman and priest), 42

Bouligny, Francisco, 39, 40

Bourbon House, 244

Bourbon Street: A History (Campanella), 47

Bourbon Street Black (Barker), 269

"Bourbon Street Parade" (Paul Barbarin), 168, 221, 258, 268

Boutté, John, 3, 79

Boyd, Valerie, 207

Brady, Patricia, 125

Brands, H. W., 82

brass bands, 79, 151, 166, 171–83, 216, 324; removed from white funerals, 180–82; younger generation, 269, 281–82. *See also individual brass bands*

Braud, Mark, 309

Braud, Wellman, *226*, 274

Braun, Philip, 309

Brewster, Gary, 295

Brice, Bruce, 248–49

Bring New Orleans Back Commission, 302

Brinkley, David, 249–50

British, 16, 102; 1812 events and, 98–99; at Manchac, 48–50; Natchez and, 18–19; Non-Importation Act and, 97; Spanish crown prohibits trade with, 48; Washington, D.C., burning of, 102–3

British jazzmen, 276

Brock, Jerry, 109

Brother Isaiah (John Cudney), 211

Brothers, Thomas, 173, 267

Brown, Kerry, 270, 272

Brunious, John, 276

Brunious, Wendell, 276

Brunner, Larry, 277

Buddy Bolden and the Last Days of Storyville (Barker), 270

"Buddy Bolden's Blues" (Morton), 170–71

Buerkle, Jack V., 269

burglary, 34

"Burgundy Street Blues" (Lewis), 287, 291

burial societies, 71

Burke, Raymond, 310

Burr, Aaron, 81, 83, 90–91, 105

Burt, Hilma, 192

Bush, George H. W., 300

Bush, George W., 298, 299

Butler, Benjamin, *137*, 156, 158–59, 164

Cabildo, 37, 39–40, 51–59, 192; construction of, 64–65, 71, 73; funeral for Carlos III and, 56–59; rivalries within, 51–52; termination of, 76–77

Cable, George Washington, 43, 104, 178, 225

Cadillac, La Mothe, 16–19

Cadillac, Madeline, 16–17, 19

Cagnolatti, Ann, 214, 216–17

Cagnolatti, Anna Shelby, 213–15

Cagnolatti, Antoine, 213

Cagnolatti, Ernie Antoine, 213

Cagnolatti, Ernie Joseph ("Cag"), 213–16, 218–19, 247, 249

Cagnolatti, Leonce, 213–15

Cagnolatti, Ruth Johnson, 214–15, 217, 218

Cahn, Jules, 295

Cailloux, André, *136*, 155–56, 159–61

Caldonia Inn, 305–6

call-and-response, 41, 265

Calloway, Cab, 265, 272, 273

Campanella, Richard, 12, 23–24, 47, 123, 168, 206

Canada, 6, 13, 16, 25, 35, 75

Claiborne, William C. C., 76, 77, 78, 80–84, 117, *128*; death of, 117; deaths of family members, 88, 91, 117; 1811 slave revolt and, 95–96; free Africans and, 86–87; Haiti and, 91–96; Jackson and, 82–83; Laffites and, 97–98, 100, 103–5; militia and, 77, 81, 84, 86–87, 91, 97–100, 104; Sedella and, 88–90; "war of the quadrilles," 84–85, 88; Wilkinson and, 77, 81, 84–85, 90–91

clarinet, 280, 288

"Clarinet Marmalade" (Original Dixieland Jazz Band), 202

Clark, Daniel, 91

Clark, Emily, 22, 85, 86

Clark, Emily Suzanne, 157, 163

Clarkson, Jackie, 293

Clay, Emile Victor, 225

Clay, Henry, statue, 189–90

Clay, Sacha Borenstein, 253

Clayborne, William, 82

Clement XIV, 46

Clevenger, JoAnn, *223*, 244, 245

Clevenger, Max, 245

Clinton, Bill, 300

coartación (petition for freedom), 37

Code Noir (1724), 27–29, 32, 36–37, 76; loopholes, 33, 41

cod liver oil (Vitamin D), 212

Cody, John, 284

Coffee, John, 101, 110

Cohen, Dave, 298

College of the Immaculate Conception (Jesuit High School), 147

Collins, Lee, 193

Colored Waif's Home, 200, 215

Comité des Citoyens, 191

Committee for Public Safety, 106

Committee of Fifty, 188, 189–90

"Compagnie des Mulâtres et Nègres Libres de cette colonie de la Louisiane, La," 49

Company of the Indies, 9, 10, 20, 22–23; pulls out in 1731, 26, 27

concessionaires, 10, 33

Cone, James H., 172

Confederacy, 155–61. *See also* Civil War; Lost Cause mythology; statues and monuments

Congo, Luís, 32–33, 34

"Congo Circus," 119

Congo Square (Place Congo), 27–30, 38, 40, 44, 70–71, 78–79, 119, 161, 281, 305

Congo Square: African Roots in New Orleans (Evans), 29

Constitution, United States, 89–90, 103, 153

Constitution of 1868, 163

Contessa Entellina Society, *140*

Conti Street, 143

Convention Center, 308

cooperationists, 154

Corcoran Museum of Art, 256

Corpus Christi, feast of, 72–73

corruption, 34, 240; gay bar payoffs, 243, 245 , 250; Ring machine, 185–87, 192

Corte, Pascal, 189

Costello, Elvis, 2

Cotton Club, 261, 265

Cottrell, Louis, 249

crack cocaine, 308; at funerals, 275–76, 281, 296

Crawford, Davell, 2

Creole Jazz Band (Original Creole Orchestra), 260–61

Creoles, 34, 41; Claiborne and, 98; clans, 283; colored, 143–44; French Revolution and, 61–64; rebellion, 1768, 36–37; refugees from Saint-Domingue, 61–62; royalty, belief in, 57; spiritualism and, 157; white, 49, 178

Creoles, black, 70–71, 110, 143–44, 157–59, 161–62, 167, 174–75, 182–83, 239, 321; Comité des Citoyens, 191

Crescent, 158

Crescent City Lynchings, The (Smith), 186

Crescent City Serenade (White), 296

Crescent City White League, 4–5, 164, 186, 189, 318; "Battle of Liberty Place," 177–78, 190

Crockett, David, 101

Crossman, A. D., 148–49

Francs Amis, 258

Franklin, Benjamin, 89

Franzoni, Giuseppe, 117

Frazier, Cie, *224*

free Africans (*gens de couleur libres*), 50,
68, 85, 143; artisan class, 143–44; Civil
War and, 155; French Revolution and,
61–62; marriages, 86; slave ownership,
144

"Freedman's Case in Equity, The" (Cable),
178

Freedom Riders, 250

*Freemen of France to Their Brothers in
Louisiana* (Genêt), 63

French Caribbean colonies, 27–28, 35. *See
also* Saint-Domingue

French Enlightenment, 53

French Market, 51, 71

French Quarter, 8, 192–93, 205, 243

Friedlander, Lee, 244, 250–51, 255

Friends of Order, 156, 160, 161

Fromont, Cécile, 70

*From the Kingdom of Kongo to Congo
Square* (Dewulf), 70, 71

funerals, 1–5, 13, 120, *142*, 149; 1809 ordinance, 92–93; African customs, 30,
120–21; Alvaro III (Kongo), 70; Bannock, Larry, *230*, 321–22; Barbarin,
Paul, *221*, 268–69; Barker, Danny,
275–78; burial assemblies prohibited,
30; burial societies, 71; business of, 258;
Cailloux, André, *136*, 160–61; for Caldonia Inn, 305–6; Carlos III, 56–59, 70;
changing, 1990s–2000s, 295–97; crack
cocaine and, 275–76, 281, 296; Davis,
Jefferson, *138*, 178–79; Dunn, Oscar J.,
163; embalming, 151–52; France and
Canada, 13; "freedom rising" message
of, 180; for homicide victims, 296–97;
jazz music in parades, 171–72, 179–80,
277–80; Lewis, George, 282; musicians,
149–51, 160–61, 258; Native American sacrifices, 17; at night, 30; Roman
Catholic music and, 66; social class not
important, 194; transmigration of souls,

30–31, 281; white, removal of music,
180–82; "widow's wail," 280; yellow
fever and, 149–50. *See also* second-liners

funerary architecture, 117–18

Gaillot, Mrs. B. J., 284

Gaines, Ernest, 270

Gaines, William, 263

Gallier, James, 117

Gallier Hall, 187, 192, 275

Gálvez, Bernardo de, 48–51, 85

Gambit Weekly, 272

Garrison, Jim, 274

Gathering of Old Men, A (TV movie), 270

Gaudet, Jerome Klebert (Claibere), 213

Gay Carnival Ball, *232*

gay culture, 242–43, 250

Gehman, Mary, 144

Gem Saloon, 163

Genêt, Edmond-Charles, 63–64

gens de couleur libres. See Creoles, black;
free Africans (*gens de couleur libres*)

German bands, 190

German Coast, 37, 95

Gertrude Geddes Funeral Home, 217

Gill, James, 164, 188, 294

Gillespie, Dizzy, 265, 269

Gioia, Ted, 171, 267

Girod, Nicholas, 107

"Go Down, Moses" (Bolden), 171

Goldberg, Jeffrey, 317

Golden Starhunters, *230*, 321

Gouan (women's secret society), 31

Grady, Henry W., 178

Grand Isle, 97, 103

Grand Village (Natchez Village), 17–18

Grant, Ulysses S., *137*, 164, 186

Gratz, Roberta Brandes, 311–12

Gravier, Bertrand, 55–56

Great Depression, 211, 243, 246

Great Mother cults, 209

Great Sun (Natchez Emperor), 17–18, 21, 23

Greenleaf, Richard E., 59

griff (black-Indian offspring), 33

Grimes, William, 200

indigo plantations, 21, 27, 35
infant mortality, 168
Ingersoll, Thomas N., 21, 32
Inner Harbor Navigational Canal, 206
Innocents (gang), 186
Inquisition, 53–54, 59–60
In Search of Buddy Bolden (Marquis), 170
Inskeep, Steve, 102
insurance industry, 301
International Migration Society, 195
Interstate Highway Program, 305
Interstate 10, 298, 306
In the Shadow of Statues (Landrieu), 299
"In the Sweet Bye and Bye," 277
Intimate Enemies (Vella), 51, 52
Irish immigrants, 146–47, 161, 185
Islam, African resistance to, 31
Isle au Chat (Cat Island), 100
Isleños (Canary Islands), 49
Italians, 184. *See also* Sicilians
Italy, 184, 189

Jackson, Andrew, 82–83, 91, 98–99, 104, *131*, 210; black military and, 109–13; duels, 99, 100–101; as president, 118; trek to Tennessee, 100–103; visit of 1840, 148; War of 1812 and, 106–8, 110–12, 125
Jackson, Elizabeth, 82–83
Jackson, Elizabeth Lewis, 83
Jackson, Jesse, 314
Jackson, Mahalia, 307
Jackson, Rachel, 101–2
Jackson, Stonewall, 179
Jacksonland (Inskeep), 102
Jackson Square, *140*, 148
Jacobins, 61, 68, 69, 125
Jaffe, Allan, *224*, 247–50, 252–53, 290
Jaffe, Ben, 255
Jaffe, Russ, 255
Jaffe, Sandra (Sandy), 247–48, 253
James, C. L. R., 42, 62
Jansenists, 35
"Jass and Jassism" (*Times-Picayune*), 203–4
jazz, 4, 166–83, 244–45; blues, 167–71, 174,

179–80, 186, 193–94, 199, 210–11, 262–63, 267, 279, 282, 288; church background, 166–67, 169, 173–74; clash of politics and, 247–51; Depression-era, 246–47; ensemble style, 166; family structure and, 166; Hurricane Katrina and, 300–301; mixed bands, 250; New Orleans Style, 200; origins, 166–67; post-Katrina, 246; rhythm sections, 199; Sicilians and, 190, 201–2; story lines about city, 168–69; syncopated rhythms, 171, 175; white musicians in, 201–2. *See also* Bolden, Charles Joseph (Buddy); Borenstein, Larry; Jaffe, Allan; Jaffe, Sandra (Sandy); Lewis, George; Morton, Jelly Roll (Ferdinand LaMothe); Ory, Kid; Russell, William (Bill); White, Michael
Jazz at Lincoln Center, 279, 296, 317
Jazz at Preservation Hall: The George Lewis Band (recording), 287
Jazz Hounds, 270–71, 273
Jazzmen anthology (1939), 246
Jazzola Eight, 289
Jazztimes, 270
Jean Lafitte (town), 114
Jean Lafitte National Historical Park and Preserve, 114
Jefferson, Betty, 304
Jefferson, Mose, 303
Jefferson, Thomas, 63, 74, 76, 81, 83, 99, 105–6, 117
Jefferson, William (Bill), 303–4
Jelly (Dirty Dozen), 271
Jenkins, Charles, 308
Jenkins, George, 214
Jenkins, Nanny Cowans, 211
Jesuit High School (College of Immaculate Conception), 147
Jesuits (Society of Jesus), 6, 11, 21; *Code Noir* and, 27–28; return, 1830s, 147–48; slave-owning, 35–37
Jews, 28, 122, 169, 190, 200, 243, 248–49, 295
Jim Crow laws, 307

Nelson, Medard, 259
neoclassical design, 117–18
neo-Confederate mentality, 177–78
Neville, Aaron, 2
Neville, Cyril, 3
Nevis (island), 14
New Basin Canal, 146, 168, 205
New Lusitanos Benevolent Association, 180
New Orleans: as black majority town in
    year ten, 32; breaking ground, 19; Civil
    War defeat, 158–61; drug culture, 296;
    fire of 1794, 65; food supply, 51; Good
    Friday fire of 1788, 54–56, 62; interior
    cypress wetlands, 14, 114, 146, 168, 239;
    as largest slave market, *133*, 146; levee
    system, 20, 206; mid-1700s, 23–24; mu-
    nicipalities, 145; oil slump, 281; post–
    Civil War, 161–62; Prohibition era, 205;
    recovery, 315–16, 325–26; as second-
    largest port, 146; swamps, interior, 168;
    as symbol of America victorious, 118;
    three-tier society, 68; tolerance, 123; as
    tourist destination, 239, 240, 252, 280,
    300, 313; Ursuline convent, 22–23; as
    winter vacation spot, 192
—locations and neighborhoods of: Algiers
    neighborhood, 205–6; Back o' Town,
    141, 168, 173, 184, 195; Bayou Road, 27,
    32, 78; Bourbon Street, 92, 152, 186,
    246–47; Canal Street, 5, *139*, 145, 147,
    188–90, 196, 199, 205, 239, 318; Carroll-
    ton Avenue, 304, 321–22, 324–25;
    Central City, 183, 197, 210, 241, 285,
    289, 303; Claiborne Avenue, 206, 235,
    239, 300, 304–6, 316; Congo Square
    (Place Congo), 27–30, 38, 40, 44, 70–71,
    78–79, 119, 161, 281, 305; Dauphin
    Island, 9; Decatur Street, 184; District
    (French Quarter, Storyville), 192–95,
    203, 205, 239; Dryades Street, 169;
    Elysian Fields Avenue, 168; Faubourg
    Sainte-Marie, 56; Faubourg Tremé,
    78–80, 119, 145, 167, 191, 239, 304–8;
    French Market, 51; Garden District,
    168; Gentilly Woods, 168, 241; Gert

Town, 322–25; Iberville project, 239;
    Industrial Canal, 235, 284, 299; Lafitte
    project, 239; Lakeview, 14, 239; Lake-
    view neighborhood, 14; Louis Arm-
    strong Park, 27; Milneburg, 168–69,
    180, 238–39; New Basin Canal, 146,
    168, 205, 298; Ninth Ward, 205–18,
    242, 249, 255, 282–83, 299–300; North
    Claiborne Avenue, 235, 239; Palmetto
    Avenue, 323–25; Place d'Armes (Jack-
    son Square), 11, 27, 40; Place Publique
    (Place des Nègres), 30; Plaza de Armas,
    39–40, 46–47, 51, 76; rampart area,
    46; Rampart Street wall, 27; Robert E.
    Lee Boulevard (Lakeview), 3; Royal
    Street, 11, 236; Seventh Ward, 184, 241,
    257–59, 271, 302, 305–6; South Liberty
    Street, 289; St. Bernard Parish, 49, 206,
    284; St. Charles Avenue, 3, 48, 289; St.
    Claude Avenue, 206; St. John the Bap-
    tist Parish, 169, 285; St. Peter Street,
    242–45, 247; St. Peter Street cemetery,
    30, 46, 52, 56; Uptown, *139*, 147, 210,
    282–83, 288–89, 300; Vieux Carré, 184,
    185, 191–92, 244; West End, 168; West
    End seawall, 238–39
—population of: 1732, 25; 1788, 46; 1791;
    1850, 147; 1920s, 206; 2016, 325
New Orleans, Battle of, 109–14, 116, *131*,
    261
New Orleans Argus, 143
"New Orleans Blues" (Morton), 200
New Orleans City Directory, 143
New Orleans Country Club, 167, 204
New Orleans Jazz Club, 266
New Orleans Jazz Festival and Louisiana
    Heritage Fair (1970), 253, 268, 284, 285,
    313
New Orleans Levee Board, 206
New Orleans Masters programs, 296
New Orleans Museum of Art, 236, 253,
    256
New Orleans Revival, 221, 246, 265–66,
    288, 290
New Orleans Rhythm Kings, 169

ABOUT THE AUTHOR

Jason Berry is renowned for his landmark reporting
on the Catholic Church crisis in *Lead Us Not into
Temptation*, *Vows of Silence*, and *Render unto Rome*,
which received the Investigative Reporters and
Editors Best Book Award for 2011. An award-winning
documentary producer, his books include the music
history *Up from the Cradle of Jazz*. For his New Orleans
research, he has received fellowships from the National
Endowment for the Humanities, the Alicia Patterson
Foundation, and the John Simon Guggenheim Memorial
Foundation.